FORTUNE'S
A RIVER

FORTUNE'S A RIVER:

The Collision of Empires in Northwest America

By Barry Gough

HARBOUR PUBLISHING

Harbour Publishing Co. Ltd.
P.O. Box 219, Madeira Park, BC V0N 2H0
www.harbourpublishing.com

Printed and bound in Canada
Text design by Martin Nichols
Cover painting original watercolour by Steve Mayo, courtesy of David Syre collection.

Harbour Publishing acknowledges financial support from the Government of Canada through the Book Publishing Industry Development Program and the Canada Council for the Arts, and from the Province of British Columbia through the British Columbia Arts Council and the Book Publisher's Tax Credit through the Ministry of Provincial Revenue.

THE CANADA COUNCIL | LE CONSEIL DES ARTS
FOR THE ARTS | DU CANADA
SINCE 1957 | DEPUIS 1957

BRITISH
COLUMBIA
ARTS COUNCIL
Supported by the Province of British Columbia

Library and Archives Canada Cataloguing in Publication

Gough, Barry M., 1938-
    Fortune's a river : the collision of empires in Northwest America/ Barry Gough.
    Includes bibliographical references and index.

    ISBN 978-1-55017-428-1

    1. British Columbia—History—To 1849. 2. Northwest, Canadian—History—To 1870. I. Title.
FC3821.G683 2007   971.1'01   C2007-903867-0

for
James W. Scott
and
Roland L. De Lorme
partners in many beginnings

I took pains to determine the flight of crook-taloned birds, marking which were of the right by nature, and which of the left, and what were their ways of living, each after his kind, and the enmities and affections that were between them, and how they consorted together.

Aeschylus, *Prometheus Vinctus*

Our descendants will one day know many things that are hidden from us, for some knowledge is reserved for future generations, when all memory of us will be gone …. The world would be small indeed if there existed no possibility of new discoveries …. A moment will come when all that has been concealed will surge to light as the result of time and prolonged study. There will be a time when our ignorance will startle our descendants, because all these things will appear perfectly clear to them.

Seneca, *Naturalium Quaestionum*

Contents

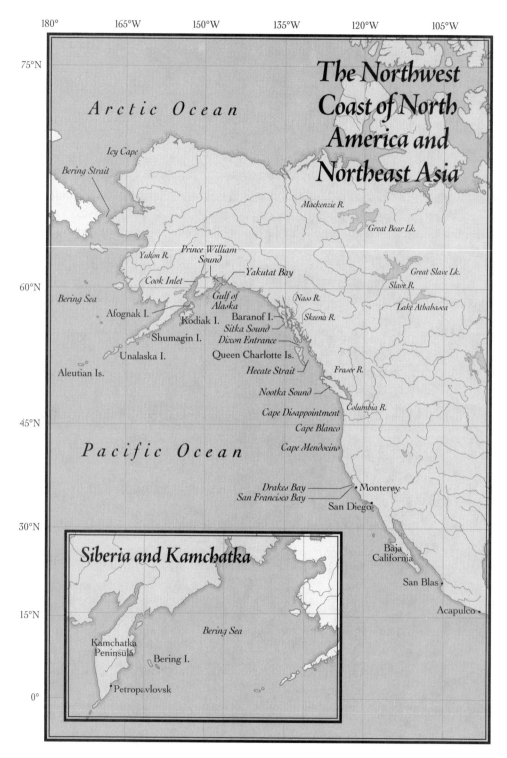

The Northwest Coast of North America and Northeast Asia

Arctic Ocean

Icy Cape

Bering Strait

Mackenzie R.

Great Bear Lk.

Yukon R.

Prince William Sound

Cook Inlet

Yakutat Bay

Great Slave Lk.

Slave R.

Bering Sea

Gulf of Alaska

Nass R.

Lake Athabasca

Afognak I.

Kodiak I.

Baranof I.

Skeena R.

Sitka Sound

Shumagin I.

Dixon Entrance

Unalaska I.

Queen Charlotte Is.

Fraser R.

Aleutian Is.

Hecate Strait

Nootka Sound

Columbia R.

Cape Disappointment

Pacific Ocean

Cape Blanco

Cape Mendocino

Drakes Bay

San Francisco Bay

Monterey

San Diego

Baja California

San Blas

Acapulco

Siberia and Kamchatka

Bering Sea

Kamchatka Peninsula

Bering I.

Petropavlovsk

180°   165°W   150°W   135°W   120°W   105°W

75°N

60°N

45°N

30°N

15°N

0°

Preface

I n researching and writing this history of the struggle of nations for control of the mouth and watershed of the Columbia River, I have taken a tour through my own childhood and youth when, with my parents and sister, I explored what were then primitive roads and campsites of the greater west— south from central British Columbia and southwestern Alberta through all the northern tier states west of North Dakota, and south again toward the great basin of Utah and northern California. In the late 1940s and the 1950s, this greater west inspired many by its simple beauty and unadulterated landscape. The legacies of that beauty and majesty are still to be seen, though diminished in grandeur by human pressures on land and waterways. Unforgettable was our visit to Grand Coulee Dam, then under construction. We marvelled at man's capacities to harvest the water resources of the Columbia River, hardly appreciating what devastation and destitution might accompany the construction and ongoing operation of the dam. Our innocence was understandable, for North America's abundance seemed everywhere apparent, and man's assurance about what might be done with it was almost unquestioned.

A century and a half before my first travels in this vast collection of mountains, plains and rivers, Meriwether Lewis and William Clark had entered the Columbia country from the east, crossed to the shores of the Pacific Ocean, wintered, and made their return passage, eventually reaching St. Louis, then the metropolis of the west. The image of the garden, as sanctified by Ken Burns's documentary film history of the Lewis and Clark journey,[1] still inspires us to view The West in the way we all want to see it—as something pristine, something unadulterated. However, the west that Lewis and Clark were examining was already largely familiar to those who occupied the ground or traversed it. On the northwest coast of North America, maritime traders and naval explorers had made known the particulars of the coastline and the trading possibilities of the area. *Fortune's a River* is about the rivalry for control of western North America, and it portrays the Lewis and Clark expedition as a necessary expedient of a United States government headed by Thomas Jefferson.

Jeremy Adelman and Stephen Aron's cogent review of recent historical literature shows that contemporary historians have substituted the idea of "borderlands" for "frontiers."[2] They have moved from an Anglocentric, triumphalist narrative of continental expansion, even conquest, to a re-engineered formulation that shows the divergent forces of European imperialism at work. In doing so, these historians have emphasized newcomers' relations with aboriginal peoples, stressing accommodations or forms of resistance. They have made imperial history local, inadvertently revitalizing that history. This book falls into the category of comparative imperial history or, more correctly, the history of empires in rivalry and conflict. As it recounts the details of the struggle for the farthest west, it reveals how those who shaped imperial purposes were more often than not explorers and traders—agents of empire. As Adelman and Aron argue, in the Great Lakes region it was the British who most completely understood and exploited the middle ground. But in the coastal zones of Pacific America, from the Aleutians to Alta California, the *maritime* preceded the *continental* in imperial influence and heightened the rivalry or made it more complex.

The epic of greater America, as Herbert Eugene Bolton reminded us a century ago, was much more than the Anglo-American westward push from the Appalachian Mountains, across the wide Missouri's valley, and over and beyond the Continental Divide to the Pacific shores. It also involved the French and British empires to the north, the Spanish empire to the southwest, and the Russian empire on the Pacific coast of North America. This book is an extension, or demonstration of Bolton's postulation, with particular emphasis on Canadian traders' influences on and responses to the Lewis and Clark expedition.

Since Bolton's time, scholars have been energetically tracking French, Canadian, Spanish, British and Russian activities in relation to their several borderlands, or zones of influence. Now it is time to bring all this information together and—the specific purpose of this book—to show how these influences shaped the course of America's westward reconnaissance in the form of the Corps of Discovery, the remarkable, state-sponsored expedition that constituted President Thomas Jefferson's answer to encroachments on the northern, westernmost and southwestern regions. Jefferson and Congress sent Lewis and Clark to explore and, by implication, to claim and secure, if only nominally, the remaining quarter of what became the continental United States, excluding Alaska. (It was then too late to obtain Alaska, though that was acquired later, by purchase.) The remarkable journeys of the American explorers occurred against a larger canvas of international rivalry and intrigue that brought forth Jefferson's response.

Related to this, and often forgotten in the larger account of "how the west was won," are the following activities and events: American trade and navigation on the northwest coast of North America, principally by Captain Robert Gray, a discoverer of the mouth of the Columbia River; the Spanish push north and northwest from New Orleans, western Mexico and Alta California; British and Canadian activities that gave British imperial interests prior knowledge of the Missouri River and its potential for aboriginal trade; Russian expansion southward from Sitka, Alaska, to the Columbia River (never effected) and to Fort Ross, Alta California; and the explorations of Alexander Mackenzie, the first European to cross the continent north of Mexico to the Pacific coast, in 1792–93, which was the immediate cause of Thomas Jefferson's decision to send Lewis and Clark west. After Mackenzie's journey, Simon Fraser and that most remarkable of all western explorers, David Thompson, also took up the search for the headwaters and courses of the great rivers of the west on either side of the Continental Divide. The battle for control of the mouth of the Columbia River, fought bitterly by John Jacob Astor's New York-based Pacific Fur Company, successor to the Winships of Boston (who had attempted to build on the Columbia River in 1810), on the one hand, and the British-Canadian firm, the muscular North West Company based in Montreal, on the other, constitutes the result of all these forces. The maritime enterprise on the Pacific coast, exercised by competing American and British traders, came to a head with the overland quest for dominance by rival American and Canadian commercial concerns.

Fortune's a River also aims to demonstrate the true Canadian rivalry on the northern frontier of US interests. And it seeks to examine the struggle that developed in the immediate aftermath of the Lewis and Clark expedition, a rivalry that pitted Astor's abilities and attempts against those of the Nor'Westers. This contest was made dramatic, even tragic, by the voyage of the ship *Tonquin* and the successive losses and difficulties of other Pacific Fur Company vessels. Coupled with these difficulties was the Royal Navy's intervention at Astoria, near the mouth of the Columbia, in 1813, which, oddly enough, compromised British claims. The War of 1812 was waged without violence at this western margin of empire, and it represents, or symbolizes, the Anglo-American rivalry for western North America advanced in the age of Mackenzie and Thompson and of Lewis and Clark—four giants of western overland exploration and imperial expansion.

To complete the story, this history examines how claims to the Columbia River mouth and watershed were dealt with by diplomats in Washington and London respectively. Astor's thrust to the Columbia had diplomatic and political consequences far beyond any commercial hope of establishing a workable base of operations at Astoria and posts upriver. Similarly, the War of 1812 in this area, specifically at the mouth of the Columbia, brought the question of sovereignty to a head. As claims to sovereignty based on priority of discovery and exploration suffered a long, slow death, they were replaced by more tangible matters: occupation or on-the-spot control. Realpolitik replaced any pre-eminence of Robert Gray's discovery of the Columbia River and, similarly, Alexander Mackenzie's first passage overland to Pacific tidewater. The resolution, when effected in 1846, completed a natural cycle of diplomatic intrigue resulting in mutual exhaustion and a division of the Columbia River watershed.

Many books have been written on the intriguing subject of the search for the Northwest Passage. This is not one of them. Rather, it is an inquiry into economic influence, business activity, some scientific investigation, statecraft and diplomacy, and the making of borders. Various concepts of a northwest passage, and various voyages and charts that indicated the existence of same, nonetheless provide an enchanting backdrop for the activities of nations in the struggle for the farthest west. In Appendix 1, the reader will find a synopsis of these fanciful concepts and a note on relevant sources.

Had Lewis and Clark found a navigable passage to the Pacific and to India, as Jefferson had hoped, all might have been different. Geography stood in the way of empire; it retarded the westward movement for at least a generation. Meanwhile, Yankee mariners sailed that same far coast, enriching the coffers of Boston, New York, Providence and other seaports. Even before Lewis and Clark, and certainly after, the United States was at a disadvantage in the Anglo-American rivalry for Oregon. However, colonization, driven by organized associations and, particularly, missionary zeal, was a powerful political additive that Congress could neither ignore nor neglect and the British government (and all its naval, military and commercial instruments and might) could not counter. In the early phases of this rivalry, the United States government, like the British, preferred trade to dominion. But Lewis and Clark opened new pathways to occupation for the swelling American population, and against this, as against any other settlement it had faced, the Hudson's Bay Company, the last legatee of the Russian, North West Company, Pacific Fur Company and Spanish commercial interests, was powerless to react.

Members of the human race make history, and in this book I have sought to provide abundant profiles of the principal personages who form the historical narrative and analysis. I begin with John Ledyard, who takes pride of place as precursor of Lewis and Clark, and I have drawn his pithy story into that of Jefferson's western designs. He was followed by Sir Alexander Mackenzie, noted Scottish fur trader and explorer, who was even more celebrated for his famous book of discoveries. Tied to Mackenzie's story is that of a shadowy figure, the enigmatic Peter Pond of Milford, Connecticut. The Russian background to this narrative is told through the overlooked navigator Alexei Chirikov and the remarkable Alexander Baranov, manager of the Russian-American Company. A further Russian personage is Baron Rezanov, whose ill-fated quest to plant a Russian base at the mouth of the Columbia in March 1806 is little known. The Spanish undercurrents are told by way of Bruno de Hezeta, true discoverer of the mouth of the Columbia River, and Esteban Martínez, highly charged commandant at Nootka. The North West Company cast long shadows across Lewis and Clark's pathway to the west, as demonstrated by the story of that fascinating fellow David Thompson, followed by the likes of Alexander Henry the Younger, Charles Mackenzie and François-Antoine Larocque. The faltering Spanish quest for control of the upper Mississippi, the Missouri River and the

Illinois country is illustrated by the tale of two adventurers in the employ of a Spanish corporation, James MacKay (ex-Nor'Wester turned servant of the King of Spain) and John Evans (the man seeking to find the white Welsh Indians). Against this larger panorama stands Jefferson, with his westward vision. He forms a centre of gravity, carrying through his response to Mackenzie's prescient book with its warning of British imperial commercial designs. Not least in this story are the Yankee mariners of the sea otter business, who became masters of the northwest coast's trade, obliged the Russians to trade with them and do their bidding, and carved out intended places of occupation. Robert Gray, John Kendrick, Joseph Ingraham, Jonathan Winship Jr. and Nathan Winship play enticing roles herein. Hard-luck John Jacob Astor, of New York, becomes for a time the most prominent of these, but he, too, is all but destroyed in this branch of commerce. The book closes with Thompson's discovery of the source of the Columbia River, the North West Company's purchase of Astoria, the intervening and reinforcing presence of the Royal Navy during the War of 1812, and the diplomatic arrangements that settled, for a time, the destiny of western North America between Russian America and Alta California.

In the process of writing, I grew aware that I was composing a chapter in the greater epic of America, with the far west as the focus. I make no apology for its wide-ranging scope. I have sought to provide a comprehensive account of international rivalries and results. If this book goes some way to diminish parochial national understandings, American and Canadian, I shall be pleased and encouraged.

I thank various readers, known and unknown, who gave me the benefit of their knowledge and guided my interpretation of the documents. Among the numerous repositories from which evidence has been gathered I thank the Oregon Historical Society, Liisa Penner at the Clatsop Historical Society, the Missouri Historical Society, the Montana Historical Society and the Washington State Historical Society. I thank David Nicandri and the Washington State Historical Society for arrangements that allowed me as Curtiss Hill Lecturer to research aspects of Lewis and Clark near Pacific tidewater. Similar thanks are due Bob Doerk and Ella Mae Howard and the Great Falls chapter of the Lewis and Clark Trail Heritage Foundation for the invitation and arrangements for me when I was William Sherman Lecturer. Equally parallel thanks are due to Andy Motherwell and the committee that made arrangements for the Lewis and Clark Trail Heritage Foundation to visit Montana—and eastern Idaho—so that I could launch the prototype of what became the first third of the present book. It was on that occasion, in 2000, that I stood where the Missouri flows out of the ground in Lewis and Clark's own sea of mountains. And so it has all come together, a journey through time and space. Pacific tidewater, the Great Falls of the Missouri, and the source of the Missouri—these completed, for me, my personal discovery of the waterways of North America. Rivers run through this history.

So do the documents of the past. In Canada I thank the Library and Archives Canada, the Archives of Ontario, the British Columbia Archives and Records Service, and the Provincial Archives of Manitoba, custodian of the Archives of the Hudson's Bay Company. In Britain I thank the British Library, the National Archives, the National History Museum, the National Maritime Museum, the Hydrographic Record Office of the Ministry of Defence (Navy), Scott Polar Research Institute, and the University of Cambridge Library. I owe personal debts to W. Raymond Wood for advice on precursors of Lewis and Clark, to William Billeck for estimating routes from North West Company posts to the Great Bend of the Missouri River, and to James P. Ronda, for his insights into Lewis and Clark, indigenous peoples, and Astoria. Ronda, James Axtell, the late Donald Jackson and the late Abraham Nasatir have been for me sources of inspiration and therefore support. Jackson and Nasatir, now deceased, are not forgotten. John Logan Allen gave me the benefit of his vast knowledge and insight. Robin Inglis and Robert King helped interpret French and Spanish activities in the Pacific. Bill McDonald advised on Peter Pond. Daniel Kyba did likewise on David Thompson. Eric Grove opened doors of natural history. Michael Barritt, Andrew Cook, Andrew David and Adrian Webb gave assistance on hydrographical matters. Over many years I have benefited from the works of Glyn Barratt, the late John C. Beaglehole, James Gibson and Glyndwr Williams. Colonel E. Giesecke aided my inquiries about the Russians, Winships and the *Tonquin* tragedy. David W. Griffiths of the Tonquin Foundation updated particulars on the possible location of that tragedy. Barbara Belyea shared her knowledge of textual analysis of the works of explorers. Sandford Bederman, Angelo Borras, Adele Boucher, Martyn Clark, Norman and Dale Collingwood, John Crosse, Kim Davies, Penelope Edwards, Brenda Guild and John Jenkins provided help and encouragement. Elsie Grogan brought the text to its final state. Steve Mayo provided his marine art, models of authenticity. I thank Audrey McClellan for skilful editing and Howard White for his avuncular support. To these persons, and others without whose help and knowledge this book could not have been completed, I extend my gratitude. The errors are mine alone.

Barry Gough
Victoria, British Columbia

Prologue

JOHN LEDYARD: "THE VERY FOOTBALL OF CHANCE"

E ven in his own time, a legend formed around John Ledyard. He enters
our story like a meteor, a streak of flame illuminating the affairs of
northwest America and the North Pacific Ocean on the eve of Alexander
Mackenzie's voyage. For a time he cast a radiant glow over the links between
Asia and America, Russia and the United States before fading from the scene
and, almost, from history.[1]

His Majesty's Ship Resolution, *462 tons, workhorse for Pacific discoveries, is here portrayed
entering Nootka Sound 1778. Persons shown include Captain James Cook, beneath the mizzen,
or aft, sail, William Bligh, master, all in black beneath the ensign; Midshipman George Vancouver in the mizzenmast rigging with telescope, and to the left, near the mainmast, Corporal John
Ledyard, the white cross belts indicating him as a Marine. These four, and others, were global
travellers in the age of fighting sail. The* Discovery *is in the distance. Courtesy Steve Mayo*

John Ledyard—canoeist, traveller among the Iroquois, Royal Marine and deserter from the service of King George III—was a solitary voyageur in search of wealth and fame. Though considered by many to be cocky, he set in place the visionary tendency and commercial zeal that dominated American activities in the Pacific Northwest. Courtesy of Dartmouth College Library

The Reverend Andrew Kippis, Captain Cook's first biographer and Ledyard's contemporary, assessed Ledyard and his eye-catching activities this way in June 1788: "This corporal Lediard is an extraordinary man, someone whose history cannot fail of being entertaining to my readers." Another observer, John Ledyard's shipmate Captain James Burney of the Royal Navy, wrote that Ledyard had perhaps the most romantic enthusiasm for adventure of any man in his time. "With what education I know not, but with an ardent disposition," recalled Burney, "Ledyard had a passion for lofty sentiment and description."[2]

Thomas Jefferson, then the United States Minister to France and resident in Paris, was similarly much taken with Ledyard, even if slightly perplexed by him. Jefferson liked what he saw in the thirty-four-year-old adventurer, who was only eight years his junior. But he rightly qualified his tribute. Jefferson called Ledyard "a man of genius, of some science, and of fearless courage and enterprise," but also commented privately to a friend: "unfortunately, he has too much imagination."[3]

Born in Groton, opposite New London, Connecticut, with sea air in his nostrils and with love of distant horizons in his blood, Ledyard was the son of a local merchant sea captain who had died at age thirty-five. His widowed

In his hand-hewn canoe, young John Ledyard, avoiding scholarly obligations at Dartmouth College, finds his downriver course more than he can handle. His Bible has flown from his grasp into the water and his hat flies from his head as he seeks to avoid disaster in the whitewater below. This view is an allegory of his life, though his wild antics still inspire canoeists of Dartmouth and other New England colleges. Courtesy of Dartmouth College Library

mother remarried and moved to Long Island. John Ledyard was never a waif or a stray, but like his brother and his sister he was sent to live with relatives. The boy was taken into the home of his stern grandfather in Hartford, where he attended grammar school. But before long his grandfather also died, with little love lost to the boy, and so he came into the care of his uncle, under whom he began an apprenticeship in law.

By invitation from the founder of Dartmouth College, the Reverend Eleazar Wheelock, John Ledyard became one of the charter students at this remote campus in Hanover, New Hampshire. It had been intended, or so it is recorded, that young John would become a missionary to the Indians. He could not keep to his books, however. He took to the amateur theatrics of Dartmouth. Free spirit that he was, he wandered in the summer months of 1772 among the Iroquois of Quebec. The next spring, with help from fellow students, he built a dugout canoe, fifty-five feet long and three feet wide, which he launched in the Connecticut River. Ledyard did the downriver run from Hanover to Hartford, past falls and rapids, while reading the Bible. A portage made just in the nick of time, when he had to lay his Bible aside for his paddle, saved his neck. To this day, remembrance of his daring exploit inspires the John Ledyard Canoe Society of Dartmouth College and, by extension, all other groups in the greater North East Canoe Association.

Young Ledyard was not much for discipline, the Reverend Wheelock could see with regret, and though obviously bright enough, could not submit himself to the demands of scholarly life. He was not cut out for theology any more than he was for law. His nonplussed uncle had neither the funds nor the leverage with Wheelock to keep him in Dartmouth College, and so John Ledyard began his independent search for new prospects in life.

He decided to follow the sea paths of his father. In 1773 at New London, he shipped as a common sailor in a merchant ship bound for the Barbary Coast for a cargo of mules. However, the merchant marine offered no prospects, no glory. At Gibraltar he deserted and impulsively joined a British regiment. The commanding officer, discovering the details of his desertion, ordered him sent back to his vessel. Thus the Connecticut mariner made the return passage via the West Indies to New London, completing the triangle run. By 1774, Ledyard found himself back in Connecticut. After a brief love affair in Boston, the young sailor decided to make a career in the service of the king. He went to New York, shipped in a merchant vessel to Falmouth, England, and travelled to Bristol, his grandfather's original home, where, he says, he joined a British regiment.[4]

Somehow, in Plymouth, he presented himself to the master mariner Captain James Cook, then about to sail on his third voyage of discovery to the Pacific Ocean with the aim of finding the western entry to the fabled Northwest Passage. Ledyard enlisted in the Royal Marines, took the oath of allegiance to His Majesty and was posted to the 24th Company, Plymouth Division, with the rank of corporal. The record is silent as to how Ledyard got into the Marines. It could have been on the recommendation of Cook. More likely it was through the intervention of a fellow American, Lieutenant John Gore, who sailed in the expedition.

Ledyard joined HMS *Resolution* in Plymouth on July 9, 1776. The expedition sailed on July 12. The United States had just declared its independence from the British Empire, and a state of war existed. However, the British government had fixed up an arrangement with Jefferson's august predecessor in Paris, Benjamin Franklin (whose credit among English statesmen was mighty), by which the United States had agreed not to molest Cook's ships or otherwise interfere with his great expedition with its lofty scientific goals and intentions.

For four long years Ledyard sailed the seas with the Royal Navy's ships of discovery. The wealth offered by the pelts of North Pacific sea otters was an instant attraction for him, as it was for many members of the expedition. "We purchased while here [Nootka Sound] about fifteen hundred beaver, besides other skins, but took none but the best, having no thoughts at the time of using them to any other advantage, than converting them to the purposes of clothing; but it afterwards happened that skins, which did not cost the purchaser sixpence sterling, sold in China for one hundred dollars."[5] Several officers and men speculated in the peltry business "on the side," coming away with handsome profits in Canton and Kamchatka. The Russians' rich traffic with the Chinese was similarly impressive. As Cook remarked, this sea otter trade was potentially one of the most valuable branches of commerce. Perhaps direct trade in British hands from the northwest coast of North America—from Nootka Sound and the Gulf of Alaska, embracing the Sandwich Islands—would prove advantageous to the British nation, adding to its profit and power.

Lieutenant Gore recommended Corporal Ledyard to Cook for a dangerous baidarka (kayak) mission to gain information about Russian activities from Deramonshk (or Yearmosk), an indigenous hunter and his party. If Ledyard met the Russians, or others, he was to endeavour "to make them understand that we were English, Friends and Allies." Ledyard did meet some Russian traders, and in the most telling part of his account of the expedition, flattering to himself, he says: "I was at this time and indeed ever after an intimate friend of John Gore, Esq.; first lieutenant of the *Resolution,* a native of America as well as myself and superior to me in command, he recommended me to Captain Cook to undertake the expedition, with which I immediately acquiesced. Captain Cook assured me that he was happy I had undertaken the route as he was conscious I should persevere."[6] Cook deemed Ledyard "an intelligent man" and recognized his exceptional physical abilities in extreme situations, his record-keeping and his enthusiasm for adventure.

At Kealakekua Bay, Hawaii, Ledyard was one of four marines on the beach with Cook when the famous mariner was murdered and dismembered by Hawaiian warriors. With no chance or hope of saving his captain, Ledyard used his powerful swimming abilities to escape to the safety of the ships. John Gore led the dispirited expedition home via Canton, where the sea otter skins, gathered with much enthusiasm but little care for quality, garnered astonishing prices. They were sold to make warm, prestigious robes for mandarins.

The ships returned to England, where Ledyard sought a discharge, but in vain. In 1782, his current ship headed for North America and came to anchor in Long Island Sound. He obtained a week's leave to see his mother, who lived across the sound, and nearly surprised the wits out of this nervous, obsessively religious woman. He stayed longer than he should have, deserted the king's service, and went home to his Connecticut haunts. There a new opportunity presented itself.

Nathaniel Patten, an energetic Hartford publisher, possessed a keen instinct for hungry readerships. He imagined that the bright tale of a Yankee sailor turned explorer under the protective mantle of the great and much lamented Cook would have a good sale. In 1781, an unauthorized London publication containing the story of the voyage and the great mariner's death at Kealakekua Bay had appeared, authored by John Rickman, who had also sailed with Cook. Ledyard set to work on his own account of the voyage. Using Rickman's book heavily, and lifting some sections verbatim, Ledyard constructed his narrative. Careful scholars should note that Ledyard added many of his own details that would otherwise have been lost to the record of adventure and science. His book contains the first published description of the Russian presence at Unalaska in the Aleutian Islands, the first permanent Russian settlement in northwestern North America.[7] His account of New Zealand and Australia included his observation that "the island of New-Holland (for its boundaries are now ascertained) is by much the largest known, and most eligibly situated on the map of nature ... even the Empress of Russia might be gratified with such a portion." Ledyard's descriptions of the Hawaiian Islands, of his travels inland there and of the death of Cook recount the essential details. They also, Jefferson noted with regret when he read Ledyard's book, cast the great captain in a lesser luminescence, for Ledyard's unflattering portrayal of Cook had the effect of "lessening our regrets at his fate."[8] Patten issued the work in two serial parts and then, in 1783, released the whole under the title *A Journal of Captain Cook's Last Voyage to the Pacific Ocean, and in Quest of a North-West Passage between Asia & America,* now an extremely scarce item in the book trade. Ledyard, to secure his literary primacy, petitioned the Connecticut Assembly for the exclusive right of publication of his narrative. When this was granted, it provided the basis for a copyright licence, the first such in the United States.

Ledyard—and Patten—knew that the interested publics in the United States and Britain wanted to know all about Cook's death. Ledyard did not disappoint. Readers also learned the details of the reprisals carried out by the sailors and mariners—the summary punishment and lesson—that followed on as a matter of judicial course in that age. Such pieces of Cook's hacked-up body as could be collected together were placed in a purpose-built box made by the ship's carpenter of the *Resolution.* When the vessels sailed for the entrance of Kealakekua Bay, his remains were committed to the deep in the time-honoured fashion of the Royal Navy, with the customary solemn salute fired.

Ledyard's narrative did not stop there, as well it might have if it were just intended to satisfy readers' curiosity. He went on to address two themes—one old, one new—that were, or became, passions of the age and that are central to our larger story. Ledyard knew that many European nations were interested in the search for the Northwest Passage that would link the European world with Asian ports and trade. In his book, therefore, he plays on this theme, noting that Cook's last voyage was the first to tackle the problem of finding an entrance to the passage from the west, or Pacific, end. Ledyard stresses that in the course of the endless, even tedious, search, he and all the others seemed to abandon the possibility of such an opening while the redoubtable, thorough and reliable Cook, pursuant to his instructions and in keeping with his own high expectations of himself, persisted with the reconnaissance until it could be categorically stated "No Northwest Passage here."

On May 27, 1778, Ledyard's account tells us, they found themselves "in what we conjectured to be a vast river, having a strong southerly current—sounded 40 fathoms. This gave us hopes again of a passage."[9] And thus Cook's River made its appearance on the drawings and, eventually, charts of the northwest coast. Cook's River was no passage and no river. Later discoverers were to find it an inlet, now bearing the placename Cook Inlet. But it was due to the jotting down of this incorrect, undefined coastal particular that North West Company trader Peter Pond, working in the Athabasca district and headquartered at what trader and traveller Alexander Mackenzie would later call Pond's House, on Elk River, about forty miles south of Athabasca Lake, came to believe that he was perched near the headwaters of what must be Cook's River.

In time, this curious link between Alaska and Athabasca produced an extraordinary set of results: it sent Mackenzie out to the Pacific with expectations

"Cook's River," drawn by George Dixon in 1789 and published in A Voyage Round the World, *is actually Cook Inlet, located in present-day Alaska. In May 1778, James Cook described it as a river, for even after a week of exploration it seemed to stretch inland without end. This conjecture led Peter Pond and Alexander Mackenzie to believe that the "river" might possibly flow from a spot east of the Rocky Mountains westward to the Pacific, a watery northwest passage.*

of meeting Russians at Unalaska (as Rickman and Ledyard had advertised), induced Jefferson to seek to pre-empt the British in their various imperialist and scientific schemes and actions in that quarter, and pushed the Nor'Westers to greater, wider trading arrangements with the indigenous peoples of the Rocky Mountains and Pacific shores.

The second theme, one overshadowing the saga of Cook's death but running in parallel with the search for the elusive strait, centred on the northwest coast itself, for its geographical features, its resources, its arable lands, its indigenous peoples—all these and more—were as yet unknown to the Americans. The urge to find out what existed in northwest America was quickened by Ledyard's text.

Ledyard also hinted at the relationships between aboriginal languages on the northwest coast with those he knew from his vagabond missionary days among the Iroquois of Quebec when he was enrolled at Dartmouth. His book was the first by an American on this subject. Ledyard wrote as an American, conscious of his New World membership. "It was the first time too that I had been so near the shores of that continent which gave me birth from the time I at first left it [to enlist in the Royal Marines]; and though more than two thousand miles distant from the nearest part of New England I felt myself plainly affected," he wrote with longing for home, "all the affectionate passions incident to national attachments and early prejudices played round my heart,

This portrait of a Nuu-chah-nulth man, engraved by W. Sharp, from the original by John Webber (the artist on Cook's third voyage to the Pacific), reveals the subject's intense attention to physical appearance. The tattooed forehead, tightly woven locks of hair, nose ring and fur-fringed garment of woven cedar are among the features shown. It was originally published in James Cook and James King, A Voyage to the Pacific Ocean (London, 1784), the record of Cook's last voyage.

and induced them because they were prejudices. I was harmonized by it. It soothed a home-sick heart, and rendered me very tolerably happy."[10]

At Nootka Sound, Ledyard and his mates had found Mowachaht and Muchalaht people with copper bracelets and rough wrought knives. Where did these items come from, the sailors wondered. Ledyard contended that they came a great distance, from Hudson Bay. "Commerce is defusive and nothing will impede its progress among the uninformed part of mankind, but an intervention of too remote a communication by water, and as this cannot be the case with regards to the inhabitants of a continent, it seems entirely conclusive to suppose no part of America is without some sort of commercial intercourse, immediate or remote."[11] His postulation that transcontinental trade existed among the continent's indigenous peoples has been borne out by social scientists and historians. Trans-Pacific links, especially across Siberia and northwestern Alaska, have likewise been demonstrated. Ledyard's understanding of North America as a single geographical unit bears on the obvious. New to the logic was the fact that the Pacific Northwest, and the northwest coast from California to Bering Strait, fronted on the Pacific Ocean, an avenue of commerce.

Ledyard set in place the visionary tendency as well as the commercial zeal for American activities in the Pacific Ocean and on the Pacific rim. His significance in the maritime expansion of American commerce is profound. His biographer, Jared Sparks, indicates that, as a traveller and visionary, Ledyard stood at the forefront of the American quest for new worlds to conquer by commerce.[12] The Ledyard destiny for the United States was gathering momentum. He was lighting the lamp for Lewis and Clark.

Patten's investment paid handsomely. As for Ledyard, the twenty guineas he received as a fee for his narrative spurred him to his next project.

When it was published, Ledyard's book gave him an entree into the world of the savants and the merchant capitalists outfitting ships of trade. His star was rising. In that same year, the independence of the United States meant that the ex-Marine was no longer a "deserter." History saved him, gave him a new lease on life. He travelled extensively, seeking support for his favourite scheme: sending a trading ship to the northwest coast. Capital, investors and shipping were scarce. One ship, the *Empress of China*, which in 1784 made the first American voyage to China, escaped his grasp. In New London and Boston he faced similar difficulties. In New York, Ledyard's scheme was described as wild, visionary and lacking in sober, mature judgment. "No merchant was found willing to hazard his money, or his reputation, in an adventure so novel in its kind, or so questionable in its purpose; a scheme not only untried, but never before thought of," writes Ledyard's biographer.[13] Ledyard made inquiries in Philadelphia. Almost everywhere, indifference greeted him. But Robert Morris, prominent financier of wide vision and purpose, took up Ledyard's concept and arranged to furnish the outfits for a voyage according to the plan Ledyard drew up.

In Boston, New London and New York, Ledyard could not obtain a ship. There was a flash of promise when a shipping agent in New York, Daniel Parker, procured a vessel. But Morris's backing for fixing such outfits was badly timed. Then the impatient Morris backed out. Then came another chance. A captain in New London, Deshon, who had sailed with Ledyard to Gibraltar and was a chum, and who had at his disposal a new ship perfectly suitable for a northwest coast voyage, first agreed, then shied away. Prudence ruled. Captain Deshon came to regret his unwillingness to back Ledyard when he learned that later investors in the maritime fur trade were rewarded with extraordinary success, purchasing lands from the indigenous peoples and making plans to establish factories or colonies. Boston shipping interests also got cold feet. "The Americans were too busy at reconstruction after the Revolution to listen long to a penniless theatrical fellow who promised them incredible wealth if they would pay for a ship and its complement," writes one authority.[14] That may be. But the complexity of linking concept, business plan, capital, a ship, a crew and an outfit for trade was not easily mastered. Ledyard sailed on the whims of chance.

At least he had the nominal backing of the Philadelphia financier Morris, who as a kind of consolation prize provided the adventurer with letters of introduction to prominent French merchants. In Paris, Ledyard sang the praises of a seaborne expedition to the northwest coast and to China. He came close to success on one occasion. A syndicate in Lorient, a port in Brittany, arranged for a 400-ton vessel. It never sailed. From June 1784 to 1786, Ledyard worked away at the project without reward. After knocking on many doors, he came to that of Thomas Jefferson. He must have been in a state of desperation.

Jefferson, with his enlarged vision of things, was bound to listen to Ledyard with care, even fascination. His systematic, methodical mind would have absorbed all that Ledyard recounted. Seated before him was a fellow who had sailed with the legendary Cook, who had encountered the Russians in Alaska, met the Chinese in Canton and, in an earlier cruise, gone to the Barbary Coast, that constant source of American worries about security of its citizens and trade. Here before Jefferson sat a world traveller, a seasoned mariner, an author. No dreamer this, no closet geographer. Rather, here was a sailor without a ship, an adventurer bent on new worlds to discover and exploit.

The two had much in common. They were patriots and expansionists alike. Jefferson understood the systematic nature of power and nation-states. Ledyard was merely an individual actor on the larger stage of empire building and commerce. Both shared an interest in the origins of the indigenous peoples of America and recognized that the links between Siberia and Alaska perhaps explained the diffusion of races and languages. Jefferson had read Ledyard's book on Cook's last voyage and liked it so much he had lent it to General Lafayette's wife, who promptly and carelessly passed it on to friends, never returning it to Jefferson. Jefferson had also been presented with the "vocabulary" prepared by Ledyard under the puffed-up, or august, title "Comparative View of Chipeway, Naudowissie & Nootka Languages being the newest known on the northern continent of America, analogically considered with respect to any other language ancient modern improved or unimproved."[15]

Jefferson shared Ledyard's passion for aboriginal languages and had studiously compiled an extensive catalogue of the aboriginal nations of the United States based on British, French and American records dating from Deputy Agent George Crogan's 1759 report gathered for Sir William Johnson, the superintendent of Indian Affairs.[16] His interest in these matters extended to the diffusion of languages, a key index of the history of races and peoples. Jefferson speculated on the subject of how the American tribes had come from Asia and had written on this matter in his *Notes on the State of Virginia*, a privately circulated compilation first printed in Paris in 1785, the year before he met Ledyard. In 1787, this work would also appear in French translation and in English printings issued on both sides of the Atlantic, in London and Philadelphia.

In the *Notes*, Jefferson reflected the then current belief that indigenous people had passed to America from Asia. He even speculated that the American tribes were older than those of Asia:

> Great question has arisen from whence came those aboriginal inhabitants of America? Discoveries, long ago made, were sufficient to shew that a passage from Europe to America was always practicable, even to the imperfect navigation of ancient times ....

> ... the late discoveries of Captain Cook, coasting from Kamschatka to California, have proved that, if the two continents of Asia and America be separated at all, it is only by a narrow straight. So that from this side also, inhabitants may have passed into America and the resemblance between the Indians of America and the Eastern inhabitants of Asia, would induce us to conjecture, that the former are the descendants of the latter, or the latter of the former: excepting indeed the Eskimaux, who, from the same circumstance of resemblance, and from identity of language, must be derived from the Groenlanders, and these probably from some of the northern parts of the old continent. A knowledge of their several languages would be the most certain evidence of their derivation which could be produced. In fact, it is the best proof of the affinity of nations which ever can be referred to .... It is to be lamented then, very much to be lamented, that we have suffered so many of the Indian tribes already to extinguish, without our having previously collected and deposited in the records of literature, the general rudiments at least of the languages they spoke.[17]

Likely Jefferson judged Ledyard much as did other contemporaries, including his biographer Jared Sparks. Gentlemanly in behaviour, Ledyard gave the impression of being singularly independent. He dressed unusually, as if to gather attention. Tahitian tattoos graced his hands, alarming or attracting females as the case might be. Self-possessed, bold but not obtrusive, he had great powers to win the approval of others when so inclined. Sparks mused that Ledyard was dignified, independent, and enthusiastic about life. He was well deported and a good conversationalist. But Ledyard could be cocky, haughty and unappreciative of his superiors and those in power. Jefferson did not know the latter particulars. He took Ledyard at face value, only later learning of these sad limitations.

For three years and more, Jefferson had been pondering the future of the United States in lands beyond the western boundaries of the nation. Here was a man who could open the door to that future. But there existed something too fantastically wild in Ledyard's scheme. Besides, such commercial ventures as the traveller spoke of lay beyond the immediate scope of the diplomat.

Next Ledyard met the US naval hero John Paul Jones, then in France collecting prize money due him. For a time the two shared shining prospects of a lucrative venture to the North Pacific. Jones designed an expedition to the northwest coast, similar to one organized by Jean de Galaup, Comte de Lapérouse, that would involve persuading Louis XVI to finance a pair of vessels, one a ship of 250 tons in which Jones would sail as master. The venture would steer for Hawaii via the Horn, then to the sea otter habitats of Vancouver Island and Alaska. While the principal vessel traded there, Jones would sail the tender to Japan to offload his furs. If that failed, he would then go on to Macao or Canton. A hold full of tea, silk and porcelain would be a handsome cargo for the homeward track to Brest. Whether Jones intended to raise the Stars and Stripes rather than the *fleur de lis* at the factory he planned to erect there on the Northwest Coast is anyone's guess.

Jefferson, anxious about French colonial resurgence in Northwest America, asked Jones to find out all he could about the expedition of Lapérouse. Jones reported, on Spanish intelligence, that the French intended to establish a trading factory on the northwest coast but not a settlement; they also planned to examine New Holland (Australia) for future settlement possibilities. It seemed as if the French meant to drive a wedge between Russian and Spanish territories on the Northwest Coast. Lapérouse, backed by Parisian savants, had gone in imitation of Cook's expedition; his intentions were scientific in the main, but these concealed the imperial purposes of the French government, to the alarm of the Spanish. Jefferson had cause for worry.[18]

On June 23, 1786, the French frigates *Boussole* and *Astrolabe* made a landfall in 58° north latitude, and Mount St. Elias came into view through a damp, foggy veil. Gloom prevailed, and Lapérouse had no reason for cheerfulness: masses of snow covered barren cliffs that came down to the crashing surf, presenting a black, burned appearance. He coasted south and east, and near Mount Fairweather he picked out a promising entrance, possibly a strait, but it was a bay—Lituya Bay, Port des Français as he called it. He calculated this safe position as being ninety-nine miles northwest of the northward extremity of Spanish voyages and three hundred miles south of Prince William Sound, which was near where the Russians were. If the French government wished, it could establish a factory on this coast, for here, so he thought, no other nation could have the least pretext for opposing it. As authority Robin Inglis remarks, this was a location strategically placed between the limits of Spanish activity to the south and Russian to the north. Here Lapérouse planted the flag, true to instructions, then sailed for Monterey (where he met the Spanish mariner Martínez and gave him reports on Russian activities in Alaska) and laid a course for Kamchatka, where he sent his journals and recommendations to Paris. He entered Botany Bay just as the British were planting their colony in January 1788. Then he sailed once more and disappeared, wrecked on Vanikolo in the Santa Cruz group. The search for him, his men and the frigates consumed years and deflected any resumption of empire at Lituya Bay.[19]

All nations, speculators and investors were grasping at the possibilities of this sea otter rush. One biographer of Jones, Samuel Eliot Morison, says that Ledyard and Jones could have, in combination, made a killing in the northwest coast fur business. True. But this same author strangely states that the King of Spain, listening to Louis XVI of France's appeal, killed the scheme. More likely Jones's entanglements with the Russians shattered Ledyard's commercial chances—and they may even have blown the cover that Jefferson's hastily arranged passport gave the adventurer so that he might cross Russia unmolested. Even so, it is hard to quarrel with Morison's naming Ledyard "the celebrated rolling stone from Connecticut."[20]

Jefferson's relationship with Ledyard cooled, leaving Ledyard still further on the margins of influence in Paris. But for a brief moment fortune smiled. An English acquaintance, Sir James Hall, MP, got him passage on an English merchantman then lying in the Thames. The vessel was bound for the northwest coast on a fur venture. Ledyard imagined that once he was at Nootka Sound he would make his way back to Virginia overland. Just before the ship was to sail, he purchased two great dogs, an Indian pipe and a hatchet as accompaniments for his trek home from Nootka Sound across America. Again, circumstances lay beyond his control. English monopolies tied up trade with China and beyond the Capes. The vessel was seized by His Majesty's customs officers, and the project died. Ledyard once again found himself high and dry.

Ledyard returned to Jefferson, "panting for some new enterprise."[21] What could Jefferson suggest? His choices were limited. He could not offer capital, nor could he refer Ledyard to a suitable shipowner. The commercial world of the sea lay beyond him, was not in his gift.

Jefferson's mind roamed across all the remaining possibilities. Then he hit on an idea. Ledyard could explore the northwest coast of North America by going overland from St. Petersburg to Kamchatka, sailing on a Russian trading vessel to Unalaska or even Nootka Sound, and then crossing North America by land—exactly the reverse of the journey proposed to Alexander Mackenzie the next year by Peter Pond, the Connecticut Yankee trading for a North West Company firm near Lake Athabasca.

Jefferson states that he made the suggestion to Ledyard, not the other way round, though Ledyard's biographer demurs. "That patriot," writes biographer Sparks of Jefferson, "equally ardent in love of science, and friendly to every enterprise which had for its object the improvement of his country, received Ledyard with great kindness, and approved most highly of his design of an expedition to the Northwest Coast of America."[22]

Introducing Ledyard to General Lafayette in February 1786, Jefferson wrote:

Dear Sir

The Mr. John Ledyard, who proposes to undertake the journey through the Northern parts of Asia and America, is a citizen of Connecticut, one of the united states of America. He accompanied Capt. Cook in his last voyage to the North-western parts of America, and rendered himself useful to that officer, on some occasions, by a spirit of enterprise which has distinguished his whole life. He has genius, an education better than the common, and a talent for useful and interesting observation. I believe him to be an honest man, and a man of truth. To all this he adds just as much singularity of character, and of that particular kind too, as was necessary to make him undertake the journey he proposes. Should he get safe through it, I think he will give an interesting account of what he shall have seen.[23]

Jefferson knew Ledyard's expedition, if successful, would translate into immediate mercantile benefits and in the long run would redound to the commercial and political interests of the United States. The northwest coast, indeed western North America, remained largely unexplored and unclaimed except for those areas visited by tireless Canadian traders and infrequent Spanish mariners. To that point, only Cook's visit to Nootka Sound had breached the wall of ignorance and set down a marker for future British dominion in the far west. If Ledyard were successful, the United States might soon embrace the northwest coast of North America.

Jefferson regretted that Ledyard had so little support in the United States and also that, in European circles, he was hostage to fortune. As Ledyard wrote to his brother Isaac, he was left in the metropolis of France "the very football of chance." But now fortune shone on him. From a gloomy garret and with nothing more than a clean shirt, he had been invited "to the splendid Tables of the first characters of this Kingdom." In fourteen days, he told his brother, he would set off from Paris for St. Petersburg, then Moscow, Kamchatka and the coast of America, travelling overland to New York. "I will write you from St. Petersburg after I have seen Kate of the North."[24]

Ledyard arrived in St. Petersburg in March 1787, having travelled by foot via Stockholm, Lapland and Finland. His shoes were worn thin, his purse empty. The empress Catherine the Great, now in the twenty-fifth year of her reign, was, alas, away inspecting her dominions in the Crimea when Ledyard reached St. Petersburg. It is tempting to imagine what would have transpired between the two of them had they met. Ledyard would have been well received, doubtless welcomed into the warm bedchamber of "Kate of the North," as he dubbed her. General Lafayette had backed Jefferson's assurances of Ledyard's good behaviour and undoubted prospects, and he told Catherine's minister of state, Baron von Grimm, that Ledyard was completely preoccupied with remarkable voyages, his dominant passion, and that Catherine, who reigned supreme in the arts, letters and sciences, would be pleased with "the ardent traveler."[25]

In St. Petersburg, Peter Pallas, a scientist and a person known to Sir Joseph Banks, the botanist on Cook's first voyage, befriended Ledyard. So did the Portuguese ambassador, who cashed an unauthorized warrant in Banks's name for the credit of the penniless American. William Brown, a Scottish physician in Russian service, took Ledyard three thousand miles eastward, to Barnaul in western Siberia. At Yakutsk, farther east again, on the Lena River, Ledyard encountered Captain Joseph Billings, an English mariner, now in Russian imperial service, engaged in a projected survey of Catherine's northeastern territories and shores. Billings and Ledyard had been shipmates in the Cook expedition, with Billings an astronomer's assistant. Billings intended to take Ledyard with him to Okhotsk on the Pacific seaboard the next spring, but Russian officials got word of this non-resident alien among them on unauthorized business. The diary of Catherine's personal secretary in Moscow says: "It is ordered to send back the American John Ledyard, making his way from Okhotsk to America, from this place; he was a naval cadet with the famous Cook."

Ledyard was only two hundred miles from Pacific salt water when the cold hand of Russian officialdom clamped itself on his shoulder. There is speculation that Russian fur-trading interests conspired to have Ledyard arrested, but this theory does not pass scrutiny. Russian intelligence agents had deduced from such intercepted sources as a Jefferson letter to Lafayette and a document showing Ledyard's petition for safe passage through Russian realms that Ledyard was on foreign, private and, therefore, dangerous business.

Martin Sauer, an Englishman and secretary to Billings's expedition, gives us eyewitness details of the arrest made in the depths of the Russian winter:

> At Yakutsk we found, to our great surprise, Mr. Ledyard, an old companion of Captain Billings, in Cook's voyage round the world; he then served in the capacity of corporal, but now called himself an American colonel, and wished to cross over to the American Continent with our Expedition, for the purpose of exploring it on foot.
>
> In the evening of the 24th February, while I was playing at cards with the Brigadier and some company of his, a secretary belonging to one of the courts of justice came in, and told us, with great concern, that the Governor-General had received positive orders from the Empress, immediately to send one of the Expedition, an Englishman, under guard to the private inquisition at Moscow; but that he did not know the name of the person, and the Captain Billings was with a private party at the Governor-General's. Now, as Ledyard and I were the only Englishmen here, I could not help smiling at the news, when two hussars came into the room, and told me that the Commandant wished to see me immediately. The consternation into which the visitors were thrown is not to be described. I assured them that it must be a mistake, and went with the guards to the Commandant. Here I found Mr. Ledyard under arrest. He told me, that he had sent for Captain Billings, but he would not come to him. He then began to explain his situation, and said that he was taken up as a French spy, whereas Captain Billings could prove the contrary ... but the Captain

assured me that it was an absolute order from the Empress, and he could not help him. Ledyard took a friendly leave of me, desired his remembrance to his friends, and with astonishing composure leaped into the kibitka, and drove off, with two guards, one on each side. I wished to travel with him a little way, but was not permitted. I therefore returned to my company, and explained the matter to them; but, though this eased their minds with regard to my fate, it did not restore their harmony. Ledyard's behaviour, however, had been haughty, and not at all condescending, which certainly made him enemies.[26]

The Russian guards escorted Ledyard first to Moscow and then to the border of Poland, where, at Mogilëv, he was set free.

At the beginning of May 1788, a weary, impoverished and perhaps chastened Ledyard made his way back to London and the sympathetic companionship of Sir Joseph Banks. He had experienced, he told his benefactor, "a miserable journey, in a miserable country, in a miserable season, in miserable health, and a miserable purse; and disappointed of his darling enterprise." Ledyard also told Banks that "though he had been retarded in his pursuits by malice, he had not travelled totally in vain; his observations in Asia being, perhaps, as complete as a longer visit would have rendered them."[27] Indeed what he did write—though not all of it survives—forms a traveller's tale for the ages. What might have been the results of his intended walk across America? One can only wonder.

Banks and other scientific and literary worthies of his circle exhibited unflagging generosity to the American. Before long, Banks introduced Ledyard to the kindly Quaker Henry Beaufoy, a member of parliament, a man who was becoming the chief fixer of African discoveries and who had the ear of the British ministry of the day. Banks told Ledyard of the Association for Discovering the Inland Countries of Africa, which was then being established at St. Alban's Tavern, off Pall Mall, London.

The African Association, as it was generally called, represented growing economic interests in west Africa, but it had other goals, lost to time, including emancipating slaves and ending the slave trade. The British government would soon establish the colony of Sierra Leone to further these purposes. For these reasons, geographical discoveries in Africa had a political overtone.[28] A succession of explorers was sent forth under the agency of the African Association, and Ledyard was among the first, if not the first. Banks gave Ledyard fair warning when he told the American that the expedition lying ahead of him would be almost as perilous as that which he had just come from.

Beaufoy, secretary of the Association besides being its heart and soul, takes up the story: "Before I had learnt from the note [of introduction from Banks] the name and business of my visitor, I was struck with the manliness of his person, the breadth of his chest, the openness of his countenance, and the inquietude of his eye."[29] Beaufoy spread a map of Africa before Ledyard and indicated the objectives. When asked when he would be able to accept the invitation to lead the expedition, Ledyard replied that he could do so the next day. Beaufoy, as quick as a wink, though doubtless delighted with Ledyard's self-assurance and willingness, replied that he and the committee would not be able to frame the exact instructions quite by then. But a deal had been struck. Ledyard was to travel from Marseilles to Cairo and Mecca, then across the Red Sea and west to the Niger River, and then back to London from European forts on the West Africa coast.

Ledyard left London on June 30, 1788, woefully underfunded, for the Association's membership, recently formed, had not yet completed its subscriptions. Fifty days later, having assumed the necessary dress of a traveller in Egypt, he arrived in Cairo on August 19. Here he was befriended by the Venetian consul and assisted by some Carmelite nuns. He travelled locally but could not advance his expedition. Ledyard intended to attach himself to a caravan heading for Sennar, a town in Sudan on the Blue Nile, but the very day that he was to have left, January 4, 1789, bad weather delayed the caravan.

The British ambassador in Cairo, George Baldwin, reported to Beaufoy that Ledyard flew into a violent rage at the conductors. He became so deranged that he tried to treat himself with an emetic, but he took a dose so strong that he vomited excessively and burst a blood vessel. In three days he suffocated and died. Thus ended, on January 10, 1789, the life of the American Marco Polo.

Thomas Paine, then residing in London, wrote Jefferson to confirm the truth of the rumour of Ledyard's passing and enclosed a copy of Beaufoy's report to Banks on the affair.[30] The kind-hearted Beaufoy spilled over with grief. Although he blamed Ledyard's impatience for the disaster that had overcome his friend, yet he found much to admire in Ledyard's splendid and unusual character:

> To those who have never seen Mr. Ledyard, it may not, perhaps, be uninteresting to know, that his person, though scarcely exceeding the middle size, was remarkably expressive of activity and strength; and that his manners, though unpolished, were neither uncivil nor unpleasing. Little attentive to difference of rank, he seemed to consider all men as his equals, and as such he respected them. His genius, though uncultivated and irregular, was original and comprehensive. Ardent in his wishes, yet calm in his deliberations; daring in his purposes, but guarded in his measures; impatient of control, yet capable of strong endurance; adventurous beyond the conception of ordinary men, yet wary and considerate, and attentive to all precautions, he appeared to be formed by Nature for achievements of hardihood and peril.[31]

Jefferson greeted the news with confirmed sadness. His mind would have raced back to that first meeting with the young Yankee from Connecticut in Paris, and to the expansive scheme they had dreamed up that saw the undaunted sailor traversing two continents, first Eurasia and then America, even as far as his home on the east coast of North America. "Thus failed the first attempt to explore the western part of our northern continent," he wrote of the adventure. But it would not be the last attempt. Before hearing of Ledyard's death, Jefferson had informed a friend: "My last accounts from Ledyard ... were from Grand Cairo. He was just then plunging into the unknown regions of Africa, probably never to emerge again. If he returns, he has promised me to go to America to penetrate from Kentucky to the western side of the Continent."[32]

Nearly forty years later, Sparks speculated that those details of the scheme that Ledyard had told Jefferson "were deeply impressed on the mind of Mr. Jefferson, and in them originated the journeys of Lewis and Clark overland to the Pacific Ocean, twenty years afterwards, which was projected by him, and prosecuted under [his] auspices."[33]

In later years, and in his autobiography (1821), Jefferson distanced himself from Ledyard. He took pains to note that the empress Catherine had never granted Ledyard permission to cross Russia, and that the American explorer had done so of his own volition. The empress "refused permission at once, considering the enterprise as entirely chimerical. But Ledyard would not relinquish it, persuading himself that, by proceeding to St. Petersburg, he could satisfy the Empress of its practicability, and obtain her permission. He went accordingly."[34]

And so Ledyard disappeared into time and space, an enigma even to his end in Africa. He had sailed with Cook and been there at his death. He'd known the presidents of Dartmouth and of Yale, dined with the great and the good in Paris and London, and invited the support, moral if not financial, of the weighty promoters of science and exploration in London. His passion inspired respect. To Beaufoy goes the last word, for it was he who last saw Ledyard outward bound from London. He knew the mettle of the man as well as Jefferson did and probably better:

> He seems to have endured the utmost pressure of distress. "I am accustomed … (said he, in our last conversation—'twas on the morning of his departure for Africa)—I am accustomed to hardships. I have known both hunger and nakedness to the utmost extremity of human suffering. I have known what it is to have food given one as charity to a madman; and I have at times been obliged to shelter myself under the miseries of that character, to avoid a heavier calamity. My distresses have been greater than I have ever owned, or ever will own to any man. Such evils are terrible to bear; but they never yet had power to turn me from my purpose. If I live, I will faithfully perform,

in its utmost extent, my engagement to the Society; and if I perish in the attempt, my honour will still be safe, for death cancels all bonds."[35]

The dreamer from Groton, by episodes of daring and fortune unknown to common man, lit the way for those who came later to success. Ledyard was a forerunner of Lewis and Clark in a strange, indirect way. He had no intention of carving an American empire out of the great region between the Mississippi and the Pacific, and we cannot be sure of his ultimate intentions save for speculating on his wandering nature, his mercurial disposition and his unbounded imagination.

He lives with us still, this strange and irrepressible character, who we like the more with the knowing and the new details that continue to come to hand, especially from New England, English and Russian texts. No man of commerce this, but a traveller and voyager across continents and seas. Only two sections of the northern hemisphere escaped him: the two hundred miles from Yakutsk to Okhotsk and then the three thousand plus miles from Nootka Sound to Philadelphia. Otherwise he saw the vast bulk of it—and set others to thinking of how geography and science were ending speculation and of how nations and empires and their agents, such as those who had detained him in the wilds of Russia and deported him on promise that he should never return, were shaping the course of history.

Chapter 1

DREAMS, SCHEMES, REALITIES

Visions, perceptions and dreams of western destiny—intangible as they may seem—were often the basis for North American discovery, for surely Champlain and La Salle, Carver and Fremont, to give only a few examples, were driven by visions of finding proof that would end speculations. By contrast, pragmatic pursuits, such as the lure of Eldorado, the quest for land or furs, and the necessity of surveying, drove the actual discovery of America's interior and shores. Dreams and visions suggest romance, while the pragmatic encompasses the workaday, even the prosaic. The imagination fuels the pragmatic, and the pragmatic, in turn, modifies the visionary. The navigator Amerigo Vespucci told his sponsor: "Rationally, let it be said in a whisper, experience is certainly worth more than theory."[1]

By the last quarter of the eighteenth century and the first decade of the nineteenth, there remained visions of a northwest passage by water still waiting to be found; every hard-earned detail of geographical rendering that had been worked out along the margins north of the Canadian Shield pointed farther north for such a passage. The possibilities of a *mer de l'ouest* were receding, and British naval explorers, Captain George Vancouver

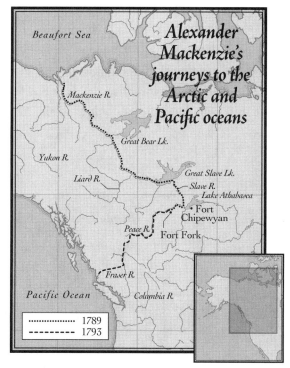

Beaufort Sea

Alexander Mackenzie's journeys to the Arctic and Pacific oceans

Mackenzie R.

Great Bear Lk.

Yukon R.

Liard R.

Great Slave Lk.

Slave R.

Lake Athabasca

Fort Chipewyan

Peace R. Fort Fork

Fraser R.

Pacific Ocean   *Columbia R.*

················ 1789
---------- 1793

among them, were trying to end speculation about what was termed a great hyperborean sea to the north. The great Salt Lake of what is now Utah was hardly known, and Palliser's Triangle, the dry belt of land in the southern regions of present-day Alberta and Saskatchewan, had yet to be uncovered. Indeed, at the turn of that century, a vast quarter of northern and western North America had yet to be explored.

If the particulars of that space were as yet unknown, the probable features were beginning, year by year, to fall into place. Aaron Arrowsmith, distinguished London cartographer, kept track of all such continental discoveries, and he updated his edition of the great map of North America as new information trickled into his office. Cartographic companies were so confident the details would be filled in that they supplied explorers with a blank version of the map and asked them to add their discoveries. Arrowsmith benefited much from the empirical research that Canadian fur traders provided. Lewis and Clark benefited in turn.

While armchair geographers of the Atlantic world pressed on with their imaginings, mariners were already in the Pacific, pragmatically surveying the actual coastline. Spain's Vizcaíno and Cabrillo, England's Drake and Cook, Russia's Bering and Chirikov, France's Lapérouse—these and many others were delineating such vital spaces on the western North America map as Bering Strait, San Francisco Bay, and Nootka Sound on Vancouver Island. These were enough to indicate the tendencies of the coast from Baja California to northwestern Alaska. Thus when Alexander Mackenzie, of the Montreal-based North West Company of Canada, or when Meriwether Lewis and William Clark, commanding the United States of America's Corps of Discovery, arrived at Pacific tidewater, which they did respectively in 1793 and 1805, they were coming to a shoreline already known. Captain George Vancouver had been to the same Dean Channel as Mackenzie that summer of 1793. Cook had been only one hundred miles away from the spot fifteen years earlier. John Meares, the sea otter trader, had been at Nootka in 1788 and had provided charts and maps of the area, though these were, admittedly, in error and in dispute. Even so, Mackenzie had them in his map case and consulted them on occasion. Similarly, Lewis and Clark knew where the mouth of the Columbia River was from the discoveries of Bruno de Hezeta, Robert Gray and especially William Broughton. By the time Lewis and Clark reached Pacific tidewater, a great number of maritime fur-trading vessels had come that way. If we understand the larger context of North American exploration, we better appreciate the role of Lewis and Clark. We see them as North American explorers, not American ones. Their role is not diminished but is more correctly understood. Of equal significance, Mackenzie's explorations—and explorations by agents of the North West Company, including David Thompson and Simon Fraser—loom at least as large as Lewis and Clark's in historical importance.

It is a matter of record, though one hardly known, that Thomas Jefferson was the conduit between Mackenzie's journey and the Lewis and Clark expedition. Mackenzie's discoveries prompted and accelerated an American response. Fear that Britain would outdistance the United States on the northwestern margins of American territories spurred the president to effect a journey of exploration. Once decided upon, the expedition was quickly mounted—and we shall return to it and to the Jeffersonian "connection," as it may be called. For the moment, however, Alexander Mackenzie's amazing feats require description and analysis.

Alexander Mackenzie, a prince among fur-trading explorers, though strangely independent of many of his partners in the North West Company, was driven by inner logic that a devotee of Freud might find appealing. He was ardent, thoughtful and well-educated. Early biographical particulars of note include a

In 1789, Mackenzie canoed to the Arctic by way of the Mackenzie River, which he once referred to in private correspondence as "River Disappointment." In 1793, he was the first European to cross the continent, an arduous transit. In 1802, Mackenzie was knighted for his accomplishments as an explorer. British Columbia Archives, PDP-02244

downwardly mobile family thrown out of the Hebrides; a childhood and youth without parents; the life of a boy soldier, then a counting-house clerk and finally a fur trader sent out to the wilds of what are now central Saskatchewan and northern Alberta. In this latter location, Mackenzie became the understudy of a Connecticut Yankee, the enigmatic Peter Pond—violent in style and action, yet a powerful visionary who imagined from aboriginal accounts that a river flowed west from Great Slave Lake to the coast, where Captain James Cook reported that he had found a river. This was "Cook's River," and so it showed on Cook's charts. Here surely was a northwest passage. But Pond was a murderer, or so it was claimed by maligners or rivals, and such criminal behaviour was not countenanced by partners of the North West Company or by the British government in Quebec, which was then seeking to expand its jurisdiction, and way of law, into the First Nations territories.[2] He was obliged to sell his shares in the North West Company and leave the fur trade.

To Mackenzie fell the task of following up on Pond's musings and dreams. Mackenzie had a hard-driving Scots Presbyterian outlook, and he saw rivers and lakes as vectors of trade and commerce—and thus of profit, corporate and personal. On the eve of his May 9, 1793, departure from his advance base

The celebrated inscription by Alexander Mackenzie was originally marked with vermilion mixed in melted grease. The Government of Canada later had the inscription chiselled out and painted, as is shown here. It is located in Alexander Mackenzie Provincial Park, British Columbia. Library and Archives Canada, C-003131

at Fort Fork,[3] near the fork of the Peace and Smoky rivers, destined, he hoped, for the Pacific Ocean, he wrote his expectations to his cousin, confidant and trading chum Roderick Mackenzie: "I send you a couple of Guineas. The rest I take with me to traffick with the Russians ...."[4] His object was to reach Muscovite trading posts at Unalaska and even, if necessary, Kamchatka. We do not know if he hoped to reach the Winter Palace of Catherine the Great in St. Petersburg, but in the end he undertook no Russian journey, nor did he reach any Russian post in Alaska. We now know that his real intent was to reach the Pacific overland. This he did. On July 22, 1793, he wrote on a rock these famous though straightforward words: "Alex Mackenzie from Canada by land 22^d July 1793."[5]

Not to be forgotten in all of this is the fact that his overland journey was the second he made in quest of a northwest passage by land. In 1789, hoping to find the route mentioned to Pond by the Cree, and spoken of by Pond, Mackenzie made an arduous river journey to the Arctic Ocean by way of what the Dene called *Deh Cho*, Great River—now the Mackenzie River. Mackenzie, on only one occasion, spoke of this as River Disappointment—it led north not west. But after regrouping both his finances and his trade, and after upgrading his scientific and surveying skills in London, he undertook his second great quest, the successful one. It remains one of the most remarkable journeys of North American history and, indeed, one of the unique human achievements in all of history.

Mackenzie was driven by personal demands for achievement, success and wealth, but it is important to appreciate that he was also working out the last chapter of a great and larger drama that was begun by Columbus and Vespucci, and pursued by Jonathan Carver, Robert Rogers, Peter Pond, Alexander Henry the Elder and others, including La Vérendrye and La Salle. Remarkable, however, is the fact that Mackenzie writes as if he stands alone, separate from all those who preceded him in the quest. One can excuse an explorer for failing to give credit to those who have gone before. Yet it seems penny-pinching in the extreme that he did not give Pond even a credit. In the history of the fur trade that forms part of Mackenzie's *Voyages from Montreal* (1801), his superb book of travels describing his two great quests, any prior discoveries are spelled out as fur-trade achievements—new posts, new Native alliances, new zones for exploitation. That age saw commerce as a vehicle for development, and Mackenzie stood at the forefront of his age, characterized by Adam Smith as one in which labour could be the means of bringing wealth and prominence. Mackenzie was Smith's credo personified. Mackenzie connected fur trade with empire.

On his return to Canada, Mackenzie lobbied both the lieutenant-governor of Upper Canada, John Graves Simcoe, and the governor of Lower Canada, Lord

Dorchester, about the necessity of protecting and enlarging Canadian trade to the west, the object being trade to China, Japan and elsewhere in the Pacific rim. Mackenzie did not stop there, for two factors compelled him to enlarge the trading world of the counting houses of Montreal. One was the Hudson's Bay Company, the chartered giant registered in London, which had historical pre-eminence in North America and held a monopoly on the use of rivers and bays draining Rupert's Land toward Hudson Bay. The other was the growing worry, as fur traders saw it, of settlement infringing on trading prospects. When land was divided up and farmed, it hampered the abilities of trappers and hunters to catch animals and collect furs, and it diminished wetlands. For many years Mackenzie fought against the Earl of Selkirk's scheme to plant a colony of Scots settlers—"oatmeal eaters," the Montrealers derisively called them—at the forks of the Red and Assiniboine rivers. Mackenzie and Selkirk were buying up HBC shares to thwart or advance the plan respectively. Mackenzie lost that corporate stock-grabbing war. He later lobbied the British Colonial Office, the department of state responsible for regulating trade and commerce in British dominions, for support. But despite the enthusiasms of this scheme, and his careful preparations to arrange business links with other corporations, crown-authorized and other, Mackenzie was never able to break through existing systems. "Imperial schemer" he might have been; "imperial fixer" he was not. It was not for want of trying. Simply, political power to direct British commercial policy lay beyond his grasp. In the end he was a corporate promoter of empire, and certainly within his own sphere as discoverer, trader and capitalist he was without equal.

In a way he speaks to an older Canada, an older North America, for he was the last of the fur-trading barons, and when the Hudson's Bay Company was reorganized and swallowed up the North West Company name in 1821, Mackenzie's dream of a Montreal-based Canadian fur trade had already died with him in 1820.

That was all in the future, however. When Mackenzie returned to Montreal from the Pacific in 1794, Jefferson, urbane and learned (and cut from an entirely different cloth than Mackenzie), had already been gathering bits and pieces of information about western North American discovery and development since the early 1780s. By the end of the eighteenth century, the United States was beginning to garner the remnants of French and Spanish borderlands in America. Florida and Texas lay ahead as objects of imperial ambition, manifest destiny or continental desire and consolidation, and Spanish claims to California and Oregon also needed addressing by diplomacy or war.

In 1801, Jefferson was the newly elected president of the United States. A pre-emptive impulse coursed through his veins. Other presidents had it, George Washington among them. The urge to provide security against foreign, principally British, encroachments (real or imagined) played a major part in Jefferson's actions. Enlarging the republic, or the federation, was problematic at the time. Who would pay for policing such an enlarged federation? How would the Union be kept secure? Indeed, what was the role of the US Army in defining the west and the boundaries of the nation? Jefferson was keen only to have protection for immediate waters and lands of the United States, as his naval policy shows. He was interested, too, in the idea of federated republics, all of them in sympathy to Washington, understandably. But the worry of imperial overextension had to be matched to the pre-emptive impulses of his age. In the long course of American territorial expansion, Jefferson stands at a unique and important time. The Lewis and Clark expedition may therefore be seen as having been thrust upon him by the requirements of the age. Any president might have acted similarly.

At the same time that Mackenzie was reading proofs of his book and compiling the great maps, Jefferson hired Meriwether Lewis as private secretary. "[The President] was a man whose virtue and talents I have ever adored, and always conceived second to none," mused Lewis, who was buoyed up by the prospects, raised in his own estimation, "insomuch that I have almost prevailed on myself to believe that my abilities are equal to the task."[6] Here was a different fellow than Mackenzie. The position of private secretary was ill-defined but promising for someone who could make something of it. Jefferson wanted a person with knowledge of frontier travel and of the army (and its politics), someone who might be able to provide information to himself and the public about western lands and possibilities. At the time, Jefferson was probably considering sending

Lewis to investigate the Ohio Valley, the current interest of western settlers and frontier folk. Lewis was in his assignment two years before Jefferson was compelled to act on different information.

"Have you seen McKenzie's account of his journeys across the Continent & to the Northern Ocean?" Dr. Caspar Wistar of Philadelphia asked Jefferson in one of several letters to the president. "He had very peculiar advantages for such an enterprize, & happily availed himself of them. It is reported here that he is at New York, on his way to the North West Country, & that he has provided himself with the vaccine virus for the benefit of the unfortunate natives. His melancholy account of the effects of the Small Pox in that country must add greatly to your satisfaction on account of your exertions to diffuse the benefits of that very happy discovery."[7]

About this time, Polish diarist Julian Niemcewicz, a contemporary who met Mackenzie, referred to him in correspondence with Jefferson as "the celebrated traveller" who "has made a journey which is the most astonishing that has ever been undertaken, having crossed the whole breadth of the immense continent of North America."[8] London was taking note of him, and scientific circles were also beginning to pay attention to Mackenzie, the man who had made a fabulous northern as well as western tour of North America—and reached the Pacific.[9]

Voyages from Montreal was admittedly an outstanding book, well received. Two months after its publication, the king, George III, made the young Scot a knight, no small distinction. But despite this, Mackenzie was entrammelled in the politics of corporations and crown-based schemes for trade and dominion.

It was in Monticello, not London, that Mackenzie made his mark. In the summer of 1802, Jefferson ordered a copy of Mackenzie's book of travels and the most recent edition of Aaron Arrowsmith's map of North America. As early as 1795, Arrowsmith had showed Mackenzie's routes, and the newer editions, such as that of 1802, filled the now diminishing gaunt and yawning spaces of northwestern America with new details. Riddles were being solved, river courses plotted, mountains marked down on pieces of paper—time seemed to be running out for American discoveries.

Voyages from Montreal was the most important geographical work in Jefferson's library. Jefferson may have learned about the famous fur-trading explorer before—from a sea otter pelt brought east from the Pacific coast by the traveller, or from Mackenzie's visits to New York and Philadelphia to promote cross-border trade.

Had Mackenzie's book not dealt with political and geostrategic concerns, Jefferson might not have paid it so much attention. However, when Mackenzie talked of opening a great commercial intercourse between the Atlantic and Pacific oceans, and developing a great new Canadian dominion suitable for settlement of a civilized people, with interior establishments linked to coastal communities and places for merchant trade that would control the fur trade north of the forty-eighth parallel to the pole (leaving the Russians their existing quarter)—alarm bells rang in Monticello. Mackenzie pointed specifically to the Columbia River as the great line of communication on the Pacific coast. And to all of this would be added "the fishing in both seas, and the markets of the four quarters of the globe."[10]

Jefferson knew that if Canada, an imperial extension of Britain, stretched to the mouth of the Columbia River, it would outflank any intended US claim to that locale. Jefferson also knew that British and Canadian traders retained an informal empire in Michigan and Wisconsin, and that the Canadian–American border only stretched as far west as the Lake of the Woods. By 1803, when Jefferson was consulting Mackenzie's book, the American imperial quest was gathering momentum with the western tide of settlers, followed by government action, political, diplomatic and military. Details of the Missouri River valley remained uncertain in the eastern American mind at the beginning of the nineteenth century, and defining these became the first task of a Corps of Discovery, with the delineation of western rivers to the Pacific the corollary.

"The object of your mission," ran Jefferson's instructions to Lewis, "is to explore the Missouri river & such principal stream of it, as, by its course & communication with the waters of the Pacific Ocean, may offer the most direct & practicable water communication across this continent, for the purposes of commerce." The aims of the expedition were thoroughly described and detailed, and thoroughness—not speed—was of the essence. Great pains were to be taken to provide accurate descriptions. Answers were needed for a great number of questions. The whole expedition was to proceed with a view to safety, and there is an expressed concern by the patron, Jefferson, on behalf of government, that the explorers should go and return safely.

No such statement was given to Alexander Mackenzie. Indeed, his only instructions were those he commanded of himself with North West Company backing. Where a terrible compulsion sent him forth on his journey, as had driven Balboa before him, Jefferson alone—in the words of Jeannette Mirsky, one of the first to draw the comparison—was the creative agent, the propelling factor, for the Corps of Discovery. Lewis and Clark were but agents serving his vision. "Capable they were, but they lack the glamour that glitters around the other two. The agonized urgency, the lonely unshared vigils, are gone; their place is taken by conscientiousness, by a meticulous adherence to the full spirit of instructions. These men are carrying out a job capably; they are not giving form to a vision."[11]

Lewis and Clark, captains on a mission of science and empire, kept their instructions closely at hand and always on their minds. They followed the rivers and noted the tributaries, made detailed descriptions of courses and possibilities of the same, and maintained a riverine mentality entirely in keeping with the tasks at hand. "Behind Jefferson's instructions," writes Albert Furtwangler, "lay the president's understanding of how important rivers were and would be to the development of the continent."[12] Throughout the great interior, the St. Lawrence, the Ohio, the Missouri-Mississippi and now, possibly, the Columbia offered new passageways. In fact, as is well known, it was possession of the mouth of the Mississippi, and of New Orleans in particular, that drove a worried Jefferson to effect the Louisiana Purchase in 1803 and remove it from France's hands. Should the United States have to go to war against France, should the latter attack New Orleans, the United States, Jefferson reasoned, would become a slave to international realities. "The day that France takes possession of N. Orleans ... seals the union of two nations who in conjunction can maintain exclusive possession of the ocean. From that moment we must marry ourselves to the British fleet and nation."[13] In other words, security of continental rivers and control of river estuaries and ports were the Jeffersonian rule.

Control the perimeter and thereby control the interior: this is a powerful logic in the making of continental aspirations and is a great legacy of this Jeffersonian era. Asia—China, Japan, India—is absent from the president's logic. Even so, the security of commerce on and over the seas remains a principal notion of Jefferson. And in that age it was trade to China and security of trade in the Mediterranean (where the Dey of Algiers and others posed risks to American shipping and the Stars and Stripes) that compelled his attention.

Bringing the Mackenzie expedition and Lewis and Clark's Corps of Discovery together reveals fundamental differences between the two. It also brings into sharp focus the differences of substance that separate Canadian from American history. Mackenzie was a Scot, a trader, a Montreal-based agent of commercial empire. Lewis and Clark were US-born nationals, army officers and servants of the state. Mackenzie wrote his own instructions, unhindered by the requirements of his masters, both corporate and national or imperial. He had corporate backing but he defined his own movement. Lewis and Clark kept to the letter of instructions written for them by higher authority. Mackenzie led a lightly equipped party of eight Canadian voyageurs, one fellow countryman and two Natives to act as guides/hunters/interpreters through some of the toughest terrain imaginable. Lewis and Clark also covered difficult terrain, but with a party four times larger. Mackenzie's scientific and geographical discoveries led to no immediate political or imperial result. Lewis and Clark's led to a more ready opening of western realms, even though they pointed to difficulties with certain groups of indigenous people. Mackenzie was no surveyor. Lewis and Clark were surveyors and minute recorders of detail. In consequence, Mackenzie's legacy was that he pointed out the prospects for the future. It was fully a century after his explorations before the details of the Canadian northwest were completely revealed. Mackenzie opened up the fur-trading conduits of the north, and for many years, until the 1870s, the Canadian northwest remained very much a trading realm. By contrast, Lewis and Clark opened the rivers and watersheds to fur traders, travellers and pioneering settlers—and they indicated ways westward that others readily followed.

Population pressures in the United States, and immigration to America, aided the westward quest. Where Mackenzie offered a northern destiny toward the west, Lewis and Clark offered a western destiny to the west. Mackenzie showed in his book an agreeable relationship with aboriginal people, one that the fur trade understandably fostered. Lewis and Clark more than hinted at difficulties that would arise—infractions and eruptions—in the westward journey of a nation.

In the end, neither Mackenzie nor Lewis and Clark nor Thompson, whom we will meet presently, stand alone in achievement. They are all part of a larger, longstanding body of explorers, dating to Vespucci and others, who sought to uncover the secrets of the last unexplored quarters of North America. We look back through their books and records with not a little wonder, for the world they were describing was one newly revealed to the wider world. They witnessed the last age before settlement and exploitation, yet they presaged such development. Neither expedition carried with it the moral concern that today's students of history preoccupy themselves with. It would be a mistake to argue that they were, in their several ways, heralds of a destiny that would crush all before it in its wake. Mackenzie and Lewis and Clark did not see their missions that way. Nor did Thompson. Those who are interested in this age are attracted to it because by studying it they are resituated in the continuum of time. Thus we see Mackenzie, rightly, as an individual seeking fame and fortune in a world of intense corporate rivalry, and we admire his pluck and drive, rather unusual then as now. Thus, too, in Lewis and Clark we see the corporate world of government and science stamping itself on the American west, presaging a greater government control that is soon to follow. Indeed, in the recent historical literature of "what is the west," the concept of government preceding settlement, rather than the other way round, has certain validity. In the northern realm of commerce and discovery promoted by Mackenzie, we see, too, an urging and a requirement for rivers as conduits of commerce. In the northern destiny, which Mackenzie heralded, commerce predated western development. In the western destiny, which Lewis and Clark advertised, commerce and settlement marched hand in hand.

Chapter 2

VISIT OF THE STRANGER FROM THE WEST

A s he came into the clearing at the southern fringe of the bush garden of Upper Canada on September 8, 1794, the traveller spied a timber structure known locally as Navy Hall. In the days when the British, Canadians and their aboriginal allies used to defend the imperial frontier against the rebellious Americans, this building at Newark (now Niagara-on-the-Lake, Ontario) had been a well-sited garrison and storehouse. The observer wondered if it would ever be used again for combat. Since 1783, peace had reigned on the border between the British dominion and the new republic of the United States. Still, he recalled that not far from where he now stood, he had fought for the Loyalist cause as a boy soldier in the American Revolutionary War. The Mohawk Valley had been the scene of terribly brutal warfare and reprisals. Since then, animosities between the empire and the new nationalists had never completely died down. Fires that had not been extinguished remained glowing embers. Gusts of wind could quickly bring them to flame. And resumption of such frontier war seemed a dreadful thing to contemplate. This he knew not only from his own

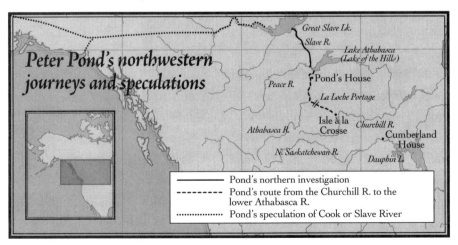

experience but from the loss of a parent. His father, an officer in a loyal regiment, had died a prisoner on a remote island in the St. Lawrence.

Alexander Mackenzie, the explorer whose fame had not yet arrived, walked on toward Navy Hall. Such a pleasant prospect rose before him. A Union flag, or jack, waved listlessly from the flagpole, and the whitewashed structure gleamed in the midday sun. Gardens for the imperial larder lay close at hand. Soldiers posted on guard duty, some smoking, others cleaning their Brown Bess muskets, added spectacular brightness to the scene. They were not in uniform and were not expecting inspection that day. Yet there was no doubting their readiness to defend the frontier on that or any other occasion. A small number of enlisted men from the famed Royal Artillery lingered there too, ready to serve the guns that defended the nearby blockhouse and pointed across the Niagara River at this strategically narrow spot. American forces, both regular and irregular, had come this way ten years before. Who knew when they might come again.

There had been recent American rumblings about the rights of Canadians trading on American soil, but that had been cleared up when the American jurist John Jay had gone to London and negotiated a treaty with the British. Now the indigenous people could pass back and forth across the border in a form of free trade, provided they carried their goods only in small bundles and packages. Canadians could trade south of the line, too. But in order to extract this special concession, the British had promised to withdraw from their several garrisons and fur posts, some deep in American sovereign territory, and abandon them to their rivals. Detroit, Michilimackinac, and Prairie du Chien numbered among these posts.

Now Navy Hall and the forts of the Niagara River formed the bastion of British Empire in Upper Canada. On the northern shore of Lake Ontario stood Fort York (now Toronto), key to the communications that led to the vast interior of the continent via the upper Great Lakes. To the west, on the Detroit River opposite bustling Detroit, stood the British post of Fort Malden and the shipyard at nearby Amherstburg. Only two anchors of empire existed north of Detroit. First was Fort St. Joseph, a post on St. Joseph Island, not far from Michilimackinac in the northwest corner of Lake Huron. This garrison, thought by its older inhabitants to be like a Siberian exile, guarded the straits leading to Sault Ste. Marie, and it was thus the watchtower for all the commercial traffic between the Canadian northwest and the great port of Montreal or the administrative capital of Canada, the town of Quebec. The fur trade, lifeblood of the colonies of Upper and Lower Canada, flowed back and forth along this North Channel. Sault Ste. Marie, the second locus of power, had a small garrison, but its real function was as a shipping place, an entryway to Lake Superior and thus to the grandest fur region on the globe, the boreal or northern forest of Canada. There was none finer, and it seemed to become an even greater Eldorado the more the likes of Alexander Mackenzie worked and explored its hinterland. Profit and power—these were the intertwining maxims of the British Empire, as true in Canada as in Jamaica, Barbados, India or Cape Town, and the young Scot, only thirty-three years old, seemed to personify this union of imperial drives and purposes.

Mackenzie strode, a little lamely, to the door of Navy Hall. He knocked. We do not know if his hosts expected his arrival, but perhaps it was not necessary to have an appointment when you were on such important business. A servant greeted him and invited him inside. Among the mahogany furniture, plush drapes, lace curtains, oriental carpets and bright candles and kerosene lamps, Mackenzie stood out in his roughness. The years of wilderness travel had made his roman bearing even more striking. In one hand he carried his black broad-brimmed hat. He had a gun, used on both his journeys,[1] and at his side hung a short sword, or hanger. He wore a shirt of coarse but sturdy cotton. A white scarf surrounded his neck almost like a clerical collar, and an old dun vest covered his front. His long dusty jacket, or frock coat, had the cutaway form of his times. But it was below the waist that the true frontiersman was revealed. Tough breeches and leggings, or spats, buttoned up on the outer sides, fitted snugly over his stout boots of fine but well-trodden leather. In his pocket was his prized chronometer, a time-keeping instrument, acquired in London in 1790, which allowed him to determine longitude wherever he might be—at Navy Hall or at the wild Pacific shore. He had with him, too, a telescope in a leather case; a package of journals, records and field notes; a tube of charts, maps and sketches; and, not least, a bag of trophies and curiosities to show the governor. His golden red hair shone brilliantly and accentuated his pleasant, radiant demeanour. His sharp, kindly and knowing eyes were a treat to gaze at. They revealed, as the portrait made by the court painter Sir Thomas Lawrence a few years later shows, a hint of surprise and achievement, or, perhaps more accurately, surprise *at* achievement.

As everyone of that age who took an interest in these things knew, young Alexander Mackenzie had arrived in this world from very disadvantageous circumstances—thrown out of his own family's holdings on the Isle of Lewis, near Stornoway, his birthplace, by the viciousness of new landlords who had ruined the old economy and the old tribal lives of the Highland Scots. He'd made a new life for himself in North America, on the Loyalist side, and he had every intention of recovering his fortunes through the commerce of the fur trade. He was a businessman, but he was also an explorer, a visionary. By itself, the fur trade could be a means to wealth and fame, but when combined with exploring it could offer a route to imperial attention and notoriety. Mackenzie's visions for new realms of trade; bolstered connections with China, Japan and Russia; and fresh fields to conquer at the expense of American, French, Spanish or any other rivals in North America placed him far ahead of the ordinary post trader. Though of diminutive stature, he was a giant in his line of work.

Colonel John Graves Simcoe, first lieutenant-governor of Upper Canada, spurred Alexander Mackenzie to think in British imperial terms about the prospects for Canadian trade and trans-Pacific links. Mackenzie paid a visit to Governor and Mrs. Simcoe in September 1794, en route to Montreal and London, and brought the governor a sea otter pelt as proof that he had reached the Pacific coast. Library and Archives Canada, C-008111

Before long, John Graves Simcoe made his appearance in the great room of Navy Hall and welcomed Mackenzie. Simcoe held the rank of colonel in the British Army. He, like Mackenzie, had fought against the rebel Americans in the previous war. They had much in common. They were both relatively young men. Simcoe was King George III's viceroy in the Upper Canadian bush, administering all British dominions to the north and west except Rupert's Land, the preserve of the Hudson's Bay Company. Canadian fur traders like Mackenzie might be the commercial barons, but Simcoe, the lieutenant-governor of the Province of Upper Canada (established in 1786 and formally made a colony in 1791, two years before Mackenzie's visit), was the guardian of imperial destiny in Upper Canada. He ruled all the settlements near and far, and all legal matters came under his purview. He was also the architect of the colony's road systems. He planned all the major arterials of Upper Canada—the western road leading from York on Lake Ontario to Fort Malden on the Detroit River, and another, the northern one, leading from York to Penetanguishene on Georgian Bay. He conceived of a system of defence along Roman lines—main routes and arterials, with forces sent from key points such as London, Upper Canada, or York or Kingston as circumstances and emergencies might require.

As an empire builder, Simcoe had few equals. He had the full confidence of his superior, Sir Guy Carleton, Lord Dorchester, the governor of Lower Canada, resident in Quebec. Carleton, too, had fought in the American Revolutionary War. Simcoe had a free hand in framing the nature of Upper Canada, and despite the paucity of resources at his disposal, his energetic zeal and sound business acumen combined to make Upper Canada, by 1793, the most enviable province of the British dominions in America. Simcoe disposed of lands. He controlled the War Office's activities on the frontier. He dispensed patronage and largesse. By these means he engendered alliances with aboriginal peoples. He or his agents signed treaties with them, including one that would allow a naval base to be built at Penetanguishene some day. He knew that a naval anchor of empire would eventually be needed there on the shores of Georgian Bay. He entertained any and all good proposals for the betterment of the vast fiefdom under his control. That is why he listened attentively to the young, bronzed Scot now seated before him.

Governor Simcoe knew the rapacious Canadian fur traders were constantly searching for new watersheds where they could trap beaver. After all, that trade, which had gone on for almost three centuries now, depended on sustained yields in known areas but, more, on windfalls in new areas. There was no point in trapping out the old places unless you wanted to keep the Russians or Americans at a distance (the Spanish did not much care for the trade or were otherwise engaged). The key to augmented wealth lay in new territories, those farther west such as Île-à-la-Crosse (in what is now north-central Saskatchewan), Lake Athabasca and the Peace River district (in present-day Alberta). At this time the Yukon River, Snake River country, the Columbia River watershed, the upper Fraser River and others were still largely unexplored. A few trappers and Iroquois, who seemed to be present in all watersheds, were venturing into these areas. Some were freemen. Others had connections to small firms or partnerships.

Simcoe would have known the history of the Canadian fur trade to that time. He knew, too, that Mackenzie and the Nor'Westers were continuing the exploration begun by French and Canadian traders in the first half of the eighteenth century. Sieur de la Vérendrye, with the aid of his sons, had put up a series of posts on the Red and Assiniboine rivers near the forty-ninth parallel. They had travelled farther to the south, even to Pierre, now in South Dakota, and they had gone west yet again, not quite to the Rocky Mountains. Then the War of the Austrian Succession and the titanic Seven Years War put an end to their schemes and dreams and to the French empire in northern North America. When the British captured Quebec in 1759 and Montreal the next year, all that the King of France and his deputy in Quebec had done to build a string of powerful forts in the Mississippi and Illinois country linking Montreal with Detroit, Chicago, St. Louis and New Orleans had been destroyed by British military might.

Soon after the French and British signed the Articles of Capitulation at Montreal in August 1760, English and Scottish traders began to make their appearance in the interior country known to Canadian inhabitants as *pays d'en haut*. Within months, Natives reported to the master at Moose Factory that these "pedlars from Quebec" were "as thick as mosquitos" on the streams leading to Hudson Bay.[2] This may be an overstatement, yet it signifies the speed with which English and Scots, and Americans besides, came into the St. Lawrence-based fur business after the fall of New France. Instant partnerships sprang up between conquered French and conquering English and Scots in Montreal. New agencies were established to build up trade in the interior. Gregory, McLeod and Company was one such, and after his time of frontier fighting, Mackenzie became a clerk in that partnership and learned accounting. So fast was the trade growing, in Detroit, Michilimackinac and Île-à-la-Crosse, that Mackenzie was vaulted upward at a ripe young age into great responsibilities, first at Detroit and then at Île-à-la-Crosse. He never disappointed his bosses. Rather, he surprised and delighted them with his brilliance and forethought. His ambitions outdistanced their expectations. He intended to become king of the interior trade, and he did.

Simcoe knew of the tenacity of the Scots and how ferocious they were in combat. He knew, too, that Scots could be nasty rivals of each other, even among their own clans and kin. The Celtic tribal system had its built-in rules. Simcoe, as a military man himself, knew that even if the Battle of Culloden stifled the last gasp of Scottish military independence and made the Scots a conquered people, Scottish instincts and drive that bordered on the fanatically independent would result in rival firms questing for dominance in the fur trade. In fact, the North West Company, nominally headquartered in Montreal, was no united company at all. Rather, it was a cluster of firms, such as Mackenzie's employers Gregory, McLeod and Company, thrust together for mutual convenience. The partners—some were the heads of member firms; others were senior traders in the field—regulated everything by votes at their annual rendezvous each July. They would meet at Grand Portage, at the head of Lake Superior, to vote new partners into the company, give out shares or authorize sales of shares. They planned new fields for exploitation of beaver and other fur-bearing animals. They pooled resources and credit and thus determined personal futures and fortunes.

In 1794, when Mackenzie visited Simcoe at Navy Hall, Nor'Westers (as they were called) were trading from the Missouri River near the great bend of that stream, throughout present-day Illinois and Michigan, and westward into Minnesota and North Dakota. They exploited the Qu'Appelle Valley of southern Saskatchewan and controlled the Saskatchewan River. In the 1780s, they had gone far to the north by way of Methye Portage and found themselves in Arctic waters that flowed through Lake Athabasca and Great Slave Lake to the northern sea. Samuel Hearne of the Hudson's Bay Company had ventured west from Hudson Bay to the Coppermine River but had developed no trade of any consequence with the Dene or the Inuit. In fact, the Nor'Westers were coming through the western doorway of the HBC traders, skirting around them via the river system known to the Dene as *Deh Cho*, which flowed to Arctic salt water. This was the northern river of destiny. Its entryway, for commercial purposes, was Lake Athabasca, the hub of rivers, the crossroads of Native peoples.

In 1778, Peter Pond, penetrated to the shores of Lake Athabasca, where Mackenzie joined him a few years later. Pond was a quizzical fellow, a strange, rough and enigmatic character. He had joined the king's colours without hesitation during the Seven Years War—the French and Indian War they termed it in his hometown of Milford, Connecticut—when the fife-and-drum crops and the recruiting sergeant had arrived. Pond was a shoemaker, just as his deceased father had been, but was now breadwinner for a very large number of brothers and sisters. He had been a sailor for a while and then a soldier in one of the royal regiments that fought against the French at Fort Oswego, just across the Niagara River from Navy Hall. When the business of soldiering came to an end, Pond used his frontiering instincts in another equally profitable war: the fur trade. He was inured to wilderness travel and life, and like many of his kind he hated competitors. He would raid another's post, start a damaging fire, lure away his rival's aboriginal trappers and guides—even, if necessary, murder a former ally. News of these depredations reached the Nor'Westers' headquarters and even London. Suspicions grew in Montreal. A dark cloud hovered over Pond. Meanwhile, the Athabasca trade grew. His trading arrangements with parent organizations and suppliers had to be two-year ventures rather than the usual annual outfits; he could not come out every year because the trip took so long. He wintered in the Lake Athabasca territory—first at his old post, then at Fort Chipewyan—and came out in the springtime heavily laden with furs, travelling south across Methye Portage, then east on the Saskatchewan River out to waters and carrying places leading to the great depot and rendezvous at Grand Portage.

Mackenzie joined Pond as his second-in-command in 1787. Long nights around the stove in those snow- and ice-bound trading houses in stockaded posts left ample time for talk and for the study of maps and charts. Pond was a visionary. Mackenzie was the pragmatic trader. Pond had only a rudimentary education and little knowledge of surveying, astronomy or mathematics. Mackenzie was well educated, and in addition to his native Gaelic and English he had mastered French as a schoolboy besides Latin and some Greek as well as mathematics, geography and classics. He'd been a student in the laird's school in Stornaway. When in 1774, age twelve, he'd shipped as an emigrant on the square-rigger *Peace & Plenty*, bound for New York, he had been listed in the Board of Trade Emigration List as "scholar." On that occasion, all the others who had sailed for America in various states of destitution were listed as servants or labourers. Much has been made of Mackenzie's lack of navigational and astronomical skills as of this time, demonstrated by the fact that when he pursued Pond's dream of finding a river route west to Russian settlements at Unalaska he, Mackenzie, was lost in terms of precise longitude and latitude. But it was not Mackenzie's fault, it was Pond's. Mackenzie was left to pick up the pieces from his superior's misconceptions.

After Pond was removed from the fur trade by the North West Company partners, he returned to Milford, where he started to lobby, quite successfully as it turned out, the president of Yale University, Ezra Stiles. Pond's intention was to get Americans, and the United States government, interested in northwestern exploration, trade and colonization. For Stiles, and on another occasion for Congress, Pond prepared maps showing his routes, his posts, his Native allies, various indigenous warpaths or trails, and even the places Russian and English traders sailed to or had bases at on the Pacific coast of America and the Gulf of Alaska. Employing his excellent spatial memory and knowledge of river systems and lakes, Pond drew a grand map. It is a remarkable construction, no doubt, but it is wrong and misleading. Along the way, Pond learned of Captain James Cook's visit to Cook Inlet, Alaska, in 1778. Cook suggested that the unexplored inlet might indeed be a river, and so Cook's River shows itself on Pond's map, or more correctly on one version of Pond's map. Pond imagined that the waters draining north and west from Lake Athabasca flowed to Cook's River.

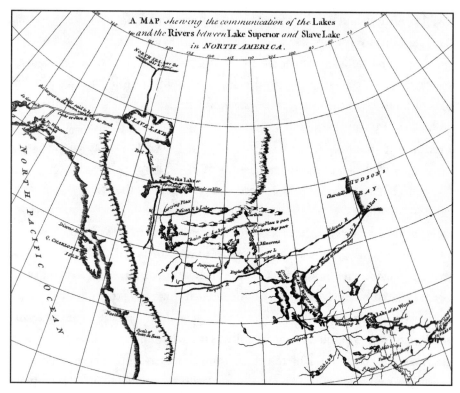

This map of the greater northwest, drawn by Peter Pond and published in London's Gentleman's Magazine *in March 1790, illustrates the state of geographic knowledge and conjecture on the eve of Alexander Mackenzie's voyages in search of a waterway to the Pacific. Pond tutored Mackenzie and deserves more credit than he is given for the latter's achievements.*

Here was a revival of the idea of a northwest passage in these latitudes, that old bugaboo of North American geography (see Appendix 1). Navigator Juan de Fuca had proposed it after his reported voyage in the late 1500s, and the idea had been passed down by Michael Lok, a geographical theorist and visionary, who had, like the Welsh astrologist John Dee, worked up Elizabethan-age concepts of a passage west from Davis and Hudson straits. The idea died a slow, frozen death. In Pond's day, and Mackenzie's too, however, the dream of finding a northern sea route was kept alive in order to get government sponsorship, and Pond and Mackenzie exploited it to their benefit.

At the same time as Mackenzie reached Pacific tidewater overland, disproving the existence of a southern northwest passage, Captain George Vancouver of the

Royal Navy was nearby, extending his discoveries on the Pacific coast in HMS *Discovery* and *Chatham* and the several gigs and cutters that penetrated such inlets or fjords as Dean Channel, where Mackenzie and his men paddled in their large cedar dugout canoe on the welcome salt waters of the western shore. Vancouver did not encounter Mackenzie, the more's the pity, as it would have been a strange yet wonderful conjunction of the two vectors of northwestern discovery: Vancouver in his great armed ships bearing the White Ensign, backed by the muscle of the Admiralty and the British government; Mackenzie almost solo, in his borrowed canoe, there on company business, theodolite at hand, taking altitudes using an artificial horizon and then a natural one, putting down in his notes the latitude of his rock (52° 20' 48" north), observing the immersion of two of Jupiter's Galilean moons to fix his longitude at 128.2° west of Greenwich, and sketching out the configuration of the coastline in the vicinity.[3]

At Navy Hall, Mackenzie could tell Simcoe and his wife, Lady Elizabeth Gwillim Simcoe, of these adventures and of the journey back to Upper Canada. Simcoe and his wife listened with care, even awe. A solitary Scot, their guest, had traversed the continent of America. He began his expedition from his advance base on the Peace River—Fort Fork, he'd called it—on May 9, 1793. He'd gone west and had crossed the 119th meridian on May 13, camped below Hudson's Hope on May 18 and reached the head of Peace River on the 24th. Approaching the Continental Divide via Parsnip River and Arctic Lake, he had crossed the Divide on June 12, 1793, and ventured into the headwaters of what he thought was the Columbia River, but he still used the indigenous name of the river, *Tacoutche Tesse.*

He had followed the tributaries of the *Tacoutche Tesse,* he told Governor and Mrs. Simcoe, and reached such a position on the river that Dakelh informants warned him against going farther south in his great canoe. They told him of great dangers downstream—narrow gorges, impassable rapids, navigational hazards major and minor. They were warning of Hell's Gate Canyon, and it would take another bold Nor'Wester, Simon Fraser, on orders from the Company, to explore the river in 1808 (his journey is described in Chapter 11).

Mackenzie, ever reliant on aboriginal advice, heeded the warnings. He went westward from near the present-day location of Quesnel, BC, via the Blaeberry and West Road rivers, across a height of land on a journey that consumed nearly two weeks. In what he terms "a sea of mountains," he and his party negotiated frightful mountain passes where the winds blew so ferociously that the men had to seek shelter in the lee of large rocks. Before long, still following existing trails, they were in the upper waters of the Dean River. Descending rapidly on foot, three thousand feet in a long afternoon, they eventually reached a village, Rascal's Village as Mackenzie termed it, where thieving was duly matched by generous hospitality. There or nearby, Mackenzie bought some sea otter pelts. These were no beaver pelts; they were the ermine of Asia.

By the time Mackenzie proudly displayed his sea otter skins to Governor and Mrs. Simcoe, the Yankees and British were waging a fierce rivalry on the northwest coast. The trade was bringing them into sharp competition with the Russians farther north, who in 1799 were obliged to seek the support of the state and get a charter for a trade monopoly, in the name of the Russian-American Company, from the Russian czar. The traders also faced attacks from the local indigenous people, for the Bostonians had brought guns and ammunition to trade for furs, along with flour and other foodstuffs, rum, gin and whisky. So rapid

Rascal's Village, as Mackenzie called it, was known by its inhabitants as Gom Goltes. It was here that Chief Sears Kille gave a reception for Mackenzie and his companions. Nearby was Friendly Valley (Burnt Bridge) and farther downriver was Bella Coola village. British Columbia Central Coast Archives, Iver Fougner, circa 1920s

was the arms buildup among the many rival and already ferociously warlike aboriginal peoples of the northwest coast that no Yankee ship would sail those waters without being well armed for its own defence. With a touch of sadness and much regret, Captain Vancouver observed that he had come none too soon to make his systematic hydrographic examination, for the aboriginal people, heavily armed, had become troublesome and aggressive, and he feared reprisals and conflicts.

Mackenzie did not know, could not have known, about such incidents as John Kendrick's terrible shaming of the Haida chief Koyah and the vicious, justified reprisals that went on thereafter (see Chapter 6) until the British navy established a *Pax Britannica* on the coast by the late nineteenth century.[4] However, Mackenzie had evidence of internecine ferocity from his own experience near Mackenzie Rock when rival tribes threatened war. He had just had time to make his astronomical readings and test them against those that could be calculated using the chronometer's revelations. Fortune attended him at a critical hour: the sky was clear enough that day to take the readings. Mackenzie safely extracted himself and his men from life-threatening circumstances, and he brought home the ultimate prize: the precise longitude and latitude of that lonely rock on the Pacific coast, the crown jewel of coordinates showing that he had reached the Pacific coast overland for the first time. He'd thus disproved the existence of the northwest passage in those latitudes beyond a shadow of a doubt, though heaven knows the British Admiralty and government had spent a fortune disproving the existence of such a passage.

There was thus much to talk about at Navy Hall that lovely late-summer's day. Mackenzie related the salient details of his travels. He described the salmon of the Pacific Ocean, which he pointed out to his hosts was a different genus than the Atlantic salmon he had known as a child. They would have discussed fur-trading posts and the rivers and lakes on which they were situated. There would have been talk of the perils of crossing the Continental Divide, both outward and homeward bound. Not least, they would have conversed about the nature and characteristics of the many aboriginal peoples, perhaps speaking of Mackenzie's Cree wife, The Catt, and of their Métis children at Fort Chipewyan, who, in company fashion, were carried on the books of the

North West Company and thus entitled to food, clothing, shelter and whatever medical aid was to hand. They would have chatted about the implementation of Jay's Treaty, the US courts' reluctance to compensate Loyalists for the loss of their abandoned lands stateside, Canadian arms sales into the United States and the remarkable informal empire that Canada had in the northern US territories. And there would have been talk about the frontier wars of America and of General George Rogers Clark's activities in the Old Northwest during the Revolutionary War, which had secured that area for the republic. Perhaps they discussed what the United States government would do to counter Mackenzie's revelations of the route to the west. Who knew what the official American response would be once Mackenzie's planned book on the subject appeared? Certainly it was Mackenzie's intention to get his account of his voyages into print as soon as possible. Generous and well-deserved book royalties, national acclaim, even a knighthood might await him. But more than that, commercial benefits would accrue to him and his partners, for, truth to tell, he saw in the empire of the beaver and sea otter a means, perhaps his last chance, to increase the profit and power of the British Empire.

Simcoe and his wife were much taken by the young Scot. The day passed quickly and then it was time for him to renew his eastward progression. Shortly after bidding adieu to Alexander Mackenzie, Elizabeth Simcoe noted in her journal, under the date September 8, 1794:

> Mr. McKenzie [she spelled it that way] who had made his way from Grand Portage to the Pacific Ocean is just returned from thence & brought the Gov. a Sea Otter Skin as a proof of his having reached that Coast. He says the Savages spear them from the Rocks, as the Indians here do Sturgeon. These animals are amphibious but generally in the sea.
>
> Mr. McKenzie went down the River of Peace near 2 degrees north of L. Superior & came to the Rocky Mountains on which rise some Rivers that fall into the Atlantic & others which empty themselves into the Pacific Ocean. He went down a River which falls into the latter, & rises not 700 yards from

the River of Peace. He afterwards travelled 17 days by land. There are a kind of large sheep on the Rocky Mountains their horns the size of a Cow's. The Indians near the Coast live on fish which they are very dextrous in catching, they dry salmon in boxes in a kind of upper story in their Huts. They prepare the Roes beating them up with sorrel till it becomes a kind of caviar & when the salmon are dried boil & mix them with oil. These Savages never taste meat, & think if any was thrown into the River the fish would go away. One of Mr. McKenzie's men having thrown a bone of a deer in the water an Indian dived & fetched it out, nor would they suffer water to be ladled out in a kettle in which Meat had been boiled. Are these not veritable Ichthyophagy [fish-eaters]? Mr. McKenzie observed those Indians who inhabited the Islands on the Coast to be more Savage than the others. The Otter Skins are sold at a great price by those who trade on the coast to the Chinese.[5]

Simcoe, like Elizabeth, was enchanted by the visitor from the west. The governor marched to the imperial drum. In Mackenzie he recognized the living embodiment of explorers of the Canadian west and north who had gone before: Jacques Cartier, who in three voyages, beginning in 1534, had discovered for European science the St. Lawrence River; Samuel de Champlain, empire builder extraordinaire, who had not only founded Quebec as a fortified town but had also explored west to the Ottawa River and into Georgian Bay and "the sweetwater sea" (Lake Huron); and Jean Nicollet, who in 1634, under Champlain's instructions, had ventured as far west as the shores of Lake Superior, carrying in his valise a splendid damask robe that he would wear when he reached the court of Kublai Khan. Nicollet intended to arrive, as custom dictated, as Marco Polo had advertised, with correct precision. Mackenzie embodied La Vérendrye, Louis Jolliet and Pond as well as a score or more of less important traders and trappers. They had all worked with aboriginal people. They had imported traps, beads, woollens and cottons, Brazilian tobacco, rum and brandy, axeheads, pots and pans. They had used indigenous modes of travel—canoes and snowshoes—and they lived in the fashion of the country. They had found freedom in the *pays d'en haut* and taken comely Indian wives, thus fixing alliances with certain chiefs and tribes and learning their languages and ways. By the same token, those aboriginals with whom they were in most intimate touch became more European. They, too, bridged two worlds. Mackenzie, when he met Governor and Mrs. Simcoe, already had his feet placed firmly across these cultural, racial and linguistic divides. He trod the middle ground. He was perhaps more Canadian at that time than any man living. He had embraced the North and the West. He had delineated the courses of the Mackenzie and the upper Fraser rivers. He had made a fortune in that new Eldorado, Athabasca. So highly did other Nor'Westers regard him that, shortly after his great western journey and return to Montreal, they made him their agent and thus their representative in all their transactions at the annual rendezvous as well as in their banking and agency business. His star was on the rise.

Even so, in the tightly knit world of British politics, no person alone could shape imperial strategy or direct the course of financial benefit. In 1793, Britain had just gone to war against Napoleon Bonaparte and France. That meant that any scheme for imperial aggrandizement in the Canadian Northwest or the North Pacific, both relative backwaters in imperial geopolitics, would stay on the margins of statecraft. For another, all trade, commerce and regulation was tied up with an immense body of legislation, rules and regulations known as the Acts of Trade and Navigation. The Glasgow political economist Adam Smith had noted the octopus-like prevalence of these rules in his *Inquiry into the Wealth of Nations* (1776). But even his distinguished highlighting of these dominating regulations did not bring an end to them. The Board of Trade, which oversaw them, began to combine and simplify these rules, but it was not until the repeal of the Corn Laws in 1846 that anything resembling free trade was effected.

Thus Mackenzie, the bushranger, found himself working within the requirements of a paper world. He did so out of necessity. He tried to change things through the cracks and around the margins. He sought partnerships with the Hudson's Bay Company. He sought a lease to gain rights of shipment and passage through the HBC's chartered territory to Hudson Bay. These attempts failed. He sought to go around the rules, to trade freely across the border to the United States and to ship his furs in Philadelphia or New York ships bound for China ports. All of these ventures he attempted, with differing degrees of success and much obstruction from bureaucrats, officials and rivals.

But Simcoe liked what he saw in Mackenzie. The governor's duty was to encourage trade and settlement. He asked the young explorer to prepare a memorandum of his journey and findings. Accordingly, Mackenzie wrote to Simcoe:

Sir

Agreeable to your Excellency's request I beg leave to acquaint you that on the 9th May 1793 I in a Bark Canoe left one of our Settlements [Fort Fork] in the North West on the Unjigah or Peace River Latitude 56° 9' North and longitude 117° 43' West from Greenwich,[6] for the purpose of penetrating to the Western Ocean. I followed up the Waters of this River to their Source, carried over the Height of Land which is only 700 yards; from hence I continued my route down a small River which I found discharged itself into the branch of a larger one that the Natives call Tacoutch Tesse or Tacoutch River [Fraser]. We were carried down this River by the strength of the Current with great velocity. I found that it took too much a Southern Course to bring me to the sea as soon as I expected, and from the best information I could procure judged it did not discharge itself to the Northward of the River of the West, a Branch if not the whole of which I take it to be. I was sensible that this was the best, but not the shortest communication with the Sea. My then situation could not admit of my taking it; therefore, I returned up the River five days Journey, left my Canoe, and what of her Landing we could not carry with us in Latitude 50° North and Longitude 122° 43' West. Travelled 15 days and arrived on the Western Ocean; the Sea along the Coast being much interspers'd with Island. I borrowed a Canoe from the Natives, went about 20 Leagues out amongst them. Here I found myself in the Latitude 52° 23' North and Longitude 128° 15' West. From this I returned the 23rd July by the same Road I went and arrived safe with my people the 24th August at the place[7] from which I had taken my departure.[8]

Mackenzie had made a grand diversion on his eastbound travels so as to pay a call on Simcoe. This was not his usual route to Montreal. He had come south from Sault Ste. Marie by lakes and rivers previously unknown to him. From Niagara he hastened by sailing vessel to Kingston and thence to Montreal.

Simcoe told Mackenzie to pay a call on Governor Dorchester and get his good advice. Illness prevented such a visit. Sickness had dogged Mackenzie for much of the previous year. During his crossing of the Continental Divide, he had suffered a mild inflammation of his ankles and legs, perhaps caused by the virus that results in Bright's Disease (a terrible attack on the kidneys). He was in such physical difficulty that his legs were numb when he walked in the cold river waters during portaging. His men had to carry him so as to minimize the pain. Always before he had travelled under his own power. Now he was nearly immobilized. Once in his canoe, as it raced on the swift current downstream toward Fort Fork and Fort Chipewyan, the swelling and pain seem to have eased, and the life-threatening crisis passed. But the damage done lingered and contributed to his death in 1820 at age fifty-eight.

Mackenzie could not attend on Dorchester. His health determined that. Earlier, having decided that he intended to get out of the confounded interior country as soon as possible, he had made it abundantly clear to cousin Roderick that he was so exhausted by his travels, so delirious in consequence of his disease, so infirm by all that was engulfing him that he did not know if he would ever be able to write his record of great experiences. After such exertions, such pain, such illness, he could not put pen to paper for long. This state of affairs continued for months on end.

His visit to Navy Hall and his discussions with Governor Simcoe lifted his spirits and charged him with new zeal. Simcoe, whatever he said to the young traveller, placed an imperial stamp on Mackenzie. Thereafter Mackenzie's writing speaks not only of profit but of power (and imperial advantage). Rivalry with the Americans and, to a lesser extent, the Russians begins to assert itself as a theme. The tone of his writing and memoranda becomes more strident, more cautionary, more political and more urgent. Western expansion by the United States cast a long shadow over Mackenzie's path and intentions.

Mackenzie wrote to Dorchester on November 17, 1794, to explain his inability to attend on him:

My Lord

It was my intention to have done myself the honor of waiting on your Lordship, but the state of my health deprives me of that Satisfaction. Circumstances at present have made me determine to go to England by way of the States, previous to which I think it my duty to give your Lordship a short Sketch of two Expeditions I have performed across this Continent, humbly hoping it may not be disagreeable to you.

The 3rd June 1789 I took my departure in a Bark Canoe, accompanied by five Canadians, and three Indians, from one of our Settlements [Fort Chipewyan] in the North West, Latitude 58° 38' North, Longitude 110½° West from Greenwich. I followed the course of the Waters which had been reported by Mr. Pond to fall into Cook's River. They led me to the Northern Ocean, in Latitude 69½° North, and about 135 of West Longitude, by the 16th July the Sea was then covered with Ice at some distance from Land. We saw a number of white Porpoises, and observed there was a small Tide. Further, it was needless for me to go, besides it would have been very dangerous to attempt to cast with such a slight Vessel as I had. Therefore we returned by the way we went.

Tho' this Expedition did not answer the intended purposes, it proved that Mr. Pond's Assertion was nothing but conjecture, and that a North West Passage is impracticable. Not having been furnished with proper Instruments to ascertain the Longitude in my first Expedition, I made myself but little known during my residence in London the Winter 1791/2, but to prevent the like Inconvenience I then purchased proper ones, in case I should make a second attempt.

I left the Downs the 7th April 1792, and passed the following Winter at one of our Westernmost Settlements in the North West, on the Banks of a large River which the natives name Unjegah [Peace River], in Latitude 56.9 North and Longitude 117.40 West of Greenwich.

The 9th May 1793 I proceeded in a Bark Canoe, ten of us, *viz.* an Assistant, six Canadians and two young Indians, to the source of this River, carried over the height of Land (which is only 700 yards broad) that separates those waters, the one empties into the Northern Ocean, and the other into the Western, in following the latter, they soon increased to the Size of a large River [Fraser], which I continued going down for a considerable distance. The rapidity of the Current, the Natives Account of it &c., convinced me that I could not go to its Mouth and be back that Season: *From its course, and the information I received, I conclude it to be part, if not the whole of the River of the West* [Columbia]; this determined me to leave my Canoe in Latitude 53° North and Longitude 122° 43' West, and go over land by a Route the Natives frequent in going to the Western Ocean, to procure Iron and Trinkets for which they give Furs in Exchange to the Inhabitants of the Coasts, where I arrived the 18th of July, there being many islands which prevents the View of the Main Ocean, I borrowed a Canoe from the Natives in order to go and get a sight of the Open Sea. I went about Sixty Miles yet was not gratified, the Inhabitants becoming troublesome, made it dangerous to proceed any further.

The Latitude here I found to be 52° 23' North and Longitude 128° 15' West, which situation answers to Sir Chas. Middleton's Sound.

The Inhabitants are well furnished with European Articles, few of them of any material use except the Iron, we could not understand those people, therefore could not procure much intelligence from them.

We came back the way we went, and arrived at the place of our departure the 24th of August.

I am sorry I cannot give Your Lordship a more particular Account of this Expedition, my Journal being as yet undigested.[9]

Dorchester, a soldier and administrator who had spent a lifetime trying to preserve the British Empire in North America, had been the architect of the Quebec Act of 1774, which was an attempt to keep Quebec in the empire and engender the loyalty of the French-speaking Canadians, or Quebeçois. Dorchester shared Simcoe's keenness for empire, trade and settlement, and he sent his endorsement of Mackenzie's warning, plan and proposals to his superior in London:

Mr. McKenzie who has been employed by the Associated Merchants of Montreal to make Discoveries in the Northwest parts of America has sent me a short Narrative of two Expeditions performed by him across this Continent. The great Importance of the Trade carried on by those Gentlemen may render it of consequence for His Majesty's Ministers to be more fully informed of Mr. McKenzie's Discoveries, and as he is about to proceed to England for the purpose of presenting a more particular account of them to Your Grace, I take this opportunity of recommending him to your notice.[10]

There the matter stood until 1802, when Mackenzie began to knock on the doors of the Colonial Office in Downing Street. Such lobbying as he had done with Simcoe, and enlarged upon with Dorchester, he now pressed on ministers of the British government. They are the subject of the next chapter.

In the meantime, Mackenzie's health had made a remarkable turn for the better. Medical treatment and rest proved beneficial. The return to Montreal and London were agreeable. He began to sort his papers and revise his thousands of pages of journal entries and notes. He knew that the record of his travels would best be viewed against a context of the general features of the fur trade of Canada. Accordingly, he invited his cousin Roderick to write a general history of the Canadian fur trade as an introduction. Alexander Mackenzie reviewed this text and made his own points. In itself, Roderick's history is a vitally important compendium of details on the evolution and state of the interior trade at the end of the eighteenth century. Mackenzie's 1789 journal of his voyage to the Arctic Ocean was the first of his two segments of the book proper. It was followed by his account of his transmontane journey to the Pacific in 1793. Additional pages include aboriginal vocabularies. When published by a prominent London publisher in 1801, *Voyages from Montreal* became an instant success. The work was dedicated to King George III. Alexander Mackenzie's sometime travelling companion the Duke of Kent (father of Queen Victoria) played a key role in fixing the dedication.

The king seemed duly pleased, as was, presumably, the prime minister of the day, for in 1802, Alexander Mackenzie, age forty, the wee Scot who had suffered so much deprivation and faced such danger, trial and tribulation, was made a Knight Bachelor. In his book, Mackenzie had concluded the account of his western travels with a description of his return to Fort Chipewyan in 1793 that contained an excellent premonition of the royal honour soon to be bestowed:

> At length, as we rounded a point, and came in view of the Fort, we threw out our flag, and accompanied it with a general discharge of our fire-arms; while the men were in such spirits, and made such an active use of their paddles, that we arrived

before the two men whom we left here in the spring, could recover their senses to answer us. Thus we landed at four in the afternoon, at the place we left on the ninth of May.

Here my voyages of discovery terminate. Their toils and their dangers, their solicitudes and sufferings, have not been exaggerated in my description. On the contrary, in many instances, language has failed me in the attempt to describe them. I received, however, the reward of my labours, for they were crowned with success.[11]

Chapter 3

THE MACKENZIE TOUCH

Although Mackenzie had reached his destination—Pacific salt water—he was as aware as any member in his party that he had not found a navigable passage for boats, canoes, rafts or any other waterborne conveyance. He had only uncovered a trail or track, hardly a great artery of commerce. Even so, Mackenzie formulated commercial schemes to exploit the rich fur-bearing territories of the far west and northwest and to profit in the trade to China, Korea and Japan using merchant vessels. Mackenzie developed his ventures as a late-eighteenth-century entrepreneur at the leading edge of business theory and practice.

For Mackenzie, time was of the essence. Time misspent was time lost. It brought no profit, no benefit. When he travelled from Fort Chipewyan to the Pacific, he was on no scenic tour. Even scientific advancement lay beyond his concern. He left that to the Sir Joseph Bankses and Alexander Dalrymples of his age. Shooting the stars, reading the astronomical tables and using a chronometer were of a different order to him. With them he could literally pinpoint his position on the map. He was his own global positioning system, filling in the blanks and joining one point to the previous or to the next, tracing his own route across the page, his ant-like progress across the vast terrain of the rugged northwest. "I do not possess the science of the naturalist," he had written in the preface to *Voyages from Montreal*, "and even if the qualifications of that character had been attained by me, its curious spirit would not have been gratified. I could not stop to dig into the earth, over whose surface I was compelled to pass with rapid steps; nor could I turn aside to collect the plants which nature might have scattered on the way, when my thoughts were anxiously employed in making provision for the day that was passing over me." He did not disparage the savants or learned men of his time. Science was indeed king in those days, but in the British Empire, commerce was emperor. Mackenzie targets geology and botany, two ruling passions of scientific minds of his time, but he does not intend any offense. He mentions them only to explain what propels his own self. He thus defines his own requirements, and in doing so personalizes his discoveries. His genius always comes home—a little selfishly, as genius will do—to himself.

To the above explanation he added, "I had to encounter perils by land and perils by water; to watch the savage who was our guide, or to guard against those of his tribe who might mediate our destruction. I had, also, the passions and fears of others to control and subdue. Today I had to assuage the rising discontents, and on the morrow to cheer the fainting spirits, of the people who accompanied me." His leadership skills were frequently tested, as we will see. He always found a way out of a jam, always offered a solution to crisis and showed the road ahead. His charges had reason to complain or threaten to quit and go home to their sweethearts, children and friends. "The toil of our navigation was incessant," he explained, "and oftentimes extreme; and in our progress over land we had no protection from the severity of the elements, and possessed no accommodations or conveniences but such as could be contained in the burden on our shoulders, which aggravated the toils of our march, and added to the weariness of our way."

Mackenzie, and three centuries of Canadian explorers before him, sought the "Western Sea" and the "Southern Ocean." In its quest for profits in the China market, the North West Company, composed of a group of Montreal traders operating together under a series of agreements going back to 1776,[1] was obliged to observe mercantilist regulations emanating

Perseverance was the watchword of the North West Company, an association of partners and firms whose hub of operations was Montreal and whose tentacles of trade influence stretched northwest into Athabasca and west to the Rocky Mountain cordillera and the watershed of the Columbia River and its tributaries. Underappreciated as a corporate giant, it was a precursor of transcontinental Canadian dominion.
Library and Archives Canada, C-00871

from London. The Nor'Westers did not enjoy the privileges of trade that their great rivals, the Company of Adventurers of England Trading into Hudson's Bay, had possessed by charter since 1670, and they had to resort to subterfuge in order to circumvent the powers of the British East India Company, another chartered firm whose monopoly also dated from the seventeenth century. At one time or another, these two giant chartered companies and, to a lesser degree, the South Sea Company (which had some rights of licensing ships sailing in the Pacific between Cape Horn and the Cape of Good Hope) sought to keep rival British traders out of their domains. And even though the East India Company allowed the North West Company to trade in China, it imposed stringent regulations. No doubt the monopolistic nature of British colonial and commercial policy obstructed the growth of the Canadian fur trade to China. On the other hand, competition with the Hudson's Bay Company on its northern flank and with the Astorians on its southern flank (both in the Old Northwest and on the Pacific slope) pushed the Nor'Westers westward. Essentially, the Nor'Westers had to choose between expansion or elimination, and the latter was out of the question for the Nor'Westers, whose motto was "Perseverance."

The "Adventure to China" originated in the 1760s, shortly after the Treaty of Paris (1763) brought Canada under British control. In 1768, Sir Guy Carleton (later Lord Dorchester), the governor of Quebec, advised Lord Shelburne, president of the Board of Trade, that British traders should proceed across the continent to the Pacific coast. There they would select "a good port, take its latitude, longitude, and describe it so accurately as to enable our ships from the East Indies to find it out with ease, and then return the year following."[2] Here was a concrete proposal for trans-Pacific trade emanating from Montreal on the St. Lawrence. Similar schemes involving a search for a northwest passage by sea and land, as well as the founding of a post near the imagined western entrance of the Strait of Anian, were proposed by American explorers Robert Rogers and Jonathan Carver, among others, in the 1760s. Carver believed that a British settlement on the northwest coast of North America would aid trade, discovery and communication with China and English settlements in the East Indies.[3] Partners and traders in the North West Company never tired of sending memoranda to the home government requesting British support for their enterprises. This was especially true of Peter Pond, who realized that Athabasca could be a base for a new trade to the Pacific coast and the far east.[4]

The East India Company showed no interest in the maritime fur trade that had been identified by James Cook in the late 1770s (see the Prologue), but in 1785 it gave grudging assent that allowed certain British entrepreneurs trading under the name of the King George's Sound Company to trade with the Chinese. The East India Company was apprehensive of this intrusion as it seemed to foreshadow the advent of free trade. Thus the company's Court of Directors framed regulations to protect their interests.[5]

Though there was at least one attempt, in 1793, for the East India Company to cooperate with the Hudson's Bay Company, the East India Company's regulations remained in force until they were relaxed later that year by government demand. The maritime fur trade fell increasingly from British into American hands. While it is easy to blame this development on British mercantilist regulations, it is also true that in 1793 Britain was at war with France. In 1812 the country was again at war, this time with the United States, and both conflicts were detrimental to commerce in the North Pacific.

Meanwhile, the North West Company had commenced its China trade. It did so through Moscow, Irkutsk and thence to Beijing. Indeed, a quarter of all furs that came onto the English market were destined for Russia, and from there the largest portion went on to China. Not only did the Nor'Westers seek to expand this trade, but they wanted to trade directly with Canton. Thus in 1792 they lobbied the government to request that Lord Macartney, the British emissary to Beijing, negotiate with the Manchu emperor Ch'ien-lung for admission of furs to China. Macartney's mission was unsuccessful: he refused to *kowtow*.[6] Consequently, the Nor'Westers had to continue conducting their business via Russia, and from 1792 to 1795 they sent furs to the annual value of £40,000.

However, there were many difficulties associated with carrying on commerce across the North American continent and the vast Pacific Ocean. These included the necessity of a large capital outlay for a long period, the risks of war and storms (beaver pelts could and did get wet and spoiled), the need to develop roads and canals in Canada to encourage the export of the staple, and the reliance on illegal means of commerce to circumvent the rigid British commercial regulations. (This involved smuggling furs from Montreal into the United States, from whence John Jacob Astor of New York forwarded the cargo to Canton in American ships, which were not subject to British law.)

In 1792, two years before Mackenzie met with John Graves and Elizabeth Simcoe, and a year before he reached the Pacific coast, the partnership of McTavish, Frobisher and Company and Alexander Henry, and possibly Astor, chartered the ships *Washington* and *America* to convey pelts to China via Cape Horn. The return cargo of yard goods, tea and semi-porcelain purchased in Canton was sold to Astor. This direct and profitable Canadian venture to China was followed by a second and more ambitious undertaking, the outlay for which was estimated at £279,894. The trade, involving the conveyance of four thousand beaver pelts, was undertaken by an 800-ton vessel chartered in New York.[7]

By 1794, McTavish, Frobisher and Company, leading partners in the North West Company, had run up a deficit of £23,000 on their China account. Alexander Mackenzie believed he had a solution. In his scheme, trade via the Pacific was less expensive and less difficult than trade through the St. Lawrence. A post at Cook Inlet, another at the southern limits of British trade (possibly on Vancouver Island), and a conciliatory approach to the indigenous people would secure the Pacific coastal trade for the Nor'Westers. The China trade would increase—a matter of importance to the East India Company because the importation of furs would lessen the need for that company to import silver from India or England to China. British maritime interests would also advance with the development of trade via Hudson Bay, and in time of emergency, Upper Canada might be made more secure.

Mackenzie, who was now a principal partner in McTavish, Frobisher, was "confirmed in his view that the salvation of the fur trade lay in the north-west, in access to the Pacific and in the absorption of the Hudson's Bay Company's rights; not in collaboration with the Americans."[8] Having convinced his partners to extend their capital outlay, Mackenzie went to New York in 1798 and purchased in the name of William Seton and William Magee Seton, citizens of the United States and residents of New York, the 340-ton ship *Northern*

Liberties. He had it coppered and fitted out for a voyage to the Pacific. He also convinced Messrs. Seton, Maitland and Co. of New York to invest $25,000 in the project.[9] He had the venture insured for the total cost and for a voyage from New York to Canton and thence to any European port with leave to call at Falmouth, England, for "orders warranted American property."[10] Thus was the subterfuge of using foreign cargo ships complete.

The success of this voyage encouraged the Nor'Westers to consign furs of first quality to China. Regrettably, the company had insufficient first-quality pelts for both London and Canton markets. In consequence, the former began to suffer, much to the regret of the London partners, and the Montreal interests soon were at odds with their London counterparts. The "Canadians" (McTavish, Frobisher and Company) wanted to extend the new field of commerce, while the "British" (McTavish, Fraser and Company) warned that the enterprise would weaken its position on the London market *vis-à-vis* the Hudson's Bay Company, to say nothing of running afoul of East India Company regulations and French warships at large on the high seas.

This actual extension of markets tied in naturally with Mackenzie's strategy of extending, with deliberate speed, company trade across the continent. From his own experience, he believed that the Athabasca region was the westernmost point from which furs could profitably be sent east to Montreal and then to markets.[11] Why not send the Athabasca returns westward to the Pacific? Here was the origin of what later became known as the "Columbian enterprise." At this germinal stage, Mackenzie was pressing for a division of company exports. On the one hand, pelts could be sent via Hudson Bay (thus avoiding the expensive Montreal route). On the other, western furs would be taken to the Pacific, where company ships would transport them to China ports.

In 1799, this vision led to a split between Mackenzie and Simon McTavish, director of the North West Company, and Mackenzie left the Nor'Westers to head the New North West Company—better known as the XY Company (this split is covered in more detail in Chapter 9). With great energy, he pressed on government and public the necessity of developing the trans-Canada trade route. He put forward his suggestions in *Voyages from Montreal,* which deserves to be quoted here at some length:

The discovery of a passage by sea, North-East or North-West from the Atlantic to the Pacific Ocean, has for many years excited the attention of governments, and encouraged the enterprising spirit of individuals. The non-existence, however, of any such practical passage being at length determined, the practicability of a passage through the continents of Asia and America becomes an object of consideration. The Russians, who first discovered that, along the coasts of Asia no useful or regular navigation existed, opened an interior communication by rivers, & through that long and wide-extended continent, to the strait that separates Asia from America, over which they passed to the adjacent islands and continent of the latter. Our situation, at length, is in some degree similar to theirs; the non-existence of a practicable passage by sea, and the existence of one through the continent, are clearly proved; and it requires only the countenance and support of the British Government, to increase in a very ample proportion this national advantage, and secure the trade of that country to its subjects.

... the Columbia is the line of communication from the Pacific Ocean, pointed out by nature, as it is the only navigable river in the whole extent of Vancouver's minute survey of that coast: its banks also form the first level country in all the Southern extent of continental coast from Cook's entry, and, consequently, the most Northern situation fit for colonization, and suitable to the residence of a civilized people. By opening this intercourse between the Atlantic and Pacific Oceans, and forming regular establishments through the interior, and at both extremes, as well as along the coasts and islands, the entire command of the fur trade of North America might be obtained, from latitude 48 North to the pole, except that portion of it which the Russians have in the Pacific. To this may be added the fishing in both seas, and the markets of the four quarters of the globe. Such would be the field for commercial enterprise, and incalculable would be the produce of it, when supported by the operations of that credit and capital which Great Britain so pre-eminently possesses. Then would this country begin to be remunerated for the expenses it has sustained in discovering and surveying the coast of the Pacific Ocean, which is at present left to American adventurers, who without regularity or capital, or the desire of conciliating future confidence, look altogether to the interest of the moment. They, therefore, collect all the skins they can procure, and in any manner that suits them, and having exchanged them at Canton for the produce of China, return to their own country. Such adventurers, and many of them, as I have been informed, have been very successful, would instantly disappear from before a well-regulated trade.

It would be very unbecoming in me to suppose for a moment, that the East India Company would hesitate to allow those privileges to their fellow-subjects which are permitted to foreigners, in a trade that is so much out of the line of their own commerce, and therefore cannot be injurious to it.

Many political reasons, which it is not necessary here to enumerate, must present themselves to the mind of every man acquainted with the enlarged system and capacities of British commerce, in support of the measure which I have very briefly suggested, as promising the most important advantages to the trade of the united kingdoms.[12]

Mackenzie, a businessman of immense vision, thought in expansive, global terms about how he could outflank the East India, South Sea and Hudson's Bay companies. He reasoned that the fishery of the North Pacific coast offered immense possibilities. He planned to set up a new company: the Fishery and Fur Company. Whaling ships would take trade items to the northwest coast. An entrepôt of trade and an organizational centre would be built at Nootka Sound, with smaller posts on the Columbia River in the south and at Sea Otter

Fur traders and Natives transact an exchange in this rare illustration. The location is likely the eastern woodlands or Mississippi headwaters. The chief trader stands in white as the spokesman for the Natives holds up his hands to indicate the fair measure demanded in exchange. Voyageurs tend to the canoe while others, on both sides of the transaction, look on.
British Columbia Archives, PDP-00368

Harbor in the north at latitude 55° north. Mackenzie laid his plan before Lord Hobart, the Secretary of State for War and the Colonies, in January 1802 under the august, stuffy title "Preliminaries to the Establishment of a permanent Fishery & Trade in Furs &c. in the interior and on the West Coast of North America."[13] Nine months later, on October 25, 1802, Mackenzie again appealed to the Colonial Office for support—this time of a military nature—to build an establishment on the northwest coast and to forestall foreign rivals.[14]

At this stage, the greatest opposition Mackenzie faced came not from the government nor from the chartered companies but from certain Montreal traders. Mackenzie had told Hobart that a coalition between the North West Company and its Montreal rival, his own Sir Alexander Mackenzie or XY Company, would be necessary to achieve the desired end. As he anticipated, his scheme for company union met resistance, especially from Simon McTavish, who did not want to see his own role, and that of Montreal, reduced. Weaving a safe course through the many hazards of imperial affairs taxed Mackenzie to the full, and a man of lesser zeal and belief would have gone peacefully into retirement. But history is seldom if ever shaped by indifference. Mackenzie never surrendered his dream or faltered in his progress, and he had a powerful influence on Jefferson's actions to stop the Canadians, as did the Russians, whom we will meet next.

Chapter 4

SOFT GOLD: THE RUSSIAN THRUST TO ALASKA, COLUMBIA RIVER AND ALTA CALIFORNIA

A lexander Mackenzie knew all about the Russians. When he ventured west in 1793, he intended to reach the Russians at Unalaska, and all evidence pointed to the fact that they would be there in wait for him. Cook, with John Ledyard's help, had discovered them perched on the shores of the continent in 1778. Who knew where they might be found in force, and who knew the dimensions of their southward migrations? The Russian bear seemed never to sleep for long. Contemporaries of the late eighteenth century who had followed the course of Russian expeditions to the Pacific Ocean and northern seas, such as the Reverend William Coxe, curate to the British ambassador at St. Petersburg, recorded and therefore warned that Russian imperial ambitions seldom rested. Coxe's hot-selling book—published in 1780 and continuing through four editions, the last in 1804—registered the

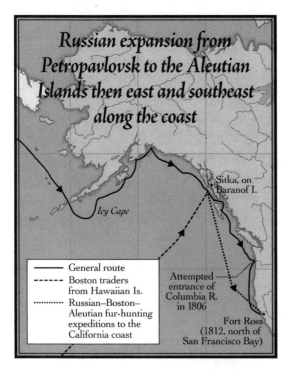

Russian expansion from Petropavlovsk to the Aleutian Islands then east and southeast along the coast

Sitka, on Baranof I.

Icy Cape

——— General route
----- Boston traders from Hawaiian Is.
··········· Russian–Boston–Aleutian fur-hunting expeditions to the California coast

Attempted entrance of Columbia R. in 1806

Fort Ross (1812, north of San Francisco Bay)

eastward growth of the Russian empire and showed that Russian designs in North America extended well beyond Alaska proper.[1]

When Empress Catherine reviewed the previous fifty years of Russia's eastward expansion in discovery and trade, a truly notable progression, she expressed profound shock and horror that it had taken an Englishman, Coxe, to tell the heroic saga of Russian pursuits in such distant and barren regions while all the time the original papers were housed in the Archives of the Admiralty at St. Petersburg. Catherine wanted results. Catherine wanted to make her own contribution to Russian exploration and discovery. To achieve this, Dr. Peter Pallas, professor of natural history at the Imperial Academy of Sciences in St. Petersburg, took up the advice Coxe had given in his book and devised a secret astronomical and geographical expedition from Kamchatka that would navigate and chart the waters between Asia and America. To command this expedition, the Russian Admiralty hired Lieutenant Joseph Billings, who had sailed with Cook on the *Resolution* (and who chanced upon Ledyard, his former shipmate, in deepest Russia).

Coxe, Pallas and other foreign students of Russia's progress knew that an amazing set of circumstances, not unlike those that had sent Columbus, Cabot and Cartier to the New World, had led to the discovery of Alaska and northwestern North America from Asia or, more particularly, from Kamchatka. Geographical revelations should remind the curious of the obstacles, terrestrial and marine, that had to be overcome. This point does not need elaboration but must be kept in mind when we trace the progress of the Russians—from the royal residence and the offices of state in St. Petersburg to the far-off frontier shipyards and outposts of Kamchatka and the even more distant, mystery-enveloped shores that these hard-driving adventurers probed, often at the cost of their lives.

The search for tributes to exact, wheatfields to harvest, and silver to mine were among the first reasons for the eastward extension of Muscovy. Russian trappers moved across the forested taiga in search of the extraordinarily valuable sable and reached the Sea of Okhotsk in 1639. They would have turned south at the mouth of the Amur River, but the Chinese barred the way. The Chinese, suspicious of Russia's southerly march, insisted that Russia advance no farther than the tributaries of the Amur River, and after driving the Russians back by force in the 1680s, they obtained Russian signatures to this effect in the Treaty of Nerchinsk of 1689. Any Russian posts built on Chinese territory had to be dismantled. Hunters who crossed the line were to be put to death. "From the day that this perpetual peace between both empires shall be sworn to, neither side shall receive any fugitive or deserter: But if any subject of either empire shall fly into the territories of the other, he shall be immediately secured and sent back."[2] The border was sealed. Henceforth, of necessity, Russia had to move north, northeast and across the Pacific Ocean. Nearly two centuries were to pass before the Governor of Siberia, Count N.N. Muraviev-Amursky, was able to confirm the final details of the Russian-Chinese boundary in 1858 (the same year that British Columbia was proclaimed a crown colony). Vladivostok, an ice-free port, was founded in 1860, becoming Russia's warden of the North Pacific. All that lay ahead, but it indicates the difficulties of the achievement and hints at the parallel structure of developments on the west coast of North America.

Peter the Great (1672–1725) exacted wide-ranging reforms. He had much to change, it is true, for the serfdom of mediaeval Russia still existed, wrapped up in political and religious heavy-handedness. Besides reorganizing the army and building a modern navy, Peter established secular schools, restructured the administration of the state, promoted the emancipation of women and redirected the country's economic development. Very little passed his desk unread, and he supervised the affairs of his subjects with strict discipline.

He was an empire builder, perhaps the most prominent in Russia's long history, and it is this which principally concerns us. The measures he put in place to find out about the "big land," Alaska, led to a hitherto unheard-of quest for fur-bearing resources in the North Pacific world. In this case, trade followed the flag and, like a bursting star, cast a fascinating light over a watery waste hitherto known only to its powerful, warlike indigenous inhabitants. Peter was also driven by scientific pursuits, and in this he reflected the enlightened dispositions of other leading monarchs of Europe. All motives taken into consideration, the czar's powers eventually extended over half a continent, and they did so within the passage of a mere half century. The Russian Admiralty

College became the life and soul of twenty-five years of expeditions and in due course accumulated an impressive list of findings: that the northeast passage was impracticable; that the Asiatic coast stretched farther east than imagined; that Japan was an archipelago not a peninsula; and that the American coast shaped itself northwesterly from Cape Blanco. Secrecy cloaked all arrangements of imperial discovery and growth.

Peter stood at the centre of the venerable Russian quest for new territory, subjects and tribute. Lands lying to the east of imperial control were added to the Russian bear's lair. Accessions were made with local consent when possible, with brutal force when necessary. Thus the Russian flag found its way to Irkutsk and then to the mouth of the Amur River. Peter sent orders to explore farther eastward, to the shores north of Kamchatka. Beginning in 1719, Peter sent Ivan Evreionov and Fedor Luzhkin to Kamchatka to discover and record details. Their mission involved determining if Asia was linked by land to America, and Peter may have given them secret instructions to lay claim to America. They sailed to the Kuril Islands and also interrogated some veteran Cossacks, garnering from them specifics of the physical conformation of the North Pacific rim. They assembled the particulars on a great map, true fruits of their work, and presented it to Peter on their safe return in 1722.

It is worthwhile to pause and remember the logistics of these developments. The distances these early Russians travelled by land and sea in the North Pacific places their activities among the prize feats of human endurance. Overland, they preferred to travel in the winter, along icy rivers and lakes, on sleighs and sledges. The fur traders of Russia, known as *promyshenniki*, had no equivalent in wilderness travel except the Canadians, whose geographical circumstances were surprisingly similar (as Mackenzie noted more than sixty years later). The riverine craft the Russians used on the Amur were supplemented by Baltic-designed and -tested flush-decked vessels with one or two masts. The Baltic and Pacific lay thousands of miles apart, but the tradition of Baltic ship design and construction, which owed much to Dutch advancements (and Peter's encouragements), made such vessels as were put together in the shipyards at the Amur estuary, Okhotsk, Avacha Bay (where Bering established the settlement of Petropavlovsk), Kamchatka and later at Unalaska and Sitka ideal for northern, heavy weather voyaging. It was inadequate foodstuffs that did the mariners in, leading to scurvy and therefore less efficient crews. To this was coupled ageing and weakening ships' timbers, sails, lines and rigging, caulking and gear. These material forces came into play in Peter's quest for claiming and dominating America.

In 1724, Peter came under pressure from the savants of his time, specifically the Paris Academy of Sciences, to find out how far east America lay from the northeasternmost borders of Kamchatka. Peter drew up the instructions in his own hand and told his counselor, the General-Admiral Count Apraxin, "I have reference to the finding a passage to China and India through the Arctic Sea. On the map before me there is indicated such a passage bearing the name of Anian. There must be some reason for that. In my last travels I discussed the subject with learned men and they were of the opinion that such a passage could be found. Now that the country is in no danger from enemies, we should strive to win for her glory along the lines of the Arts and Sciences. In seeking such a passage who knows but perhaps we may be more successful than the Dutch and English who have made many such attempts along the American coast."[3]

In the instructions, dated December 23, 1724 (just weeks before his death), Peter ordered an expedition headed by a thirty-seven–year veteran of the Russian navy, Captain-Commandant Vitus Bering, a

A pre-eminent mariner of the early eighteenth century, Vitus Bering (1681–1741), a Danish captain in Russian service, unlocked the secrets of the North Pacific in two scurvy-wracked voyages with the Russian Alexei Chirikov. He discovered and described the shores of the Aleutians and part of Northwest America, opened the region to Russian hunters and traders, and inaugurated Russian expansion to America. He was in charge of all logistics of these undertakings, including the building of the ships, but never saw home again. Vitus Bering-1, Alaska State Library Photograph Collection

God-fearing Lutheran, to proceed to Kamchatka or some other place controlled by the Russians and there to construct one or two vessels. In these craft, Bering was to shape a course to "near the land which goes to the north, which (since no one knows where it ends), it seems is part of America." Bering was to find out about these coasts and report on them, with an eye to any foreign claims or places of occupation. Bering was to indicate the sites of any rival occupations on a map he would compile.[4] Again, orders to claim sovereignty were not explicitly stated but were understood.

In the decked boats *Fortuna* and *Sv Gavriil*, Bering, with the incomparable Alexei Chirikov, his second-in-command, and forty-four sailors passed through the fog-shrouded strait that came to bear Bering's name. They reached 67° 18' north latitude but never saw America. Bering made a spirited attempt to find the American shore, but a storm checked progress. The return was bittersweet, for the navigators had found only half of what they had been looking for.

Peter's successors were impatient but true to his vision. Academicians continued to cry out for specific details of the empire's eastern margins. Thus a follow-on project, known formally as the Second Kamchatka, Second Bering, Great Northern and First Academic Expedition, was sent forth in 1733, with Bering and Chirikov again the respective leaders. This time no doubt existed as to its purpose: the explorers were to find and claim for Russia the shore of western America. The vessels were different this time—the Baltic-designed packet boat *Sv Peter* and the similar *Sv Pauel*—and there was a combined ships' complement of seventy-five. Naturalist Georg Wilhelm Steller, the first naturalist of Alaska, whose journal lays out the details of the expedition with scientific clarity, sailed with Bering.

On July 16, 1741, Bering spied mountains, and four days later, Steller stepped ashore on Alaskan terrain with a view to finding precious ore—the first sourdough. They were at 58° north latitude, between the mouth of the Copper River and Cape Suckling. Bering shaped a southeasterly course, discovered Kodiak and Ukamok islands, and, later still, to the west now, chanced upon the Shumagin Islands. Storms and scurvy haunted the ships and men. The *Sv Peter* was cast ashore on what became known as Bering Island (Ostrov Beringa), one of the Komandorskiye group, adjacent to Kamchatka.

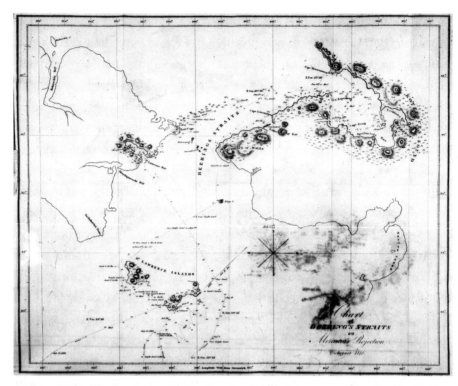

A chart of Bering Straits, August 1816, undertaken by Russian cartographic authorities. Beginning with Dezhnev, Bering and Chirikov, the Russians explored the waterways of this crossroad of continents. Inspired by the stimulus provided by Britain's James Cook (who went to very high latitudes), Billings (1789–92), Lisianski (1804–5) and Kotzebue (1815–18) continued the quest. Kotzebue's track to Kotzebue Sound, his principal discovery, is shown here. Alaska State Library, Alaska Purchase Centennial Commission Photograph Collection P20-209

Bering closed out his life on the rocky, grim island that bears his name. The crew crafted a new vessel out of the bones of the old, launched it and named it for the holy apostle Peter. "On the morning of August 14," wrote an elated Steller, "we besought God in a special prayer for his blessed help and support for a successful voyage. Then we weighed anchor." They skirted Bering Island, recalling their miserable arrival there the previous November, their miraculous survival thanks to the nourishment of sea mammal meat and oil, and their return to health and strength that had been sufficient for them to build their new vessel. They now had the means to sail the relatively short distance to Petropavlovsk on the Kamchatka Peninsula.[5]

In the meantime, Chirikov, luckier than his chief, coasted the southern shore of the Alaska peninsula and the Aleutian Islands. He added precious details to the Russian chart. On the Alexander Archipelago, which lies just above 54° 40' north latitude, he sent a ten-man party ashore to reconnoiter. The work was hazardous, full of the unexpected. The party failed to return. The men were either lost altogether in tides and water surges or, less likely, taken into custody by the local Tlingit. A second reconnaissance team sent inshore found no trace of the first. Chirikov decided to cut his losses and terminate his search of the American shore. He shaped a straight course for Kamchatka, joining the new Sv Peter with the remnant of Bering's crew.

Thus ended the first epoch of Russian sea exploration in the North Pacific. Bering and Chirikov and their men had discovered a new, hazardous and potentially profitable realm. They had revealed to the wider world an island-infested littoral rich in fur-bearing animals. Steller had not neglected the opportunity that presented itself. Sea mammals of various types were described in bulging notebooks and classified by the inquisitive Steller (who also named Steller's jay), working with strict German efficiency. Sea lions, seals and walrus, whales and porpoise were listed according to the observed cannons of European taxonomy. None of the mammals was so remarkable as the "sea beaver," as the Russians usually called it. In fact it was the sea otter, *Enhydra lutris*. The "big land" had now been reached, placed on the chart. But of all its treasures, that of immediate profit was the lustrous skin of the sea otter, what the Russians came to call soft gold, which was beautiful in appearance and so sensuously soft to the touch.

"The skin of a sea-otter is preferred in China to every other, but is used only by the opulent," wrote a Russian naval officer.[6] The sea otter trade drove Peter the Great's concept of empire to its second phase. This had real consequences for those who would control the continental fringe of northwestern North America, placing brutal pressure on the Tlingit and Aleuts in the process. Exploitation now supplanted discovery, and alliances with the Tlingit—by peace if possible, by enslavement if necessary—followed reconnaissance.

In those days, the breeding ground of the sea otter stretched in a six-thousand-mile arc from the Kuril Islands, Kamchatka, the Aleutians and southeast Alaska to the Queen Charlotte Islands and the shores of British Columbia (except the inshore or interior channels) as far south as Juan de Fuca Strait and the bays of California, and for the Russians and the hired Aleuts the pickings were easy; the hunts, destructive. Between 1743 and the end of the eighteenth century, one hundred Russian ventures exploited the sea otter habitat, obtaining, by one estimate, more than eight million silver rubles in wealth.[7] One trader, Andrei Tosltykh, made three voyages at mid-century and took over ten thousand sea otters, including 821 cubs. His success was duplicated. Two Russians at Saint Paul Island took five thousand one year and another thousand the next year. At tremendous cost—sea otter depopulation—the value of soft gold continued to mount, and this was long before the British and the Americans entered the maritime fur trade. Russian traders moved inexorably and rapidly south, toward the Queen Charlotte Islands, Vancouver Island, the Columbia River and Alta California.

When non-Russian voyagers first came to the Gulf of Alaska in the late 1770s, they were much surprised to hear that the Russians had already taken possession there. The Russians had not come to Alaska and the northwest coast by stealth, but they had not advertised their presence either; they had no need to. Trade and empire was their business, and as long as the Chinese would let them trade across the border at Kiakhta, at the southern reaches of Siberia, that was all that mattered. An inkling of the Russian expansion eastward was not made public to the English-speaking world until the narratives of Captain Cook's third voyage were first printed, in 1781 at the earliest. They related that in September 1778, Cook had found the Russians at Unalaska, and the master mariner had sent John Ledyard from Samgoonoodha Harbour to investigate (an episode referred to in the Prologue). Some Russian traders came back to the British warships with Ledyard, and Cook laid out, on his great table in the *Resolution*, his own grand chart of the Pacific Ocean. This showed the islands and coasts of America, with recent additions. "I laid before them my chart," noted Cook in his journal entry for September 8, 1778, "and found they were strangers to every part of the American coast except that what lies opposite them."[8]

From the principal trader Gerassim Gregoriev Ismailov, Cook learned that the Russians called "the great island" of land *Alaschka*. But Cook says that the Russians and Tlingit also knew it by the name *America*. From Ismailov, Cook also learned that the Russians had made repeated attempts to "get a footing upon that part of the Continent which lies adjacent to the islands, but have always been repulsed by the Natives, whom they describe as a very treacherous people; they mentioned two or three Captains or chief men, that had been Murdered by them and some of the Russians have shewed us wounds which they said they received there."[9]

In the wake of Cook's voyages, British merchant mariners chanced on Russian traders from time to time. Such episodes were accidental and spasmodic. When Nathaniel Portlock and George Dixon, in their trading vessels, came off Cape Bede, Cook Inlet, in 1786, they were greatly surprised—shocked might be a better term—to hear the report of a large gun from the shore. The heavy weather lay thickly over the land and they could see no smoke. The English traders answered this salute. They fired a gun and hoisted their colours, and before long a boat rowed out toward the ships. "I found the people to be Russians," recounted Portlock, who in disbelief stated, "If I understood them right, they came last from Kodiak, an island near the Schumagins, on a trading expedition; that they left their vessel at Kodiak, and proceeded to Cook's River in boats." The Russians, twenty-five in number, had put up a summer trading station, or base of operations, on a pleasant piece of flat land and had brought Tlingit from Kodiak or Unalaska to that location to do the hunting for them as there were no aboriginal habitations there. The English received a quantity of fine salmon (the Russians seemed to have only a fish diet, which was not customary for English mariners) and in return gave the Russians beef, port and a few bottles of brandy. The Russians feared that the local Indians would attack them, so "they were constantly on their guard, with their arms always ready, and ... no man slept without a rifle-barreled piece under his arm, and his cutlass and a long knife by his side." They also made certain they did not become intoxicated and thus put themselves in a state that would lower their defences. Portlock and Dixon took similar precautions. When a shore party went to gather wood, a chest of arms was sent along with the boats.[10]

How far south and east the Russians had progressed by the end of the 1780s was any outsider's guess. Dixon, with Portlock, went so far as to say that it was impossible to ascertain how many furs the Russians procured on the coasts of America. He reasoned that because the Russians did not trade directly to Macao and Canton, but did so via Kiakhta, they did not influence the price of sea otter on the China market. "We are pretty certain, that their traffic extends very little to the Eastwards of Cook's River, and that place certainly does not produce so many sea-otter as King George's Sound; so that I should imagine they do not collect 500 skins annually."

The British traders pondered how they could set up their own base in opposition to the Russians. They would need a safe and accessible port providing good refuge and a place to refit. They would have to guard against the indigenous people or make them their allies. Fortifications might have to be erected, and gun emplacements too. And, of course, there would have to be pelts available in abundance. Many fine ports existed, but some location between the Gulf of Alaska and Alta California seemed best, as it would be central to the sea otter habitat on North American shores. Dixon thought that the northern Queen Charlotte Islands would be the best place for such a base.[11] Others contended that Nootka Sound would work well, and that is where John Meares, trading out of India and China, eventually set up his fort (as described in Chapter 5).

On August 3, 1784, Grigorii Shelikhov established the first permanent base in North America under the Russian flag at Three Saints Harbor on Kodiak Island. This marks a turning point in the international contest for control of the resources and territory of the northwest coast. "It was not an ordinary venture of a common fur trader to gather a few skins for a temporary profit," wrote one authority, who explained that "it was part of a far-reaching plan devised for the extension of Russian dominion over the larger part of the western coast of what is now Canada and the United States."[12] Shelikhov's plan was well in place before, during and after his arrival at Three Saints Harbor. From this base the Russians extended their hunting and trading operations to the neighbouring islands and mainland. This, the first outpost of their American empire, was established almost a decade before Vancouver made his surveys of southeastern Alaska or Mackenzie came to Pacific tidewater, and twenty-one years before Lewis and Clark made their winter stay near the mouth of the Columbia River.

The state of Russian trade and expansion was disclosed to the wider world by the various narratives—of Meares, Dixon and Portlock—that were published

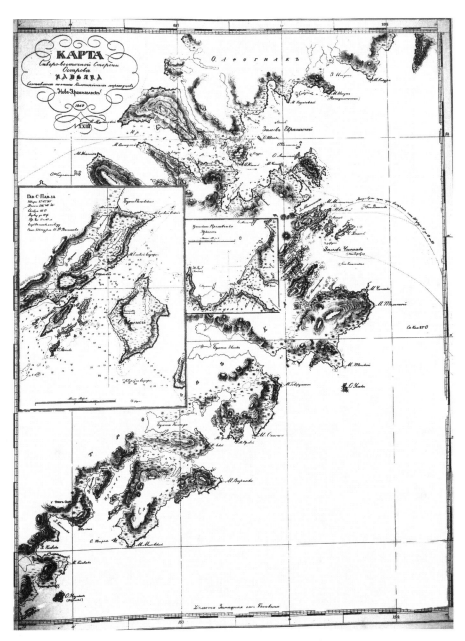

This chart shows the east coast of Kodiak Island, Alaska, with Kodiak town inset. Grigorii Shelikhov, merchant trader and expansionist, built the principal base here, which gave him command of the central coast. The chart is from Mikhail Dmitrievich Tebenkov's Atlas sie verozapadnkh beregov Ameriki *(1852). Alaska State Library, Alaska Purchase Centennial Commission Photograph Collection P20-229*

in London and, some of them, translated into German, French and Russian. The word spread, and Russian America began to appear on maps. Mackenzie and Jefferson knew of these narratives and had them in their libraries.

More than a decade later, in 1799, the Russian government under Paul I (1796–1801) chartered the Russian-American Company, on the advice of associated merchants, to regulate their trade and empire in Alaska. With a twenty-year monopoly, the firm would be a government within a government, maintaining its own armed forces, trading where it wished, making such treaties as it required and spreading the Greek Orthodox faith. Three Saints Bay would do as a post but not a base for American operations. Accordingly, Alexander Baranov, governor and superintendent, presented his plan to establish a new base of operations far to the south and east at Sitka on Norfolk Sound in the Alexander Archipelago. Once again, the headquarters of the Russians had moved closer to the Spanish sphere of influence. The articles of the company theoretically made it possible to occupy the Queen Charlotte Islands and Nootka Sound. Baranov considered this in 1800 or so, but likely decided that interference from the Haida, Nuu-chah-nulth and Kwakwaka'wakw would check any ambitions there.

Baranov could never get enough muskets, ammunition, cloth, molasses, wheat and other necessities from Kamchatka, but American shipping solved his problem. When the *Enterprise*, from New York, arrived at Kodiak in May 1801, two years had passed since the previous ship. Baranov embraced the mate, the Irish-American Joseph O'Cain, like a brother.[13] (In fact, O'Cain was well known to the Russians. He had already visited them on the Alaska shore in 1792 as first mate of the Calcutta-based schooner *Phoenix*, under Captain Hugh Moore, an East India Company trader in the sea otter business.) The Russians traded two thousand pelts for all the supplies the *Enterprise* carried and extracted a promise from O'Cain that he would return again as soon as possible. The Russians needed all the foodstuffs, metal pieces, clothing, arms and ammunition they could possess, for the local Tlingit sought revenge on white traders for the barbaric acts of an Englishman, Captain Henry Barber of the *Unicorn*. Violence begat violence, and the Tlingit eventually took Sitka, and with it half its arms.

O'Cain, who did return as promised, forged an alliance with Baranov to prop up sagging Russian authority on the northwest coast of America. He established powerful partnerships with various Boston traders, most notably the Winships (of whom more later), so as to keep the colony supplied with foodstuffs. The Yankee mariners also recruited workers for Baranov—shipwrights, metalworkers and other tradesmen—and made plans to sell the Russian bounty of fur in Canton, developing a triangular trade—Russia, the United States, China. This brought the Boston mariners more closely in touch with the Hawaiian Islands, which offered easy places for rest, resupply and repair. King Kamehameha sent Baranov best wishes for the re-establishment of Sitka.

American shipping was a mixed blessing for Baranov and the Russian-American Company, for while Yankee traders brought desperately needed supplies, in doing so they subverted company control. In 1802, headquarters sent Baranov strict instructions to keep foreign shipping out and to extend territorial interest as far south as the 55th degree—even to Nootka Sound. "Try to insist on certain rights, even on Nootka Sound," ran the directive, "for should the Court of England present its demands, it ought to be possible to insist on placing the frontier as far as the 50th degree ... After all, this part of the world is still unoccupied, so Russia has predominant rights there."[14]

Now the Russians flexed their naval muscle. In 1803 the Russian Imperial Navy frigate *Neva*, commanded by Captain-Lieutenant Yuri Lisianskii, was sent from Kronstadt in the Baltic by way of Cape Horn to conduct naval diplomacy in the realm of the Tlingit, or Kolosh, as the Russians called them. For four days the Kolosh put up a stout defence, but they could not continue it against the *Neva*'s firepower and thus determined to abandon their native shores and withdraw to the interior. "In pursuance of this resolve," says the Bostonian William Sturgis, who got the information from the Russian captain, "they collected together and, shocking to relate, cut the throats of all the infants and old People of both sexes who were unable to support a journey through the desolate wilderness, choosing rather to massacre them with their own hands than suffer them to fall alive into the hands of their enemies from whom they expected no mercy."[15] Baranov decided to put his headquarters on a new, better footing and established a fortified post, New Archangel, on elevated ground four miles from the old Sitka. He sent a sloop to the Hawaiian Islands for food, and it came back laden with pigs, taro, bananas, yams and coconuts. Meanwhile the two hundred or so Russians holed up in New Archangel lived on their guard, fearful of a Tlingit attack.

Despite these difficulties, Baranov began to plan the first expedition to southern waters in 1802, and the scheme went into effect the next year. The Russians, employing Aleuts as hunters, exploited the sea otter to near extinction. They did not act alone, for at the turn of the century there were many more American ships in Alaskan waters than vessels from any other nation. In consequence of the sea otter's decline, the Russians ranged farther south in search of fur seals, and this hunt forged a new, strange link between Muscovite and Bostonian. The Russians hired the Aleuts as hunters and with them their kayaks and baidarkas. Each hunter was issued one musket only. The Americans supplied the foodstuffs and also provided the vessels whereby the Russian furs were shipped to Canton at a charge of usually 5 percent of the cargo plus freight costs both ways. The Russians had Bostonians share the sea otter catch fifty-fifty. The arrangement worked perfectly, for the Americans lacked able hunters, the Russians had few ships, the Americans had access to Canton and the Russians had the ability to engage the Aleuts. The new combination edged down the coast to poach on the more plentiful rookeries of Baja California. The American ships kept well off the coast, in international waters, so as to avoid Spanish capture.

In the summer of 1805, the initiative for planning these southern voyages passed to Baron Nicolai Petrovich Rezanov, a chamberlain at the Russian court, son-in-law of the pioneering Grigorii Shelikhov, and a powerful political force in Russia's eastward destiny. Rezanov had been given full plenipotentiary powers to negotiate a commercial agreement with the Emperor of Japan that would allow the Russians to obtain provisions and dispose of commodities there. Earlier correspondence had been encouraging and had produced an invitation for him to visit Nagasaki. With understandable optimism, he sailed to Japan in the Russian imperial vessel *Nadeschda*, under the command of Captain-Lieutenant Ivan Krusenstern. All his approaches were met with prevarication, obfuscation and resistance.[16] It had been a false dawn in Russia's attempted closer relations with Japan.

Taking a different tack, Rezanov laid an enhanced expansionist blueprint before Baranov. Rezanov was a latecomer to Russia's dream of moving south, but he made it official. He wanted to wrestle California from Spain, and he saw occupation of the Columbia River as a means to that end. It might take a decade, he thought, but the Spanish were weak and might in time become weaker. In the meantime, opportunities awaited Baranov's traders as far south as California, urged Rezanov. The Spanish showed weakness there, and thus two posts should be erected immediately to tap the trade: one at the mouth of the Columbia River; the other at Nova Albion just north of San Francisco Bay, the Spaniards' farthest post north. The object was to develop agricultural foodstuffs for the Russian-American Company. The Hawaiian Islands could be made a place for special diplomacy and for possible concessions, even annexation. "To accomplish this it would be necessary to build as soon as possible an armed brig to drive away the Bostonians from this trade forever," Rezanov told the company's directors—never mind that the Bostonians were currently their partners. "From the Columbia we could gradually advance toward the south to the Port of San Francisco, which forms the boundary line of California. I think I may say that at the Columbia we could attract population from various localities, and in the course of ten years we should become strong enough to make use of any favorable turn in European politics to include the coast of California in the Russian possessions."[17]

Around the same time as Rezanov put forward his proposal, the Boston captain Jonathan Winship Jr. told Baranov that sixty men had started overland from the United States the previous autumn (1804) to settle the Columbia River. In fact this was misleading, although Baranov may have misinterpreted Lewis and Clark's expedition of discovery as a venture in colonization. The news alarmed Rezanov, who noted that four Boston vessels were cruising and trading in the sounds of the northwest coast. With a strong touch of the proprietorial he asked, "When shall we drive these unwelcome guests away?"[18]

Rezanov now advanced his plan for establishing a base on the Columbia River. He saw that place as one to attract trade and settlers, and he also saw it as a base from which to expand south to San Francisco. He intended to enter the Columbia River in March 1806 to reconnoiter for his proposed settlement and marine depot. At New Archangel, the Russians purchased the ship *Juno* from a Rhode Island skipper, John D'Wolf, and readied it for the voyage south to the Columbia River.[19] "We left [New Archangel] on February 25 aboard the ship *Juno* which I had bought from the Bostonian [John D'Wolf] but my men soon fell ill," wrote Rezanov. "I had intended to survey the Columbia River in spite of all this ... We sighted the mouth of the river on March 14 [1806]. But head winds forced us to stand off ... We approached it [again] on the evening of March 20 and dropped anchor. We planned to enter the river the next day, but the tremendous current and the great breakers in the channel hindered us."[20] The captain, Lieutenant Nikolai Khvostov, made two further attempts, one each on March 31 and April 1, to cross the Columbia River bar. He nearly lost a boat and crew in the process.[21]

It is not inconceivable, using Rezanov's dates of the *Juno*'s approach to the Columbia, that the ship was there at the same time as Lewis and Clark were camped at Fort Clatsop, near the mouth of the river. They had been there all winter and broke camp on March 23, three days after the *Juno* made a second attempt to enter the Columbia River. On March 31, when the *Juno* was lying off Cape Disappointment (and Rezanov was hoping to get across the bar), Lewis and Clark were camped close to the eventual site of Fort Vancouver. The next day they were near Sandy River. One historian, Stephen Haycox, who carefully reconstructed these various movements, concludes, correctly, that if Rezanov's *Juno* had made it into the river, Clatsop runners would have been sent after Lewis and Clark. He explains that the American explorers had already lingered at Fort Clatsop, delaying their departure in hopes they might make contact with an American or British trading vessel. "What would these agents of their respective governments have discussed if they had met, and what might have eventuated in terms of a Russian presence on the Columbia and in the Pacific Northwest?"[22] An excellent question, displaying great insight into these competing rivalries for the Columbia River. If the Russians had put up their post, as proposed by Rezanov, the US claim to the mouth of the Columbia River would have been greatly weakened.[23] Not for the last time, the Columbia River bar shaped the destiny of empires.

Rezanov was obliged to abandon the attempt. Sailing to Hawaii was out of the question, so, using Captain George Vancouver's charts, he ordered a course for San Francisco Bay. On March 28, 1806, the *Juno*, flying the Russian flag, dropped anchor off the Spanish presidio. Spanish authorities had long worried that the Muscovites would arrive sooner or later. Rezanov, who stepped ashore in his finery, was received as a gentleman by Captain José Darío Argüello, the commandant, and made it known that the purpose of the visit was to purchase provisions for the Russian colonies. Spain's laws forbade any such transaction. But the commandant's eligible daughter, the charming Doña Concepcíon, found Rezanov, a widower, exceedingly handsome, and the feeling of attraction was mutual. On the grounds of trading among family, or at least betrothed persons, the governor permitted the exchange of Russian gifts and Spanish provisions. After six weeks Rezanov sailed for New Archangel, exchanging salutes in recognition of the new arrangement. Meanwhile, papal dispensations were sought so that the Greek Orthodox baron could marry the Roman Catholic Doña Concepcíon. But shortly thereafter Rezanov died from an illness that led to a fatal fall from his horse at Krasnoyarsk in Siberia. Doña Concepcíon, it is said, did not learn about this until forty years later. So ended the first attempt to bring Russia and Spain into closer cooperation on the Pacific coast of North America.[24]

That same year, 1806, the ship *O'Cain*, commanded by Jonathan Winship, sailed from Sitka with nearly a hundred Aleuts and Kodiaks (including twelve women) and three Russian supervisors, and with seventy baidarkas and some leather boats stored in the ship. This constituted another remarkable voyage to the Spanish waters of California. Russians, aboriginals and Americans were drawn together to exploit sea otters and fur seals. On this occasion, Humboldt Bay was discovered and charted.[25]

Back in New Archangel, Baranov strengthened the palisades and erected a wooden castle. The capital of Russian America grew in its commercial and ecclesiastical power, a mighty headquarters for local shipping and ship repairs. Baranov sent an agent to Hawaii to increase influence there, but King Kamehameha, aware of these proceedings and worried about Russian ambitions, drew closer to the British.

Although he did not fully embrace the policy of extension promoted by his masters, Baranov could not ignore the wishes and instructions of his superiors. He had to regenerate and pursue the Rezanov dream of a Columbia River settlement.[26] In consequence, in the fall of 1808 he sent more expeditions south to build forts and establish settlements.The first expedition, under the command of Nikolai Bulygin, travelled in the brig *Sv Nicholas*, a vessel acquired from the Americans. It came to grief on the rocks north of Gray's Harbor. The survivors clambered ashore and were eventually enslaved by the local Natives.[27] A relief ship, the *Lydia*, out of Boston, rescued the survivors and brought them back to New Archangel.

Ivan Kuskov, Baranov's jack of all trades and deputy governor, who had already made four voyages south, was sent to establish "a settlement in New Albion near the Columbia River." Still another expedition was to build a fort just north of San Francisco. All employed Captain Vancouver's charts. Afanassi Shvetzov anchored in Bodega Bay, and the Russians subsequently developed the port there in 1812, establishing several farms and sending a hunting party to the Farallon Islands off the Golden Gate.[28]

Also in 1808, Sysoi Slobodchikov, on the ship *Kodiak*, claimed territory at Trinidad Bay (41° north latitude) for Russia by placing a copper plate bearing the imperial coat of arms on the shore.

The climax of the southward quest came in 1812 when the Russian-American Company established Rossiya (Fort Ross) on an elevated plain in what is now Russian County, California. They built a stout post of redwood cedar, fortified it with twenty cannons, and ran it with a hundred Russians and eighty Aleuts, as well as some convicts from Siberia. It was a useful agricultural and hunting base, and it caused no end of aggravation to the Spanish authorities, who objected to this Russian intrusion but did little to oust the Muscovites. When eviction orders were finally issued in 1818, the Spanish governor lacked sufficient means to make the Russians comply.[29]

Yankee merchant traders were the Russians' strong partners in exploiting the marine resources of the coast, ranging as far south as the Farallons and the Santa Barbara Channel. They cut a deal with the Russians at New Archangel to take Kodiak fur hunters south in their baidarkas and baidaras (larger leather-on-frame craft that employed up to a dozen natives). The Americans placed gangs ashore on islands such as Guadalupe, Natividad, Ceros and Redondo to take fur seals, and sent other parties to hunt the sea otter among the island waters. Between 1803 and 1812 there were thirteen joint expeditions involving American ships and Russian supervisors. Thirteen Yankee sea captains were involved, and 21,000 sea otter pelts were taken.[30] These expeditions ranged south from the Columbia River to San Diego Bay.

The regular and persistent visits to California waters from the north alarmed Spanish authorities. The Spaniards, "with a portended jurisdiction, attempted to prohibit other nations from taking the fur-bearing animals on their coast," William Dane Phelps, one of the Boston traders, said.

> Consequently, when the ship rode at anchor in ports on the main, it was ostensibly for the purpose of trade with the Spaniards; and the canoe hunters were kept away from the ship, giving the appearance that they were not connected with her. The Spaniards would sometimes capture and confiscate a stray canoe with its contents, and the Indians of the missions would occasionally meet with the Kodiaks and have a scrimmage … the fortune of war generally terminating in favor of the Kodiaks …. The management of such a body of more than half savage men, to keep them under proper discipline, and profitably and safely employed, and at the same time to navigate a large ship and crew, and conduct the whole to a successful termination, was no small matter.[31]

By 1813, in spite of the lucrative joint Russian-American sea otter hunt, the difficulties of the Russian-American Company were becoming acute. It was in a state of desperation and disappointment that Baranov learned of John Jacob Astor's proposal to found a colony on the Columbia (see Chapter 12).

The Russians tried to rejuvenate their own expansion schemes. In 1815, Dr. Georg Anton Schaeffer, a Russian agent on Hawaii, ill-advisedly built a fort and raised the Russian flag, but Hawaiians, Britons and Americans united and caused his precipitate departure to China. A few years later, Russian sympathizers Peter Dobell and A. Ljungstedt, who saw the Hawaiian islands as the key to the Pacific, tried unsuccessfully to secure Russian domination. The Russian government was well aware of British and American resistance to Russian annexation of Hawaii, but that was not a difficulty on the continental shore of America—except for the north shore of Alaska, where Russian naval discoveries cast a long shadow over British claims for a seaborne passage from the Atlantic to the Pacific. Explorations by Otto von Kotzebue in 1815–17 prompted the British Admiralty to send out various expeditions, including that of John Franklin, Royal Navy, to explore from the mouth of the Coppermine River eastward. It would be mortifying, said an Admiralty secretary who sensed the danger, "if a naval power but of yesterday [Russia] should complete a discovery in the nineteenth century, which was so happily commenced by Englishmen in the sixteenth."[32]

Baranov lasted until 1819, when the Russian-American Company underwent a corporate reorganization. He was relieved of responsibilities, bringing to an end the old era of independent management under the man Washington Irving called the "old Russian potentate," and who the same British Admiralty secretary described as "a rough, rugged, hospitable, hard-drinking old Russian; somewhat of a soldier; somewhat of a trader; above all, a boon companion of the old roistering school, with a strong cross of the bear."[33]

Still the Yankee vessels arrived in strength. Each year about ten or fifteen foreign vessels came to Sitka to trade, a signal of potential intrigue and unwanted influence. American vessels were well armed and amply furnished with munitions of war. "Separated from the civilized world," one contemporary, William Sturgis, wrote of the Russians at Sitka, "and cut off for a long time from all communications with it, they have been accustomed to rely on their own resources for protection and defense; and to consider and treat as enemies all who attempt to intercept them in the prosecution of their lawful pursuits." Business on the northwest coast, though buoyant, lay in others' hands. Russian officials grew even more nervous, and the Americans refused to relinquish this commerce or be coerced in any way.

In 1821 the czar issued an ukase, or decree, claiming the coast south to 51° north latitude and forbidding all foreign ships from approaching within one hundred miles of the coast. The United States and Britain protested this action, the Hudson's Bay Company increased its trading activities on the coast, and the Royal Navy continued its marine surveys in the high Arctic, advising the Russians that they intended to do so all the way west to the Bering Sea. American merchant mariners pressed on Washington their need for redress and support.[34] Eventually the matter was settled by treaties between Russia and the United States (April 17, 1824) and between Russia and Great Britain (February 28, 1825), by which Russian claims to sovereignty were confirmed to territory north of 54° 40' north latitude and west of 141° west longitude.

Rezanov's dream of moving south to the Columbia River suffered the fate of so many voyages of adventure in that river—disaster at or near the bar. The Russians never established their hoped-for post at the Columbia River or, for that matter, on the Queen Charlotte Islands or Vancouver Island either. Why they did not settle the Queen Charlotte Islands or put up a post at Nootka Sound may puzzle some. The truth of the matter is that they could not raise crops, principally grains, there. This drove them south to the Columbia River and, when that eluded them, to Alta California. They kept up an agricultural station at Fort Ross and its neighbourhood until they sold it in 1842. By this time the Hudson's Bay Company—successor to the Bostonians—had solved all the Russian traders' problems of supply, had worked out an arrangement for dominating coastal shipping and trade, and had leased the trade of southeastern Alaska, the original heartland of Baranov and the Russian-American Company. Hawaii always lay beyond Sitka's reach and, after a while, Alaska too passed from Russian commerce and became more a benefit to the British traders, another informal realm of the British Empire. This was a prelude to the sale of the territory to the United States in 1867, an arrangement from which the British were excluded by Russian design.

The lure of furs that had drawn the Russians across Siberia and then to Alaska and California lessened with the years. In 1842, according to Captain Otto Von Kotzebue, who visited Fort Ross in the ship *Ruryk*, the Russians had almost exterminated the sea otter on the California and Baja coast. Russian imperial overstretch had been achieved; processes of contraction begun.

Chapter 5

RISING TIDES OF EMPIRE:
FLAGS AT NOOTKA SOUND

A ll the time the Russians seemingly had no foreign rivals in North Pacific waters and sailed unopposed to the Aleutians and the Gulf of Alaska, the Spanish watched with growing anxiety for any and all potential intruders. As early as 1750 the Spanish were aware of Russians in the North Pacific. French mapmakers, Jesuits, Russian voyage accounts, and Spanish ambassadors' reports from St. Petersburg all gave early warning. Although Sebastián Vizcaíno had explored the California coast in 1602, it was not until 1768 that Monterey was ordered to be occupied so as to thwart the Russians. At that date, Spain was the first power in Europe. It had the most extensive empire and was dominant in the Western Hemisphere. Consolidation and protection were watchwords of the Spanish imperial state, and these guided every action of ministers of the crown and their subordinates. The king of Spain, Carlos III, an enlightened, clever and scientifically minded monarch who ruled from 1759 to 1788, directed the affairs of state, but he had no shortage of home-grown or colonial-born aristocrats, gentry and other place-seekers to do his

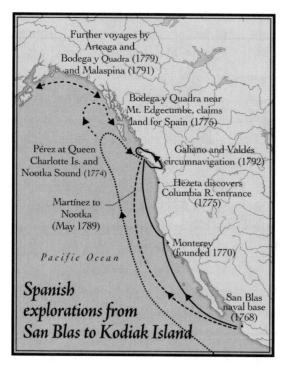

Further voyages by
Arteaga and
Bodega y Quadra (1779)
and Malaspina (1791)

Bodega y Quadra near
Mt. Edgecumbe, claims
land for Spain (1775)

Pérez at Queen
Charlotte Is. and
Nootka Sound (1774)

Galiano and Valdés
circumnavigation (1792)

Heceta discovers
Columbia R. entrance
(1775)

Martínez to
Nootka
(May 1789)

Pacific Ocean

Monterey
(founded 1770)

Spanish
explorations from
San Blas to Kodiak Island

San Blas
naval base
(1768)

bidding. The old order of medieval Spain still ruled the Iberian empire, though it was tempered by the infusion of new royal blood, and any early indication of revolution or religious non-compliance was quickly crushed and swept away. Administrative improvements, agricultural and military reorganization, and scientific pursuits reflected European preoccupations but particularly the zeal of Carlos III. This was no moribund empire but, rather, an expansive, if self-contained, world. It was an empire of the sword and the cross.

Throughout Texas, New Mexico and Arizona, the Spanish organized their frontier posts so as to provide a rational scheme of defence against various indigenous nations including the Apache and the Comanche, though the vastness of the territory and the varieties of these geographical locales made a uniform administrative and military structure impossible. In addition, the Spanish governor in New Orleans knew of the mounting enemy presence on the northern perimeter, notably in the upper Mississippi valley, which included Spanish Illinois (the situation there is discussed in Chapter 7). The British from Canada, who were advancing in the wake of the Canadien traders from the old French regime in Quebec, and now the Americans, progressing via the Ohio River and Kentucky and pressing toward Spanish St. Louis, posed a frightening combination to Spanish rule. Who knew how far west they might go? In the last year of Carlos's reign, Manuel Antonio Flóres, viceroy of New Spain from 1787 to 1789, warned about the "republican and independent" American states aspiring to get a safe port on the Pacific. The United States might furthermore "try to sustain it by crossing the immense land of this continent above our possessions of Texas, New Mexico, and the Californias ... and, in truth, it would obtain the richest trade of Great China and India if it were to succeed in establishing a colony on the west coasts of America."[1] Put differently, the northern frontier of the Spanish American empire was in possible jeopardy without military reinforcement. From Spanish officialdom's perspective, the Anglo-American threat was real enough—and growing.

What gave further cause for alarm, and is the subject of our immediate concern, was the steady approach of the Russians south and east from the Gulf of Alaska.[2] In 1768, Spain's authorities worried that the Russians had got as far south as 44° north latitude, where they might find the Río de Martín Aguilar, a riverine northwest passage. Spanish policy makers reasoned that foreign incursions should be halted by scouting the coasts for rivals, checking any illicit trade and developing appropriate plans to promote Spanish occupation. As Antonio María de Bucareli y Ursúa, viceroy from 1771 to 1779, put it, "any establishment by Russia, or any other foreign power, on the continent ought to be prevented, not because the king needs to enlarge his realms, as he has within his known dominions more than it will be possible to populate in centuries, but in order to avoid consequences brought by having any other neighbours [there] than the Indians."[3]

In Baja and Alta California, the problems facing Spanish administrators were similar to those in the upper Mississippi. Military posts and missions had to be established and sustained, but, in addition, a maritime arm of authority had to be established at the same time—for policing and for consolidation. So while Spanish administrators advanced the exploration of Alta California by land, they also set forth a plan for maritime ascendancy. The first requirement was to have a proper marine base, and in 1768 they built a fortified naval yard at San Blas, on the mainland of the Gulf of California.[4] Warnings about its many weaknesses were unadvisedly swept aside in the haste of its founding. Farther north, San Diego, Los Angeles and Monterey were all founded, and the rich promise of San Francisco revealed. By the mid-1770s, the Pacific Coast frontier in these latitudes had been secured to the Spanish crown. The indigenous people, swept up in the Iberian imperial tide, learned Spanish, became Roman Catholic and intermarried with the Spaniards. They, too, became agents of empire, and in decades that lay far ahead, some of them would join with others, oust their imperial masters and found the Republic of Mexico.

For the moment, the combination of Spanish military power and missionary zeal ruled the Californias. From the marine bastion of San Blas and the Alta California capital of Monterey, expeditions of coastal exploration northward could spy out new ports for imperial consolidation so as to buttress the north-western maritime frontier of Spanish America. This was an empire of defensive expansion. In the circumstances, the antiquated proscription of the papal bull of 1493 and the Treaty of Tordesillas of the next year, which had given Spain the Americas and west as far as the Philippines—in short, the whole expanse of the Pacific Ocean, its islands and littoral—seemed now a dead letter. The old order had passed; the new reality was that occupation counted most for imperial purposes. Even primacy in discoveries—who got there first—mattered less and less in the rising tides of empires. Putting up a fort and raising the flag for king and country, that was what counted.

Regarding all foreign traders and agents as poachers (and thus subversive), Spain's colonial authorities in Mexico and California were on the watch for the Russians coming south out of the fog and mists of the Aleutians and the Gulf of Alaska. What they had not counted on was the British and the Americans arriving, almost simultaneously, by sea at Nootka Sound on Vancouver Island. British mariners James Hanna (who was first there in 1785), James Strange (1786) and John Meares (1788) formed the vanguard of British commercial activity in this annex, or backyard, of Alta California. When the American

The ship King George, *of King George's Sound Company of London, is shown in Coal Harbour, Cook Inlet. Captain Nathaniel Portlock found a vein of coal there; hence the name. Burning Mountain, from which smoke issued, can be seen in the distance. "The natives behaved with becoming civility and decorum," the ship's surgeon recorded, "and we treated them with respect and good nature." This drawing by J. Woodcock was originally published in Nathaniel Portlock's* A Voyage Round the World.

skipper Robert Gray, then in the sloop *Lady Washington* out of Boston, arrived at Ship Cove on Bligh Island in Nootka Sound in September 1788, Meares's vessels were at anchor in nearby Friendly Cove, and their crews provided a rousing welcoming committee to the Americans.[5] For the time being, and until May 1789, when the Spanish arrived and the commotion began, the British and the Americans had Nootka Sound all to themselves. The local tribes grew wealthy, enriched by becoming part of global trade.

It was the British who challenged and ultimately ended the Spanish proscription. Various secretaries and their advisers in British offices of state, especially the Board of Trade and the precursor of the Foreign Office, were keen to protect British interests and to safeguard the profit and power of the British nation and empire at every turn. Commerce ruled the corridors of Whitehall. Strident voices of the merchants, shipowners, insurance agents and bankers of Britain echoed through parliament. Some members of the merchant class intended to follow to the letter the project of the sea otter trade as described by Cook in his published voyages of 1784 and advertised as early as 1782 in unauthorized accounts of the expedition, including John Ledyard's. Hanna, Strange, Meares and others had done just that; others would follow including Nathaniel Portlock, George Dixon and Charles William Barkley.

The Americans were observers, even innocents, in the transactions that followed. They kept out of trouble, having no quarrel with the Spanish. If anything, they had a greater suspicion of the British, for the British were their former imperial masters and in the present circumstances were their greatest trading threat. Blood may have been thicker than water, but here it was every ship's master for himself, and the British competed among themselves just as the Americans did. The American merchant mariners had no interest in planting the Stars and Stripes on this distant shore in the early years of the sea otter trade. They might buy land from the indigenous nations and enter into agreements of trade and friendship with them, but they had no interest in claiming sovereignty. In fact, United States law forbade self-proclaimed agents to set up American territories or sign treaties with foreign indigenes. Nootka Sound, for the Americans, was a convenient place to trade, to rest and to resupply or repair their vessels. For the moment, the Americans were transients on this far shore (see Chapter 6).

The British and Americans had penetrated the defences of Alta California, including its northern shore, without so much as an alarm bell going off at the nearest presidio or mission at Monterey, Carmel or San Francisco. Similarly, it was news out of St. Petersburg from the Spanish ambassador that drew attention to Russian discoveries "on our Northern Coasts of California." This was what James Cook, and John Ledyard, had discovered, also to their surprise. The word passed quickly from St. Petersburg to Madrid, from Madrid to Havana, and from Havana to Mexico City. The viceroy in Mexico City, Bucareli, received orders that he should ascertain what the Russians were doing and take steps to dislodge these intruders, first by warning and then, if necessary, by force.

Bucareli knew that the Russians were in constant fear of starvation and that life on the Alaskan frontier was precarious and thus vulnerable; the supply lines from the Amur River and Kamchatka were thin and irregular, and he speculated, quite correctly as it turned out, that sooner or later the Russians would overcome these difficulties either by trading with others who could supply their wants or, even more alarming, by coming south to California to grow crops from which they could make their bread and distil their vodka. He concluded that his administration ought to take the opportunity "to put a stop to foreigners in the vicinity of our Peninsula [Baja California] & California." He knew that the Spanish presidios of San Diego and Monterey were weak and that Spanish military resources were thin. But with true northern vision he saw that the San Francisco presidio, with its garrison and excellent port, would be vitally important in the northern scheme of consolidation and defence, with the missions of Alta California giving the Spanish a true advantage by promoting self-sufficiency and supplying, in turn, the ships of the Spanish Armada, its royal navy.[6] It was in this last point that he expressed his coastwise, or oceanic, vision.

He urged, further, that preparations be made at San Blas naval base so that a sufficient number of sailors were available for service and a greater number of warships were prepared for distant voyages of exploration to the northwest coast. As San Blas lay in 21° north latitude and the Gulf of Alaska in 60° north, such a voyage would be at least 2,340 miles if made in a straight line, and would more likely be three or four times that distance given the necessary tacking required, all of it indicative of the immense sea voyaging required. This was no voyage of following the winds and currents across the Atlantic from Cadíz or Seville to Hispaniola, as difficult as that might be, but rather the reverse, travelling against prevailing winds and currents in high latitudes.

In keeping with the plan to extend Spanish influence northward and forestall Russian movements southward, in 1774, Juan Pérez, a pilot in the Spanish navy, received orders from Viceroy Bucareli to sail from San Blas. Pérez had trouble finding a suitable vessel for a northwest coast cruise, and in the end he had to settle for the *Santiago*, a 225-ton frigate somewhat unsuitable for close coastal reconnaissance. Pérez had instructions to locate foreign—that is, Russian—trading factories and settlements. To deter any Muscovite advance, he was to put down markers of claim stating that all this coastline belonged to the Spanish crown. He also carried more pious orders to attract aboriginal people to the faith and spread the gospel.[7]

Santiago cleared San Blas on January 25, 1774, and sighted Graham Island, in the Queen Charlotte Islands, on July 18. Two days later, at 55° 45' north latitude, the Spanish made contact with some Haidas near Langara Island. Then Pérez, short on water and worried about weather, shaped a course to the south, to Nootka Island. Once off the southern entrance to the sound, he ordered a launch to find a safe approach to a suitable anchorage. Foiled by a fresh wind that threatened to put the frigate on the dangerous lee shore, he gave up on his attempt to find an anchorage. Instead he lay off Nootka while the Mowachaht came out to the vessel and offered pelts in trade. Neither Pérez nor Esteban Martínez, there with him as a junior officer, realized the commercial prospects of this encounter. Trade was not their business. That was for others who legislated the Spanish world of commerce. But Martínez, seeing around him fine harbours and timber, waxed ecstatic in his report: "It is certain that if with time this land is conquered and populated and some ports are discovered in it, our Catholic Majesty will be able to say, 'I have another world of Spaniards and of land as rich and luxuriant as Spain, since thousands of ships and perhaps even more can be constructed.'"[8]

Pérez found no Russians, the reconnaissance was incomplete and unsuccessful, and thus closed the first and feckless attempt by the Spanish out of San Blas to find the Russians. On March 16, 1775, two mariners, Bruno de

Hezeta and Juan Francisco de la Bodega y Quadra, were sent in the *Santiago* and the tender *Sonora*, respectively, to find the Russians. In particular, they were ordered to reach at least 65° north latitude, to locate Russian or other foreign settlements (while avoiding contact with the foreigners), to claim all the land for Spain, and to contact and maintain friendly relations with the indigenous people. Once again the Spanish had difficulty with long-range voyaging. They also suffered from scurvy. When a boat crew from the *Sonora* was sent ashore for water near present-day Point Grenville, Washington state, it landed in heavy surf and seven men were murdered. Bodega y Quadra opened fire but withdrew the ships. He might have lost more men had he persisted and may even have had to abandon the mission.

Hezeta sailed north to about 48° 26' north latitude and then drifted south in the current. On August 17, 1775, at 46° 16' north latitude, he noticed strong offshore currents, which led him to believe the mouth of some great river could be emptying into the ocean here. He named the entrance Asuncion Bay but did not take a closer look. Scurvy and fatigue necessitated a quick turn to the south for relief. But Hezeta had put this entrance on the map, and the various names for the mystery river—Río San Roque (or Roc), the Bahía de las Asuncion, the Entrada de Hezeta—lured mariners who came to test the hypothesis of the River of the West (see Appendix 2).[9]

Bodega y Quadra zealously carried on to 57° 2' north, near Mount Edgecumbe, where he landed and took possession for the king of Spain. Then he steered south. At Kruzoff Island in the Alexander Archipelago of southeast Alaska, the Tlingit demanded items in exchange for wood and water, and they menaced the Spanish with implements of war. Once again the Russians proved to be phantoms. The Spanish might have found the Muscovites had they gone as far north as the Gulf of Alaska or west toward Kodiak Island, and they might have had enough military force to send the Russians a clear message or to oust them altogether. But at least the Spanish planted their actual physical claim to sovereignty by an act of possession at Mount Edgecumbe.

The next year, 1776, Viceroy Bucareli learned that Captain Cook intended a third voyage to the Pacific, one that, if carried out, could seriously encroach on Spanish ownership. Bucareli feared that if Cook traced the shore and found a northwest passage, it would endanger Spain's sovereignty over the coast of California. Bucareli knew that Cook was on an exploring expedition, but he classified Cook as a poacher masked by science and sent orders to authorities in California to be vigilant and to foil the British mariner as best they could without resorting to force. Bucareli did not want an altercation between his vessels and those commanded by the illustrious Cook. Bucareli's superior, José de Galvez, alarmed at the viceroy's seeming timidity, sent explicit orders: According to the Laws of the Indies, which regulated Spanish commerce, foreign vessels entering Spanish colonial ports were to be seized. Therefore, if *il famoso* Cook were found in a Mexican port, he was to be arrested.

True to his instructions, Cook arrived on the coast of Oregon in March 1778. (Almost two centuries earlier, in 1579, Drake had sailed here, claimed this territory for Elizabeth I of England, and named it Nova Albion.) Cook sailed into Nootka Sound on March 30, 1778, remaining there until April 26, unnoticed and untouched by the Spanish. Then the British warships steered north to Bering Strait and thence to Hawaii long before the Spanish were aware of the British presence.

Next Bucareli sent the frigates *Princesa* and *Favorita*, commanded by Ignacio Arteaga and Bodega y Quadra respectively, and these vessels sailed to high latitudes, landing at Bucareli Bay in early May 1779. Again Native resistance deterred the Spanish. And once again the Spanish came away empty-handed, finding neither British nor Russian interlopers.

On February 24, 1786, in Chile, the Frenchman Lapérouse gave Spanish officials an early hint that Russia had posts on American shores. Lapérouse was then en route to Alaska, but he knew of Russian advances from diplomatic intelligence. One of the four Russian posts that Lapérouse gave notice of was at Nootka.[10] This was false intelligence, though clearly indicative of the pursuits of the British sea otter traders using that port.

Two years later, in the summer of 1788, Esteban Martínez sailed to the Gulf of Alaska for a reconnaissance. Martínez had been with Pérez on the voyage in 1774 and had since studied accounts of Cook's explorations. Unlike his fellow Spanish navigators, Martínez was energetic and resourceful, with a strength of will to carry out imperial purposes. He may have been rash and impulsive, prone to heavy drinking and unstable behaviour (he was quite capable of high-handed conduct with his junior officers), but he was also dutiful, strict and patriotic—altogether a volatile combination.

Using a variety of intelligence at his disposal—some of it gained by the hard-working pilot José Narváez, the first to encounter the Russians in person; some gleaned from consultations with Lapérouse in Monterey after the Frenchman's sojourn on the Alaska shore in 1786—Martínez confirmed the double fear that the Russians were heading south to Nootka Sound and the British merchant ships were already there, using it as a locus of operations.

Martínez or his officers encountered Russians who revealed that there were 462 Russians on that coast at the time, at seven posts and watchtowers.[11] In Cook Inlet, then the most important settlement, there were 70 Russians and a galliot (sailing vessel); at Unalaska Island, 120 Russians and two galliots. There were other locations at least as active. Martínez learned that the Russians were sending hunting parties south to Nootka Sound.[12] The Russian informants told Martínez that the British had their eyes on Nootka Sound and that the Russians, never to be outdone, intended to get there first.

From his inquiries in high latitudes, Martínez concluded that the Russians intended to garrison Nootka. He took this news in stride, as it suited his purposes. He told the viceroy, now Manuel Antonio Flóres, that if the Spanish could take Nootka Sound, it would provide all the requirements for a naval base. Moreover, such a conquest would give Spain full dominion over the land between Nootka Sound and San Francisco and over a multitude of aboriginals. The window of opportunity was narrow. The Spanish needed to take Nootka Sound by May 1789, according to Martínez.

He worked up a grand scheme that called for a fortified garrison at Friendly Cove (to be called San Miguel), a fur-trading company to be established and working from Nootka Sound (along the same lines as the Russian-American Company, which was set up a few years later), a victualling place to be set up in the Hawaiian Islands, and Nootka and Clayoquot sounds to be developed as settlements, bulwarks, as it were, against foreign encroachment. Martínez's design resembled what Mackenzie or John Meares, the British sea otter trader, would have proposed. The viceroy might have thought it attractive, but although the Spanish did ship sea otter pelts out of Nootka Sound to California and freighted same in American vessels, they took no permanent measures such as they were to do in establishing the Missouri Company (discussed in Chapter 7). Martínez got no support from the merchant community of Mexico, and the only real trans-Pacific trade link for Spain's North American colonies remained the Acapulco-Manila galleon.

In any event, on the basis of the firm advice he had to hand, Flóres ordered Martínez to Nootka to protect Spain's interests, and the latter set sail from San Blas in February 1789. Martínez, flush with power and authority, arrived on May 5 at what Pérez had named San Lorenzo de Nutka. He did not find the Russians. Instead, he found three vessels, one English and two American, in Cala de los Amigos (Friendly Cove).

About eight months earlier, on September 17, 1788, the Boston sloop *Lady Washington*, then commanded by Robert Gray, had arrived at Nootka Sound. Seven days later, the flagship of the enterprise, the *Columbia*, commanded by John Kendrick, joined the tender at anchor. Kendrick loved ceremony and was in a festive mood. On October 1, anniversary of the day the vessels sailed from Boston, he ordered a suspension of routine duties, the striking of eight bells, a federal salute of thirteen guns, one for each state in the union, and a sumptuous feast. This was a grand plan of celebration, and the salute was repeated by the *Lady Washington*.

There was an English ship there at the time, the *Iphigenia Nubiana* under Captain William Douglas, which was sailing for the firm headed by John Meares, and another Meares schooner, the *North West America*, built at Friendly Cove, was then making ready for coastwise trading. Meares had constructed a sort of house-fort in the northern corner of the cove at Yuquot, and so that the Mowachaht might not have it when the mariners departed, Kendrick and Douglas had agreed to divide the dried timbers for firewood. The English vessels, which sailed under the Portuguese flag for the sake of convenience in order to avoid the dreaded East India Company monopoly, quit the harbour by the end of October, leaving the Americans in solitary and quiet possession.

The Yankees spent that unusual winter in confinement, even exile. They traded with the Mowachaht, hunted when necessary and brewed some lovely spruce beer. They also kept a sharp lookout against the depredations of stealthy aboriginal thieves. As was his style, Kendrick proved to be heavy-handed when attempting to recover articles apparently stolen, but he could not arrange for their return, even by force. And so the Americans passed that winter in splendid, melancholic isolation. The Mowachaht departed their summer village of Yuquot and returned the next spring. The crews beefed up their armament and defences, and in the spring the *Lady Washington* made sail for coastal trade, now under Kendrick's command.

The *Columbia* and the *Iphigenia* lay undisturbed in Nootka Sound when Martínez arrived in command of the *Princesa* early in May 1789. Martínez naturally wanted to know what Gray was doing there, for that port was claimed as a Spanish possession. Gray hedged on a reply. But Meares later wrote that Gray told Martínez that the American expedition was "equipped under the patronage of Congress, to examine the Coast of America, and to open up a fur-trade between New England and this part of the American Continent, in order to provide funds for their China ships, to enable them to return home teas and China goods."[13] If Gray had orders and authorization from President Washington, none are extant. He may have lied to Meares, or the latter may have made up the details.

At this juncture, Kendrick returned in the *Lady Washington* from a successful cruise to the Queen Charlotte Islands, and he, too, was asked by Martínez why he had been there that past winter. His reply was that he had had to put in to port for repairs, having sprung the mizzen mast and damaged his rudder and sternpost in a gale. Scurvy had made savage inroads. Kendrick wanted no complications. In any event, he told Martínez, the *Columbia* and *Lady Washington* would soon be departing.

Relations with the Americans and English were on a good footing for a time. On June 21, 1789, a Sunday, Martínez ordered all work stopped, and he invited Kendrick, Gray and Thomas Hudson, captain of the *Princess Royal*, and all their officers, and also all those of the packetboat *San Carlos*, to a magnificent banquet.

That evening the commandant sent the schooner *Santa Gertrudis*, commanded by Narváez, south to 48° 20' to find a creek that Martínez said he had located in 1774 and to survey in the vicinity. Narváez sailed into the sunset, and in subsequent days he worked south, entering the Strait of Juan de Fuca, to that point only the subject of rumour and speculation. When Narváez returned to Nootka two weeks later, on July 5, he told Martínez about the great waterway: "From side to side it measured 21 miles, continued on land for almost the same width as far as one could see, no horizon being visible in the east-southeast, and is the strait which they call Juan de Fuca. Inside is a port called San Juan [Port Renfrew, Vancouver Island] which is a good place to anchor in, to take water and wood and to provide oneself with timber for planks and masts. It is at the farthest north and west point."[14]

Meanwhile, the Spanish had built the fort of San Miguel on Hog, later Lighthouse, Island and were putting finishing touches to the entrenchment for ten pieces of artillery. Ashore, a parapet was being erected where cannon would be mounted.

On June 24, 1789, the day having dawned clear and serene, and everything being ready, as Martínez recorded in his journal, he landed from his vessel on the shore of this port of Santa Cruz, as they called it, situated at the entrance to San Lorenzo de Nutka, accompanied by officers and men of the two Spanish ships. With them went four monks, Franciscan missionaries from the Colegio of San Fernando in Mexico, and the Catalan soldiers of the garrison, marching with all due solemnity and pomp. When all were ashore, Martínez, as commandant, took possession of the port, coast and adjacent islands in the name of the king. He did so, he wrote, "with the usual ceremonies." The Holy Cross was put up, the Holy Gospel heard, and a sermon preached by the Very Reverend Fray Severo Patero. Many Englishmen and Americans took part in the event. "We left carved on the cross the name of our Lord Jesus Christ, that of August Sovereign Carlos III, and the years when I had visited this port, 1774 and 1789." The troops fired a salute; the *Princesa* returned a reply of fifteen guns, as did the *San Carlos* and the cannon of the Fort San Miguel. The party returned to the flagship for further festivities, and, once aboard, the salutes were repeated all round. Seven vivas were made to the king. A magnificent banquet was served, and there were many more vivas and toasts. And how was this locale to be claimed as a permanent Spanish anchor of empire? Martínez says: "The

Document of Possession was placed in a bottle, carefully closed with pitch, and buried at the foot of a little pile of stones on the shore, from which place the bearings of Sta. Clara Point were N.E. 1/4 E. those of S. Ignacio to the N.N.E. and those of S. Francisco to the N.E. 1/4 N all by the Compass."[15]

As for the Franciscans, they lacked any knowledge of the indigenous language. The spiritual conquest of the Mowachaht, "these miserable idolaters" as Fray Severo called them, seemed impossible given the scant chance of raising grain or stock in the forested, mountainous terrain. Those men and women they did convert—seventeen by 1791—they did by purchase.[16]

That spring and early summer, a number of English ships had come and gone from Nootka Sound, and although Martínez had issued demands and claims of ownership, he had not yet played a hand likely to cause an incident. However, when, on July 2, 1789, Captain James Colnett arrived in the ship *Argonaut*, sailing for the Meares syndicate, Martínez met his match. Colnett resented Martínez's demands and imperious demeanour. In any event, said Colnett, the coast belonged to Great Britain, and Captain Cook had discovered it. Martínez countered by saying that he had been there three years before Cook, which was true.

These two antagonists make a curiously well-matched pair of *agents provocateurs*. Both were unbridled patriots. Both possessed a boundless attachment to duty in the name of their respective kings and countries. Both had a tendency to be heavy-handed. Colnett was plagued by a tendency toward mental instability under stress. For his part, Martínez had orders to follow, and although at first he hesitated, in the end, fearing censure from superiors, he took action.

We now know that Martínez detained Colnett as a poacher and seized the *Argonaut*. Colnett, angered beyond reason, insulted Martínez by calling him a "God-damned Spaniard." It is said that on one occasion Colnett attempted to jump overboard; on another he climbed through the cabin window and dove into the icy water. He was fished out, half-drowned, but safe enough now to be shipped to a Spanish prison in pestilence-ridden San Blas. Colnett was eventually released and crossed Mexico to return to London, all the while grumbling about the nasty treatment he had received at the hands of the Dons. Many other English sailors captured by Martínez did not survive the voyage to the fetid tropics or incarceration at the disease-ridden naval base.

Meares, who followed the altercation with the tetchy Colnett from a distance, recorded most of the prominent details. Later he prepared a memorandum for government and testified before the Privy Council in London, providing evidence confirming what the British ministry began to call high-handed Spanish action.[17]

Rumours of these events at remote Nootka Sound circulated around the world, for those who gossiped about the details knew that sooner or later this Anglo-Spanish dispute would involve other powers. For the moment, Russia took no action; had the Russians had ships or a garrison at Nootka, their implication in the proceedings would have led to many complications, possibly war. The American vessels were largely bystanders, but the United States would be hard pressed to remain neutral should Spain and Britain go to war. Spain and France were bound by the Bourbon family alliance of mutual aid and assistance; thus, if Spain were in need, France was supposed to provide assistance.

As news of the episode at Nooka drifted into London, press and parliament treated it as a *cause célèbre* of victimization at the hands of the Spanish Dons. Cartoonists had a field day, and a pantomime on the subject proved all the rage in Drury Lane. Anti-Spanish sentiment rose and became more strident. Bellicosity was not in short supply. From London in 1790, John Rutledge Jr., described to Jefferson in Paris the burgeoning war spirit in the House of Commons:

> As soon as the house rose, I went amongst the members I was acquainted with, afterwards dined in company with others, and in my life I do not remember to have been amongst such insolent bullies. They were all for war, talked much of *Old England* and the *British Lion*, laughed at the idea of drubbing the Dons, began to calculate the millions of dollars they would be obliged to pay for having insulted *the first power on Earth*, and seemed uneasy lest the Spaniards should be alarmed at the British strength, ask pardon for what they have done and come immediately to terms.[18]

The British government of Prime Minister William Pitt took a strong diplomatic position against the Spanish and used Meares's sworn evidence as proof. The Admiralty began to prepare what is now called "the Spanish armament." By hugely bolstering the fleet and number of seamen, the government intended to make it clear, through brinkmanship, that it had every intention of checking Spanish pretensions at Nootka. The British hated any interference with their shipping, and Martínez's seizure of two British-owned vessels was all that was needed for them to issue a clear warning: unless the Spanish admitted their error and made compensation, the British would make war.

As part of the war preparations, the British government made plans to strike at Spanish dominions in North America. The cabinet made unofficial representation to the government of the United States, inquiring about the possibility of obtaining US permission for British troops to cross American territory and strike New Spain's garrisons and forces in the Louisiana Territory from the rear, as it were. The representation came through a Major George Beckwith, who was under orders from the Governor of Lower Canada, Lord Dorchester. The major visited New York, where he made contact with some intermediary, detailed the sensitive aspects of the imbroglio with Spain and assured the American intermediary that England's cause ought to be joined by the United States.[19]

President Washington, who heard about the proposal via Alexander Hamilton, Secretary of the Treasury, brought the matter to cabinet for discussion. He asked members of cabinet for their advice in the event that the British should attack and conquer Louisiana, which was a Spanish possession at the time. Hamilton had no objection; in fact, he encouraged the idea of the passage.

But Jefferson remained wary of obligations and commitments, and he wanted to pursue a strict neutrality. He prepared a memorandum, "Heads of a Consideration on the Conduct we are to Observe in the War between Spain and Great Britain, and particularly should the latter Attempt the Conquest of Louisiana and the Floridas." He leaned toward Spain, for he worried that if Britain ever got hold of New Orleans and neighbouring territory, it would be "calamitous," a perpetual danger for the United States. Jefferson proposed to the president that no response be given to the unofficial inquiry, and other members of cabinet agreed neutrality was the best course in the circumstances. Jefferson was concerned that the British would get more territory in North America, and he was particularly worried that such land might be adjacent to US territory: "We wish to be neutral, and we will be so if they will execute the treaty fairly and attempt no conquests adjoining us." The British might take Spanish lands by conquest, but, said Jefferson, "If war takes place, we would really wish to be quieted on these two points, offering in return an honorable neutrality." Jefferson feared the possibility of further foreign encroachment on North American lands, lands that he, as a continentalist and expansionist, believed the United States ought to possess, of necessity. The Nootka Sound crisis, therefore, prompted discussions among the principal officers of government about ways and means of continental security—and freedom from further encroachment. In Jefferson's responses we see the statement of principles that later became the Monroe Doctrine.[20]

As for President Washington, he held the view that "having so formidable and enterprising a people as the British on both our flanks and rear" would be alarming.[21] His views accorded perfectly with those of Jefferson.

As the crisis unfolded, the French, invariably self-interested, did not uphold their obligation to help Spain in a fight against Britain. They had good reason, for the French Revolution was in full flower and the world seemed turned upside down in Paris and the provinces. Spain, isolated and abandoned, could not face the British navy and, in consequence, was obliged to admit British claims to rights of trade and navigation in the Pacific Ocean. Nootka Sound was a mere symbol of these rights. The Spanish agreed to pay compensation for the loss of Colnett's vessel and much else besides.

In spite of this setback, they remained extraordinarily active in their political and scientific pursuits on the northwest coast in the early 1790s and continued to send vessels of discovery to Nootka Sound and the northwest coast as high as the Gulf of Alaska. Salvador Fidalgo sailed in the *San Carlos* to Prince William Sound. Manuel Quimper examined the Strait of Juan de Fuca in the *Princesa Real*. Alejandro Malaspina searched for the fabled Strait of Anian, mentioned by Ferrer Maldonado, in the *Descubierta* and *Atrevida*. Francisco de Eliza continued this search, and so did Francisco Antonio Mourelle. In 1792, the *Sutil*, under Dionisio Alcala Galiano, and the *Mexicana*, under Cayetano Valdéz, explored the upper reaches of Juan de Fuca Strait, the Strait of Georgia and beyond, circumnavigating Vancouver Island.

In 1791, Captain George Vancouver sailed for Nootka as British commissioner to receive from his Spanish counterpart, Bodega y Quadra, the lands and establishments that Martínez had seized. En route, Vancouver's two vessels, *Discovery* and *Chatham*, encountered two small Spanish warships under Galiano and Valdéz, and the four ships sailed through the inner passage between Vancouver Island and the mainland for a time during the summer of 1792, carrying out shared duties of hydrographic assignments and adding noteworthy scientific detail to the chart at the same time as they put to rest the

Spanish navigator Alejandro Malaspina, a man of the Enlightenment, was ahead of his time politically. He commanded the Descubierta *and* Atrevida *on a five-year voyage to the Pacific. His account of his travels to Acapulco, Monterey, Nootka Sound, Botany Bay and many other places was suppressed at first but later published and became a classic. Museo Naval, Madrid*

speculation of the old closet geographers and mapmakers. Vancouver also had orders to look one last time for the entrance to the Northwest Passage between 30° and 60° north latitude, of which more later in this chapter.

Vancouver arrived at Nootka Sound in August 1792. Bodega y Quadra, taking advice from the Yankee trader Joseph Ingraham, decided not to return all the houses, gardens and occupied premises as they stood. When the Spaniard showed him the acreage he could receive, Vancouver wisely declined and wrote home for new instructions. "Can this chasm possibly be considered as the districts or parcels of Land etc. intended to be ceded to me on the part of His Britannic Majesty? Now there is little doubt I should either have proved myself a consummate fool or a traitor to have acceded to any such cession without positive direction to that effect."[22] Vancouver was exasperated, and rightly so. The matter then passed to the diplomats.

It took three Nootka conventions to finally seal the arrangement and cool all feelings. Naturally, on that distant margin of empires, representatives of the two crowns could not be sure that instructions recently sent were the true representation of what the diplomats had agreed to 18,000 sea miles away. But in Madrid on January 11, 1794, the third, and final, convention—the Convention for the Mutual Abandonment of Nootka—was signed. By this document, Britain and Spain bound themselves to a number of provisions respecting the future of the northwest coast in European hands. Subjects of either nation could erect temporary buildings at Nootka but not permanent establishments such as garrisons or factories. (Britain had abandoned an earlier scheme to put up a garrison at Nootka that would tie in with its convict settlement in New South Wales, Australia.) Moreover, neither nation could claim sovereignty to any territorial dominion at the other's expense. The two countries were also to maintain this free port against claims by any other power that might attempt to establish sovereignty or dominion there. In other words, Nootka had become, irrespective of aboriginal interests, a free port to be maintained as such by an agreement of mutual exclusion.

Nonetheless, the nagging problem of restoring the lands and buildings at Friendly Cove (San Miguel) to Britain still remained. The third convention specified that the two governments would send new commissioners to Friendly Cove, where the Spanish officer would convey "the Buildings and Districts of Land" to the British officer. Subsequently, the British officer would raise the Union Jack as a token sign of possession. Then the officers of the two crowns would withdraw their subjects from Nootka Sound.

As soon as possible, the two commissioners made their way to Vancouver Island. In March 1795, a youthful British lieutenant of marines, Thomas Pearce, arrived in Nootka Sound and there undertook, with his opposite commissioner, Brigadier-General José Manuel de Alava, the hitherto all-powerful governor of

Nootka, to stand down from all imperial holdings ashore. The Spaniard did likewise, and the five-year-old Spanish possession at San Lorenzo came to a crashing end.

Even so, Pearce's mission had a decidedly imperial intent. He explained to the great local chief Maquinna that the British government had received many good reports of his people from Captain Cook and from British traders. The British crown, Pearce confided to Maquinna, had decided to take the Mowachaht under its protective wing. "With this Account they all seemed much pleased," the lieutenant reported to London in self-congratulatory tones, "observing that the English had ever been their good Friends—but were now very anxious to know if the Spanish should return, whether they were to be friends with them; from which I inferred that they had not been treated very kindly by them."[23] After the Spanish delivered over to Pearce the site where Meares's yard and storehouse had been, Pearce went to the flagstaff. He raised and lowered the Union Jack. Then he passed the flag to Maquinna for safe-keeping, instructing him to hoist it whenever a ship appeared. This mark of confidence gratified Macquinna very much, Pearce claimed. Pearce and Alava left letters in Maquinna's care to be shown to fur traders in order that the terms of evacuation could become known on the coast.

Meanwhile, the Spanish fort was dismantled on Alava's orders, its guns and moveable property stored aboard Spanish ships there at the time, and the Spanish thus abandoned this northernmost post of their North American empire. The commissioners exchanged documents verifying the restitution and mutual abandonment of Nootka. Then they sailed away, leaving this port of hopes, dreams and tragedy in the peaceful possession of Maquinna and his people.

The Mowachaht soon demolished the village, carrying away everything of value to them, particularly nails and other pieces of metal that could be fashioned into implements or ornaments. They likewise ransacked the cemetery, taking nails from coffins. Within months the remnants of Spanish buildings had been replaced by Maquinna's lodges on the ancient site of his ancestors' dwellings. Friendly Cove, as it became known, or Yuquot, took on the appearance it had when, twenty-one years earlier, Pérez had first anchored off the sound.

Before the Spanish arrived to occupy Yuquot (Friendly Cove), Nootka Island, the place was a summer village of the Mowachaht. As early as 1786, the English had a trading base, or factory, there under a tacit agreement with the Mowachaht. A part of the Native village is shown along the foreshore, a customary layout, as seen in this 1798 engraving by J. Heath for A Voyage of Discovery ... *George Vancouver.*

We can now see that it was the British, surprisingly, not the Russians, who had prevented the northern consolidation and expansion of the Spanish empire in this quarter. The Spanish fell back on a port they had established on the Olympic Peninsula, Neah Bay, but even there the British denied them exclusive access and control. That threw them back to whatever post they had in Alta California, and that was the San Francisco presidio, their northernmost bastion of empire.

By excluding the Spanish from Nootka Sound and Neah Bay, the British inadvertently handed the United States a remarkable gift. For by refusing to accept the king of Spain's expansive claims to the waters and lands of the Pacific Ocean, the British pinned the Spanish at Nootka and ousted them from it. The British had not been spoiling for a fight on this issue. It was Martínez who set the whole affair in motion, and because he was only doing his job, and doing so zealously on the basis of his instructions, it was in the firm policies of the viceroy of New Spain that the source of difficulty lay. The Spanish inadvertently unleashed a British bulldog, and in consequence their presumptive claim for control of the northwest coast as far north as the Gulf of Alaska, where Spanish discoverers had set down markers, was now a paper empire. Their withdrawal, and the British abandonment of the area, led Baranov to think that the time might soon arrive for Russia to occupy this prize port (as described in Chapter 4).[24]

As mentioned earlier, when Vancouver was on the northwest coast between 1792 and 1794, he was to survey the coast between latitudes 30° and 60° north and determine if there was any possibility of communication by water to the countries on the opposite side of the continent. He was to have a particular look at the "supposed Straits of Juan de Fuca" between 48° and 49° north, which the American sloop *Lady Washington* was said to have entered in 1789 (this was according to the exaggerated statements of John Meares—in fact, the *Lady Washington* never made such a course) and which some people believed might connect to a river across the continent. Vancouver remained dubious about the existence of a Northwest Passage. He had been to Nootka with Cook, his mentor, who held categorically to the view that no such waterway existed where he had probed the continental shore. But the British government was not altogether convinced. Rumours persisted of passages, straits and a river of the west (see Appendix 1), so Captain Vancouver and his officers, including Lieutenant William Broughton, were thorough in charting the features of the northwest coast from Oregon to the Gulf of Alaska.

In 1792, when he first arrived on the coast, Vancouver encountered the ship *Columbia*, under Captain Robert Gray. This officer had formerly been in command of the *Lady Washington*, and Vancouver asked Gray if Kendrick had actually circumnavigated Vancouver Island in 1789, as Meares's account and chart, published in 1790, showed. According to Meares's biographer, Richard Nokes, Gray denied the circumnavigation had happened. But, says Nokes, it nonetheless remains a slim possibility that Kendrick, who exchanged commands with Gray in Clayoquot Sound in July 1789, made just such a passage en route to the Hawaiian Islands, where he died in Honolulu in 1794, taking all written evidence with him.[25] Highly problematic such a voyage may have been, but not impossible (though if it did occur, Meares had the details wildly wrong), and so the intriguing puzzle continues.

In the summer of 1793, Vancouver's surveying crews were scrupulously examining the features of the deep inlets and intricate inner waterways of the mainland shore north of Cape Caution when Mackenzie and his men came down from the mountain passes and plateaus of the British Columbia interior. British marine explorers did not meet their land-based counterparts on that occasion, but Bella Bella people told Mackenzie of the actions of the long boats and the surveying crews. Mackenzie had no hope of finding a navigable waterway in those latitudes, no seaway leading to the eastern seaboard or Hudson Bay. He had long given up on such a prospect, if ever he had believed in it, which is doubtful. After all, he had already voyaged to the mouth of *Deh Cho* (Mackenzie River) and back and disproved the existence of any passage in northern latitudes. Now he had done the same thing in southern latitudes not far north of Nootka Sound. For these stout reasons, Mackenzie thought the chart showing the route of the *Lady Washington* through the coast range of mountains entirely false and misleading, and he doubted Meares's evidence and advice on that score.

Vancouver held a similar view. When the tedious work of the surveying parties was concluded on the Alaska shore in August 1794, Vancouver wrote trenchantly that a principal object of the voyage had been brought to a successful conclusion. "The little squadron now proceeded to a cove ... where they took up their abode for the night," he wrote. "In the course of the evening no small portion of facetious mirth passed amongst the seamen, in consequence of our having sailed from old England on the *first of April*, for the purpose of discovering a north-west passage, by following up the discoveries of De Fuca, De Fonte, and a numerous train of hypothetical navigators."[26] The survey ended at what they called Port Conclusion. In his narrative and his folio of charts, Vancouver provided as full details as he thought necessary to kill the beast of speculation. "The perusal of these parts of our voyage to persons not particularly interested, I am conscious will afford but little entertainment," he wrote without apology, "yet I have been induced to give a detailed account ... for the purpose of illustrating the charts accompanying this journal; of shewing the manner in which our time day by day had been employed; and, for the additional purpose, of making the history of our transactions on the north west coast of America, *as conclusive as possible*, against all speculative opinions respecting the existence of a *hyperborean or mediterranean ocean* within the limits of our survey."[27]

It is certain that Vancouver and Mackenzie together ended speculation about a sea channel to the Atlantic in these latitudes, and it now seems strange that reaching this conclusion took so long, consumed so much in finances and talents, embraced so many international rivals. The fact of the matter was that the environment delayed any easy revelation. In that distant dominion, explorers, by sea and by land, worked in a complex and tortuous environment, a wild terrain where desolation was matched by splendour and scientific gains were made piecemeal and by risky ventures.

Once the existence of a northwest passage in southern latitudes was disproved, control of the Columbia River mouth became all the more important. Vancouver had missed the entrance of the Columbia, and there have been many jests that such a great mariner should have missed it. He did the same with the Fraser River. But nature keeps its own secrets as long as it can, and without today's ship-based radar or aerial photography, the abilities of a hundred or so men working from two sailing ships plying unknown waters in less than perfect weather is a reminder of the limits and hazards of discovery in the age of reason. The Spanish, who contributed mightily to the charts of the northwest coast, even as their empire was at flood tide and soon to ebb, had first noted the presence of a river at Bahía de las Asuncion, though they did not explore it. Which left it to the Americans to lay their claim, as we shall see in later chapters.

Chapter 6

THE EMPIRE OF
SAFE HARBOUR RETREAT

D uring the winter of 1787, when Alexander Mackenzie was holed up in his snow-covered, windswept post on Lake Athabasca with Peter Pond, at the same time as John Ledyard was walking to St. Petersburg, and a year before Esteban Martínez arrived at Nootka Sound to establish a northern fort for Spain, a number of well-fed, prosperous gentlemen were gathered before the flaming hearth of Dr. Thomas Bulfinch at his Boston residence. Bulfinch was a prominent physician and a good friend of another person then present, Joseph Barrell, a well-respected and equally prominent merchant and shipowner. Talk turned to adventures overseas. Charles Bulfinch, son of Thomas, had recently returned from two years of architec-

In 1787, Joseph Barrell, far-seeing Boston merchant and chief partner in the voyages of the Columbia *and Lady Washington, led a syndicate of six to finance an American-based sea otter trading venture. Other Bostonians fared well in "the golden round" of around-the-world trade, but it is Barrell who gets credit for the initial impulse that connected the eastern seaboard of America to the northwest coast.* Courtesy of the Massachusetts Historical Society

tural study in Europe. He had visited Jefferson's residence on the Champs Élysées. There he had met John Ledyard, who told a tale of woe about his inability to get any banking, mercantile and shipowning support for his projected voyage to hunt and trade sea otters in Nootka Sound, Alaska and Canton. The outstanding topic of that day continued to be Cook's last voyage—how Cook had been killed by some Hawaiians, details of which remained murky. But keener minds such as these fellows possessed turned to the trade possibilities of the North Pacific. Charles Bulfinch knew of Ledyard's grand scheme, and he had heard of other rivals interested in the sea otter business. Perhaps he had heard of Lapérouse's voyage to Alaska. Yankee mariners such as Barrell were never reluctant to look at new fields of endeavour, for the Pacific was just opening to them as a new realm.

In consequence of the discussion at Dr. Bulfinch's residence, on September 30 of that same year, the *Columbia Rediviva*, a ship of 212 tons recently constructed in Plymouth's North River, cleared Boston destined for the northwest coast by way of Cape Horn. The second half of the name (which means "restored to life"), now forgotten and unused, was to signify the ship's intended triumph. The name and the omen were propitious, for the *Columbia* solved the riddle of the China trade by its first voyage and initiated the imperial aspirations of the young United States by the second. Few commercial vessels in American oceanic

The ship Columbia Rediviva *and the brig* Lady Washington, *under, respectively, Captain Robert Gray and Captain John Kendrick of Boston, American pioneers in the sea otter trade, are shown in Clayoquot Sound, Vancouver Island, on September 20, 1791.*
Courtesy Steve Mayo

history have played such roles in the opening of the wider world. The *Columbia* sailed in company with the sloop *Lady Washington* of 90 tons. William Sturgis of Boston, who subsequently made many voyages to the northwest coast and was an early historical commentator on this buoyant and hazardous branch of commerce, expressed warm appreciation for the magnitude of the undertaking while outlining the obstacles and difficulties that had to be surmounted to carry out the earliest expedition:

> Were I required to select any particular event in the commercial history of our country to establish our reputation for bold enterprise and persevering energy in commercial pursuits, I should point to this expedition of the *Columbia* and the *Washington*. Let it be borne in mind, that we had then just taken a place among independent nations, and had not even established a permanent form of government; that we had recently terminated a long and exhausting contest as feeble colonies against one of the most powerful nations of the world; that public and private credit were prostrate and but little capital could be found for commercial purposes; that the contemplated voyage would be, at least, of three years' duration; that those intrusted with its direction had no experience of its dangers to guide, and no local knowledge to aid them; that navigation as a science was little known; that the vessels were such as would now hardly bear the inspection of an insurance Company, or be deemed safe and sufficient for the coasting trade. Taking these, and other circumstances that will readily occur to you, into consideration, I think you cannot fail to concur with me in the opinion, that this was one of the boldest and most remarkable commercial enterprises ever undertaken from this Country.[1]

Owned by a merchant syndicate headed by Barrell and including Samuel Brown, Charles Bulfinch, John Derby, Crowell Hatch and John M. Pintard, the expedition was commanded by Captain John Kendrick of the *Columbia*. Robert Gray was skipper of the *Lady Washington*. The purpose of this voyage was to exploit the fur trade of the northwest coast, the pecuniary prospects of which had been made public by Captain Cook's voyage. Ledyard had proposed such an American venture in 1783, with himself as principal, but that scheme had been cut down to a single ship, *Empress of China*, that had gone directly to China. Now Ledyard's idea was being revived in a different guise. As noted in Chapter 5, the *Lady Washington* reached Nootka Sound, Vancouver Island, on September 16, 1788, followed by the *Columbia* a week later, after a long, hard voyage. However, Gray undertook no aggressiveness in trading, leaving that to Kendrick, with whom he exchanged vessels (of which more presently). Gray steered for the Hawaiian Islands, China and then Boston, which he reached on August 9, 1790. The *Columbia* thus became the first vessel to carry the Stars and Stripes around the world. Gray sailed again for the northwest coast on September 28, 1790, traded on "the Coast" and went into winter quarters at Clayoquot Sound, Vancouver Island. In May 1792, he sailed the *Columbia* into the great River of the West—which he named for his ship. The *Columbia* reached Boston with a rich cargo of oriental goods on July 29, 1793.

As mentioned above, in the course of the *Columbia's* first northwest coast cruise, John Kendrick shifted to the *Lady Washington* while in Clayoquot Sound on the west coast of Vancouver Island. It seems he did this for several reasons, not the least of which was that *Lady Washington* was the smaller of the two vessels and thus handier and safer for navigation in unknown and unsurveyed waters. Kendrick also intended to winter on the coast (he was the first to do so) and thereby undertake multiple trading seasons before sending pelts to Canton.

The bright glare of history has cast much illumination on Gray, given his circumnavigation and his subsequent Columbia River reconnaissance, and has tended to put Kendrick in the shade. But Kendrick was no less a great sailor and navigator, and in his time he ranked high among his peers. Captain Amasa Delano, author of a highly esteemed account of voyages published in 1817, wrote that Kendrick taught many of his countrymen the way to wealth and the method of navigating distant seas with ease and safety. "He was a man of extraordinary, good natural abilities, and was noted for his enterprising spirit, his good judgment and superior courage. As a seaman and navigator, he had but few equals."[2]

Kendrick was keen on establishing alliances with the indigenous peoples of the northwest coast. His intention was to set up an arrangement with the head chiefs of the many villages in and near Nootka and Clayoquot sounds, then the focus of the maritime trade in southern latitudes, so he could repeat the success of the initial trade.

The aboriginal inhabitants of the northwest coast called all American traders "Boston Men," which set them sharply apart from "King George Men" (in the local Chinook jargon, *Kintshautshmen*). Boston Men were the Yankee traders, the purveyors of spirituous liquors, the importers of goods, the gun runners and the seaborne merchant mariners who became, if only for a mere forty years, masters of the northwest maritime fur trade.

It is doubtful if a tougher breed of sea traders existed in modern human history. The Yankees conducted an annual voyage around the world. They doubled Cape Horn, reputedly the world's most hazardous passage, without the loss of a single ship. "The passage around Cape Horn from the Eastward I positively assert," wrote Captain David Porter of the US frigate *Essex*, "is the most dangerous, most difficult, and attended with more hardships than that of the same distance in any other part of the world."[3] They faced the unpredictable perils of the roaring forties. They risked the slaking thirsts of the doldrums. They persisted against the countless hazards of North America's fogbound west coast. Not least, they conducted business with the indigenous lords of the northwest coast, who, as circumstances were to show, were no docile breed. Their ships were captained by some of the most hard-headed, heavy-handed officers, many of whom owned their own vessels. The Magee, Winship and Perkins families, among others, sent forth their stoutest ships and their toughest sons in a line of work that was as laborious and hazardous as it was lucrative and exotic. These sea traders embodied a spirit of free enterprise and harboured a suspicion of authority. Theirs was the law and theirs the profits. They hated interference. They were suspicious of foreigners. They were transients on a wild coast, untrammelled by government regulation and with no inclination, unlike their English competitors, to regulate the trade, to establish a monopoly or to license ships. This was an open commerce where the free-spirited Bostonians had no limits to their needs and no rivals to interfere with their business. Kendrick was the epitome of this breed of men.

On July 12, 1791, Kendrick brought the *Lady Washington* abreast the southern entrance to Nootka Sound. He had first been to Nootka Sound in 1788, and in the interim he had sailed to Hawaii and Canton with sea otter pelts. Now he was returning from Canton to gather another cargo of furs. On his way he had sailed south from the Queen Charlotte Islands, where sea otters were so abundant. He was now to enter Nootka Sound quite familiar with the details of the dispute the Spanish had had with the British a few years earlier, in 1789. The particulars of it were of no concern to Kendrick, provided he could trade as he wished with the Mowachaht and other groups nearby.

The Spanish navigator Pérez had paused off the same entrance in 1774, but had not chosen to stay and did not ponder prospects of trade or alliance with the indigenous people of Nootka Sound. In the seventeen years between Pérez's call and Kendrick's arrival, numerous mariners had dropped anchor inside Nootka Sound. Captain Cook arrived in late March 1778. His journals and letters reveal a powerful, rich society, one in which concepts of property ranked higher than anywhere else Cook had voyaged. Every blade of grass, he noted, seemed to be accounted for by these people. The timber of the forests were likewise items of trade and barter. Nothing material lacked value or price. Kendrick would also learn this.

British mariners out of Calcutta, Bombay, Canton and Macao—and even some directly from London and Bristol or sailing out of Antwerp under foreign flag—put the northwest coast on the commercial map. They predated Kendrick and Gray by only a few years. In those days, as the British minister of trade, Henry Dundas, noted with pride, the quest for new commercial opportunities by merchants and mariners knew no bounds.[4] On the distant, temperate shore of North America, so long hidden from the wider world, British mariners were pursuing a new, vital realm of commerce. The Americans, such as Gray and Kendrick, James Magee and Joseph Ingraham, all of Boston, were soon on their tail and soon to overtake them. For the moment, as of 1791, the British held whatever commercial mastery this international commerce would allow—and it bulked mightily in the political mind of the British nation and government.

Kendrick, with Boston bravado, took his own mission in stride, seemingly oblivious to the swirl of international politics that had been blowing recently around this remote, often fogbound port. His actions that summer might be judged naïve. More likely he was simply cocky or cheeky. For all he knew, Spain and Britain might still go to war. Nothing was settled on the spot, and title to land was still fair game. Yankee acquisitiveness had a new field of opportunity.

Just inside the sound's entrance stood the Spanish fort on Hog Island. And as the *Lady Washington* passed by, the Dons, using a speaking trumpet, spoke sternly to the American, warning him not to enter. Kendrick turned a conveniently deaf ear. He continued his course and brought his brig to anchor in Marvinas Bay. He then went about his business. Now it was the turn of the Spanish commandant to take action. No doubt annoyed at the American's crass disregard of the Spanish king's rules, he ordered a launch with an armed guard, all dressed in the uniform of the frontier guard of this unit of imperial Spain's forces, to row out to the brig, there to give solemn warning not to trade in Nootka Sound.

Kendrick found himself obliged to take the Spanish threat seriously, and, knowing what had happened to Meares and Colnett before, he understood that discretion was the better part of valour. He therefore promised to leave the next day. But he did not make sail. The days passed. Kendrick was still there on July 20. Dilatory and stubborn he may have been, but he probably knew that the king of Spain's writ in this distant quarter was but a paper one. And he likely did not interfere with anything the Spanish were doing there, keeping his men at arm's length, as it were, and minding their own affairs. He was left alone. He had his own work to do.

Unbeknownst to the Spanish, Kendrick went about the business of buying land from various chiefs. At Nootka Sound and elsewhere he purchased land, exchanging guns and ammunition for real estate. The English trader Meares had bought up land in these parts, but the chiefs put no credence on these transactions and even discredited Meares, whom they were quick to call a liar.

But if Meares had bought up land of his own volition, Kendrick carried specific instructions from his superiors and shipowners to do so. The American empire of trade out of Boston was now being linked to real estate. When Joseph Barrell and his associates in Boston had given Kendrick instructions concerning this first fur-trading venture to the northwest coast, they had included this guidance: "If you make any fort or improvement of land upon the coast, be sure you purchase the soil of the natives; and it would not be amiss if you purchased some advantageous tract of land in the name of the owners; if you should, let the instrument of conveyance bear every authentic mark the circumstances will admit of."[5]

Kendrick's anchorage, Marvinas Bay, was known to the Mowachaht as Chastacktoos. For ten muskets, Kendrick purchased from Maquinna, the chief, and other chiefs, the harbour "with all the land, rivers, creeks, harbors, islands, etc., within nine miles north, east, west and south of said harbor, with all the produce of both sea and land appertaining thereto." Kendrick, for his part, "does grant and allow the said Macquinnah to live and fish on the said territory as usual." Kendrick obtained the rights of free passage through all rivers and outlets of Nootka Sound. In the future, these rights were to fall to his heirs, executors and administrators. He called the place Safe Harbour Retreat.

The deed, likely drawn by the captain's clerk, John Stoddard, bears the marks of six chiefs—Maquinna,

Maquinna, "possessor of pebbles," the principal chief at Nootka, was prominent in diplomatic and trade relations of the late eighteenth century. Alexander Walker, who sailed with James Strange on his fur-trading voyage, met Maquinna in 1786 and thought him "a stout, handsome young man," the most intelligent person they had encountered. As long as the trade thrived he remained powerful, but when it faltered, his influence among his people declined. This is a contemporary engraving, based on a portrait by Tomás Suria. British Columbia Archives, A-02678

Warclasman, Hannopy, Clophananish, Tartoochtheeatticus and Clack-oeener—all of whom appear as verifiable persons in reports and journals of other contemporary voyages, such as Vancouver's *Voyage of Discovery*.[6] The Kendrick deed had some validity at the time. In 1792, Joseph Ingraham of the *Hope* stated that Maquinna acknowledged Kendrick to be the proprietor of lands round Mahwinna. Yet, strangely, Maquinna had no reluctance six weeks later, on August 27, to sign a deed with the Spanish explorer Esteban Martínez that "ratified the cession of land previously made for the present settlement"—that is, the cession of land on which the Spanish village at Friendly Cove, or Yuquot, was built.[7]

We infer from this that Maquinna and other chiefs were keen to satisfy European and American acquisitiveness for land but that they were not bartering away aboriginal title or sovereignty. As for Kendrick, he continued his purchases. On August 2 he took the *Lady Washington* into New Chatleck harbour, called Hoot-see-ess by the Mowachaht, which Kendrick refers to as Port Montgomery. Three days later he purchased the harbour, with all the lands, mines, minerals, rivers, bays, sounds, harbours, creeks and islands, "with all the produce of both sea and land appertaining thereto"—all for two muskets, a boat's sail and a quantity of powder. This was Nuchatlitz, an inlet near Esperanza Inlet.

Kendrick's hunger for land knew no bounds. On August 5, at Cheninkint, Port Elisa in Esperanza Inlet, Kendrick swapped six muskets, a boat's sail, a quantity of powder and an American flag for eighteen miles square (over 300 square miles), with the same rights of access as before. The next day he bought nine miles of real estate around the port at Tashis. Again, at Clayoquot Sound, he bought a parcel eighteen miles north, south, east and west of Opitsat, Meares Island, from Wikaninnish and five chiefs, all for four muskets, a large sail and a quantity of powder—articles of trade that Kendrick noted ruefully were of great value and in growing short supply. Another deed was supposed to have been signed to cover lands south to the Chehalis River, though Kendrick never traded south of the Strait of Juan de Fuca.

It was Kendrick who signed these deeds, and his owners, in deference to instructions, are not mentioned.[8] True copies of these deeds were certified by

John Howell, who sailed with Kendrick and may have been a supercargo and actuary; certainly Howell was Kendrick's confidential adviser.

The original deeds, five in number, were kept by Howell, an acquisitive and secretive chap, but on March 1, 1793, Kendrick sent the attested copies to Jefferson, then the Secretary of State of the United States. Taken together, the deeds cover 72 miles square, or 5,184 square miles. Another estimate, by Barrell, stated that they covered 240 miles square, or 57,600 square miles.

Barrell and his associates would have welcomed some benefit from their investment in the voyages of the *Columbia* and *Lady Washington*. Kendrick's real estate purchases offered dubious compensation for the long outlay of equipment and capital. Howell had no illusions, warning Barrell: "If you knew the lands [of Nootka and Clayoquot Sounds, etc.] as well as I do, you would not be very anxious about the fate of them." The lands were of no value, he stated later. "I have had an opportunity of seeing most parts of Captain Kendrick's purchases on the No. Wt. Coast of America; and cannot flatter you with any hopes of profit from them even to your great, great grandchildren. They cost but little it is true; and when the Millenium shall come and all the nations of the earth shall be at peace, your Posterity may, perhaps, settle them."[9]

Kendrick, in his correspondence sent to Jefferson, claimed the land as his own. Barrell had different ideas and was completely unaware of Kendrick's claim to ownership, contending that four degrees of latitude on the northwest coast, that is, 240 miles square (an area larger than England), belonged to him and his associates. Barrell believed that Kendrick had registered the deeds and lodged them in the office of the American consul in China.

With time, Barrell's imagined empire grew in size. "The company's territory embraced all Quadra's [Vancouver] Island not sold to Kendrick or the king of Spain, and likewise the possessions of Tatooche and other chiefs of the coast, extending as far south as the 47th parallel of latitude. These lands, embracing about four degrees of latitude, are bounded on the east by the whole extent of the westerly shores of the northern and southern areas of de Fuca's straits." So concludes a House of Representatives document, number 43, of 1840. By that time the zeal for an empire in Oregon knew no bounds, and exaggerated claims were commonplace.

Even in 1795, Barrell was convinced that he could turn the deeds to account. Through the firm Barrell and Servante, he floated a circular in four languages (English, French, German and Swedish), issued in London, inviting the public to invest in these lands and settle them. The expansiveness and glitter of the French Revolution was still apparent. "The Era of Reason is now dawning upon Mankind," the advertising circular begins, "and the restraints on men's laudable endeavors to be useful will cease." The agents invited interested parties to apply to the American Agency Office at 20 Threadneedle Street, London, to purchase whatever lands they wished, any amount, and on very low terms, "as perfectly secure Tenure." Leasehold lands could be arranged for those on limited means, with future freehold fixed by purchase within ten years. For those with even less wealth, freehold estates would be granted to those who would assist "their still poorer neighbors" by going out as managers.

And then we find the grand finale of benefit and public good:

> That such as may be inclined to associate for settling a Commonwealth on their own Code of Laws, on a spot of the Globe no where surpassed in delightful and healthy Climate and fertile Soil—claimed by no civilized Nation and purchased under a sacred treaty of Peace and Commerce and of a valuable consideration of the friendly Natives, may have the best opportunity of trying the event of such an Enterprise and Finally,
>
> That Men under the guidance of rationality, in every rank, may have opportunities to becoming essentially useful to their Neighbours while they proportionably mend their own condition.

Besides community service and benefit, there is a touch of redemption or rehabilitation in this statement. The agents never shied away from the prospects of taking up land on distant Vancouver Island. They were, they stated, "authorized to treat with any Gentleman, or Association, for purchase of a tract of Land, no where exceeded for fertility and Climate, and which may by a prudent management of some wise Institution become of the utmost importance."[10]

The Barrell scheme went nowhere. No investors came forward. The war against Napoleon commanded the shipping and capital of the age, and even after the peace of 1815 there were many better places for English, Scottish and Irish emigration than Vancouver Island—for example, the Fish River of South Africa, the available lands of Upper Canada, and the tracts of New South Wales. Jefferson never took up the scheme as an example, or prospect, of some sort of satellite dependency of the United States or even associate republic, as well he might have had it been authentic. Barrell and Servante's domain was a paper empire.

Kendrick was accidentally killed in Honolulu Harbor on December 12, 1794, and his descendants endeavoured to claim much real estate on the northwest coast based on his deeds. For some years during the mid-nineteenth century, congressional committees evaluated the evidence and concluded that the heirs had no case.[11] Charles Bulfinch and others sought confirmation of their title to certain lands purchased from the Nuu-chah-nulth in 1791, but the US non-intercourse acts, forbidding trading with aboriginals without government sanction, made these deeds questionable as well.[12] In any event, in the early twenty-first century, the Kendrick deeds are receiving mention, if only in passing, in the Meares Island case, one of the major aboriginal land claim cases in British Columbia courts. Kendrick allegedly undertook an arrangement with Chief Wikaninnish and others of Meares Island and Clayoquot Sound, as did the British trader Meares, after whom the fourteen-square-mile island is named. Meanwhile, as historians and others continue to examine these early records, the heirs of Wikaninnish and others, represented by the Nuu-Chah-Nulth Tribal Council, have petitioned that they never bargained away their aboriginal rights to the crown or any other party. The court has enjoined the timber giant MacMillan Bloedel, which holds the tree-harvesting licence to the island, from logging Meares.[13] The great trees, many of them of primeval origin and some showing aboriginal use dating from long before Kendrick, Gray or Meares ever made an appearance and disturbed their way of life, continue to grow and mature.

The family of Captain Gray proceeded similarly to that of Kendrick. In 1852, the heirs and widow of the great mariner, the first American to enter the Columbia River from the Pacific, joined a petition for recognition and confirmation of land grants, or other form of compensation. These heirs and successors brought a claim against the United States for compensation for lands acquired by the US under the Treaty of Washington in 1846. The family was quick to point out that John Kendrick, in his attested copies of deeds sent to Jefferson in 1793, refers to conveyance of land to Kendrick and his heirs forever by "the resident chiefs of those districts." "I knew not what measures are necessary to secure the property of these purchases to me, and the government thereof to the United States," he wrote. Elsewhere, Kendrick speaks of his claim being allowed by the Spanish crown—"for the purchases I made at Nootka were expressly excepted in a deed of conveyance executed in September last to El Senor Don Juan Francisco de la Bodega y Quadra, in behalf of his Catholic Majesty, by Maquinnah and the other chiefs of his tribe to whom those lands belonged"—and, not least, of his own scheme as agent of American expansion: "When I made these purchases I did it under an impression that it would receive the sanction of the United States, and that should an act of the legislature be necessary to secure them to me, I should find no difficulty in obtaining it."[14]

The lure of empire, the promise of real estate, the expectation of sovereignty—all these and more motivated Kendrick, Gray and Barrell (with his associates). Theirs was a naturally expansionistic age. The Northwest Ordinance of 1787 had recently given promise that new states would be created out of old territories, and the spirit for extending the American republic seemed boundless. Kendrick, Gray and Barrell never spoke of utopian community, though the last did promise that men under the guidance of rationality might establish a commonwealth "on their own Code of Laws"—that is to say, a republic.

Certainly the enterprise of Kendrick had drawn attention to "a tract of delightful Country," as the agents for Barrell and Associates put it. Even so, colonies, states and nations did not grow from advertisements but rested on sterner stuff: corporate finance, emigration agencies and collectives, transportation linkages and, above all, the need or hunger for land. All of that lay in the far distant future. Even Kendrick's minder, Howell, had no illusions when he referred to the fact that when the millennium would come and when the nations of the earth were at peace (and the Napoleonic wars over), some of Barrell's posterity, Bostonians undoubtedly, might settle there. Yuquot, at Nootka Sound, might become the new Cape Cod; Clayoquot the new Salem; Barkley Sound the new Back Bay.

That millennium never came. The settlement of Bostonians, and other Americans, was diverted south to the Columbia River. Within three years of Lewis and Clark's wintering at Fort Clatsop, and their reconnaissance of the lower reaches of the Columbia, another Boston concern, the Winships, founded the nascent, transitory settlement near Oak Point (described in Chapter 12). These American destinies, then working themselves out on the western continental rim, answered to different masters than the president and Congress of the United States. The commercial world preceded actions of the state. Trade went before the flag. But the dreams of the Barrells, the Winships, the Howells and others of Boston and Massachusetts, probably little understood by the Virginia planters and statesmen who dominated the politics of the early republic, became realities in a later age, when colonizers put the stamp of approval on distant schemes by voting with their feet and inhabiting the far shore. "At present," Howell wrote Barrell, in January 1793, of the lands deeded by the Nuu-chah-nulth to Kendrick, "they appear to be of little value, but in some future time they may possibly be worth possessing."

Kendrick never completed his circumnavigation of the globe, never returned to Boston. His life disappears in the shadows of the early relations between New England, the northwest coast, the Hawaiian Islands and Canton. A rough-and-tumble mariner, he could be brutal and vicious in his dealings with northwest coast aboriginal people (as described below), but besides this Kendrick was a keen trader, offering higher prices than any of his fellow countrymen and thus garnering more sea otter pelts and the adherence of aboriginal traders and suppliers who liked the cut of his jib, so to speak. He was a pioneer of Massachusetts global commercial expansion, and his name is writ large in the history of New England's enterprise on distant seas. He never reached the distinction or recognition accorded the great Gray, with whom he had sailed to the Pacific in 1787. Gray came home after two circumnavigations and could claim to be the first non-aboriginal to travel up a portion of the Columbia River. Kendrick, by contrast, slips from our vision and dies in Honolulu, the Pacific world having consumed him and all his endeavours.

We have noted how Kendrick received what he portrays as officious treatment at the hands of the Spanish at Nootka Sound. The Spanish armed guard had to visit him in Safe Harbour Retreat when the cocky Kendrick should have submitted himself, as courtesy and protocol dictated, for Spanish examination. Kendrick chose to disregard niceties of protocol. The Boston mariner played by his own rules.

The customs and protocols of the indigenous people were also disregarded, which often led to trouble. Kendrick was probably not alone in issuing orders that traders be circumspect in all their relations with aboriginals, that they treat them with care and respect and not take anything from them except with fair compensation. Those high-minded principles were not always observed in practice. On his 1791 voyage in the *Columbia*, Gray built winter quarters on Meares Island. (The site of this station has recently been positively identified on Lemmens Inlet, and its Boston-fired bricks and various artifacts are testaments to the links established between two margins of the same continent two centuries ago. Captain Gray's Fort Defiance, as it is called, is now a British Columbia heritage site.[15]) Here as elsewhere on the northwest coast, the indigenous people were jealously protective of their resources. The Bostonians were intruders. As the trade advanced between the men of the *Columbia* and the *Lady Washington* and the Clayoquot at the village of Opitsat, Meares Island, so too did the armed power of the Clayoquot. The Bostonians grew nervous; they feared a reprisal for infractions against indigenous customs. A well-armed party was sent on a pre-emptive strike to burn Opitsat, and the journal of young John Boit, then a third mate, clearly demonstrates the inhumanity of the sordid action.[16]

This constituted but one of several violent encounters between Bostonians and indigenous people in the trade. The captivity of blacksmith John Jewitt of the ship *Boston* at Nootka Sound in 1803 became a Boston legend, well known to every school child.[17] The dispute between Captain Kendrick and the Haida chief Koyah, another celebrated encounter, was the subject of "The Ballad of the Bold Northwestmen," a favourite in the forecastles of the vessels in that trade.[18] The location of that clash was Houston Stewart Channel (otherwise Barrell's Sound) in the Queen Charlotte Islands, and the date, the balladeer attests, was June 16, 1791. The Haida, trading on deck, had seized the keys to two chests of arms. Kendrick immediately took action. He ordered officers and men to arms. They fired at the Haida, killing sixty of them. The Bostonians then went to a nearby village and forced the return of some stolen property. It was an act of revenge, but it fathered desperate legacies. Koyah was placed in irons, which demeaned him in the eyes of his people; accordingly, he swore revenge and engaged in three unsuccessful attempts to restore his own dignity among his people. The Haida did not forget past wrongs, as the balladeer stated in this quatrain:

> I'd have you all take warning and always ready be,
> For to suppress these savages of Northwest America;
> For they are so desirous some vessel for to gain,
> That they will never leave off, till most of them are slain.

A coda to the Kendrick episode comes with the visit to Nootka Sound of the 72-ton brigantine *Hope*, likewise of Boston, in 1791, a month before Kendrick's *Lady Washington* dropped anchor at Safe Harbour Retreat. And while Kendrick scurried round the sound and visited nearby inlets and sounds such as Esperanza and Clayoquot, buying up real estate, the young master of the *Hope*, the well-educated and sympathetic twenty-eight–year-old Joseph Ingraham, was playing a cozy and rewarding game with the Spaniards.

Ingraham, when a mere slip of a boy (he was the same age as Alexander Mackenzie, born in 1762), had first sailed to the Pacific—and to Nootka Sound—as second mate, or officer, of the ship *Columbia* in 1787. Ingraham's talent had been spotted in Canton by the equally young Boston merchant mariner Thomas Handasyd Perkins, "the fixer," who had also sailed as a lad on the ship *Astrea* to China and the East Indies. Perkins was of a wealthy merchant family of Boston that was soon to become richer by the northwest trade. One of the "solid men of Boston," as their first historian called them,[19] Perkins met Ingraham, now first mate of the *Columbia*, when the ship reached Canton with its sizeable cargo of sea otter pelts. Perkins made all the arrangements with Boston.

Five short weeks after the *Columbia* came home from its celebrated circumnavigation, having paraded the Stars and Stripes around the world, Perkins outfitted his own vessel, the *Hope*, for the Pacific and gave the command to Ingraham. This voyage, one of many, takes precedence in this narrative because it serves as a counter to the Kendrick land-purchasing ventures and adds a scientific understanding of northwest coast geography. It also provides a window on the Spanish doings at Nootka Sound and Neah Bay (on the coast of Washington state, east of Cape Flattery on the Strait of Juan de Fuca). We follow Ingraham in his sometimes halting progress, and in doing so we are instructed in the complexities of the commercial and diplomatic winds about Nootka Sound. We gather an affectionate understanding of the Spanish commandant and mariners and, further, an appreciation of the incessant and driving zeal of British mariners on the same coast, whose warships were coming to show the flag, to coerce the Spanish and to win their rightful place among the merchant mariners of the Pacific.

We start this coda to the Kendrick story in Boston, and we pick up the story in Ingraham's own words, from his remarkable journal:

> ... we discharged the pilot abreast of the lighthouse [Nantasket Road, September 17, 1790], and I took a parting view of my native shore which sunk deep into my heart. But making all sail, I launched my little bark into the bosom of the ocean. Night soon came on and tore every object from my sight except the starry heavens and foaming seas. Inured to the boisterous elements and almost become amphibious, I endeavoured to reconcile myself to my narrow prison hoping the variety of objects which usually occur on such voyages would tend to make it pass away lightly—thus deceiving myself in the best manner now left me to practice.[20]

He sailed via the Falkland Islands, the Marquesas, the Hawaiian Islands, the Queen Charlotte Islands, the Hawaiian Islands again, and then to Canton. In the Queen Charlottes, where trade was energetic, he met up with Captain Gray and the *Columbia* on July 23, 1791. The two vessels lay alongside one another, rising and falling in the swell. So deep was it there, they could find no bottom with a fifty-fathoms line. Gray and Ingraham exchanged pleasantries, and Ingraham received from the *Columbia* letters from his friends in Boston, letters which, though dated ten days after the *Hope's* departure from Boston, "were yet great satisfaction." These letters had been smuggled on board the *Columbia* and passed to Ingraham by his friend Robert Haswell, another young officer, "who brought them unknown to the owners of the *Columbia*. These gentlemen, filled with envy against all who meant to share with them this valuable trade, gave orders that no letters should be borne out in their ship to anyone on board the *Hope*." This mean-spiritedness cut deep but served to highlight the cut-throat rivalry among the Bostonians. Captain Gray then shaped a course for the continental shore, and Ingraham continued his trade southward toward Cape St. James, the southern extremity of the Queen Charlotte Islands.

In the Queen Charlotte Islands, Gray had informed Ingraham that the Spanish had augmented their settlement at Nootka and established another in the Strait of Juan de Fuca, "from which it seem these Dons have become very jealous of the territories," Ingraham had written in his journal on July 30, 1791.

> Some of them, I believe, they have a just claim from their being the first discoverers, yet if being the first discoverers establishes a right to claim agreement to the laws of nations, I believe many parts of the N.W. Coast of America may with propriety be disputed as being Spanish property. Indeed it has already been the cause of the disturbance between England and Spain and cannot end there as there are no less than five nations to contend for it. But to drop this point, to be discussed by parliaments and national assemblies when it may become a matter of more serious consequence, I shall again resume my narrative.

Nine months after sailing from Boston, after much treacherous coastal navigation, Ingraham entered Nootka Sound on September 16, 1791. The *Hope* dropped its hook in Ship Cove, where Cook had been thirteen years before. Ingraham, unlike Kendrick, submitted himself to the protocols of the Spanish.

In Canton, Ingraham met up with Kendrick and alerted his fellow countryman to what was going on at Nootka, where, to his way of thinking, the Spanish were tightening their grip of authority. "They [the Spanish] did not molest him," Ingraham wrote when recording his discussion with Kendrick on December 7. "However, lest they should attempt to detain him in his way out, he came out by another passage to the northward of the one he entered, by which he got off clear after purchasing many valuable skins." Ingraham showed this passage on his great chart as Massachusetts Sound. It was during this Canton meeting that Ingraham recorded the sordid details of the struggle between Kendrick and Koyah and the "very disagreeable skirmish with the natives on the southern part of Washington's Isles [the Queen Charlotte Islands], where Koyah is the chief."[21]

In later years, Kendrick's deeds and Ingraham's connections with the Spanish grew in historical significance. American navigators' discoveries and acts of possession on the northwest coast became, by the 1820s and in the years leading up to the Oregon crisis, material particulars to the veracity and strength of the United States claim. "These acts, without the benefits of similar acts performed by Spain," wrote Hall J. Kelley, the champion of the Kendrick deeds, "vest our country with a just and complete title to all that part of the territory on the Western side of American, between the forty-second and fifty-fourth parallels of latitude." Some, like Kelley, argued that among the many titles acquired by the United States on the northwest coast "there is none so clear and complete as that derived from *lawful purchases of Indian lands*."[22] Land hunger began early for the American republic on the northwest coast and acted powerfully among statesmen and legislators for years and decades to come.

In the decade after 1795, many US-flagged vessels, mostly from Boston, the successors of Kendrick, Gray and Ingraham, continued to visit at Nootka and other sounds and harbours on Vancouver Island and the northwest coast. By 1805 the Spanish flag, fort, battery, garrison and church were but a distant memory. The foundations of the church and the governor's house could still be seen. Onions, peas and turnips, remains of the Spanish garden, still sprouted from the ground. But the new Mowachaht village of Yuquot, twenty houses in a long row newly arisen from the ashes of conflicting imperial fires, sat on the precise ground the Spanish garrison had occupied. The new village stood where its predecessor had been before the Dons arrived, demolished the split-planked cedar houses and forced the inhabitants to retire into the country. The upheaval had been momentous for the Mowachaht, and the new village brought a sigh of relief and a remembrance of past pain. The armourer of the *Boston*, John Jewitt, who was captive there from 1803 to 1805, recounted this turnabout in village affairs: "With great sorrow, as Maquinna told me, did they find themselves compelled to quit their ancient place of residence, but with equal joy did they repossess themselves of it when the Spanish garrison was expelled by the English."[23]

Yuquot—"the place where winds blow" (in more than just a physical sense it had turned out)—reverted to Mowachaht control and to the powerful *Tyee* Maquinna. No nation or imperial power came to occupy it again, save for Canada, which designated an Indian reserve there and put up a lighthouse as an aid to navigation. Vessels engaged in the maritime fur trade invariably made it a port of call, less to trade, for there were greater pickings elsewhere, than to take on wood and water. Maquinna and other chiefs maintained their influence, and the customary tribal society continued much as before. Eventually the round of slavery, warfare and internecine rivalry dried up too, and a general peace reigned.[24] As for the slave Jewitt, he was liberated when the Boston brig *Lydia*, Captain Samuel Hill, sailed into the harbour and cast anchor. Now it was Maquinna who found himself in irons. Now it was Jewitt's turn to intervene. On his assurance of good conduct, Maquinna was released.

The *Lydia* sailed for the Columbia River in order to procure spars (it had suffered badly in a recent gale). The brig entered the great river and sailed about ten miles upriver to one of the Clatsop villages. There Captain Hill, Jewitt and other sailors heard that Lewis and Clark had been there two weeks before on their return journey overland. They had left several fine medals that the Clatsop showed the mariners.[25] The *Lydia* sailed back to Nootka, completed trade on the coast and then pointed for China, then home, completing the golden round of trade.

And so a Boston syndicate's assembly of real estate on the mid-reaches of Vancouver Island's western share, like the Spanish garrison, disappeared to memory. Nowadays the details of Kendrick's and Gray's claims pop up periodically in aboriginal land claim cases. Otherwise they are a subject of curiosity and a veiled showing of Boston intentions in these lands and waters. But history passed Boston by, as well, for the locus of imperial rivalry, now that the Spanish and British were effectively barred from occupying Nootka Sound, shifted both north, to the pretended borders of Alaska, and more especially south, to the mouth of the Columbia River, where the geopolitical rivalry in succession to Nootka now focused.

Chapter 7

CANADIAN TRADERS ON THE MISSOURI AND THE SPANISH RESPONSE

I n the same years that Kendrick, Gray, Ingraham and other American mariners were carving out a new sphere of influence on a distant shore, another form of international rivalry and intrigue was playing out at the great crossroads of the North American continent, the Missouri River, its valley and its tributaries. "The Missouri Valley is a valley of strangers," wrote noted authority Rufus Terral in 1947. "Jacques Marquette in 1673 discovered the river that unlocked the door to it. For more than a century that door swung open almost idly. The valley lay in the known continent like a dark empire."[1] Gradually, word of what existed in the valley flowed out with the corn raised and traded by the Mandans, and because the Mandan and Hidatsa villages were a great mart for horses and corn, traders from the east and north took an increasing interest in this nexus of trade. By 1790, the trade between the Nor'Westers' post Pine Fort on the Assiniboine River and the Missouri River was

The Missouri River valley as documented in the late 1790s

Lake Winnipeg

Assiniboine R.

Souris R.

▲ Turtle Mountain

Missouri R.

Red R.

Fort William (Kaministiquia)

Snake House

Little Missouri R.

Hidatsa Villages

Mandan Village

Mississippi R.

Missouri R.

Platte R.

established enough for Peter Pond to note it on his map. The Mandans brought corn to Pine Fort, Pond stated, adding, "Our people go to them with loaded horses in twelve days."[2]

Little by little the "dark empire" became known to the wider world. But the traders who came overland from their posts on the Assiniboine, Souris and Qu'Appelle rivers kept no scientific record, no accumulative written knowledge of the routes to the Mandan and Hidatsa villages. Year after year, however, they made the passage. As they became more accustomed to the routes and less worried about interference from the Sioux and Assiniboines, they began dreaming of farther ventures.[3]

As early as 1738, Pierre Gaultier de Varennes, sieur de La Vérendrye, and a handful of tough Canadian traders had come out of the northland destined for the Mandan and Hidatsa villages at the Great Bend of the Missouri. For at least twenty years before Lewis and Clark arrived in the valley, the Canadians

Fur traders and explorers such as Lewis and Clark and David Thompson noted with interest the mole-like houses of the Mandans at the Great Bend of the Missouri River. These signified permanence or lack of wandering habits. The number of these lodges was considerable, and their structure was unique at this great mart of the plains. National Park Service

The interior of a Hidatsa house, also at the Great Bend of the Missouri River, is shown here. Smaller in population than the Mandan, the Hidatsa lived in close proximity and were subjects of care and diplomacy by traders and government representatives. The Mandan and Hidatsa populations suffered severely because of subsequent diseases. National Park Service

had crossed from the Red and Assiniboine rivers or their tributaries, following increasingly well-worn trails. They came on foot, in parties of two to eight, and probably never as single travellers. They preferred spring, fall or winter travel—especially February, strangely—when, despite wind and cold, the travel was fastest and safest along trails made familiar by sights along the way—Turtle Mountain, for instance—or along frozen river and creek bottoms. Ground was hardest in winter and mosquitoes, happily, nonexistent. Plains First Nations used the horse and dog travois to haul their articles, and the traders did likewise. Sleds and snowshoes eased their travel and sped them to their destination. The traders travelled with indigenous conductors and linguists, and although they were guided to the Mandan villages, their journeys were hazardous nonetheless, endurance tests with food and drinking water not always available. These epic voyages across bald hills and through wooded valleys and breaks still invite our imagination, still call forth our appreciation of the grit and brawn of these Canadian entrepreneurs entering a different world from that of the Crees and Assiniboines to the north. At the Mandan and Hidatsa villages the Canadians traded for many goods and commodities, and here they obtained horses so necessary for their overland expeditions toward the headwaters of the Yellowstone River, where they traded with the Crow Nation.

Canadian traders maintained a handful of posts on the Red and Assiniboine rivers and their tributaries. In 1738, La Vérendrye built Fort La Reine on the Assiniboine, and this became the base for trade and for efforts to reach the Missouri and the fabled Western Sea. From there, in 1742 and 1743, La Vérendrye and his sons went south to the Mandan villages, then made a long loop to the foothills of the Rockies and back via what is now Pierre, South Dakota, on the Missouri.[4] Other posts—Pine Fort, Fort Dauphin, Brandon House and Fort Souris—were built by La Vérendrye or, later, by the North West Company or the Hudson's Bay Company. Attendant to these were the smaller seasonal locations of the circuit traders who traded *en derouine*, as travelling salesmen.

In the days of La Vérendrye, the Canadians had the trade to themselves. But rivals were not far distant. There were freemen in the fur business—private trappers and tenant traders owing no allegiance to company or country. More likely than not they hailed from St. Louis or Montreal. More serious still were men of the New North West Company (also known as the XY Company), who contested the old Nor'Westers whenever they could, and that included the area between the Assiniboine and the Missouri rivers in the years immediately before Lewis and Clark reached the Mandan and Hidatsa villages. If this were not enough, the Hudson's Bay Company had sent traders to penetrate this borderland of commerce. By the turn of the century, therefore, the rivals had multiplied.

The Canadians—and the North West Company—rightly claimed historical precedence. The Canadian system of trade licences issued at Quebec over the signature of the governor had always encouraged their activities. It invited them to penetrate the country to trade with more distant tribes. The system, based in the ancient French administration of New France, aimed to regulate traders, who were confirmed by licence to the particular post or posts fixed upon for their trade. The arrangement favoured the boundless and energetic Canadians and British who came to the area in and around the Missouri-Mississippi confluence, where in 1764, one trader, Pierre Lacadeda Liguest, had founded St. Louis of Illinois five miles from that strategic union of waters. The licence system was the gift of the colony of Quebec to the merchant traders of the peltry business, and the entrepreneurial state, as well it might be termed, gave force and impetus to these traders, great and small, in their expansion. The system, inexorably augmenting itself, presented an undoubted challenge to the fur traders of the infant United States after 1783, a subject of persistent interest in this book.

After control of France's North American colonies passed to Great Britain, the British enlarged their posts in the interior, erected stockades at public expense, and on the Great Lakes built schooners and gunboats at Detroit, Chicago and Michilimackinac to provide assistance and assurance to the traders. The British also garrisoned the main posts and established militia units with the Nor'Wester partners, clerks and traders as the officers, and the *voyageurs* and other *engagées* as other ranks. The aboriginal alliance system was built up on the back of the British War Department and effected through agents of the British crown, who were often former traders and officers of militia. They shaped the alliances with the tribes near and far. British largesse flowed freely in the interior, in time of war or peace, until 1815. Meanwhile, the wealth of the Canadian economy flowed out of the Old Northwest, the forks of the Red and Assiniboine, and the Saskatchewan country. The northern lakes—from Grand Portage and Duluth through Michilimackinac and Sault Ste. Marie across to the French River, northeastern Lake Huron, and the entrance to the Ottawa River, that remarkable commercial highway to the St. Lawrence—saw the passage of the wealth of the forested interior. In short, the guiding arrangements of the governors and military establishment at Quebec, with long tentacles to the interior, paid mighty dividends. The free-trading fur barons of the interior had the might of Britannia behind them. The British trading empire extended to the heart of North America.

Under these arrangements, the Mandans and Hidatsas found themselves the subject of special consideration. They did not fail to appreciate their special circumstances. Their relative isolation from the worlds of European and eastern American commerce had been breached by these traders from the north, and as lords of the Great Bend of the Missouri, they grew even more powerful as a result of the energetic commerce brought to them in the packs of traders. English guns, ammunition, knifes, nests of kettles or pots, Venetian beads, Brazilian tobacco, English cloth, French brandy and much else made the long overland passage from the northern posts. In return flowed bundles of furs, containers of corn, and a few horses. Diverted northward from the watersheds of the Missouri and Mississippi, these items formed part of the lifeblood of the economies of the St. Lawrence River and Hudson Bay.

In the late seventeenth century the traders were French only. In later years the Canadian French, or Canadiens, came from Quebec or Montreal or Trois Rivières. Still later we find the Metís, or mixed bloods, trading at the Missouri. The Scots and the English came down from the north in increasing numbers after the conquest of Quebec, working hand in hand with the Canadiens and Metís; even if they had been born in the Highlands of Scotland or in London, they had become masters of frontier travel and trade. Those in charge of business dealings could keep the trade books, for they had to account to their partners and superiors for all goods sold, traded or received. Some had tolerable literacy skills, but few bothered to keep journals or diaries. They were the sons of Martha, work-a-day veterans in the peltry business. A rare few stood above the rest.

David Thompson is one of these, a giant in North American empirical science. He entered the Mandan and Hidatsa villages in 1797. Before his years in the wilderness of America were completed, he had uncovered the sources of the Saskatchewan and Columbia rivers and drawn the first and reasonably complete map of the watersheds, lakes and rivers of the greater northwest. He discovered one of the sources of the Mississippi. The greatest of all North American explorers, he went to the Missouri on the business of science and cartography; business and diplomacy were also his concerns on that occasion, as we will see. We return to him presently.

David Thompson, surveyor, explorer and mapmaker extraordinaire, is shown here taking an observation with his sextant. The location is most likely in the Alberta foothills, with the Rocky Mountains in the distance. This pen and ink illustration is by Charles William Jefferys, noted artist of Canadian history. Library and Archives Canada, C-073573

Another Nor'Wester of note, the New Jersey son Alexander Henry the Younger, revealed no pretensions of a literary life, no inclination to keep a journal other than for his personal amusement and commercial advantage. Through his literary record, first uncovered by Elliott Coues, a surgeon in the US Army, we are able to trace his route—the preferred passage of many others who had gone before—from the Souris, or Mouse, River, a branch of the Assiniboine, to the Missouri Great Bend. His journal for the years commensurate with Lewis and Clark's visits, outward and inward bound from the Pacific, ranks among the treasured portraits of the Mandans and Hidatsas at this time, a window on a world now lost to view.[5]

The René Jusseaumes, the Jean Baptiste Cadottes and the Jean Baptiste Lafrances of the Missouri world represent the deepest traditions of the

Canadian trade. The blood of Normandy and Brittany coursed through their veins. Native themselves in so many ways, they embodied different gradients of power and influence in the fur business. Some were clerks, others tenant traders; still others were guides, packers or canoemen. They were representative of an older Europe and an older Canada, one before the British took Quebec and Montreal. But they had become one with the British in the northern fur trade. Although a handful of them are to be found in the service of the Hudson's Bay Company, we discover most of them working as Nor'Westers. Not a few of them were prominent and powerful clerks and partners, or *bourgeois*. They worked in easy harmony with the Scots and English and even the Welsh and Irish traders who flowed in after 1759. Neither nationality nor language divided them in the fur business. Invariably they had aboriginal wives, and so they were in time tied together by ties of blood—"many tender ties" is the way the Scots West Indian James Douglas, who became governor of British Columbia at the time of the gold rush, put it. And he knew, for his wife was Metís. Thompson and Henry, like Mackenzie and Daniel Harmon, were to take aboriginal wives. They were truly married "in the custom of the country," living multilingual lives, breeding and raising a new nation of mixed bloods, the Metís, literally a breed apart (who acquired constitutional status as aboriginal peoples in Canada in 1982, the only such in the western world), and acquiring small fortunes over the course of years, sometimes decades, in the interior.[6]

Truly this Missouri was a world where European and American empires were intersecting: the Canadians from the St. Lawrence, the British from Hudson Bay, the Spanish from the Gulf of Mexico and now the Americans from the eastern seaboard. It was indeed a valley of strangers. The Missouri River represented something else, as well. James Ronda has it right when he says "it is a river of promise, of dreams, and of dreams denied."[7]

In these days of the Nor'Westers' southward penetration to the Missouri River, imperial Spain held the sovereignty of the Mississippi River's west bank and its tributaries, including the Missouri. The burgeoning Canadian empire was one of commerce. By contrast, Spain's imperial edifice in America rested on the sword and the cross, and, save at New Orleans and St. Louis, commerce and business concerns ran a distant third in the order of priorities. Spain's wealth was acquired elsewhere than in the heartland of America.

Spain cast a cloak of secrecy and silence over the vast, still-undefined area west of the Mississippi. The Iberian empire and its managers had not yet unlocked the area's secrets that were known to the aboriginal inhabitants. In the last decade of the eighteenth century, Spanish maps of North America usually indicated the territory as a blank void belonging to His Catholic Majesty. Just as they kept secret their charts and other hydrographical data from the British, their rivals at sea, so too did they lay a veil of mystery over the western interior of North America. On the perimeters and margins of a quarter of a continent they still did not know, they, figuratively speaking, posted signs that read "No Trespassing."

Spanish officialdom feared any foreign encroachment, especially from the north and east. From the north came the Canadian threat that, though it "seemed a dream to us on account of the distance, is today at our doors," according to a contemporary Spanish official who was concerned about the endangered frontiers of Spain's enlarged empire in Louisiana, New Mexico and California.[8] The Spanish began to mount expeditions from St. Louis and from Santa Fe with a view to strengthening their hold on the river routes and inter-tributary links that would join the Mississippi and Missouri basins with the Green River, the Colorado River and the Gulf of California. All of a sudden the Big Horn, the North Platte and the Missouri's tributaries took on new significance. Madrid's traditional policy of buttressing imperial interests on the Pacific coast by means of naval forces based in San Blas, Mexico, had its parallel, under the minister Manuel de Godoy, in the exploitation of Spanish Illinois and Louisiana, thereby consolidating approaches to the southwest with its wealth of minerals.[9] The Spanish administration grew aggressive in defence of its northern frontiers.

On the Mississippi, the Spanish made a concerted attempt to exploit and monopolize the fur trade of the Illinois, Wisconsin and Dakota areas. Upriver from St. Louis they sent keel boats, armed with cannon and manned by soldiers, to such places as Prairie du Chien on the upper Mississippi River. And they turned to the problems of the Missouri, seeking to cut out the private or independent traders. Spanish officials sent agents or spies to determine the nature of the threat from Canada. Their expeditions were private rather than official. In these duties, the Spanish turned to French and British traders, "since no native has been found with sufficient intelligence."[10] By that was meant knowledge, languages, experience and savvy. The multilingual Canadians, masters of the waterways leading south from Detroit, Chicago, Green Bay and, even farther west, Duluth and the forks of the Red and Assiniboine, had been travelling in the upper reaches of the Mississippi and the lower Missouri for nearly half a century. The Spanish employed them out of necessity.

In the vanguard was Jacques d'Eglise, a Spanish subject. He left St. Louis the summer of 1790 and proceeded up the Missouri for the Mandan villages, "to which no one had ever gone in this direction and by this river."[11] He returned to St. Louis in 1792, full of information—some good, some bad and some indifferent—about the various tribes of the Missouri all the way up to the Great Bend, and about the extent of Canadian commercial activities among them and to the north. The Mandans told d'Eglise about the Assiniboines to the north, a wandering people, they said, with whom the traders of Canada "traffic in peltries." The Hidatsas told him additional news of mighty portent: that the Yellowstone River was navigable and that it flowed directly from the Stony or Rocky Mountains, but that it was hard to say whether it connected with the waters of the west.

The findings of d'Eglise sparked a fire in the official Spanish imagination at St. Louis, New Orleans and elsewhere. Would not this northwestern thrust, foreshadowed by the explorer, allow the Spanish to oust the Canadians from the interior country, or to forestall their further advances? Would not this quest capture the aboriginal trade of the Missouri and turn it to the benefit of Spanish traders and officials? And, finally, would not this scheme reveal a route to the South Sea and join the Mississippi with Mexico and California, fulfilling imperial dreams of old? Spanish imperial desires were rejuvenated. The pulse of trade and dominion quickened. The Spanish intended to consolidate their control of the upper Mississippi and the Missouri and its tributaries. They also intended to promote exploration that would, perhaps, even produce an overland link to San Lorenzo de Nutka on distant Vancouver Island.

No one carried a heavier burden of office than Francisco Luis Hector, baron de Carondelet, the governor-general of Louisiana, headquartered at New Orleans. He gave every consideration to the problems of the upper Mississippi and Missouri, and his military report of November 1794—so full of worries, for requirements outdistanced resources—makes specific the difficulties of defence and points out the problems of securing these distant zones by commerce.[12] Carondelet linked the Canadian trade with the expansion of American fur merchants in the Ohio country. He did not differentiate between the interests of the British Empire in America and the traders of the United States. He feared them in combination. He often spoke of them in one breath. Americans, he urgently warned Madrid in 1794, if not checked, would "demand the possession of the rich mines of the interior provinces of the very kingdom of Mexico."[13]

The Spanish policy for "Spanish Illinois" thus rested in three interlocking rings: oust the British traders or anticipate them, capture the fur trade, and discover a route to the west linking the Mississippi and Missouri with California and Mexico.

The vehicle to achieve this policy was a new company, La Compagnie de Commerce pour la Découverte des Nations du haut du Missouri, otherwise known as the Missouri Company. In the autumn of 1793, when d'Eglise had returned to St. Louis from one of his distant journeys, the entrepreneurs of St. Louis put their heads together over the Missouri scheme and incorporated the company on May 12, 1794. Jacques Clamorgan headed up a board of stockholders numbering eight in total. The investors came from a variety of nationalities and pasts: Spanish, French, Canadian and other. Clamorgan himself derived from Welsh, Portuguese, French and possibly African stock and was a leading spirit of St. Louis's commerce. He was well placed to influence the resident lieutenant-governor of Spanish Louisiana, Zenón Trudeau. Clamorgan, rich and self-made, embraced dreams of exclusive trade on the upper Missouri that squared nicely, even perfectly, with Trudeau's perceptions about how the northern frontiers of New Spain could be made secure. In ambitious combination, they imagined that the profits of the trade would offset the initial outlays of the various intended expeditions. Trade would accompany exploration and vice versa. Trudeau sent pressing letters to his superior in New Orleans, Carondelet, urging that a monopoly of trade be granted to Missouri Company investors and including the alluring detail that an old man had told of a journey to the headwaters of the Missouri, beyond which he had seen at a distance a great river flowing westward.[14]

Carondelet and Trudeau gave the scheme their support and encouragement. Carondelet granted 2,000 Spanish dollars as a reward to any Spanish citizen who could find the route from the upper Missouri to the Pacific coast, and a few years later he boosted the prize money to $3,000. He put an interesting proviso on the claim of any who should reach the Pacific: that person would have to have a certificate from the Russian commandant verifying that the subject of His Catholic Majesty had, in fact, reached the Pacific. This may seem fantastic, but Carondelet knew he could not fritter away prize money on some would-be traveller and speculator. (Similarly, it took instrument maker John Harrison years to get British compensation for his perfection of the chronometer.) Carondelet was keen to advance exploration and to check Americans, whom he described to the captain general of Havana in late 1794 as "advancing with an incredible rapidity."[15]

Clamorgan and the investors turned to Jean-Baptiste Truteau (not Trudeau), a Montrealer and an ex-schoolmaster, to lead their initial expedition of exploration. Truteau was made field general, in charge of operations. D'Eglise, independent and aloof, declined the lieutenant-governor's invitation to join the party. Instead, he continued his own unencumbered pursuits of exploration and trade. A trade monopoly had been denied him, but he carried on regardless; during his second trip, Sioux and Arikaras interfered with him and frustrated his designs.[16]

Truteau, with a party of ten men in a heavily loaded pirogue, all outfitted at a cost of $47,000, was already making his way up the Missouri by the time Governor Carondelet at New Orleans was warning Havana about encroachments by Americans. Truteau's men poled and paddled upstream, a painful and hazardous process. They slipped by potential enemies. In August 1794, Truteau passed the Omaha villages at night because "the policy of the savages is to prevent communication between us and the natives of the Upper Missouri [who] they keep ... in a continual fear of their firearms." He came next to the

Yankton Sioux. He noted that the Sioux tribes were those who hunted "most for the beaver and other good peltries of the Upper Missouri." As he progressed upriver, he noted all the tributaries flowing from the west to the Missouri. One of these, the Cheyenne River, was so very shallow that he believed one could not venture on it in a pirogue, but only with boats made of buffalo skins. He seems to have got as far upstream as the Arikara villages near Grand River. There he asked the residents about a river, "the waters of which might possibly flow towards the setting sun."[17]

Truteau got no farther than his courage, artfulness and, above all, trade goods could carry him. His instructions called for him to travel as far as the land of the Shoshone (also known as the Snake Indians or the Serpientes), who were said to exist on the western foothills, and to find if rivers beyond the Rockies flowed westward. He failed. In fact, the Sioux forced the surrender of much of his cargo, the Poncas pilfered goods during the first winter of the party's travels, and the Pawnees took the rest the next winter.

In support of Truteau, the Missouri Company sent a trader named Antoine Simon Lécuyer de la Jonchère from St. Louis in April 1795. The investors' wild expectation was that this expedition would reach the Pacific the following spring. This second expedition was likewise a failure—probably pillaged by the Poncas—and it did not reach Truteau. Meanwhile, the enigmatic d'Eglise went upriver on his own accord in 1795 and spent that winter among the Arikaras. He probably went farther west but, sadly, his track is lost to history. He was murdered in New Mexico sometime before November 1806.[18] Another Missouri River dream had been denied.

The Missouri Company's third and most prominent expedition of trade and discovery was headed by James Mackay. It also featured his lieutenant, a Welshman, John Thomas Evans, who was a traveller and ethnographer. Mackay and Evans provided a combination unique in the history of western exploration. Their experiences are little known and sometimes misunderstood or disparaged, but they represent the best attempt by St. Louis to grasp the upper Missouri and secure it against interlopers from the east and north.

James Mackay, born in Arrichliney, County Sutherland, northernmost Scotland, in 1759, a descendant of ancient Irish royalty, arrived in America about 1776. For the next fifteen years he engaged in the northwestern fur trade. A near contemporary of Alexander Mackenzie, Mackay was engaged as a clerk in the Qu'Appelle River valley trade of southern Saskatchewan as early as 1786 and from there made his first passage, a seventeen-day journey from Fort Espérance in January 1787 to the Mandan and Hidatsa villages. He was a competent traveller and excellent trader, having a noted knack of surviving among the aboriginal people. Mackay was a Highlander and a Roman Catholic. He was also literate and well-educated, punctual and zealous. Those who knew him even said he was loyal, though this is surely a debatable point.

The Spanish soon talent-spotted Mackay (in New York of all places). To them, he seemed precisely the sort of fellow who, if in the service of the king of Spain (and of the Missouri Company), could do wonders where Truteau and Lécuyer had faltered. Carondelet assured Minister Godoy in Madrid that Mackay had been employed by the Nor'Westers of Canada as an explorer and that he had met with great success in his attempted search for a communication toward the South Sea.[19] He had faithfully kept a table of distances showing routes across the wilderness, point to point and fort to fort.[20] To that date he ranked as the most competent and promising prospect for the exploration of the Missouri. "A commission as captain in the army with full pay of his rank would flatter his ambitions," Carondelet wrote on June 3, 1796, "causing him to sacrifice himself for the service of Spain, and the success of the Company of the Missouri in which he is interested."[21] Under this new patronage, Mackay, Nor'Wester turned Spanish army captain, became general agent of the Missouri Company with orders to ascertain the route to the Pacific Ocean. A trader of fortune, he crossed over in his allegiance. He became a Spaniard by choice. Clamorgan and associates saw him as the new hope. They appointed him field manager of the Missouri Company's affairs in succession to Truteau. Who knew how high Mackay's star would rise in the Spanish firmament if success were to favour the Missouri enterprise?

The bosses of the Missouri Company liked what they saw in Mackay, and they invested $104,000 in an expedition expected to require six years. Four pirogues were arranged—one for the Arikara trade, another to buy the party's way past the Sioux, a third for the Mandan villages and the fourth for the Rocky Mountain requirements.

Mackay's instructions, which he shaped, called for him to open trade with distant nations on the upper Missouri and "to discover all the unknown parts of his Catholic Majesty's Dominions through that continent as far as the Pacific Ocean."[22] Posts or forts were to be built wherever Mackay thought appropriate. These were to ward off the British from the north. Spanish trade was to be protected and fostered. Mackay was issued with a passport from Lieutenant-Governor Trudeau. With a party of thirty-three men, Mackay felt confident of success upon his departure from St. Louis at the end of August 1795.

In Mackay's party was John Evans, who three years earlier had crossed the Atlantic and arrived in Baltimore, perhaps emissary of some Welsh persons seeking to determine the existence of Welsh Indians. Legend has it that Madoc—in Welsh, *Madoz*—sailed west in AD 1169 and landed in what is now Mobile Bay, Alabama, in 1170. He and his men explored some distance inland and, according to the legend, some of his men stayed behind, intermarried with an indigenous tribe and gave birth to fair-skinned, Welsh-speaking Indians. With respect to Madoc, the Tudor geographer Humphrey Lloyd wrote, in his *History of Cambria*, there were "manie fables fained" but "sure it was that there [in America] he was ... whereupon it is manifest that that countrie was long before by Brytaines discovered, afore either Columbus or Americus Vesputius lead arie Spaniardes thither." Various sailors and preachers kept the legend alive. The noted publisher Hakluyt printed Lloyd's history, thereby increasing its influence. German scientist and traveller Alexander von Humboldt thought the "Welsh Indian" claim worthy of serious consideration.

The world cries out for more details about John Thomas Evans and his mission. The known facts are that he was born in 1770 in Waunfawr, near Carnarfon, North Wales, the son of a Methodist preacher. His birthplace was in Gwynedd, from whence Prince Madoc is reputed to have come, so interest in the Madoc legend would have been powerful there. As a young man, Evans went to London where he joined two expatriate Welsh literary and drinking societies.[23] A colourful character named Edward Williams befriended him and encouraged him to go to America to find the Welsh Indians.

Evans was no dreary-eyed mystic but rather a tough, competent and literate traveller. Upon his arrival in the United States, he went west by way of Philadelphia, where a bookseller named Pritchard gave him intelligence about the interior. Also in Philadelphia, the pastor of the Welsh church at Pennepek, Dr. Samuel Jones (later to be a founder of Brown University), found him to be "boastful" about the mission that "God Almighty had laid upon his conscience." Evans left Philadelphia in March 1793 and crossed to Pittsburgh. By early 1795 he was in the Illinois country. There he received third-party advice, zoological and geographical, concerning the continental interior, including the skeptical scrap of news that the "Pacific Ocean can lie at no great distance from the Missouri's source."

Young John Evans may have seemed impulsive and tactless and certainly suspicious to Spanish authorities at St. Louis. Yet he was a proven wilderness traveller, possessing zeal and enough education and exactitude in science to become a meticulous surveyor and skilled mapmaker.[24] (Nearly a decade later, on January 22, 1804, Jefferson wrote to Meriwether Lewis: "I enclose you a map of a Mr. Evans, Welshman, employed by the Spanish government for that purpose, but whose original object I believe had been to go in search of the Welsh Indians said to be up the Missouri."[25]) Lieutenant-Governor Trudeau, apprised of Evans's designs, sent him north to catch up with the recently departed Mackay, and for several months they were in each other's close company before dividing their talents on related, interlocking schemes.

Mackay and Evans were armed with a map, likely compiled for their benefit and use by Antoine Pierre Soulard, the surveyor general of Spanish Louisiana, who was based in St. Louis. This map bears the date August 1795, the very time that Mackay is believed to have departed from St. Louis. The map collector's dream lies in having the rarest, most definitive copy, and the search to possess such has motivated monarchs and impoverished those less well-heeled. Tracing the several states, or versions, of the Soulard map has had its own fascination, and we are still trying to piece together all the wild particulars. As best as can be understood from the known details, a prototype of this map may have been in Truteau's possession when he made his ascent of the Missouri in 1794. The map shows the progress of the Missouri Company's discoveries, and it makes specific reference to "the Encroachments of the English Companies in the Spanish Possessions."

Soulard's map shows the North West Company fort established by René Jusseaume among the Mandans. It is marked with a flag of England, St. George's, as is the route to it, "the path the English follow." The line of British forts to the Rocky Mountains indicates the feared extent of the Nor'Westers' activities. These were apt representations of what the Canadian traders were doing. W. Raymond Wood, an authority on the maps of this era, concludes that "the encroachments of these 'North Traders,' as such merchants were often called, were of course the stimulus for the Spanish exploration of the river that led to developing the Soulard map and dispatching the Mackay and Evans expedition."[26] Mackay and Evans, therefore, had good advance information about what to expect in their travels, but they lacked details.

Mackay arrived at the mouth of the Platte River on October 14, 1795. A short distance above the mouth, he put up a trading house and manned it with a few traders. He wanted the goodwill of the indigenous people there, and, assuming the post could be well-stocked with goods, he reasoned that they could be persuaded from going over to the British. He remained there eleven days, and then, rested, he pressed on upstream to a point eight leagues above the Platte, where six company employees, a remnant of an earlier expedition, perhaps Lécuyer's, had been among the Poncas and other tribes. Next he reached the village of the great Omaha chief Black Bird. Mackay put the matter plainly: the Spanish had faced numerous interruptions and discomforts by aboriginal interference in their commerce. He dispensed several medals among the chiefs and gave out presents generously. Mackay's party put up a post here and settled in for the winter. He called it Fort Charles, named for Charles IV of Spain.

Black Bird responded warmly to Mackay's overtures. He entered into an alliance with the Spanish and promised to avenge injuries suffered by Spanish traders at the hands of the Poncas. He also offered to send representatives to the Sioux, with invitations for them and other tribes to come to trade at Fort Charles. The object was to secure the free, unrestricted navigation of the Missouri—free from let or interference by the Native tribes. Black Bird intended to escort Mackay to the Arikaras. However, Mackay decided to dispatch Evans to the Arikaras, and because the way by water was closed, hazardous or blocked, he sent him by a shortcut over land.

Mackay ventured west from Fort Charles during the winter of 1795–96 in search of Rocky Mountain tribes. Rather than making one grand reconnaissance, he made several short journeys, gathering such data as he could. On June 8, 1796, from Fort Charles, he wrote his friend Evans: "I have found the time tedious since you left this [place] not withstanding my being employed about some trip [?] or other, however, I begin to get accustomed to live Solletary I dare say that in the course of time hence I shall be happy alone as the Indian on the desert."[27] With this letter he sent a sketch of the Yellowstone River that d'Eglise had obtained from the Mandans. Mackay says he explored up to the Mandan villages, wintered in the interior and was back in St. Louis by May 1797. On the heels of Mackay, Evans came downriver from his equally remarkable travels. Mackay claimed more credit than he deserves for the expedition's undertakings and findings. To Evans goes undeniable laurels for distinguished imperial actions, made all the more remarkable when it is remembered that he was a neophyte among indigenous people and rival traders.

Mackay never lost his primacy in the Missouri Company's explorations, yet it is to the travels and trials of Evans that our story is attracted, for it brought Evans into contact with the old fur-trading chums and partners of Mackay, now the northern opposition.

On January 28, 1796, Mackay said goodbye to the agreeable Evans. With precision, and with a style bearing fine comparison to Jefferson's own instructions to Captain Lewis, Mackay instructed Evans to cross the continent and to discover a passage from the course of the Missouri to the Pacific Ocean. The covering orders bore all the authority of Clamorgan and the Missouri Company, backed by Carondelet as governor-general of the Province of Louisiana and Zenón Trudeau, lieutenant-governor of the Province of Illinois. Mackay left nothing to chance. He instructed Evans to keep notes on latitude, longitude, weather and winds—all in one journal. He instructed Evans to record the extent and location of minerals, vegetables, plants, animals and tribes, with details of same, in another. "You will take care and mark down your route and distance each day, whether by land or water; in case you will be short of ink, use the powder, and for want of powder, in the summer you will surely find some fruit whose juice can replace both." Mackay set down requirements that Evans find and confer with Truteau the trader, said to be among the Arikaras or the Mandans. He was to distribute gifts to the tribes and tell them that other traders would follow—in other words, assure the tribes that the Missouri Company would not neglect them in future. As to the specific geographical particulars, Mackay directed Evans to keep within the bounds of 40° north latitude and to go as far west as between 111° and 112° west longitude. Then he was to shape a course north to the 42nd parallel and, turning west again, travel to the Pacific. Mackay estimated the distance from the Rocky Mountains to salt water as 290 leagues, or 870 miles. Evans was to carve inscriptions on stones or trees as proof that he had passed that way. With unbounded hopes of success, Mackay told Evans not to incur the jealousy of the Russians. His findings were to be kept secret and were only to be revealed on his return to Mackay, Clamorgan or other representative of the Missouri Company in the presence of the lieutenant-governor.[28]

From Fort Charles, Evans crossed to the Arikara villages. There he met some Cheyennes, who said they were attached to the Spanish standard. He came next, overland once more, to the Mandan villages. The date was September 23, 1796.

Evans was not the first of the Missouri Company to reach the Great Bend of the Missouri, but he was the first to bear any sort of commission to make a show of his authority. He distributed medals, flags and other presents. He gave a speech in the cause of king and company. He took possession of the fort that belonged to the Canadian traders, called Jusseaume's Post, and renamed it for his boss, Fort Mackay. He hoisted the Spanish flag in lieu of the Union Jack. "This measure," wrote the distinguished authority Abraham P. Nasatir, who studied closely the journals of Evans and Mackay, "not only gave the Spaniards control over the Mandan, but by closing the upper Missouri to the British traders, it promised to throw the trade of the region into Spanish hands."[29] The Mandans were bound to listen to Evans's entreaties, particularly his fine promise that the Missouri Company traders would come in future years—a promise broken, in fact, as they were to tell Lewis and Clark years later.[30]

The trading post in question, now tenuously in Spanish hands, had been backed by the North West Company and kept up by the various independent traders who trekked from the Assiniboine and Souris rivers. The most recent of these was René Jusseaume, later hired by Lewis and Clark as a Mandan interpreter for Sheheke on his visit to Washington. One traveller, Alexander Henry the Younger, was severe in his description of Jusseaume: "He retains the outward appearance of a Christian, but his principles, as far as I could observe, are much worse than those of a Mandane; he is possessed of every superstition natural to those people, nor is he different in every mean, dirty trick they have acquired from intercourse with the set of scoundrels who visit these parts—some to trade and others to screen themselves from justice."[31] In earlier days, before Mackay had crossed over to the Spanish, Jusseaume had followed him down from the north and had made a steady passage back and forth from the Assiniboine River to the Missouri, bringing trade goods, taking out furs. Jusseaume was a man of considerable influence on the Missouri, especially among the Mandans, his friends and his allies. He was kind to visitors and helpful in making introductions. He had prospered in the business across the 49th parallel of latitude and was still a force to be reckoned with in the events being played out at the fort, even though it was no longer under his control.

When Cuthbert Grant, principal Nor'Wester in the region, heard about Evans's takeover of Jusseaume's Post, he wrote most politely to Evans on October 8, from Rivière Tremblante Fort. He said that he had learned, from a letter Mackay had sent to him, that the Missouri Company had been founded and even backed by government charter. He also stated that, in consequence, he, Grant, wished to withdraw what little property the North West Company still had there at Jusseaume's Post. Grant was disingenuous. He gave the vague impression that Canadian trade there had been a losing proposition for a few years past. Grant requested that Evans allow Jusseaume to settle his affairs and take home his goods. That would require Evans to deliver all the goods belonging to Jusseaume in his possession.[32]

On precisely the same day that Grant sent his agreeable if not fully frank letter to Evans, several Canadian traders marched into the Mandan villages. Jusseaume was not among them, but he had sent his most trusted aides.

Evans could offer no resistance to this show of force. He could not stop their entrance. He could not block their trade. But he gave them, to take back with them to British possessions, Mackay's proclamation "forbidding all strangers whatever to enter on any part of his Catholic Majesty's Dominions in this Quarter under any pretext whatever."[33]

Mackay, it seems, had sent this prohibition (dated May 27, 1796, at Fort Charles) to men of the Hudson's Bay Company as well as the North West Company. "This may effect the traders from Canada a little but not those from Hudson's Bay," wrote the Bay trader James Sutherland at Brandon House. The wily Sutherland sought permission to visit the Missouri to trade in horses, Indian corn and buffalo robes, "which articles we suppose not to be connected with the Fur Trade and consequently expect you have no objection."[34]

John McDonell of the North West Company sent Evans a more blunt message, one in keeping with the longstanding ties between the Souris River post and the fort among the Mandans. At the same time as Sutherland had snuggled up to Evans, so to speak, McDonell gave warning of his necessary visit—*another* visit, and one "much against our wills"—to fetch "the dearly acquired debt of Mr. Jusseaume." McDonell sent Jean Baptiste Desmarais on this unpleasant and dangerous service of retrieval, giving him and his men goods on credit as an inducement. McDonell warned them that Evans might confiscate their goods, but in light-hearted fashion these voyageurs set out to find Evans, whom they had heard was a fine fellow, a *bon garçon*. With him, Desmarais carried two European magazines, a geographical grammar or gazetteer and other items as a gift for Evans's "amusement." The loathsome Jusseaume apparently kept a little slave girl at his old post, and McDonell hoped Evans would surrender this "property," along with Jusseaume's business assets, to Desmarais and associates.

Desmarais reached the Mandan villages before Christmas and was back home at Souris River post on January 16, 1797. On their return, he and his party had lost their horses two nights out of the Mandan villages, claimed by some Pawnees. They had consequently been obliged to leave their property behind and to go again for it. Jusseaume's assets were retrieved and his debt to the North West Company cancelled.

The next to arrive at Evans's post was none other than Jusseaume, the inveterate trader, the former king of European commerce on the upper Missouri, who now intended to reclaim his throne by destroying the agent of the Missouri Company. He arrived March 13 overland from the Assiniboine. His packs bulged with presents and much merchandise for the Mandans and for neighbouring tribes. Evans said it was Jusseaume's intention to wean the people of the Great Bend from their fidelity to the king of Spain. Jusseaume used every trick and connivance known in the business. First he attempted to get chiefs to enter Evans's house under the guise of friendship; his plan was for them to murder Evans and pillage his property. Instead of following Jusseaume's design, the chiefs ratted on the Canadian trader and even promised that they would guard Evans against attack. Next, Jusseaume attempted to murder Evans himself; this was thwarted when Evans's interpreter told all.

Evans reasoned that the Nor'Westers would stop at nothing and spare no expense to reassert their commercial influence among the Mandans. He saw that the Mandans constituted the means to an end for the Nor'Westers. The latter intended to open up trade with the nations that inhabited the Rocky Mountains. And in Evans's words, that trade "at this moment is supposed to be the best on the Continent of America."[35]

Evans faced ruin. Although he had stood his ground during that eventful winter at the Mandan villages, the future looked bleak. He needed fresh supplies. He had no garrison and insufficient men for defence. The Nor'westers had come once or twice, even in force, revealing their well-known violent tendencies and roughness. It was time to go. He made his withdrawal, instructing some loyal subordinates or allies to raise the Spanish standard once a week. On May 9, he began his descent to St. Louis, arriving there on July 15. Jusseaume, it is fair to say, had driven the Spanish out of the Mandan villages. They were never to return.

Mackay was already back from his wilderness wanderings, safe in snug St. Louis, when Evans joined him. Mackay wrote up his experiences. The faithful Evans, following instructions, did likewise. Mackay boasted that he had driven the English out of His Catholic Majesty's territories, taken possession of the fort in question and broken the British traders' alliance with the various aboriginal chiefs. None of this was correct. Mackay may have made a chart of the windings of the Missouri just short of 1,800 miles in length, but it is Evans's remarkable map that survives. And Evans relied on aboriginal information for his map, which showed the Yellowstone River, the Great Falls of the Missouri, several ranges to the west, the land of the Shoshones, the Rocky Mountains and even a west-flowing river with what appears to be a fur-trading post on its banks.[36] Lewis and Clark were to carry a version—in fact, the fourth—of this map.

As for Evans's search for descendants of Madoc, the Welsh traveller, it was unsuccessful. He had travelled extensively but had found no Welsh Indians. To his friend Samuel Jones in Philadelphia, Evans wrote: "Thus having explored and charted the Missurie for 1800 miles and by my Communications with the Indians this side of the Pacific Ocean from 35 to 49 Degrees of Latitude, I am able to inform you that there is no such People as The Welsh Indians, and you will be so kind as to satisfie my friends as to that doubtfull Question." The last part of this sentence reads as an urgent plea and also a conclusive statement of fact. Jones passed the particulars to correspondents, and in a Welsh magazine published in Carnarvon, Wales, in 1800 we find this declaration: "With reference to the Welsh Indians, he [Evans] says that he was unable to meet with any such people; and he has come to the fixed conclusion, which he has founded upon his acquaintance with various tribes, that there are no such people in existence."[37]

This remarkable Welshman turned his talents to surveying in the Spanish king's employ. He suffered from malaria. He drank heavily and is said to have become deranged. He never returned to his homeland as had been his intention. He died young, age twenty-nine. His, indeed, is a sad tale.

Mackay later became less boastful of his feats. By his own admission, he had been hired as an explorer but had spent his time attempting to wean indigenous people away from British and Canadian traders. The Missouri Company had faced persistent hostility from the aboriginals. This had not been anticipated and was attributed to the activities of the English traders who had established themselves on the upper Missouri. Mackay said later that through his hands "were distributed, principally, the presents of merchandise necessary to secure the friendship of the Indians, and to estrange them from the influence and traffic of the British, Northwest, and Hudson's Bay Companies."[38] Even so, he was well rewarded. He was given command of the post of San André on the Missouri and was granted much land by Spanish officials. His time as an explorer came to an abrupt halt. He may have believed to the close of his days that his Spanish superiors had treated him less luxuriously than they should have. But he got more than Evans, and it is fair to state that had Evans not been among the Mandans that winter of 1796–97, the secrets of the Yellowstone and the upper reaches of the Missouri would not have escaped from the cloak of secrecy that Spain had placed upon the interior. It is strangely ironic that it took a displaced Highland Scot and a wandering Welsh ethnographer to lay bare, for Spain, the secrets of the Missouri River in northern latitudes.

Mackay and Evans failed to complete their trade mission, but they made mighty contributions to discovery, providing remarkable additions to the geographical knowledge of the Missouri, especially to the descriptions of the particulars and courses of the rivers. Evans's map has already been mentioned, but what about the field general of the expedition? Mackay's reports to his superiors about the features of the Missouri (as gathered from informants) predated Lewis and Clark's findings by seven years and were powerful information in Jefferson's hands. Some of the specifics were compelling. About the Great Falls of the Missouri, Mackay wrote with considerable specific detail: "After all the information I could collect it appears that the Missouri takes its source in about 40° N. from whence it runs to the north (between the chains of the Rocky Mountains) as far as 49° N. that thence running east, it falls over the east chain of the mountains … this fall it is said is of an astonishing height, from the situation of the country and the meanders of the river I suppose this fall to be 200 leagues west of the Mandaines."[39]

Mackay's report of 1795–96 confirmed, for Carondelet, information he had previously received that told of the arrival of traders from Canada into the domains of the Spanish king. They were in two locations: among the Mandans on the south shore of the Missouri, and on the Platte (or Chato) River, where the English had erected a blockhouse. This latter particularly worried the governor, for it indicated a clandestine trade with many of the "Spanish" aboriginal tribes and perhaps even with the indigenous people of Santa Fé (in present-day New Mexico). Additional evidence from the commandant of the post at Natchitoches, Captain Don Luis Deblanc, confirmed the existence of the blockhouse, but mistakenly stated that it was of American construction and origin. Carondelet had no doubts: the Americans had not yet arrived there; this was an English-from-Canada intrusion.

The "fatal consequences of such an attempt on the part of a nation as enterprising as the English" in the area of the Missouri and the Platte left no hesitation in Carondelet's mind. He proposed that an armed expedition of two hundred frontiersmen, picked from Spanish settlements on the upper Mississippi, should set out from St. Louis with aboriginal allies to destroy the post and drive the Canadians from it. This expedition would go by water, with the barges carrying some light pieces of artillery sufficient to bombard the blockhouse and scatter the inhabitants and their indigenous allies. It was imagined that the post on the Platte had no ordnance to defend it, as the English were thought to be unable to carry artillery such a distance.[40]

As late as June 1796, Spanish fears focused on the English threat from Canada, but the Spanish military project for the reduction of the post on the Platte never developed.

In the next few years, 1798, 1799, and 1800, the Missouri Company regrouped around the capital and energies of Andrew Todd, a supplier of arms, ammunition and goods from Michilimackinac. He was the principal fur baron of the Ohio country. The company placed much hope on a quick success under his leadership for "our enterprises for the discovery of the Pacific Ocean." But Todd died, and steam went out of the scheme, even though the Company still claimed unremitting zeal and ambition for its project, carrying business to the very source of the Missouri.

The Missouri Company continued to send traders to the Platte River and to various tribes of the upper Missouri—including the Poncas, the Sioux and the Arikaras. We do not know how many traders were sent north, but one of them, Joseph Garreau, met with Lewis and Clark when they came up the river in 1804. By this time the Spanish traders knew the Yellowstone River, and, in fact, Mackay's narrative and report give a reasonably accurate account of the Missouri from its mouth to its source.[41]

Just at the time that Lewis and Clark came to the Mandan villages and proceeded on their westward journey, the Canadian traders, having already turned aside the Spanish and the Missouri Company, were extending their trade south and west by way of the Missouri and Yellowstone rivers. This was a strange concurrence of historical forces. The meeting of the traders from the North West Company and the American explorers of the Corps of Discovery marked the intersection of destinies. The Missouri Valley remained a valley of strangers—and strange encounters.

Chapter 8

THE VIEW FROM MONTICELLO: JEFFERSON'S WESTS

F or all his learning, all his erudition and persuasion, all his cosmopolitan knowledge and style, his inquisitiveness and brilliance, Thomas Jefferson was yet a man of the soil. He was a Virginia planter. His life was rooted in the earth and in property. The land, in conceptual terms, afforded wealth if nourished by economy and husbandry, and it was seen as the basis of liberty as well as prosperity. The land was also viewed as redemptive, for in the newly occupied lands of America, a free man, wife and family could redress the imbalances of the Old World. New societies could be founded in these lands, and thus commonwealths and republics, creations of man in community, could, under providence and God, thrive and flourish for the betterment of humankind.

The nature of the American federal structure also preoccupied Jefferson, and with it the vexing problem of how, and in what ways, the American republic would grow—enlarging its boundaries, filling out its natural limits. Alliances with foreign powers, dreaded but necessary in some circumstances, troubled him no less. He would have preferred to have government distanced, even unengaged, from corporate aspirations and dealings. Yet, strangely, in order to counter the mercantilist ventures of the British, Canadians, Russians and Spanish, he was drawn to the European approach to political economy. "To Jefferson, the idea of divorcing government from business was no mere counsel of prudence, but a basic principle of democratic statesmanship"; yet, concludes Paul Phillips, historian of the fur trade, with remarkable insight, "of all the American presidents he best understood the fur trade and was most inclined to do something for it."[1] Regulating the western fur trade became the measure for managing aboriginal affairs.

From the west portico of his splendid Blue Hills estate at Monticello, the largest plantation, ranch or spread owned by a president to that time, Jefferson

Thomas Jefferson, Secretary of State and later president of the United States, was the presiding genius of American geographical science and exploration. Jefferson's vision, especially in light of Mackenzie's Voyages from Montreal, *was to find the River of the West that would lead to Pacific tidewater. Library and Archives Canada, C-10133*

had ample scope to consider the wests—the physical west and the west of the imagination—that lay beyond the Appalachian Mountains. He was not a tidewater Virginian but was rather a westerner. His curiosity matched his remarkable intellect. He was a student of geography, a pioneer in that field of learning. John Logan Allen, historical geographer, goes so far as to say that Jefferson can be understood as "a geographer by birth, by training, and by inclination." Allen explains that Jefferson had mastery of the geographer's trade. This included, but was not restricted to, understanding of spatial patterns, knowledge and use of maps, and appreciation that geography is not a study of a particular matter but a way of looking at things.[2] He had a keen interest in all natural history and scientific questions, it is true. He knew his native jurisdiction, Virginia, as well as anyone and perhaps even more so. In answer to a foreigner's inquiries about the nature of Virginia, Jefferson was able to describe, in terms reflecting the Age of Enlightenment science that surrounded him, and with clarity and detail, the nature of that domain, its rivers and other geographical features, its indigenous peoples and its known resources. Rivers he saw as vectors of commerce, links among peoples, avenues of communication and business. Land he saw as a means of agricultural exploitation, but, more, as a means of providing humankind with occupation and liberty. He saw cities as places of corruption, congeries to be avoided. But the physical west beyond the Appalachians offered not only opportunity but also a beneficent means for industrious farming families to prosper and to fulfil a destiny made possible by such good soil as was suitable for agriculture.

Trade, no less than agriculture, stood high in Jefferson's priorities when he became president in 1801, for trade was a natural extension of a free people's interest in human communications. Any bridling of American commerce, or commercial intercourse, would shackle American initiative and freedom. Any intervening attempt by foreign powers—Britain, Russia and Spain, for instance—would limit American growth and American liberties. But although in Jefferson's time the United States was still a relatively minor power when considered against the likes of Britain and Spain, or of France and Russia besides, freedom of action was to Jefferson a national byword, and the China trade perfectly reflected the sort of opportunity that American seaborne commerce could pursue with increasing profit. So, too, did American fishing, sealing and whaling activities in the waters of Newfoundland and Labrador, the South Atlantic and the Pacific. American merchants undercut the British in the Caribbean. Commerce was the engine driving American foreign policy, and Jefferson managed the requirements of the trading interests to the benefit of the national government, providing diplomatic and naval support to enrich the coffers of New York, Philadelphia, Baltimore and Boston merchant traders, investors and bankers.

Long before the Revolution, the wealth of these ports—and their respective hinterlands—were based on seaborne trades. Boston's and New York's financiers, investors and bankers danced to the tune of seaborne commerce: of ships arrived and departed, of cargoes clearing customs and of new ventures to distant and nearby seas. Long before the Jeffersonian concept of western expansion—by land—obtained the backing of Congress, the old sea dogs of Boston and their backers had put the northwest coast of North America on their chart. They had also discounted any frivolous concept of a northwest passage somewhere south of the 49th parallel of latitude. Instead, they had commenced the real way of commerce to China—by sea—in their ships, sloops, barks and even schooners. They had figured out the secrets of trade to China a decade or more before Jefferson foisted the Lewis and Clark Corps of Discovery project upon Congress in 1803. The *Empress of China*, owned by Robert Morriss and

Daniel Parker, sailed from New York and made Canton by the Indian Ocean in 1784. The supercargo, Major Samuel Shaw, became an articulate spokesman for American futures in the Pacific and Orient. The implication is clear: the discovery of the Missouri River and its sources and what lay westward to the Pacific shore was a prelude to American empire, whether or not foreign intruders resisted or were permissive in the process. Jefferson stands at the lead edge of American mission and manifest destiny. The times dictated this.

The west continued as a cockpit of imperial rivalries; it had been such since the Spanish first entered the southeast in 1534. By the time Jefferson was compiling his book on Virginia in the 1780s, the west was the campaign ground of the Spanish, the Russians and the Canadians. How the young United States would deal with the collection of intertwining problems created by these three rival empires on its western doorstep remained the most puzzling issue of the day. The president could send a sloop of war or a squadron to force the liberation of hostages on the Barbary Coast or could pay tribute for the same, could declare war when required with the approval of Congress and could make such alliances or diplomatic arrangements with foreign states as would buttress national purposes. But sending a military expedition to occupy western lands was out of the question and would not only invite foreign powers to declare war on the United States, but was also unlikely to win congressional support for the financial requirements that would allow such a campaign.

Jefferson worried most about Louisiana. "Every eye is now fixed on this affair of Louisiana," he said in April 1802, when faced with a sudden reversal of fortunes. By the secret Treaty of San Ildefonso, Spain ceded the vast province of Louisiana to France in order to cut its debts and lessen defence needs in the northern perimeter of upper Louisiana or Illinois. France did not actually take control until November 1803.

As soon as news of the treaty reached the United States, Jefferson and others felt a sense of alarm. In French hands, New Orleans and Louisiana would be a place of constant uncertainty and perpetual danger. France, said Jefferson, had been looked on as "our natural friend, as one with which we never could have any occasion of difference." He even went on to add, "Her growth therefore we viewed as our own, her misfortunes ours."[3]

Jefferson felt betrayed by circumstances beyond his control. Everything hinged on Louisiana, on New Orleans in particular: "There is on the globe one single spot, the possessor of which is our natural and habitual enemy," he wrote in 1802. "It is New Orleans, through which the produce of three-eighths of our territory must pass to market, and from its fertility it will ere long yield more than half of our whole produce and contain more than half our inhabitants." Jefferson contended that Spain might have held New Orleans quietly and done so for years. Even had Spain boosted its facilities there, the country's feeble state and pacific disposition meant that sooner or later the United States might have acquired the great port. Now all was changed. France placed itself at the door of the continent, the Mississippi, in an assumed attitude of defiance. "The day that France takes possession of N. Orleans fixes the sentence which is to restrain her forever within her low water mark," said Jefferson. "It seals the union of two nations who in conjunction can maintain exclusive possession of the ocean. From that moment we must marry ourselves to the British fleet and nation."[4] The prospect was too horrid to imagine, too embarrassing for words.

With this upsetting revelation of two European and continental powers embarking on a diplomatic arrangement without US knowledge or consultation, and without the United States being able to provide an effective counter, Jefferson had defined the terrible circumstance. The United States could not yet manage its own destiny. It was subject to the whim of fate. It was not master of the continent. The external world seemed chaotic. Jefferson, by forceful statecraft, urged Robert L. Livingston, the US Minister to France, to press upon the ministers of the government of France the essential point that little was to be gained by their possession of New Orleans and that, in any event, their tenure there would be short. Perhaps, he suggested, France might exchange New Orleans and the Floridas as equivalent for a quarrel?

We are hard pressed to imagine that Jefferson was threatening war against France by writing so freely to the American minister in Paris. More likely, in Socratic tone, he was working out in his own mind the powerful and affirming position of his administration: that France should be quietly and directly informed of American interests and concerns with regards to New Orleans.

Jefferson sent James Monroe as Minister Plenipotentiary And Envoy Extraordinary to France and Spain. Monroe was ordered to join Livingston in Paris, with powers to offer a sufficient sum for New Orleans and the Floridas or, failing that, for New Orleans alone, in order to secure free navigation of the Mississippi for the Americans. If the French would not bargain, the fallback position was that Monroe would press for a perpetual guarantee of the rights of navigation on the Mississippi. If all of this were to fail, Monroe was to go to London and attempt to obtain an alliance with the old imperial master, Great Britain. Jefferson was not yet threatening war; even so, this was brinkmanship of high order.

Unknown to Jefferson, Napoleon dreamed of reconquering all of France's lost possessions in the New World. To this end he acquired a copy of the first London printing of Mackenzie's *Voyages from Montreal* and translated this fascinating, forward-thinking and thus alarming book into French, analyzing it for any strategies it might suggest for an invasion of Canada by way of the Mississippi River. The details of this sketchy plan did not become known until two decades later. In 1824 it was revealed by King Charles XIV of Sweden, formerly Jean-Baptiste Bernadotte, Napoleon's first and foremost marshal, that shortly after the publication of *Voyages from Montreal*, Napoleon had "arranged to distract the affairs of Britain by attacking her in her Canadian possessions—not by a direct descent upon them, but by a route which men expected would take England quite by surprise and prove infallible." That route lay up the Mississippi, Ohio and the Great Lakes. Bernadotte was given command of this gigantic enterprise. Foremost among the dossiers for military advice was Mackenzie's book, which Bernadotte procured through smugglers and had, in an inconceivably short space of time, translated into French for purposes of military planning. Bernadotte studied and restudied the text. He believed he would be able to take Canada in reverse, from the upper waters. "Ever since I have never ceased to look upon the name [of Mackenzie] and think of the author with more than ordinary respect and esteem," said Bernadotte, admitting that it was the emperor's campaign in Russia many years later that knocked the plans for Canada on the head.[5]

However, on April 11, 1803, the French foreign minister, Talleyrand, surprised Livingston by offering to sell Louisiana to the United States, asking what amount they would pay for it. Monroe, who arrived in Paris the next day, expressed delight. On April 30 the treaty effecting the Louisiana Purchase was signed. Louisiana, with no precise boundaries, was sold to the United States for 60 million francs, or $15 million. Livingston wrote victoriously from Paris about these remarkable negotiations: "We have lived long, but this is the noblest work of our whole lives …. From this day the United States will take their place among the powers of the first rank …. The instruments which we have just signed will cause no tears to be shed; they prepare ages of happiness for innumerable generations of human creatures." Jefferson had no constitutional powers as president to extend his powers into Louisiana, but the Senate ratified the treaty in October.

On November 30 the Spanish surrendered New Orleans to France, thus allowing French nominal control. And on December 20 the French handed the province of Louisiana to American authorities. A US governor of the territory, William Claiborne, was appointed in 1804.

For the present the United States government could not—would not—declare war on a foreign power in order to secure its western boundaries, but the chaotic circumstances on western and northern lands intensified, became more dangerous to national interests. The aboriginal "menace," allegedly aided by Canadian musket and ammunition shipments and British army gifts to Native allies in the Old Northwest, became a reason for the United States to seal this northern frontier.

In these measures, Jefferson wore the mantle of George Washington. The first president looked on North America's western and northern lands as a place of disorder and restiveness.[6] General Anthony Wayne's victory at the battle of Fallen Timbers (1794) indicated a triumph for American armed forces in the Ohio Valley and led to treaty making with the confederation of local tribes. Washington issued a proclamation against potentially disruptive colonization plans, and by Jay's Treaty (1794), which he supported, Washington was instrumental in bringing about the promise of British evacuation from the northwest posts. The Treaty of San Lorenzo (Pinckney's Treaty) established the boundary between the United States and Spanish Florida in 1795 and, more, provided for the rights of American commerce and navigation on the

Mississippi River. These were no small achievements in the western progression of American authority and influence. Nonetheless, President Washington remained chary of the social and political consequences of unregulated western expansion. Jefferson, then Secretary of State, felt similarly.

This explains Jefferson's equal reluctance to enlarge the union by precipitate action. However, he did see associate republics in the west as a beneficent means of American democratic rejuvenation and even a nutriment of republicanism. Jefferson's public land policies were also shaped by the prospects of the unspoiled wilderness. Thus a growing United States merited a well-defined and orderly western lands policy. The Northwest Ordnance of 1787, which bore the signs of Jefferson's guiding hand, established a means of regulated western expansion by government, and no less than twenty western territories were added to the Union between 1788 and 1812. Jefferson saw order and science going hand in hand with westward expansion. The Enlightenment would inform the growth of the republic. "Our present federal limits are not too large for good government," Jefferson wrote tellingly to a friend in 1786. "Our confederacy must be viewed as the nest, from which all America, North and South, is to be peopled. We should take care too, not to think it for the interest of that great continent to press too soon on the Spaniards. Those countries cannot be in better hands. My fear is that they are too feeble to hold them till our population can be sufficiently advanced to gain it from them piece by piece. The navigation of the Mississippi we must have. This is all we are as yet ready to receive."[7]

Jefferson also recognized the importance of the Missouri River. Writing in 1782, when that river was not yet within the boundaries of the United States, he speculated that it could open to American traders a channel of extensive communication with the northwest and west. The Missouri, he wrote, "is remarkably cold, muddy and rapid. Its overflows are considerable." Jefferson imagined that the ascent of the river from where it flowed into the Mississippi was also considerable. "That this ascent is great is proved by the rapidity of the river. Six miles above its mouth it is brought within the compass of a quarter of a mile's width: yet the Spanish merchants at Pancore, or St. Louis, say they go two thousand miles up it. It heads far west of Rio Norte, or North River." Jefferson could approximate some of the distances between these rivers and

New Orleans, Santa Fe, Mexico City and several other cities and towns, but he could only speculate on the distance separating the navigable waters of the Missouri from those of the North River, above Santa Fe.[8] The lower course of the Missouri was known, but its upper configuration and its tributaries lay beyond current scientific understanding.

Jefferson had been urging a scheme to explore the Missouri and lands to the west for a good many years before his pet project could at last be realized. The plan evolved from the results of the War of the American Revolution and the continuing disorder in the Old Northwest. On December 4, 1783, Jefferson wrote to General George Rogers Clark, the elder brother of William Clark: "I find they [the British] have subscribed a very large sum of money in England for exploring the country from the Mississippi to California. They pretend it is only to promote knowl-edge. I am afraid they have thoughts of colonizing into that quarter. Some of us have been talking here in a feeble way of making the attempt to search that country. But I doubt whether we have enough of that kind of spirit to raise the money. How would you like to lead such a party? tho I am afraid our prospect is not worth asking the question."[9]

When governor of Virginia, Jefferson had sent General Clark, seasoned frontier traveller and warrior, with a sizeable army to capture British posts in the Old Northwest and, in particular, to neutralize the British post at Detroit. But now the circumstances were different, Clark argued. A military

Meriwether Lewis, army officer and secretary to Thomas Jefferson, president of the United States, was instructed to lead an expedition to unlock the secrets of the west as far as the Pacific. He made the journey there and back to St.Louis. Suffering from severe depression, he killed himself without completing the narrative of the Corps of Discovery that Jefferson and others expected. Independence National Historical Park

show of force would not do. In his view, "large parties will never answer the purpose. They will alarm the Indian Nations they pass through. Three or four young Men well qualified for the Task might perhaps compleat your wishes at a very trifling Expense."[10] This was good advice and fair warning based on experience and knowledge: a major expedition might well invite reprisals from the indigenous people and would certainly alert them to the intrusions. Small would be best, Clark stated, and costs would be nominal. Better to go quietly, unassumingly, into the wilderness.

Other reasons have been cited for Clark's unwillingness to venture west at this time, including alcoholism and debt.[11] All in all, Jefferson had chosen the wrong man. And for the moment, his plan for western discoveries under the Stars and Stripes lay dormant.

Evidence of the projected British imperial examination of the continent's waterways from the Mississippi to California, referred to by Jefferson in his invitation to Clark, does not survive in any specific documents or memoirs. However, since Cook's discoveries at Nootka Sound and Alaska in 1778, British enthusiasm for finding out more about the continental interior and the Pacific shore had intensified. Certainly it was driven by commercial requirements. There was much chat of it in London's business and scientific circles, and it was probably from London that American agents gleaned news of such a scheme. Transcontinental exploration was then much on the minds of the North West Company partners in Montreal, and it was advanced in an irregular serial form by the likes of Alexander Henry the Elder and his business partners. Peter Pond knew all about this; so did Mackenzie.

For the moment, Jefferson, who knew all about how the British employed science to mask imperial measures (as demonstrated by Sir Joseph Banks, who had helped Ledyard in his fatal explorations), had to content himself with pursuing scientific goals and exploiting that group of savants with whom he was on intimate terms. This was the worthy, illustrious American Philosophical Society, headquartered in Philadelphia. In 1792, Jefferson, a leading figure in the society, persuaded his associates to finance an expedition. They subscribed goodly sums of money to encourage the enterprise, with a slice of the reward given if the explorer reached the waters that flowed to the Pacific Ocean, and the full amount bestowed if he got to the Pacific and made the return journey. But woe betide the explorer who did not even reach those headwaters (or who ran off on his own errand), for they would then refuse all reward and even claw back money he had received under subscription. The Protestant work ethic ran deeply under this arrangement. The party was to accomplish its purpose "by ascending the Missouri, crossing the Stony mountains, and descending the nearest river to the Pacific," in the words of Jefferson.[12]

Captain Meriwether Lewis, who was in Charlottesville, heard of the expedition and of Jefferson's search for a competent leader. He dashed off a letter to Jefferson, putting himself forward. Jefferson replied, giving details: "I told him it was proposed that the person engaged should be attended by a single companion only, to avoid exciting alarm among the Indians. This did not deter him …." But at about the same time the Frenchman André Michaux, a "professed botanist" (according to Jefferson) and author of a work on northern flora, was chosen. Lewis was set aside.

In 1785, Michaux had been commissioned by the government of France, then royalist, to visit North America principally to investigate potential sources of ship timbers—a vital strategic mission for a resurgent naval power. He travelled widely in North America, even going to Hudson Bay via the Saguenay River of Quebec in 1792. By the time he received instructions from Jefferson dated January 23, 1793, the French government

William Clark, an officer in the US Army with surveying and cartographic skills, was co-leader of the Corps of Discovery at Lewis's request. Even-handed and methodical—and less suspicious of Nor'Westers than was Lewis—Clark was of great value to the expedition. He later became a superintendent of Indian Affairs at St. Louis and warned the US government of Canadian expansionist aspirations in northwest America. Independence National Historical Park

was solidly revolutionary and republican, and Michaux was approached by Citizen Edmond-Charles Genêt, France's Minister to the United States, to promote French aggrandizement in Louisiana and Canada. The dream of a resurgent New France never died in republican hearts in Paris.[13] Given these circumstances, the American Philosophical Society expedition was clouded by intrigue and duplicity. Jefferson knew that Michaux was more than a collector of botanical specimens,[14] but he did nothing to stop Michaux's proceedings. In fact, we now know that Jefferson planned to have Michaux carry messages and money to George Rogers Clark in Kentucky. If Clark could raise a band of frontiersmen under the French banner for an attack on New Orleans, it could help the French take New Orleans back from the Spanish. But George Washington got wind of this and would have nothing to do with plots that required French collaboration and the reactivation of the alliance of 1778.[15]

Jefferson has a different view of this. Michaux, wrote Jefferson in his memoir of Lewis, received his instructions, "and when he had reached Kentucky in the prosecution of his journey, he was overtaken by an order from the minister of France [Genêt], then at Philadelphia, to relinquish the expedition, and to pursue elsewhere the botanical inquiries on which he was employed by that government: and thus failed the second attempt for exploring that region."

Jefferson's instructions to Michaux had designated the Missouri as the preferred channel of communication between the United States and the Pacific Ocean. Its exploration was thus the fundamental object of the expedition. "You will then pursue as much of the largest streams of that river, as shall lead by the shortest way, and the lowest latitude to the Pacific ocean." But there was a more specific requirement. "When, pursuing these streams, you shall find yourself at the point from thence whence you may get by the shortest & most convenient route to some principal river of the Pacific ocean, you are to proceed to such river, & pursue its Course to the ocean. It would seem by the latest maps as if a river called Oregon interlocked with the Missouri for a considerable distance, & entered the Pacific ocean, not far Southward of Nootka sound."

Existing maps were not to be trusted, and Michaux's instructions were to find out "the real truth." He was to take note of the soil, rivers, mountains of the territories passed through on his journey, noting its productions, animal, vegetable and mineral; to note the latitudes of these places; and to note the names, numbers and dwellings of the inhabitants "and such particularities as you can learn of their history, connection with each other, languages, manners, state of society & of the arts & commerce among them." Details were requested of the mammoth, particularly, and of the llama of Peru if it were found in North America and, if found, how far north. But the first and most important object was searching for and pursuing that route which would form "the shortest & most convenient communication between the higher parts of the Missouri & the Pacific ocean."[16]

For nearly a decade, Jefferson's project for the discovery of the Missouri River, its sources and what lay beyond languished. But it cannot have been far from Jefferson's thoughts and dreams—nor, for that matter, was his worry of foreign advances in lands on the margins of American sovereignty.

Jefferson knew about Jonathan Carver's expedition to the interior west of Lake Superior, and he had followed the progress of Peter Pond, Samuel Hearne and the explorers of Canada. He knew of Cook's voyages, and Vancouver's too. Jefferson knew of the surveys that David Thompson was making along the Missouri River in 1798. In fact, in 1801, President Jefferson and his cabinet showed the liveliest interest in what Thompson had done in his traverse between Lake Superior and the Red River.[17] This backwater of American fortunes was formerly the porous northern boundary of Louisiana, but now it seemed strangely on the front line of American political aspirations, standing against encroachments of the Canadian and HBC traders coming down from the northeast and north. Whether by way of Chicago, Detroit, Green Bay, Michilimackinac or Duluth, the Canadian traders and the aboriginal agents with whom they worked controlled this informal empire. American foreign policy had to leap forward to meet this newest frontier threat. Just as alarmed Spanish officials in St. Louis had known that the Canadians and British were trading in the Mandan and Hidatsa villages and intended to progress west from this point, so did the ever-wary Jefferson know and prepare to respond.

But after the 1798 disclosure of the Thompson expedition, it becomes difficult for the historian to trace documentary proof with any hope of authenticity. Jefferson and his cabinet could hardly have known, for instance, that the North West Company partners had determined, by hard-headed resolution at their rendezvous in 1800, to advance what they called the Columbian enterprise—the plan to take furs gathered in the west to the Pacific coast, where they would be transported to Chinese ports. Nor could the Americans have known that by fall 1800, Duncan McGillivray and Thompson were laying plans to broach a Rocky Mountain pass the very next year, attempted the same and were shortly followed by deputies who succeeded. If there was a leak from the corporate decision-makers, it is not recorded. McGillivray kept the western plan of trade and discovery a secret as best he could. The Hudson's Bay Company clerk at Fort Edmonton, however, was a possible breach in security, for he followed the project with the closest interest, as his post journal notes (strange as it may seem, information about such expeditions passed freely, even among trading rivals), and the execution of such a scheme would not have escaped the notice of the US administration for long. American traders at Michilimackinac, or agents in London or Montreal, could have given away the vital secrets, and US diplomats or consuls may have passed such intelligence to Jefferson.

Even if the signs had not been read, fourteen months before Jefferson proposed an expedition of discovery to Congress in January 1803, the warning signal had come from Alexander Mackenzie.[18] Mackenzie's book was the stimulus. Jefferson, inaugurated as president on March 4, 1801, became the conduit.

William Goetzmann, the student of US science and military statecraft in the American west, contends that a number of interlocking requirements are demonstrated in the president's grand scheme for western exploration. "Judging from his intense interest in the Canadian explorers and his somewhat reckless sponsorship of the Ledyard and Michaux expeditions, it is clear that Jefferson's great passion was for an American transcontinental exploring expedition in the interests of science, commerce, and strategic geopolitics." That explains why Jefferson made his arrangements with Lewis as his personal secretary, intending him to become expedition commander. After all, Lewis possessed excellent knowledge of the western country.

The matter was gelling in Jefferson's mind. In December 1802 he spoke—casually, says Goetzmann—to the Spanish ambassador to the United States, Don Carlos Martínez, Marqués de Casa Yrujo, about some western reconnaissance organized by the United States. He wondered if Spain would object if a small caravan were to "go and explore the course of the Missouri River in which they would nominally have the objective of investigating everything which might contribute to the progress of commerce; but that in reality it would have no other view than the advancement of geography."

Here was sly Jefferson at work. The Spanish ambassador was onto it directly. He could not accept the scheme as commercial or scientific; rather, he assumed there was a grander (but covert) design in view. He wrote to the foreign minister in Madrid: "The President has been all his life a man of letters, very speculative and a lover of glory, and it would be possible he might attempt to perpetuate the fame of his administration ... by discovering or attempting at least to discover the way by which the Americans may some day extend their population and their interests up to the coasts of the South Sea."

The ambassador responded to Jefferson's query by sending dispatches to the garrison commanders at New Orleans and Santa Fe, instructing them to stop Lewis's expedition at all costs.[19] And Spain, by royal resolution, determined to "check the progress of Captain Merry's commission, if he tries to carry it forward within the dominions of the king."[20]

In subsequent years, between 1804 and 1806, Spanish authorities in the southwest sent four expeditions from Santa Fe to find and halt "Captain Merry Weather" and his exploring party. They were not successful. They did, however, locate another expedition, that of boundary surveyor Thomas Freeman and botanist Dr. Peter Custis, who, with a party of soldiers under Captain Richard Sparks and one servant (twenty-four men in all), had been sent by Jefferson to explore to the southwest. On July 29, 1806, a Spanish detachment of cavalry under Francisco Viana, from Nacogdoches, turned these Americans back on the Red River in today's eastern Oklahoma.[21]

Jefferson continued to send small parties of soldiers into Texas and into Florida. Spanish authorities became distraught, impatient with Jefferson's insistence on sending military-civilian probes into Spanish territory. Aaron Burr's mysterious activities in Louisiana were known to Spanish authorities, and they added these to their list of grievances when further news arrived about activities undertaken by William Dunbar, Zebulon Pike, General James Wilkinson and their agents. But it was "Captain Merry" that they wanted most of all, for his expedition was intended to skirt the northern perimeter of New Spain, and they believed it was also meant to incite the indigenous people against the Spanish.

However, Jefferson did not have his eyes on the Spanish mines of New Mexico. Vancouver's explorations on the Pacific coast, including Broughton's examination of the Columbia River, were far more alarming to Jefferson and the State Department than any other foreign quest for control there. He wanted to keep foreign powers, Britain and Russia, out of the Columbia. An expedition of discovery and transit would surely make official footprints where none currently existed. He needed a technical requirement so that Congress would back the expedition, and control of the trade with the aboriginal people of the western territories provided the cover. Jefferson put it this way in his memoir of Lewis:

> In 1803, the act for establishing trading-houses with the Indian tribes being about to expire, some modifications of it were recommended to Congress by a confidential message of January 18th, and an extension of its views to the Indians on the Missouri. In order to prepare the way, the message proposed the sending an exploring party to trace the Missouri to its source, to cross the Highlands, and follow the best water-communication which offered itself from thence to the Pacific ocean. Congress approved the proposition, and voted a sum of money for carrying it into execution. Captain Lewis, who had then been near two years with me as Private Secretary, immediately renewed his solicitations to have the direction of the party. I had now had opportunities of knowing him intimately. Of courage undaunted; possessing a firmness and persever-ance of purpose which nothing but impossibilities could divert from its direction; careful as a father of those committed to his charge, yet steady in the maintenance of order and discipline; intimate with the Indian character, customs, and principles; habituated to the hunting life; guarded, by exact observation

of the vegetables and animals of his own country, against losing time in the description of objects already possessed; honest, disinterested, liberal, of sound understanding, and a fidelity to truth so scrupulous that whatever he should report would be as certain as if seen by ourselves—with all these qualifications, as if selected and implanted by nature in one body for this express purpose, I could have no hesitation in confiding the enterprise to him.[22]

No man received a finer introduction or, in actuality, a finer memorial tribute, than Jefferson gave Lewis.

As a potential explorer, Lewis was deficient in scientific training, especially in astronomy (a necessary requirement for scientific geographical inquiry and surveying) but also in botany. These shortcomings could be rectified. Jefferson sent Lewis to Philadelphia, where he received training from Andrew Ellicott in making astronomical observations in woodland country. Lewis also prepared for his venture by collecting books on western travel and exploration, deciding what arms would be required for the expedition, determining how many personnel would be in the party, and planning what supplies and equipment would be necessary. He thought in larger, more expansive terms than General Clark would have proposed, and he erred on the side of more numbers, equipment and supplies. He saw the Corps of Discovery as a large venture into the wilderness.

Lewis invited William Clark, brother of General Clark, to accompany him, and William Clark, who was approved, gladly assented: "I will chearfully join you—and partake of the dangers, difficulties, and fatigues, and I anticipate the honors & rewards of the result of such an enterprise, should we be successful in accomplishing it. This is an undertaking fraited with many difficulties, but My friend I do assure you that no man lives whith whome I would perfur to undertake Such a Trip &c. as your self."[23]

In 1811, when the Philadelphia attorney Nicholas Biddle, then piecing together the history of the Lewis and Clark expedition in preparation for its intended—and long-delayed—publication, asked Clark what his relationship in rank and standing was to that of Lewis, Clark replied that Lewis had written to him stating that he would in every way be equal "in rank pretensions &c &c." On these conditions Clark agreed to make the expedition. He was a little disturbed when his commission arrived stating that he was to be a second lieutenant of artillery when he had expected to become a captain of engineers: "[M]y feelings on this occasion was as might be expected." But from Lewis he received assurance of being on equal footing, and besides, says Clark, the commission in question was only required for the purposes of military law, so that authorization existed so soldiers could be punished, essential for the discipline of this expedition. Lewis had the absolute command, for he outranked Clark, but as to the actual command and conduct of the expedition, the matter was never raised.[24]

We now retrace our steps to the point where Congress gave authorization for this expedition; it does not happen quite as quickly as Jefferson leads us to believe. In 1803, Louisiana had not yet fallen like a ripe apple into the lap of the United States, and Jefferson kept up steady communication with territorial governors on the question of aboriginal resistance and instability on the western frontiers. He sent William Henry Harrison, governor of the Indiana Territory, advice on how to deal with the frontier menace. The Mandan and Hidatsa of the Missouri needed to be brought within the realm of American commerce, said Jefferson. He knew their villages were the locus of the plains trading world and certainly the focus of Canadian and Spanish influence and intrigue. An exploring expedition would aid American trade. Thus, in a confidential message to Congress, dated January 18, 1803, Jefferson spelled out modifications to the act for establishing trading-houses and extended it to include the Mandan, Hidatsa and other nations on the Missouri. "This is an occult document, not easy to find in print," bemoaned Elliott Coues, who edited an 1893 edition of Lewis and Clark's writings, but he eventually tracked it down in an 1846 appendix to presidential messages and addresses. "Its astuteness and wariness," remarked Coues, "may be judged by the words with which it concludes:"

> The interests of commerce place the principal object within the constitutional powers and care of Congress, and that [it] should incidentally advance the geographical knowledge of our own continent, can but be an additional gratification.

The nation claiming the territory, regarding this as a literary pursuit, which it is in the habit of permitting within its own dominions, would not be disposed to view it with jealousy, even if the expiring state of its interests there did not render it a matter of indifference. The appropriation of two thousand five hundred dollars, "for the purpose of extending the external commerce of the United States," while understood and considered by the executive as giving the legislative sanction, would cover the undertaking from notice, and prevent the obstructions which interested individuals might otherwise previously prepare its way.[25]

The estimate was based on a calculation by Lewis and called for mathematical instruments; arms and extraordinary accoutrements; camping gear; medicines; transportation equipment; and presents for the indigenous people encountered along the way. It also called for pay for hunters, guides and interpreters, and for silver coin for use on the spot and contingencies. Jefferson took all this advice at face value, and he had no reason to doubt the necessity of anything that Lewis had requested.

Working closely with the president to prepare the confidential message to Congress, Lewis was wildly unrealistic about the expedition's costs. In the end it consumed $38,722. But $2,500 was something Congress could accept, and as a political reality it sufficed. So did the idea that it was the Missouri River and the aboriginal people of the Missouri that had to be connected with the trade of the Mississippi. That was an innocent, easy-to-appreciate goal for a commercial expedition.

What it masked was the westward plan of national mission and destiny, of which Jefferson was principal architect and strategist. Stealth was necessarily his method. In this confidential message, Jefferson had told Congress that he intended to propose an "intelligent officer with ten or twelve chosen men ... [who] might explore the whole line, even to the Western Ocean." In the end, the number of men in the Corps of Discovery rose to about three times that estimate.

So Jefferson continued to advance his expedition, and he chose to do it as a military reconnaissance, thus giving it a national imprimatur. This military expedition would penetrate to lands claimed by two powerful nations, France and Britain, with a third, Spain, having control to the south and southwest, and a fourth, Russia, in possession of Alaska and perhaps points on the northwest coast to the south, toward Nootka Sound. "Should you reach the Pacific Ocean," ran Jefferson's instructions to Lewis, "inform yourself of the circumstances which may decide whether the furs of those parts may not be collected as advantageously at the head of the Missouri ... as at Nootka Sound, or any other point of that coast."

Jefferson sought a diplomatic cover for this expedition, and he requested passports for the expedition leaders from Britain, France and Spain. The British willingly complied, not wishing in any way to resist an American scheme that had been couched in agreeable scientific terms of discovery. They had their minister in Washington, Edward Thornton, issue the passports directly. Lewis and Clark carried these documents on their westward journey, showing them to the North West Company at a later time (by copy sent to the posts on the Assiniboine River) as proof of their undoubtedly innocent intentions and valid credentials.

As noted earlier, Jefferson approached Spanish officials for the French permission, inasmuch as the Spanish were administering the region on behalf of France. But the Spanish ambassador, Don Carlos Martínez, objected. Jefferson ignored this and pressed ahead with his request to Congress. On February 28, 1803, Jefferson got the approval he needed, Congress's approval.

Lewis had with him a map on which he was to place his newfound particulars. Albert Gallatin, Secretary of the Treasury under Jefferson, described it in a letter to Jefferson on March 14, 1803:

> Capn. Lewis leaves this place tomorrow morning. I have requested Mr. King [Nicholas King, who had been the surveyor of Washington City] to project a blank map to extend from 88 to 126 degrees West longitude from Greenwich & from 30 to 55 degrees north latitude; which will give us the whole course

of the Mississipi and the whole coast of the Pacific ocean within the same latitudes together with a sufficient space to the North to include all the head waters of the Port Nelson River. In this I intend to insert the course of the Mississipi as high up as the Ohio from Ellicot's, the coast of the Pacific from Cook & Vancouver, the north bend of the Missouri & such other of its waters as are there delineated from the three maps of Arrowsmith & from that of Mackenzie, and the Rio Norte and other parts of the Missouri from Danville & Delisle. The most difficult point to ascertain is the latitude of the sources of the Rio Norte; and it is important in order to know whether there would be any danger in following a more southerly branch of the Missouri than that delineated in Mackenzie's [by Arrowsmith] & in the manuscript transcribed from Mr. Thornton's [English cartographer] map by Cap. Lewis. I mention this because you may perhaps have some book at Monticello, which might throw some light on that subject or at least on the latitude & longitude of Santa Fe.[26]

From Governor Harrison, Jefferson obtained a copy of John Evans's map of the Missouri, the first accurate eyewitness map of the Missouri River. This map was compiled from information given by fur traders and *engagés* Evans had met on the river upstream from Fort Charles. The details were recent and fresh, for the young Welsh explorer, working for James Mackay of the Missouri Company, had done his investigation in 1796–97. It was a road map of the first seven hundred miles of the Lewis and Clark expedition, says W. Raymond Wood, who studied and re-created the Evans map.[27]

Mackay, too, supplied details and added to the map that Evans had drawn. On January 10, 1804, Mackay paid a call on Lewis and Clark, who were now in their 1803–4 winter quarters, Camp Dubois, opposite the point where the Missouri flows into the Mississippi. Mackay gave advice and answered questions. Some few days later, Jefferson sent the copy of the map he had received from Harrison to the explorers at Camp Dubois. It was, said Jefferson in his covering letter to Lewis, "a map of a Mr. Evans, a Welshman, employed by the Spanish government for that purpose, but whose original object I believe had been to go in search of the Welsh Indians said to be up the Missouri."[28] (Jefferson, we know, was aware that Evans had been an emissary of the Welsh people to the Welsh Indians from information gained through intermediaries in London, Philadelphia and Washington.) Jefferson knew that the Evans map showed the Yellowstone River, the land of the Crow Nation, the great falls of the Missouri, the Shoshone territory, the Rocky Mountains and even that strange-looking fort on the north bank of some great river of the west beyond the Rockies. This map, though fragmentary in detail, had to be given every consideration. Sometime later, Mackay made his own notation to the Evans map. Lewis and Clark therefore had not only the map in question, but also Mackay's further, last-minute advice.

What did Lewis and Clark learn from the Evans map? That there were various place names, many of them in French, as befitted the first discoveries by Europeans or the advice from Canadian fur traders and engagés. Various rivers and their tributaries are shown with names. And to the far west there were the various ranges of mountains with valleys showing aboriginal homelands or places of dominance. Beyond the last, westernmost range was a wiggly river and on it a strange configuration denoting undoubtedly a fort or post. Was this a Russian trading post? Across the mountain ranges and the valleys of the same, Clark printed clearly the word "conjectural." The Rocky Mountain details Evans had supplied needed clarification, confirmation.

But the map gave them an inkling about some tributaries of the Missouri. Even before they left Camp Dubois, they had on their minds the Yellowstone River, fabled but largely unknown and unverified. Not on the Evans map, but added by Clark at Fort Mandan, was the track used by the Big Bellies, the Gros Ventres as the French called them, that went overland from the Mandan villages right to the foothills. They had to glean the possibilities of what lay west from the local indigenous people, and all these still had to be verified on the spot.

The Gros Ventres told of the Nor'Westers' track from the Catepoi River (actually the Qu'Appelle River, a fork of the Assiniboine River that empties to Lake Winnipeg). Mackay had reckoned this led to the Mandan villages, a distance of about 150 miles in a north-northwest direction.[29] This was useful information, indicative of how much time might be required—seven or eight days—to get a message across to the Canadian and HBC traders on the Assiniboine and Souris rivers. Then, too, there was advice tendered by St. Louis traders who had ventured north and west. One such was Pierre-Antoine Tabeau, who had wintered at the Arikara villages in 1803. He was a valuable source for Lewis and Clark.[30]

On May 14, 1804, the expedition embarked from Camp Dubois and commenced a form of discovery hitherto unseen in North American history. Unlike anything the Canadians did by canoe or by land, and different again from Spanish expeditions by horse or by ship, the Americans proceeded by heavy river barge against a four- or five-knot current. Even more significantly, this was an expedition of scientific discovery with a heavy emphasis on documenting observations and recording facts. Progress was nothing short of methodical. Diplomacy with the many aboriginal nations could not be hurried; it consumed its own necessary time.

The full 1804 season for exploration had passed and they found themselves at the Great Bend of the Missouri, with many hazards of the heroic enterprise still ahead. They would soon need to adopt the style and technique of Mackenzie and those who had come before. The heroic age of North American exploration, of small parties lightly equipped, did not die with Lewis and Clark upriver from that first year's travel; quite the reverse. And down to our own times, individuals and small groups continue the tradition of seeking out the wilds of the continent, making hazardous journeys (some of them foolhardy enterprises) using lighter and better equipment designed to make such ventures less hazardous.

Chapter 9

NORTHERN SHADOWS
ACROSS THE TRAIL:
NOR'WESTERS MEET
LEWIS AND CLARK

O n November 28, 1797, five years before Lewis and Clark set off on their expedition, David Thompson, a twenty-seven–year-old Londoner of Welsh parents, set out to the south, on horseback, from a post on the Assiniboine River known as Fort Montagne à la Bosse (latitude 49° 40' 59" north; longitude 99° 27' 15" west). He was heading for the Mandan and Hidatsa villages about which he and his bosses had heard and knew so much. He knew the exact latitude

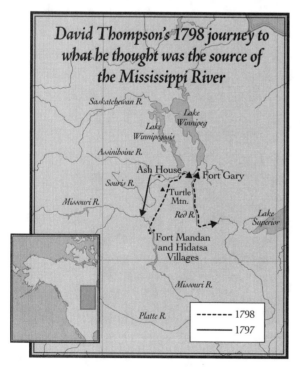

David Thompson's 1798 journey to what he thought was the source of the Mississippi River

Saskatchewan R.
Lake Winnipegosis
Lake Winnipeg
Assiniboine R.
Ash House
Souris R.
Fort Gary
Turtle Mtn.
Missouri R.
Red R.
Lake Superior
Fort Mandan and Hidatsa Villages
Missouri R.
Platte R.

------- 1798
——— 1797

and longitude of his place of departure, for he had made the precise calculations and placed the fort on his ever-more-detailed map. Bit by bit he was putting together geographical facts about how places stood west of Greenwich and north of the Equator. He never travelled light, for carefully stuffed in his packs were several instruments of his profession: a sextant of ten inches radius, with quicksilver and parallel glasses; an excellent achromatic telescope; a lesser one for common use; various drawing instruments; and two thermometers, all made by John Dollond. The surveyor, a measurer of the land, had before him half a continent to examine.

Some years earlier, Thompson, whose prominence grows as our theme progresses, would have preferred to have joined the Royal Navy, but he did not have that prospect because of filled enlistments at the time. Accordingly, he had been taken into Hudson's Bay Company employ in the year 1770. He was strangely unsettled; disaffection stirred in his blood. Given the mathematical education he had received at the Grey Coat School in Westminster, London, he had expected to have greater professional and commercial advancement than had come his way. But the Hudson's Bay Company, indifferent to his aspirations and his pride—and, truth to tell, generally indifferent to exploration and a search for a northwest passage—had sent him as a trader from post to post throughout much of the HBC's northern territory. Maybe, in the end, it was all the fault of the Honourable Company of Adventurers Trading into Hudson's Bay, or, on the other hand, perhaps it was the result of a severe leg fracture that immobilized him and gave him the rare opportunity to perfect skills in astronomical surveying.

In any event, Thompson, disenchanted, bolted from his employer and joined the North West Company as a surveyor. "How very different the liberal and public spirit of this North West Company of Merchants of Canada from the mean selfish policy of the Hudson's Bay Company styled Honorable; and whom, at little expense, might have had the northern part of this continent surveyed to the Pacific Ocean, and greatly extended their trading posts!" So wrote Thompson. To this fair comment, Thompson added this stinging rebuke: "Whatever they have done, the British government has obliged them to do. A short account of the transactions of this company will prove to the public the truth of what I assert, and will throw some light on the discoveries that from time to time have been made."[1]

Already an inveterate, tireless traveller, he was equally a man of science, ethnography and history. The Nez Percés called him "Koo-Koo-Sint," meaning "Star Man" or "He who Shoots the Stars." From the time he began with the North West Company in 1797 until the summer of 1812, he unlocked the secrets of many of the rivers of the west. Details of this were only revealed much later with the discovery of his unpublished *Narrative* (completed 1857); the disclosure of the details of his surveys, notes and maps by his first biographer, Joseph Tyrrell; and more especially through the publication of *David Thompson's Narrative of his Explorations in Western America* by the Champlain Society of Toronto in 1916. But of even greater value are his detailed journals, now in the Archives of Ontario in Toronto.[2]

Thompson, his autobiography tells us, was often as a lad a solitary wanderer among the lanes and passages of Westminster. His favourite pursuit was to go to the Abbey to read august memorial inscriptions to departed British heroes. He was a teetotaller, unusual in the fur-trading line of work, and it is said that he would not trade spirituous liquor to the aboriginals. He had a strong puritanical streak and suffered from taking offence easily from slights, real and imagined. He was not always loyal to his employers. But thoroughness in all things scientific was his byword. Thoroughness invited or necessitated slowness, and Thompson could be deliberate and methodical in carrying out duties entrusted to him (especially when it came to getting to the mouth of the Columbia River). But in his special niche in life of discovering sources of great rivers, he had no equal, charting the Saskatchewan and Columbia, and leaving Lewis and Clark to find the headwaters of the Missouri. He placed his stamp on North American geography like no other human being. His activities in western North America at the time of Mackenzie, of Jefferson and of Lewis and Clark provide us with a reminder that surveying and commerce went hand in hand with the westward-expanding destiny of the North West Company.

Thompson enrolled in the service of the North West Company upon his arrival at Grand Portage on July 22, 1797. He quickly became a true corporate asset. At that precise time the partners knew of the recent Spanish attempt to sustain a post in the Mandan and Hidatsa villages at the Great Bend of the Missouri River. Later that year they sent a party to determine if the "Spaniard" (John Evans) was still there. They feared reprisals. They understood that this was territory of Spanish claim if not sovereignty, and they doubtless knew of France's aspirations for Louisiana and the United States' zeal to try to control western lands beyond territory already under US sovereignty. In order to lobby London to protect their commercial interests on the Missouri, as well as to look after their own trade interest, including the collecting of debts run up by vaga-bond freemen and independent or quasi-independent traders such as Jusseaume and Desmarais (who were supplied from the Assiniboine posts), they needed a surveyor to define the land and the location of villages. Thompson had never traded this far south, so we can conclude that he was sent essentially on a double duty: reconnaissance and surveying, especially the latter. He was the only man available for this particular assignment. Thompson's findings were important, even if they found what the Canadians and British might not be able to hold at a peace conference (depending on certain unforeseeable twists that diplomats at some future juncture might put on where the boundary should extend west-ward from its present northwest extremity). Knowledge was power, a means to shape trade and sovereignty in this contested borderland.

At the 1797 Grand Portage rendezvous of the North West Company, Thompson received urgent instructions from Mackenzie and William McGil-livray to locate the headwaters of the Mississippi River and thus, critically impor-tant in relations with the United States, determine the position of the source of the Mississippi in relation to the 49th parallel. That line of latitude was not then the boundary, but for more than half a century it had been widely mentioned by representatives of France, Spain and Great Britain as the proper boundary. The managers of the North West Company hoped they could prove that the Mississippi rose south of the 49th, for this would indicate the northernmost extremity of Spanish-held Loui-siana. They intended to continue to exploit that fur-bearing region as much as Anglo-American arrangements would allow.

William McGillivray, principal director of the North West Company from 1804 to 1821, presided over a trade empire that stretched from the Saguenay to beyond the Rocky Mountains. Determined to find a practical canoe route to the Pacific, he pressed forward the explor-ations commenced by his brother Duncan McGillivray and David Thompson. In 1805, he appointed Simon Fraser to take charge of operations "beyond the Rocky Mountains." McCord Museum of Canadian History

Existing maps of the upper Mississippi were vague and often incorrect, and at the time peace was made between Britain and the United States in 1783, those who crafted the terms of the peace were quite in the dark about this matter of the boundary. In Thompson's words, "the commissioners on the part of Great Britain were two honest well-meaning gentlemen, who knew nothing of the geography of the countries interior of Lake Ontario, and the maps they had to guide them were wretched compilations." One map, Faden's of 1773, wildly pictured the interior as composed of rocks and swamps, quite uninhabitable for humankind; another, Mitchell's map, was incomplete, lamented Thompson. He did not think much of Pond's mapmaking either. The particulars Pond placed on his map were based roughly on compass bearings and distance measured, and these were notoriously inaccurate (it was this that had led Pond to place the western end of Lake Athabasca very near the Pacific Ocean and thus caused the mistake made by the North West Company and the esteemed hydrographer Alexander Dalrymple, who assumed the proximity of Lake Athabasca to Cook's Inlet, Alaska—a mere one hundred miles distant). These inaccurate renderings of geography by Pond irritated Thompson, who despised Pond's lack of scientific abilities and detested his record as an alleged murderer of at least one fellow trader. Pond sat "at the elbow" of the American commissioners, writes an annoyed Thompson in his *Narrative*.

Such maps gave Mr Peter Pond who was personally acquainted with those countries every advantage. A boundary line through the middle of Lake Champlain, and thence due west would have been accepted at that time by the United States for it was more than they could justly claim, had a gentleman of abilities been selected on the part of Great Britain, but at that time North America was held in contempt. To the United States Mr Pond designated a boundary line passing through the middle of the St. Lawrence to Lake Superior, through that lake and the interior countries to the northwest corner of the Lake of the Woods; and thence westward to the head of the Missouri [Mississippi], being twice the area of the territory the States could justly claim. This exorbitant demand the British commissioners accepted, and [it] was confirmed by both nations. Such was the hand that designated the boundary line between the dominions of Great Britain and the territories of the United States.

Thompson disliked those who made boundaries by diplomacy. He thus distrusted British policy makers, who (to his way of thinking) invariably gave away territory to the United States at the expense of Canada and British dominions. He saw these territorial giveaways as one long chronicle of neglect, indifference and even complicity with American officials. He knew he was not alone in his views and liked to quote Edmund Burke, the celebrated member of parliament and critic of British administrations and cabinets: "There is a fatality attending all the measures of the British Ministry on the North American Colonies."[3]

Under Mackenzie's and McGillivray's instructions, Thompson had to make sense of the geographical muddle created by the diplomats and find the source of the Mississippi (not the Missouri). He also had to determine the exact position of the villages where the Mandan and Hidatsa people cultivated corn, hunted buffalo and traded horses.

The North West Company directed Thompson to proceed from Grand Portage and take the customary voyageurs' route to Lake Winnipeg, then continue to the posts of the Assiniboine, especially to Fort Montagne à la Bosse, which was under the control of John McDonell. The latter, as we saw in Chapter 7, knew all about Mackay and Evans, who represented the Spanish quest to control the Mandan and Hidatsa villages, and he knew all about Jusseaume and the Nor'Westers' problems on the Missouri. He knew about the Assiniboines and Crees, and of their rivals, the Sioux; he knew, too, of the Hudson's Bay Company's opposition posts.

Fort Montagne à la Bosse (Hump Mountain) was one of several posts that the Nor'Westers, and the French before them, had put up on the Assiniboine River.[4] A well-built, pallisaded post, beautifully situated on a high bank overlooking the river and a vast plain opposite, it was also a sportsman's paradise.

The gentlemen of the establishment, and all visitors, had bison, antelope and deer at their disposal for hunting, and it was, besides, a great place for horse racing—"all of which cannot fail to render this a very pleasant situation," said one trader, Daniel Harmon.[5] This "enchanted abode" was stoutly stockaded, and with reason. On one occasion the gates were shut tight, for about eighty lodges of Crees and Assiniboines, "who threatened to massacre all the White People who were in it," had encamped about the fort, "and those blood thirsty Savages had the boldness to throw Balls over the Palisades & tell our People to gather them up, as they might probably want them a few Days hence."[6] The traders were able to deal with these threats, and, as excellent horsemen, they were able to outrace any Cree or Assiniboine who came after them when they left by a gate.

This post and Fort Esperance or Qu'Appelle, which lay upstream and west where the Qu'Appelle River joins the Assiniboine, served as advance bases for the 150-mile trek to the Mandan and Hidatsa villages at the Great Bend of the Missouri River. The paths from each fort joined south of the Souris, or Mouse, River and then crossed the plains or cut down into the treed valley, skirting west of the shoulder of Turtle Mountain to the destination. A journey of eight days each way would be a very quick one; it could take as long as fifteen or twenty days depending on the weather. Some northern travellers preferred wintertime for their journeys, for not only were there no mosquitoes (a terrible plague in summer except when the winds blew), but the ground was firm and thus better for horses. In spring, summer or fall, depending on the rains, traders would find their horses badly caught up in the stiff black mould of a soil. Besides, in the winter the rivers and ponds would likely be frozen (though not always, as Harmon found nearly to the cost of his life), and at that season, too, the weather was less fickle, less prone to the torrential rains that could come in the violent summer season. The trading parties might find some protection down in the forested valleys, and from time to time a welcome chinook raised the temperature magically to that of the temperate zone. Even so, it was hazardous travel for traders, horses, dogs and all who travelled with them, including aboriginal men, women and children. A customary party would number nine or ten humans and at least half a dozen horses. The dogs pulled travois, on which cargo and children would rest. There was always a threat from hostile Sioux, Assiniboines and others.

From these two posts, Nor'Westers and independent traders had been crossing to the Mandan and Hidatsa villages and independent traders for some years prior to Thompson's departure in November 1797. For example, a party of free traders left for the Missouri in December 1793; another group went in 1795. The Hudson's Bay Company may have sent men about 1795 too, but their names are lost to history. The next expedition, Thompson's, was a notch above its predecessors. To repeat, it had purposes, scientific, commercial and political. It aimed to find the source of the Mississippi River, to determine what posts existed in northern Louisiana, to encourage the Mandans to trade to the north with the Company, and to locate the projected boundary.

Thompson had as his guide that old hand Jusseaume, fully fluent in the Mandan tongue and equally conversant with that nation's ways. With the party travelled Hugh McCracken, a good-hearted Irishman, ex-artillery man and North West Company trader of some consideration in the Assiniboine River area. He knew the paths to and from the Mandan villages, too. The hard-driving and gluttonous French Canadians accompanying them as brawn of the trade had travois, two dogs to each travois, and they swore at the dogs and beat them unmercifully. Thompson necessarily had a servant with him.

The elements did not favour the travellers. The weather was terribly cruel to Thompson's two horses (one for himself, the other for his baggage) and a third belonging to Jusseaume. The visibility decreased and dropped to zero in snowstorms. Members of the party were lost in such blizzards until the others lit fires to guide them to the thickets where they took shelter. Thompson, ever curious to all around him, wondered what could cause such winds, such desolation, in the middle of the continent. "The sky was as obscure as night," he recorded on December 19, "the roaring of the wind was like the waves of the stormy seas on the rocks."[7] The thermometer plummeted to 37 degrees below zero Fahrenheit on one occasion. The men did not dare venture from their shelters. A few days later they pressed on. The going was warmer but slower in the trees. The great traverse across Turtle Mountain was delayed when Jusseaume lost his way. Even the most experienced traveller could wander in these parts. Thompson employed his compass as a guide, but the rest of the party put no faith in scientific instrumentation. They preferred to trudge instinctively, relying on the lay of the land, and to traverse from point to point as best they could.

Friendly Assiniboines had warned them about the Sioux menace. In consequence, Thompson and the others took every precaution. They advanced cautiously, often keeping down in the breaks, out of sight. On one occasion they spied a dozen or so mounted riders on a distant ridge. Their hearts pounded when they imagined them as Sioux in search of intruders. Thompson counted heavily on the Assiniboines as his friends. They were strong in numbers in the lands across to the Missouri and had longstanding trade links with the Mandans and Hidatsas. They went to the Missouri for horses. "They are friendly to the white people, a fine looking race of men and women," he recorded, "but most noted horse thieves of the horses of other tribes. It is said of a Yorkshireman, 'give him a bridle and he will find a horse,' but these will find both the bridles and the horses."[8] The Assiniboines, like many other tribes, lived in dread of the Sioux.

After thirty-three days (of which ten had been fair travelling, the rest hideous beyond belief), Thompson, Jusseaume, McCracken and the rest of the party reached the Missouri River at a point six miles above the uppermost of the Hidatsa villages. The river was frozen, so they followed its course downstream to their destination, the high banks sheltering them from the gales. Whereas La Vérendrye had found six villages altogether when he had visited in 1738, now there were five, said Thompson (Lewis and Clark would find the same number of villages six years later), and the location of these villages differed from those of La Vérendrye's time. There was upper Hidatsa, Big Hidatsa, the *Sakakawea* site (which Thompson describes as the lesser village of the Mandan), Black Cat of "mostly all Mandans," and "Deapolis," the principal village of the Mandans. Raymond Wood calculates that the villages were more diverse in composition than hitherto imagined, with a larger Hidatsa population than previously estimated. Whereas the *Narrative* indicated there were separate tribes in separate villages, Thompson's journals show more mixing, less separation and more composite communities.

At the village of Matootonha (now the Deapolis site) Jusseaume introduced Thompson to a Mandan chief whom Thompson calls "Big White Man," but who, in fact, was Sheheke ("Coyote")—known to Lewis and Clark as Big White. He was to render valuable assistance to the US explorers at Fort Mandan during the winter of 1804-5, for which he received a medal. Sheheke, with Jusseaume as his interpreter, accompanied Lewis and Clark to Washington, DC, and was later killed in a fight with the Sioux. Big White well suited Sheheke as a name, Thompson thought. He records in his *Narrative* that he told the chief that he, Thompson, did not concern himself with trade (which was patently false). This somewhat surprised Sheheke, "until told that my business was to see the countries, converse with the Natives, and see how they could be more regularly supplied with Arms, Ammunition and other articles they much wanted: this he said would be very good; as sometimes they were many days without ammunition. Our things were taken in, and to myself and my servant, Joseph Boisseau, was shown a bed for each of us."[9]

Thompson was delighted to be in the villages, for his curiosity was excited by the sight of these communities containing an agricultural population, the first such he had seen among indigenous people. He hoped to learn much of the past of these tribes, and he got Jusseaume and McCracken to help him gain as much information as he could. His journal recounts the total number of houses and tents in each village. He noted the circular nature of the houses, each the same, with a dome roof. He estimated that the Mandans had 190 houses and a population of 1,520 souls, from which they could muster about 220 warriors. The Hidatsas had 128 houses and seven tents, with a population of 1,330, of which 190 were men fit for war. "I have heard their force estimated at 1000 men, but this was for want of calculation." These were people of corn, bison, deer and horses, and they had gargantuan sexual appetites. The curse of the Mandans, said Thompson, was want of chastity, and he hoped missionaries might soon deliver them by benevolent providence. His *Narrative* is the baseline from which ethnographers and historians start their quest. His journals can also be profitably studied by historians attempting to reconstruct the demography of Native America,[10] and both journals and *Narrative* provide vital information about these people and villages just prior to Lewis and Clark's arrival.

During his travels among the villages of the Great Bend of the Missouri River, Thompson pressed the aboriginals and traders for details about the tributaries of the upper Missouri River. He wanted to know where these tributaries lay in relation to one another, and what their courses were. What distance—in days of travel—were the mountains away from the Big Bend? Were there mountain passes beyond?

In the course of his travels, on January 5, 1798, he came to Manore village, named for a Frenchman who had lived there for fifteen years and become, as it were, naturalized. Here Thompson found some Crows, natives of the Rocky Mountains south of the headwaters of the Missouri River. The importance of the encounter did not escape Thompson. He conversed with two Crows and quizzed them on certain geographical details about their distant country. On the basis of their advice he drew a sketch map of their country. Here as elsewhere he took advice from aboriginal people, made changes and corrections to his draft map as required and had the final version executed, as he puts it, or authenticated by the Crows. "They appeared to be very intelligent, as almost all the Natives of the Mountains are—[they] fully comprehend with a little explanation the drift of all my Questions, answered direct to them. When done I gave them a little Tobacco—for which they were thankful. I then returned to my quarters."[11]

Thompson had gained valuable trade intelligence, useful for future Nor'Wester quests to the Yellowstone for trade and exploration. But would there be a chance to use this information? All he could do for the present was take notes and advise his superiors upon his return.

Thompson completed his trade on the Missouri River, took his observations for longitude at noon when the weather was clear, and called on the Mandans, Hidatsas and others to come to the Assiniboine posts to trade. Better to draw them to existing posts than put up another establishment in a disputed borderland. The lesson provided when Evans took Jusseaume's post was not forgotten, nor were the hassles to get compensation. The Nor'Westers started their return on January 9, 1798, and after experiencing terrible storms and thick, high, drifting snow, they reached the post on the Qu'Appelle River nearly four weeks later, on February 3. The relief was palpable. "Thank God," Thompson closed his journal entry for that day.

Now came the time to gather thoughts, write up his journals and arrange his observations of longitude and latitude. It was also time to report to his superiors and prepare to survey the rest of the Assiniboine River and then the Red River to the Mississippi—all part of a grand cartographic scheme to show the lands and waters from Sault Ste. Marie and Lake Superior to the Mississippi and Missouri rivers, including the Red and Assiniboine. "The Gentlemen [traders of the North West Company] laugh at this Scheme as a piece of Quixotism," Thompson concluded his Missouri River narrative and added philosophically, "how far I shall succeed, Heaven Knows."[12]

Thompson took a brief respite, rare for him, but soon his attention shifted to his next assignment—finding the source of the Mississippi. He set off from Fort Montagne à la Bosse in very late winter, or earliest spring, for the Mississippi headwaters, a flat, soggy and reedy country with ill-defined topography.

In the course of his odyssey, on April 27, Thompson discovered one of the headwaters of the Mississippi River at Turtle Lake. Thompson decided Turtle Lake, with its waterway exiting to the southwest, must be the source of the Mississippi. (It is now generally understood that Lake Itasca is the source.) He also found that the source of the Mississippi was at least a hundred miles south of the 49th parallel.

The significance of his contributions to science and cartography were not lost on Mackenzie, whom he met at Sault Ste. Marie on May 28. Thompson wrote: "Here I had the pleasure of meeting Sir Alexander Mackenzie, the celebrated traveler who was the first to follow down the great stream of water flowing northward from the Slave Lake into the Arctic Sea, and which great river bears his name …. Upon my report to him of the surveys I had made, and the number of astronomical observations for latitude, longitude, and variation of the compass, he was pleased to say I had performed more in ten months than he expected could have been done in two years."[13] William McGillivray, Mackenzie's true partner in the western quest of the Nor'Westers, a fellow agent and principal partner of the North West Company, met Thompson at the same time. Mackenzie and McGillivray had arrived at the Sault to negotiate a treaty with some Ojibwas for a fur post there. They requested that Thompson continue his surveys, pointing out the need to survey the area of Lake Superior

The fulcrum of the Canadian fur trade, Fort William, on the northwest shore of Lake Superior, was the western depot of the Nor'Westers for their interior business. The post was originally called Fort Kaministiquia but was renamed Fort William after 1807 in honour of William McGillivray. Library and Archives Canada, C-24733

in and around Grand Portage, then the depot of the company. The implication of this is clear to us now: Mackenzie and McGillivray wanted to know if Grand Portage was north or south of the international boundary, which had been set along the Pigeon and Rainy rivers by the Treaty of Paris in 1783. They were seeking to avoid US trade duties and impediments. As it turned out from the surveyor's work, Grand Portage was south of the border. In consequence, in 1801 the Nor'Westers shifted their location and built a new depot at Kaministiquia (named Fort William after 1807, in honour of McGillivray). As a result of Thompson's discovery of a source for the Mississippi River, it was similarly concluded that diplomats had previously been wrong in thinking that the 49th parallel intersected that river's headwaters.

Thompson's journey to the Great Bend of the Missouri River showed that the Mandan country was not good beaver territory and that the Mandan and Hidatsa were not trappers. There was good trade there, as Thompson and Alexander Henry the Younger (there in 1806 to investigate) found, but the Mandans preferred to hunt bison and to trade in corn and horses. Thompson's reports indicated richer beaver country lying farther west, in the foothill valleys of the Rocky Mountains. The headwaters of the Missouri and the Yellowstone rivers needed to be explored and investigated, but the distances (and the costs of

travel and trade) were staggering in comparison to the transit from the Assiniboine River to the Mandan and Hidatsa villages. The commercial motivation
drove the Nor'Westers to seek out trade along the Yellowstone.

In the years after Thompson's visit to the Mandan and Hidatsa villages,
Nor'Westers continued to transit to the Missouri from their posts on the
Assiniboine. We also hear of many other Canadian traders travelling to the
Mandans and Hidatsas and a few of them going on to the Yellowstone River.
The Canadians were broadening their trade networks, enlarging their alliances
with aboriginal people to the southwest. In 1801, for instance, Charles Le Raye
from Canada, with six men, attempted to reach Osage country and open trade
with that tribe. They were set upon by a war party of Brulé Sioux and taken
prisoner or enslaved. They were brought up the Missouri to the Arikara villages
on April 22, 1802. Le Raye was slave to a Sioux chief. Soon after, another Canadian trader, Pardo, came to this place and adroitly made an arrangement with
the chief for a combined trading expedition, one that would benefit the Sioux as
well. That spring, the newly freed Le Raye went with Pardo to the Yellowstone
and on to the Powder River. They even entered the mountains and came to
the Big Horn River on October 5. Retracing some of their route, Le Raye and
Pardo wintered at the junction of the Big Horn and Yellowstone and came back
to the Missouri River on April 24, a remarkable expedition in generality.[14] If Le
Raye and Pardo could do it, Nor'Westers would surely follow.

Between 1799 and 1804 there was a deadly struggle in progress between
the Nor'Westers and their new rivals, the XY Company, headed by Sir Alexander Mackenzie. Simon McTavish, director of the North West Company,
and Mackenzie had been at war over the direction the Nor'Westers ought to
take, and this forced the split of 1799. There was no room for two Caesars in
Rome, a Montrealer observed of this fight for corporate control.[15] Thus one
of them—Mackenzie—had been obliged to remove himself from the scene.
Mackenzie never took kindly to being run over roughshod by a rival, and so
it was with McTavish, who was equally difficult, older, more experienced and
better connected among the financiers of the fur trade. He had opposed any
conciliation with Mackenzie, even though it might cost him dear. Competition
between the Nor'Westers and the XY Company was keen, and the amount

of liquor and other trade goods that spilled into the Assiniboine posts, some destined for the Missouri and Yellowstone trade, increased dramatically. New posts were put up, often side by side, in direct competition. In one location the Nor'Westers had as neighbours not only the XY Company, but also the Hudson's Bay Company. Journeys from the Assiniboine and Qu'Appelle river posts across to the Mandan and Hidatsa villages became more frequent.

The intense rivalry dissipated with the death of Simon McTavish in July 1804, and Mackenzie and his friends received invitations of mergers and compensation. By the end of the year, a merger under the old name of the North West Company was arranged.[16] And with McTavish's death and the rise of his nephew William McGillivray to ranking authority in the reorganized firm of McTavish, McGillivray and Company (a pre-eminent firm in the North West Company), conditions became more propitious for implementing Mackenzie's Columbian enterprise.

Now the La Vérendrye vision of trading west to the foothills, into the Rockies and on to the Pacific, as restated by Thompson, could be revived. Accordingly, in late 1804, Charles Chaboillez, partner in charge of the Assiniboine River, employing an unexpected surplus of men and goods in his region (made possible by the corporate merger), decided to deploy them to the Mandan and Hidatsa villages on the Missouri, and beyond to the Yellowstone River. A "hands off" agreement with his HBC opponents on the Assiniboine River, who promised that they would not establish any new outposts in that quarter, gave Chaboillez this newfound freedom of action. His arrangement coincided with Lewis and Clark's expedition. Indeed, it may well have been intended to thwart American attempts to wean the Mandans, Hidatsas and other tribes away from the Canadian traders. After all, to date the Nor'Westers had successfully checked the Spanish and the Missouri Company. They might not be able to stop the passage of the Corps of Discovery, but they could certainly assert their pressure and influence among the tribes. They came to trade and to make commercial friends.

Lewis and Clark had reached the Mandan villages of the Missouri on October 21, 1804. They had made a remarkable passage upriver to that place, passing by Zenon Truteau's post and then that of James Mackay. Diplomacy with various tribes had been difficult, unexpectedly so. "The leaves are falling fast," they noted in their journals, and as far as they could see were herds of buffalo—fifty-two herds, in fact, as counted on October 19. With friendly Mandans and abundant food at the disposal of the Corps of Discovery, the villages were the perfect place to spend the winter. They selected a winter camp the day after their arrival and named it Fort Mandan, which, like Alexander Mackenzie's Fort Fork on the Peace River of 1792–93, served as their advance base for travel westward. They were, it has been said, in "discovered" country, for Canadian and Spanish traders had been there over the course of more than half a century,[17] but they needed to find out about the Yellowstone River and how it linked to the pass or passes leading to headwaters of a river or rivers running to Pacific tidewater. As soon as the ice broke up the next spring, they would commence their travels upriver toward the foothills and ramparts of the Rocky Mountains. Mackenzie started from 56° north latitude; Lewis and Clark from 47° north latitude. History was running parallel courses north and south of the 49th parallel, and the Americans were keeping well south of the line. Jefferson wanted no interference with his scheme and no trouble with the northern traders or the British either.

Less than a month after Lewis and Clark established Fort Mandan, a party of Nor'Westers left Fort Assiniboine on November 11, 1804. Chaboillez had hired a prominent freeman named Jean Baptiste Lafrance, a veteran of Missouri travel and a trader with recent connections with the Hudson's Bay Company, to serve as guide, clerk and especially interpreter—in all, a necessary person to the success of any such travels to distant, strange parts. Lafrance and Jusseaume had acted as blood brothers, working in tight relations among the Mandans since 1793. In this strange corporate combination, one had networked for the Canadian firm; the other for the British.

Chaboillez called twenty-year-old François-Antoine Larocque to lead the expedition.[18] A contemporary, Abbé Morice, described Larocque as "a well-educated person, of great courage and fecund in deed." Canadian-born, he was fully bilingual but preferred writing in English. He was in Mackenzie's XY Company when called upon by Chaboillez to make his expedition. In fact, he had been in the trade for at least four seasons, probably escaping what are now called teenage years. Like Mackenzie, he had been thrust into business early and was already a clerk, serving in the Upper Red River Department of his firm. Mackenzie knew him personally and knew he was likely to conduct his affairs to the credit of the company. In addition to the trustworthy Larocque as leader and Lafrance as guide, clerk and interpreter, Chaboillez selected the clerk Charles McKenzie, whose journal survives from this expedition, and four *voyageurs*.

All the goods were transported on horseback this time. In the packs were trade items and favours of friendship. The men stole out of camp, their departure undertaken quietly and casually so as not to arouse the attention of the opposition traders or the Assiniboines.[19] Larocque's expedition made a safe crossing to the Mandan and Hidatsa villages.

Clark noted their arrival at Fort Mandan on Tuesday, November 27: "Seven traders arrived from the fort on the Assiniboine River from the N.W. Company one of which Lafrance took upon himself to speak unfavorably of our intentions." Lewis and Clark considered Lafrance's utterance an outrage. It prompted the Americans, on the defensive and worried about rivals, to register a protest with the principal, Larocque. The latter, along with McKenzie, "was informed of the conduct of their interpreter [Lafrance] and the consequences if they did not put a stop to unfavorable and ill-founded assertions &c. &c."[20]

On November 28, according to American account, we find Larocque giving out medals and flags. This brought to the surface the Americans' complaint that the Nor'Westers would "incur the displeasure of their great American Father ..."[21] Threatening words, these, and uncalled for in the circumstances, but empires were intersecting; patriotisms were running high and in conflict.

Lewis held the opinion that the North West Company planned to make a permanent establishment there. The Nor'Westers, he reasoned, having carried on an illicit commerce to the Missouri when it was under Spanish domination, would take advantage of the changed status of Louisiana, now in US hands, and continue trade or even increase it. The Canadian traders would trade south of the line, on American territory, in keeping with Jay's Treaty and privileges. Lewis believed that such treaty terms did not apply to Louisiana.[22] He wanted to run trade relations on his own hook, setting forth the new needs of the day by firm American control.

On November 29, Larocque and one of his men came to visit Lewis and Clark. Clark records that "we informed him [Larocque] that we had herd of his intentions of making Chiefs &c. and forbid him to give Meadels or flags to the Indians ..."[23]

Now there was a rapid about-face. The American captains reconsidered their aggressive and prosecuting position. They had second thoughts about this high-handed diplomacy. Clark recorded in his journal entry for that same date that Larocque denied having any such intentions. "We agreed," wrote Clark (in reference to the discussion with Larocque on the one hand and between Lewis and Clark on the other), "that one of our [the Corps of Discovery's] interpreters [Toussaint Charbonneau[24]] should speak for him [to the Hidatsas] on Conditions he did not Say any thing more than what tended to trade alone ..."[25] In other words, Larocque was enjoined to speak only of commerce; his lips were sealed by Charbonneau's words on matters of a political purpose, including alliances with the Hidatsas or Mandans. How successfully this measure could work is anyone's guess. Certainly it tells us a good deal about the nervousness of Lewis and Clark. They were fighting for control of the borderland.

Historians have often got the particulars of these transactions wrong, or have painted misleading pictures. Told from Larocque's position, the story is less strident, less worrisome on either side. On November 27, Larocque recorded in his journal:

> Returned to the Bl[ac] Cats [village]. Cap't. Lewis Return'd from above & stopp'd at the Lodge. Spoke to Charbonneau about helping, as Interpreter in the trade to the big Bellies, he told me that being Engaged to the Americans, he Could not Come without leave from Capt. Lewis & desired me to speak to him—which I did. Capt. Lewis told me that as he had no business for Charbonneau, but at times during the winter, he had no objection to his helping me, upon Certain Conditions, which agreeing to, Charbonneau promised me, that he would Come next morning.

Charbonneau did not return to Larocque as he had promised. The weather was bad for one thing. For another, Charbonneau had been caught up with Lewis and Clark. "In the Evening [of the 29th]," Larocque continues,

> the weather cleared, [I] went to see what was the Reason he did not come, was very politely Received, by Capts. Lewis & Clarke & pass'd the night with them. Just as I arrived, they were dispatching a man for me, having heard that I Intended giving Flags & medals to the Indians which they forbid me from giving in the name of the United States, saying that Government, look'd upon those things, as the Sacred Emblem of the attachment of the Indians to their Country. But as I had neither Flags, nor medals, I Ran no Risk of disobeying those orders, of which I assured them.[26]

Larocque denied Lewis and Clark's accusations. He countered their charges. He was well-mannered and patient. He had, he explained, his own mission to accomplish as related in his own journal. Why not travel together? Larocque requested that he be allowed to join the expedition. Lewis and Clark did not give him an answer. Larocque's suggestion stopped them in their tracks. On January 20, 1805, Larocque was again in camp, renewing his request. Lewis and Clark now refused. They did not want Nor'Wester help at this stage.[27] Gary Moulton correctly states: "The captains had no intention of helping Larocque to acquire, at United States government expense, geographical knowledge that would be of advantage to the North West Company and the British Government."[28]

The clerk Charles McKenzie, a young Scot—described many years later by Sir George Simpson of the Hudson's Bay Company as "a queer prosing long Winded little highland body"—who was with Larocque, describes the intercourse with Lewis and Clark as being most friendly. His account provides details of many acts of kindness on the part of Lewis and Clark that are not recorded by others.[29] McKenzie's journal is also rich in detail about the arrival of the Canadian trading party and their warm reception by the Mandans and

Hidatsas: "We proceeded on our journey—arriving within sight of the Missis-souri [sic], the natives flew in crowds to meet us, wishing us joy and congratu-lating themselves upon our appearance as traders amongst them—these were the *gros Ventres* nation [Hidatsas]." There were four HBC traders there at the time. They had been held hostage by some Assiniboines until they bought their way to freedom, thus diminishing their stock in trade. The Mandans, says McKenzie, had not entered into their views. The HBC trading prices had not appeared agreeable to them, but they found the Nor'Westers' much more so and consequently sold off all their furs.

"Here we also found a party of forty Americans under the command of Captains Lewis and Clark exploring a passage by the Mississouri to the Pacific Ocean," McKenzie recorded, noting that they had come up the river in a boat of twenty oars accompanied by two pirogues. Their fortifications for winter quarters were already complete. Lewis and Clark, said this Canadian trader, had held a council with the Mandans and had distributed many presents,

> but most of the Chiefs did not accept anything from them. Some time after Captain Lewis with three Interpreters paid a visit to the Gros Ventres village, and went directly to the Serpents Lodge where he passed the night; next morning he came to the village where I was—and observed to me that he was not very graciously received at the upper Village. "I sent word, said he [Lewis], to inform *Le Blet qui porte les cornes* ('the large one who wears horns') that I intended to take up my Quarters at his Lodge—he returned for answer that he was not a[t] home; this conduct surprised me, it being common only among your English Lords not to be at home, when they did not wish to see strangers ... [accordingly] I looked out for another lodging which I readily found."[30]

The Mandans were irked by the failure of the American expedition leaders to give out abundant presents, including ammunition. Charles McKenzie explains: "After haranguing the Indians and explaining to them the purport of his [Lewis's] expedition to the Westward, several of them accepted clothing—but notwithstanding they could not be reconciled to *like* these strangers as they called them:—'Had these Whites come amongst us, Said the Chiefs, with charitable views they would have loaded their Great Boat with necessaries. It is true they have ammunition but they prefer throwing it away idly than sparing a short of it to a poor Mandane.'"[31]

The Mandans admired the explorers' air gun, for it could discharge forty shots out of one load. But "they dreaded the magic of the owners." McKenzie recorded: "Had I these White warriors in the upper plains, said the *Gros Ventres* Chief, my young men on horseback would soon do for them [the Corps of Discovery], as they would do for so many wolves—for, continued he, there are only two sensible men among them—the worker of Iron, and the mender of Guns."

McKenzie further recounts:

> The American Gentlemen gave flags and medals to the Chiefs on condition that they should not go to war unless the enemy attacked them in their Villages. Yet the Chief of the wolves, whose brother had been killed in the fall previous to our arrival, went soon after with a party of fifty men to revenge his death—but not finding the Blackfeet Indians who were the aggressors, or rather having found them too numerous, the party wisely retraced their steps without making an attempt. But on their return having found some Canadians they killed four of them, and raised their scalps, which were disposed, in the course of their traffic, to the Rocky Mountain Indians.[32]

The Hidatsas held unique views on white traders and explorers, and McKenzie's recording of these and other particulars places him high on the list of ethnographers of this nation:

> White people, said they, do not know how to live—they leave their homes in small parties; they risk their lives on the

great waters, and among strange nations, who will take them for enemies:—What is the use of Beaver? Do they preserve them from sickness? Do they serve them beyond the grave? I remarked that the Northern Nations were very industrious and great friends to the white people: "We are no slaves, rejoined the Chief—our fathers were not Slaves—in my young days there were no white men—and we knew no wants—we were successful in war; of the scalps of our enemies they brought many. The white men came, they brought with them some goods: but they brought the small pox, they brought evil liquors—the Indians Since are diminished, and they are no longer happy.[33]

That winter, Larocque and McKenzie continued to live among the people of the Great Bend of the Missouri, and by and large they did so happily. Some threats came from the HBC traders, who they worried intended to do them mischief. Nor'Wester supplies ran low, and those of the opposition rose in value. Some Assiniboines became troublesome, and McKenzie feared they would seize his horses on his way back to the North West Company post on the Assiniboine River.

McKenzie records his last, telling impressions of Lewis and Clark:

Mr. La Roque and I having nothing very particular claiming attention, we lived contentedly and became intimate with the Gentlemen of the American expedition; who on all occasions seemed happy to see us, and always treated us with civility and kindness. It is true Captain Lewis could not make himself agreeable to us—he could speak fluently and learnedly on all subjects, but his inveterate disposition against the British stained, at least in our eyes, all his eloquence. Captain Clark was equally well informed, but his conversation was always pleasant, for he seemed to dislike giving offence unnecessarily.[34]

It was time for departures: the Nor'Westers for the Assiniboine, the Americans for the upper Missouri. McKenzie again:

> The Missouri was free of ice the Second of April. Then the American Gentlemen sent off their twenty oar Boat with the men for the United States; and on the 8th following the Expedition proceeded up the River towards the Rocky Mountains. It consisted of one large perogue; and seven small wooden Canoes, containing the commanding officers, thirty men, and a woman—the woman who answered the purpose of wife to Chabonneau was of the Serpent Nation [Shoshone], and lately taken prisoner by a war party: She understood a little Gros Ventre, in which she had to converse with her husband, who was a Canadian, and who did not understand English—a Mulatto [maybe La Biche who was part French, part Omaha] who spoke bad French and worse English served as Interpreter to the Captains—So that a single word to be understood by the party required to pass from the Natives to the woman, from the woman to the husband, from the husband to the Mulatto, from the Mulatto to the Captain. I was once present when vocabularies were making of the languages of the Mandane Villages. The two Frenchmen who happened to be the medium of information had warm disputes upon the meaning of every word that was taken down by the expedition—as the Indians could not well comprehend the intention of recording their words, they concluded that the Americans had a wicked design upon their Country.[35]

Larocque had been able to get a clear indication of the purposes of the Lewis and Clark expedition. From his many conversations with the American captains he drew two conclusions: first, that the expedition party had been "sent by Government for the purpose of Exploring the N.W. Countries, to the Pacific Ocean so as to settle the Boundary Line between the British & American territories" (a point never raised publicly by Jefferson or anyone else in the US government, but an undoubtedly important measure of statecraft); second, that the purpose of the expedition was likewise to "make it known to the Indians, on the Missouri, & the adjacent Countries that they are under, the Government of the big Knives, who will protect them & supply them with all their wants, as long as they shall behave as dutiful Children to their Great Father the President of the United States & which has been the Continued subject of their Harangues to the Indians, throughout the Winter." Again, this was a more imperial purpose than was ever indicated even in the instructions to Lewis and Clark.[36]

Larocque now states the new view that Lewis and Clark had adopted: "They showed me their passports & Letters of Recommendation from the French, Spanish & British Ministers at the City of Washington, which say the object of their voyage is purely scientific, and Literary, & no ways Concerning, trade, desiring all persons under their Respective Governments, to aid & assist, that party as much as in their power lies, in Case they should be in want of any thing in the Course of their Voyage." They carried drafts and letters of credit for use if necessary. Lewis and Clark, Larocque noted, had left Philadelphia in the spring of 1803, had come down the Ohio River and wintered at St. Louis. It had taken them a whole summer to come to the Mandan villages.

They made treaties of peace with all the Indian Nations they saw on their Road, excepting the Sioux's, with whom they were very near Coming to an Engagement. They made presents of a Flag, Medal, Chiefs Cloathing, tobacco, knives, Beads & other trinkets, to Every Chief of the Indian nations, which they saw, but have not given a single shot of ammunition.

They told me that it was not the policy of the United States to Restrain Commerce & fetter it, as was the Case when Louisiana belonged to the Spanish, that we & all persons who should Come on their territories, for trade or for any other purpose, will never be molested by an American Officer or Commandant, unless his behavior was such as would subject an American Citizen himself to punishment. Nor will any trader be obliged to pay for permission to trade, as was formerly the Case under the Spanish, as no Exclusive privilege will be granted. Everyone shall be free to trade after his own manner.

Lewis and Clark had gone on to talk about the American system of factories, then being experimented with in the Old Northwest, and made reference to Detroit as an example. The intention was to stop trade *en derouine*—that is, trade by circuit traders. The Americans intended to fix the trade at several locations they could control, managing the business in liquor, arms and ammunition.[37]

Nor'Westers continued to transit to the Missouri—one or two parties a year—and to press toward the Yellowstone in imitation of Le Raye and Pardo. From one trader who never went on such a venture, we find clues about the North West Company intentions as of 1805. It all boiled down to exploration and trade.

That year, Daniel Harmon, who kept a fine record of sixteen years in the country, received orders from Charles Chaboillez at Fort Montagne à la Bosse to travel with six or seven Canadians and two or three aboriginal guide hunters "to go on a Discovery." As designated leader, Harmon was buoyed by the prospect of the journey, with all its new vistas and wider horizons. He intended to start about the beginning of June. The projected route would take him first to the Mandan villages on the Missouri. Then his party would shape a course toward the Rocky Mountains in the company of some Mandans who every spring were known to go that way to meet indigenous people who came to traffic with them from the other side of the Rockies. From this rendezvous point they would make their way back home, if all went well, in November. "Mr. Chaboillez's motive for sending [me] there is in hopes that we shall discover a country abounding in beaver." Harmon became ill that spring. Not fatally so, but he had to set aside the prospect of a grand voyage of discovery with him as leader.[38]

It fell to the seasoned Larocque, who had quickly returned to the Assiniboine post from the Mandan and Hidatsa villages, to go in Harmon's stead. On June 2, Larocque and his party left Fort Montagne à la Bosse for their exploration of the Yellowstone. Larocque calls his travels of 1805 "going on a voyage of discovery to the Rocky Mountains."[39] The North West Company continued to place a high value on the Mandan and Hidatsa villages and the trade to the west to the Yellowstone River country. The Mandan and Hidatsa villages became abundant in items acquired from traders or from other aboriginal people who were in the vicinity of commercial establishments. The residents of these villages were keen on trade, and they were quite opposed to the Nor'Westers venturing further afield. As Charles McKenzie noted, "Mr. La Roque who was to ascend the Missouri upon discovery was opposed in these views by the Indians who insisted upon his return to Red River …. They said that if the white men would … extend their dealings to the Rocky Mountains, their villages would be the sufferers. They not only would lose the benefit which they had … derived from that trade but that … as the Rocky Mountain Indians would obtain arms they would become independent and insolent in the extreme." Not all information that reached Larocque was of this sort, but the evidence is strong that the Mandans and those near them did not want to see their enhanced position weakened.

Larocque made his journey with men of the Crow Nation as his guides.[40] He went to the sources of Heart River, then up the Little Missouri and to the Badlands. He marched westward to Powder River, and then he turned south, descending the Little Horn and then the Bighorn. The expedition reached the headwaters of the Yellowstone River, which James Mackay may also have reached ten years earlier.[41] Larocque found goods that the Crows had purchased from the Spanish. He followed the Yellowstone on his homeward track, then passed the Little Missouri and back. This was the last known Canadian venture to the Yellowstone River. American trade below the Mandan villages was sufficient to point out the rising tide of American influence. Gros Ventres told Larocque of fourteen small American boats downriver, below the villages.

That summer of 1805 Lewis and Clark were making their way west, and Manuel Lisa and other traders out of St. Louis were soon to follow. The North West Company threw its energies into the Rocky Mountains in higher latitudes, pushed to the heartland of present-day British Columbia in a place they called New Caledonia, and left the upper Missouri to the traders of St. Louis, who in any event, for years after, sold furs via Canadian links and purchased Canadian goods used in the trade. The Yellowstone project died as far as the Canadian traders were concerned. American political pressure didn't drive them out of this country, which at one time they were commercial masters of. Profit and loss dictated their actions.[42]

Contemplating their future prospects in the headwaters of the Missouri and the Yellowstone, the leaders of the Corps of Discovery had much to ponder. Clark especially, but also Lewis, left the Missouri villages with rich details on their draft maps about what they might find in their travels farther west. Clark, using advice from Mackay, had noted the track of the Nor'Westers from the Assiniboine River and stated it to be 150 miles in length. He knew of their intentions toward the Yellowstone. He had noted, too, the war trail of the Gros Ventres, which crossed overland toward the Yellowstone River, even to the foothills of the Rockies. The facts and figures that Clark had to record suited his personality and character, involving no judgmental position or opinion. He gathered his data from aboriginal chiefs, from interpreters and from Canadian traders.

Lewis, by contrast, saw the political and the geopolitical. If Clark noted that the Yellowstone was a subsidiary stream of the Missouri higher up, 220 miles west of Fort Mandan, Lewis looked on it differently. "If the Indian information can be relied on," he reasoned, "this river waters one of the fairest portions of Louisiana, a country not yet hunted, and abounding in animals of the fur kind." As David Freeman Hawke has said, Lewis grasped the decisive importance of where the Yellowstone joined the Missouri. The United States, said Lewis, must build a post there to check the expansion of the Nor'Westers. "If this powerful and ambitious company are suffered uninterruptedly to prosecute their trade with the nations inhabiting the upper portion of the Missouri, and thus acquire an influence with those people, it is not difficult to conceive the obstructions which they might hereafter through the medium of that influence, oppose to the will of our government or the navigation of the Missouri."[43]

Chapter 10

LEWIS AND CLARK TO
THE PACIFIC AND RETURN

W e retrace our steps. At Fort Mandan that cold and long winter of 1804–5, Clark pored over the drafts of his map and examined his various drawings and numerous notes. The geographical and other scientific data he had at his disposal seemed nothing short of prodigious. He reviewed all that Mackay, Evans and Soulard had indicated on their maps. What treasures these charts were. He compared all these findings with what he knew already of the course of the Missouri from Mackenzie's maps, and Thompson's, too, as provided by Gallatin. He readied his great map to be sent eastward, hopefully into secure hands. He laboured with a cartographer's precision. Meanwhile Lewis, the literary scholar, prepared his report for the president, measuring achievements to date against expectations of progress to that point in time and space.

It was time to take stock. Lewis and Clark and their party had gathered precious evidence at the Mandan and Hidatsa villages: the power and influence of the North West Company had been confirmed in undeniable detail,

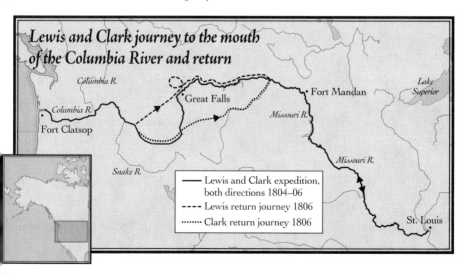

Lewis and Clark journey to the mouth of the Columbia River and return

Columbia R.

Great Falls

Fort Mandan

Lake Superior

Columbia R.

Missouri R.

Fort Clatsop

Missouri R.

Snake R.

—— Lewis and Clark expedition, both directions 1804–06
- - - - Lewis return journey 1806
········ Clark return journey 1806

St. Louis

giving American authorities increased intelligence about foreign activities and intentions. Canadian traders, Lewis and Clark revealed, intended to cross to the upper reaches of the Yellowstone River, cutting right across the Missouri River by way of the villages. All such evidence as Lewis and Clark had gathered showed the dominance of the Nor'Westers and indicated the potential for subversion of US interests in that quarter and even farther to the west and southwest.

Neither the official history of the expedition (compiled by Nicholas Biddle and published in 1814, of which more presently) nor any summary reports, such as that of Sergeant Patrick Gass, one of the expedition members, give more than a hint of the North West Company's prominence and possibilities. But Lewis, who spent his Fort Mandan winter of 1804 and 1805 in deep and inquisitive study of all the known details collected from near and far—from aboriginal sources and Canadian traders—sent east to Jefferson what can only be described as telling intelligence. Corporal Richard Warfington and his squad were detailed to return to Washington, carrying the dispatches and scientific specimens to the president. Although at first this squad was to have been sent sometime before the winter set in, it had been delayed at Lewis and Clark's call, and the information it carried eastward was now more complete, more vital in its particulars.[1]

Lewis compiled an extensive geographical report on the Missouri River, a handsome complement to Clark's 1805 map, which was likewise prepared at Fort Mandan.[2] Lewis included conjectural material about the Yellowstone River gleaned from aboriginal evidence, postulations that awaited confirmation. Based on the assumption that indigenous people could travel twenty-five miles a day, some of Clark's maps refer to distances as so many days' travel. Lewis was preoccupied with the rivers and creeks that flowed into the Mississippi and the Missouri rivers, their sources, the quality of the lands, the apparent face of the country through which they passed, the width and distance of their entrances from each other, and other details. Not least, he was interested in the information supplied by traders, aboriginal people and others, and to these he added "our own observations."

Guiding Lewis and Clark at every turn was Mackenzie's *Voyages from Montreal*. Mackenzie's account, David Nicandri attests, on the basis of close inspection, was "a methodological and literary model for Lewis and Clark." The tactics, the arguments, the analysis of terrain and topography, even Lewis's style of field instruction bore a direct resemblance to Mackenzie's. Lewis, backing Jefferson, argued that the United States needed a more hard-nosed commercial policy to check the Nor'Westers' influence on the northern frontier. If the American merchant could not venture into this area, "the field is at once abandoned to the Northwest company."[3] In short, a contest for commercial empire underscored Lewis's discoveries, reinforcing his and Jefferson's predilections and, in turn, reinforcing the pre-emptive impulse.

Before the American explorers proceeded upriver from Fort Mandan, they had some indication of what waters flowed to the Missouri River. Upstream almost two hundred miles from the Knife River, White Earth River discharged itself on the north side. Here was a stream, navigable by canoe, that flowed southeast out of the plains and was navigable even to its source. Its source was not far distant, though miles or days' travel are unspecified, from a trading post on the South Saskatchewan River. This was quite possibly the Hudson's Bay Company's Chesterfield House or, more likely, either Wills' House or Bealleau's House of the St. Lawrence-based traders North West Company and XY Company respectively.[4] "If this information be correct," wrote Lewis, "it is highly probable that a line drawn due West from the lake of the Woods, in conformity to our treaty with Great Britain, would intersect the waters of this river, if so the boundary of the United States would pass Red river between the entrance of the Assiniboine and Lake Winnipeg, including those rivers almost entirely, and with them the whole of the British trading establishments on the red Lake, Red river and the Assiniboine." This was powerful information, indicating possible future problems with the British. Lewis also noted that, "should the portage between the Saskatchewan and *White earth* river, prove not to be very distant or difficult, it is easy to conceive the superior advantages, which the Missouri offers as a rout to the Athabasca country, compared with that commonly travelled by the traders of Canada."[5] Lewis may not have had his own eye on the old trading ground of Peter Pond and Sir Alexander Mackenzie, but he was pointing out a route, via a soft underbelly, to the Eldorado of the northern trade.

Lewis, we learn through his journal entries and correspondence, at this precise moment was working out what he saw as the problems of the northern boundary, that with British dominions. The problems did not lessen with the new evidence that he had to hand. Rather the reverse. For the tributaries of the Missouri from the north cross the 49th parallel; they run "north-south" rather than "east-west," thereby complicating a merely westward and ideally easier course of the Missouri. Lewis pondered this. The strange duality was that such tributaries could become not weaknesses but strengths. They could become lines of commerce to the rich north country of Pond's and Mackenzie's Athabasca, where beaver was king. Thus if the British agreed that the watersheds of Louisiana were included in American sovereign territory, the Americans would have greater control of and influence in or toward the north country.

On the south shore of the Missouri River upriver from Fort Mandan, the geopolitics were of a different order. Lewis knew that opposite the mouth of White Earth River, three miles upstream, the rapid Yellowstone joined the Missouri. It took its rise in the Rocky Mountains, gathering in waters from a river, as yet unknown, that Lewis speculated might be Río del Norte or even waters from the Gulf of California. The Spanish, as a protective measure, had kept the aboriginal people of the area unarmed. Speculating about the Yellowstone in reference to the geographical position of the Missouri, Lewis was led to believe that it lay farther north than previously imagined. Thus he worried that the border between US and British dominions might intersect the Missouri River. The question of how to influence the indigenous people of this area caught his imagination. Lewis thought that his newly won allies, the Mandans, might be persuaded to move to the mouth of the Yellowstone if an establishment were made there. "The N.W. company intend to form an establishment in the course of the next summer and autumn, on the Missouri, near these people, which, if effected, will most probably prevent their removal to any point which our government may hereafter wish them to reside at."[6] Lewis, then, recommended that the government put up a fort, a new place for the Minetares, or Big Bellies, to wean them away from the North West, XY and Hudson's Bay companies, all of which, informants had told him, these people traded with, even though they were 150 miles distant. The pages of Lewis's report to Jefferson are peppered with references to the Canadian traders, demonstrating time and time again the dominance of trade links from the north.

As to the traders themselves, Lewis had these comments (original spellings maintained):

> The traders who frequented the nations below [Fort Mandan] heretofore were such as purchased the privilage of tradeing with the different nations, and as their terms of trade was not certain for any length of time, did not interest themselves in diswadeing the Indians from any vicious act which they might have had in view, being at all times jellous of their temporary provilegeis—The Traders who visit the Seoux are from different quarters and in Course jealous of each, which gives the Indians an unfavourable opinion of all the whites &. The Trade[r]s who frequnt the Mandans & Minetarres are from two British Companies NW. & Hudsons Bay. Those British Companies have carried their jelousy to Such hite, as to give the Indians a bad oppinion of all whites from that quarter, they not only do every thing in their power to Injur each other, but oppose each other in the presence of the Indians, several instancs of violance on the property & persons of each other & one Deaths not long since. [7]

These and other details, carried east on April 7, 1805, by the keel boat under the command of Corporal Warfington and his squad, found their way to the eagerly awaiting Jefferson.

Jefferson also learned from Lewis that the Corps of Discovery might reach the Pacific and return to the head of the Missouri, or even to the Mandan and Hidatsa villages, by the end of the season's discoveries. Optimism ran high; geographical obstacles were minimized.

The day after all the reports, charts and specimens were on their way to St. Louis and to Philadelphia, Lewis and Clark, with three sergeants, twenty-three privates and five non-military personnel—Clark's black slave York;

frontiersman and scout George Drouillard; Touissant Charbonneau, the half French Canadian, half Shawnee sign-language master as interpreter and guide; the Shoshone Sacagawea and her two-month-old Baptiste—moved upstream in two pirogues and a number of cottonwood dugouts. Far better than a bulky and hard-to-manoeuver keel boat, they were easier to progress with upstream. The party was smaller now, closer to the number best suited for light and more rapid travel. Still larger than anything a Mackenzie or Thompson would have headed up, it was now of more manageable proportions than when it had set out on May 14 of the previous year.

"This little fleet," remarked Lewis on April 7, "although not quite so respectable as those of Columbus or Capt. Cook, were still viewed by us with as much pleasure as those deservedly famed adventurers ever beheld theirs ...." Lewis had a charming sense of occasion here, and he had an undoubted sense of his place in history—rightly earned as events were to prove. He knew he was, with Clark and the others, at the lead edge of discovery, and thank goodness he had the sense to write down how he saw himself in time and space. There is much Mackenzie in him, especially in his forward-looking aspect—which Thompson lacked. Lewis sensed destiny but was more fulsome in his remarks than Mackenzie. He added: "We were now about to penetrate a country at least two thousand miles in width, on which the foot of civilized man had never trodden; the good or evil it had in store for us was for experiment yet to determine ... [yet] entertaining as I do, the most confident hope of succeeding in a voyage which had formed a da[r]ling project of mine for the last ten years, I could but esteem this moment of my departure as among the most happy of my life."

As an expedition leader, Lewis had characteristics that were Mackenzie-like in nature, including independence of thought, presence of mind in pressing circumstances, willingness to take risks, robustness in health, clearness of purpose and vision, inquisitiveness and zeal. Like Mackenzie, too, he was conscious of self, appreciative of his own role in the direction of affairs. But in other ways he stands apart from the canny wee Scot. Lewis was far less selfish than Mackenzie. He was prepared to share equal rank and even station with Clark, perhaps to pacify or placate his companion. Mackenzie, by contrast, selfishly fails to give credit to his lieutenant, Alexander MacKay, and hardly mentions him in his book. Lewis, too, had a far more anxious personality than Mackenzie, a factor of possible relevance in the death of Lewis. Like Mackenzie, Lewis faced despair and despondence in the aftermath of his great exploration. Mackenzie experienced sleeplessness, delusion, visions and an unsettled character; for months he was unable to write up his journals for publication. Lewis had a similar disposition, and he never got to the literary task that Jefferson had trusted him to complete as an imperishable record of the Corps of Discovery.

Can the fact of the matter be that Mackenzie defined his own space and Lewis was answerable to a higher purpose? Undoubtedly, for Mackenzie was leading the North West Company in its western progression, whereas Lewis was a servant of the state. Mackenzie was trade, Lewis the army. And yet within the separate spheres of each, these two explorers stand in attractive juxtaposition, and the mind races to think of what they might have talked about had they ever met.

The river temperature remained cold. The elements were not kind: the wind cut at them cruelly, and the rain drove at the men. A week out from Fort Mandan, Lewis and Clark and the party of discoverers came to a place they called Charbonneau's Creek, for Charbonneau had once been this far up the river. Lewis said that they now were as far upriver as French traders might have ventured, though he did report that two Frenchmen might have lost their way and gone a few miles farther up.

Now they were at White Earth River, pointing northeast to its source and the Canadian and British traders' posts on the South Saskatchewan River. Though this might have been attractive for an examination, Lewis knew it as a dead end and no great stream, though navigable. He preferred and wanted to trace the Yellowstone, so he headed that way, perhaps retracing portions of James Mackay's route or Larocque's. Six days upriver, beyond the Yellowstone's outlet, on the north bank, they came to Poplar River, and they speculated that perhaps it would lead to the Athabasca fur Eldorado "from which the British N.W. Company derive so large a portion of their valuable furs." Farther upstream again was another river—the Scolding, they called it, or the Milk River—another access to the Canadian trade establishments; this was, in fact, the third. It too might lead to fur-rich Athabasca. It too was too short, unsuitable for exploration given the purposes of the expedition. But it was navigable, and Lewis thought that it probably crossed the 49th parallel and therefore might be a source of difficulty between the British and United States governments in the future, should those powers quarrel about navigable rivers crossing international boundaries.

Lewis's fears were unjustified, as events were to prove. But to repeat, his point of view at that time shows that he was constantly conscious that those rivers, streams and creeks running to the Missouri from the north land could be conduits of trade and navigation and possible challenges to the northern perimeter of American jurisdiction.

Just after the middle of the month, on April 19, the Rockies came into view, puny against the horizon, but indicating things to come, difficulties. The explorers needed to find some fork that led to, and possibly through, by way of a portage, the mountain barrier. "So they must determine which fork led to the mountains," writes DeVoto,

> which was the main stream of the Missouri, and they must decide correctly. For if they decided on the wrong one and, going up it, eventually had to come back to the other—then that error "might defeat the expedition altogether." With so much time lost there could be no reaching the Pacific, perhaps no getting across the mountains, before winter. Their supplies being steadily depleted, they would have to go back to St. Louis in failure, the continent uncrossed, no route discovered, Jefferson frustrated, and the foreign and domestic policy of the United States perverted.[8]

In early June, at the mouth of Marias River, which flowed into the Missouri from the north, doubts descended on the party as to whether or not it constituted the main stream. The disagreement was strong enough for the party to divide and to make the necessary reconnaissance, consuming nine days. They undertook an examination of the two rivers, and once they were perfectly satisfied that the southern fork was the primary one, they continued together. They declared the river approaching them from the southwest the Missouri River.[9]

On July 4 the expedition celebrated Independence Day at what is now Great Falls, Montana. The festivities began about four in the afternoon and lasted till after ten. The last of the "ardent spirits" was used up, except for a little reserved for medicinal purposes. A comfortable dinner of buffalo beef with bacon, beans and suet pudding gave Lewis reason to write in his journal: "In short we had no just cause to covet the sumptuous feasts of our countrymen on this day." Private Pierre Cruzatte's fiddle worked overtime, providing music for dancing until a shower of rain put a stop to it. Songs and festive jokes continued, noted Lewis, and the men made very merry until late at night.[10]

Sixteen years earlier, on July 4, 1789, John Kendrick had celebrated Independence Day at Nootka Sound, now only 1,500 miles away. The undiscovered space between the Corps of Discovery and the Pacific coast realm of the Boston traders was closing daily.

The westward march of empire continued at dawn next day. Lewis had noted on July 4: "We all believe that we are now about to enter on the most perilous and difficult part of our voyage, yet I see no one repining; all appear ready to meet those difficulties which wait us with resolution and becoming fortitude." In the distance to the west he could see mountains, a formidable barrier, some covered in whiteness and glitter with the reflection of the sun, some not. The Corps had not yet met with the Shoshones and had no indication whether they might be friendly or hostile. It caused concern, and Lewis began to worry that the size of the exploring party was too few. He therefore concluded not to send a canoe to St. Louis with news of the expedition's proceedings the next spring.[11]

Upstream yet again, they came to the Three Forks of the Missouri and named them the Jefferson, Madison and Gallatin. Once again they deliberated, then reassembled and set out up the Jefferson. On August 12, at its headwaters, located in a small spring east of Lemhi Pass in the Beaverhead Range, they came to one of their goals, "The most distant fountain of the Missouri," Lewis dubbed it. It is a small source, a rivulet flowing out from a cut in the hillside, and if you stand there and look west—or east—all you can see, as far as the eye can reach, are folds of mountains. They were in what Mackenzie described farther north as "a sea of mountains." When I visited the spot, on much the same sort of day as the Corps of Discovery, I was struck by imaginings of the fullness of the despair that must have gripped the American party. Everything Lewis and Clark had hoped for in the way of a navigable passage, even an easy and short portage, was crushed by geographical realities. The explorers had been obliged to set aside their canoes miles before; now they were urgently in search of the Shoshones and their horses. No easy passage this; rather, the opposite. They were surrounded by mountains, Sergeant Gass remarked. These were perpetual ridges more than prominent ranges, and Mackenzie had thought that south of where he had made his transit through "the sea of mountains" the passes would be lower than the 3,000 feet above sea level that he had crossed. He had misled himself and Lewis and Clark.[12]

Sacagawea recognized this country. She assured Lewis that a stream they were tracing was the one on which her relations lived. The distance to these aides could not be far now, and so the spirits of the party were cheered. On August 17, Clark, Charbonneau and Sacagawea encountered Shoshone scouts. Sacagawea recognized her people and her brother, and soon horses were acquired. Clark, disappointed, did not discover a navigable river here. The canyon of the Salmon River was impassable, but Shoshone advice led him to a pass northward out of the Salmon valley "to the great river to the north." At the foot of Lolo Pass, their hunters and guides brought Lewis and Clark, the parties having reunited, to some Nez Percés, who told them of the way to the Columbia River and thence to traders at the sea. The most difficult, hazardous and demanding segment of their voyage was about to conclude. At one point on August 24, Gass scratched a few words in his journal about the difficulties faced by Clark when out on reconnaissance and the impossibility of proceeding along the river by land: "Our guide speaks of a way to sea, by going up the south fork of this river [possibly the North Fork Salmon River], getting on to the mountains that way, then turning to the south west again."[13]

Lewis and Clark came at last to the Clearwater River, and having built five small vessels, they set forth, on October 7, on the stream they had been in search of for so long. The course of the river made for tough going, through and around rapids. On October 16 they reached the Columbia proper—a stream remarkably clear and with many salmon. Various tribes greeted the explorers—Yakima, Wanapam, Walla Walla and Umatilla among others.

"They said we came from the clouds and were not men," recorded Clark of the Umatillas' response. The explorers were in the land of salmon, but they were famished for meat. The tribe sold them dogs for food.

On October 18 the explorers saw a mountain bearing southwest; it was conical in form and covered with snow. Mount Hood stood there in its splendour. It was seen and named by Lieutenant William Broughton, RN, in 1792. Lewis and Clark knew to look for this peak, for it was registered on their maps. They knew that once they passed by this mountain they would have completed their passage of discovery. Everything that came thereafter would be sadly anticlimactic.[14] They knew that they were on Captain Gray's Columbia River and that they were about to attain their goal. The long reach of American empire was joining with the around-the-Horn links of American merchant commerce.

The exploring party passed through the Columbia Gorge, entering that totally different world of the Pacific slope—wet and lush, even soggy, damp and foggy at certain seasons. And daily they were reminded, by the possessions of the aboriginal people they met, that the merchant traders at the mouth of the

Mount Hood was named for Lord Hood, a vice-admiral and member of the Admiralty, by Lieutenant William Broughton, who surveyed the Columbia River in October 1792. The mountain, seen here in an 1848 drawing by H.J. Warre, appeared on British charts long before Lewis and Clark arrived at Pacific tidewater.

Columbia had brought cargoes in exchange for sea otter pelts. This trade had been going on for many years.

It was winter on the northwest coast, and thick fog cut visibility down to a distance of fifty steps. On November 3, some aboriginals told the party that in the space of two days they would see ocean vessels and white people. "The persons who usually visit the entrance of this river for the purpose of traffic and hunting, I believe, are either English or American. The Indians inform us they speak the same language with ourselves and give us proofs of their veracity by repeating many words of English, as mosquito, powder, shot, knife, file, damned rascal, sun of a bitch, etc." Tidal flows also indicated their nearness to the hoped-for Pacific.

The men were weary to the point of exhaustion, hungry and ill-clad. They were at the limit of endurance. Then, near present-day Megler (site of a former fishing village, the northern terminus of the ferry coming over to the Washington side from Astoria), on November 8, the day after the fog lifted, Clark noted in his journal the oft-quoted "Ocian in View! O! the joy." He had every right to say that, even though he was not at the destination quite yet; the effort to get to Pacific tidewater had been demanding. "Great joy in camp. We are in View of the Ocian, this great Pacific Ocean which we [have] been So long anxious to See, and the roreing or noise made by the waves brakeing on the rockey Shores ... may be heard disti[n]ctly."

Clark's ebullience is fetching, attractive—and so much in contrast to the laconic, workaday reporting of Mackenzie and, later in time, Thompson. There was good cause for this elation. The Americans could be content that they had met the president's requirements. But Clark and Lewis would have been glad to have found a ship in which to take a homeward sea journey.[15] Instead they had to settle in for a long, soggy and dangerous winter. During the next week they reconnoitered the immense estuary of the River of the West, so long talked of by Carver and other visionaries.

Clark, bringing together his calculations, estimated by dead reckoning that the expedition was now 4,162 miles distant from its starting point—near where the Missouri flowed into the Mississippi. The explorers had read Mackenzie's *Voyages from Montreal*. They were familiar with the Scot's claim of having arrived at the Pacific in 1793, from Canada, by land, as Mackenzie had put it. Lewis and Clark placed their brands and other marks on trees. "I marked my name, the Day & year on an alder tree .... William Clark, By Land from the U. States in 1804 & 1805." History was repeating itself, but under a different flag in more southern latitudes.

The captains, with only one third of the whole party, travelled to the outer coast at Cape Disappointment, reached by Lewis on November 15 and by Clark three days later. They were near where John Meares had been in his trading vessel in July 1788. Here they made a temporary camp that stood in such a ludicrously stormswept location that the officers determined to winter on the south side of the cape, in a thick, lofty grove of trees on Netul Creek (now Lewis and Clark River), which flowed into the estuary. On that site they built Fort Clatsop, named for the local indigenous people who were their constant aides. Lewis and Clark continued their scientific observations, prepared accounts of their findings and traded with the Clatsops. They passed out peace medals and other gifts. Clark drew some of his maps based entirely on evidence from the Clatsops, who also told him that the Corps had come across the mountains by an unnecessarily difficult route. This enabled them to make a change of plans for an easier return, but in their Fort Clatsop memorandum dated March 18, 1806, they stated that they intended to return by the same route. Somehow this memorandum came into aboriginal hands and then into those of the merchant trader Captain Samuel Hill of the brig Lydia. Hill carried it with him to Canton and then sent it to Philadelphia. This brig, out of Boston, was in the estuary of the Columbia River in the fall of 1805 and again the following spring. On the second occasion, Hill missed meeting Lewis and Clark by a mere two weeks. The Clatsops showed Hill medals left by the explorers, proof enough of the overland conjunction with the Boston traders and the missed opportunity.[16]

The Corps departed their winter haven on March 23, 1806, and proceeded eastward, in places taking different routes from the one by which they'd arrived in order to solve geographical riddles. They crossed the mountains with sixty-six horses. At Travelers' Rest, near present-day Missoula, Montana, the two leaders separated. Lewis went east to the Great Falls of the Missouri and then explored Marias River, already identified as a tributary of the Missouri.

Clark went south to the Yellowstone River and traced it to the Missouri. Both exploring parties—and leaders—had difficulties with aboriginal people. Lewis and his men had particular troubles with the Piegans. He had sought to avoid an encounter, but when a party of Piegans stole guns and horses, a chase ensued, and Lewis shot a Piegan in self-defence. It was a nasty encounter, as are all such.

The Lewis and Clark parties effected their rendezvous and proceeded eastward in greater security. Clark tried to get Nor'Wester Hugh Heney to serve as an intermediary with the feared Sioux, but the expedition continued eastward without Heney.

They reached the Mandan and Hidatsa villages on August 14. There Sheheke consented to go east, with Jusseaume as interpreter. On September 23 they reached St. Louis and a hearty welcome.

They had been gone two years, four months and nine days. It is estimated that they travelled 6,000 miles, an average of seven miles a day, including rest periods. A dinner and ball were held in their honour on September 25.

On the next morning they began their writing—a monumental task, if completed—in a rented room at a St. Louis establishment owned by fur trader Pierre Chouteau. They hoped to complete an account of their expedition, what Clark termed "a vast, Hazardous and fatiguing enterprise,"[17] for all the world sought to learn its secrets, and this epic achievement needed a foundation in documents. They sorted through and arranged the various journal items, ethnographic notes, mineral reports and maps. They put together a catalogue. And they made a plan for future analysis and study.

Lewis's first obligation was to Jefferson, and he wrote to the president: "In obedience to your orders we have penetrated the Continent of North America to the Pacific Ocean, and sufficiently explored the interior of the country to affirm with confidence that we have discovered the most practicable rout which does exist across the continent by means of the navigable branches of the Missouri and Columbia rivers." Certainly they had done all of that, and as pathfinders of empire and commerce they had made the passage, but some historians, including John Logan Allen, counsel that we not read too much good news into the reports Lewis sent the president. It was, Allen suggests, the death knell of a water passage. In this way it completely paralleled what Mackenzie had reported five years earlier, when his book was published. Years of speculation came to a close. Now Jefferson had to review what he had previously said in his message to Congress and delete references to an "important channel of communication with the Pacific."[18]

It would await the railway age to effect the Jefferson design. Geography did not allow a navigable passage through the garden; in fact, nature put up more obstacles than had been even wildly imagined. There was no garden. The overland path, Lewis admitted, would not allow the passage of bulky, brittle or perishable goods. What could be carried? Small items on backpack or horseback was the answer. This was the country of the canoe and the packhorse, not the river barge. Lewis and Clark had discovered the best that was available, the best route across the continent that nature permitted. They had to be content with that. It was less than half a loaf.

If commerce could not benefit or triumph from the Corps of Discovery's explorations, maybe secondary considerations could shine in public acclaim. Jefferson wrote to the French naturalist Bernard Lacépède in 1808 about "addition to our knowledge in every department," and he spoke of the benefits of a voyage of discovery completely fulfilled.[19] The new central mission, in the expedition's afterglow, became scientific. As plans developed for a three-volume expedition report, a document known as the *Conrad Prospectus* was brought forward in Philadelphia on April 1, 1807. Volume one was to be a general narrative, with volumes two and three devoted to ethnography, botany, zoology and other natural phenomena. "In many ways," comments authority James Ronda, "this prospectus was the formal announcement of the new wisdom about the expedition. Jefferson's passage and the failure to find it was lost in glowing promises of memorable scientific advances."[20]

Jefferson's hope for an on-schedule publication of the report suffered numerous setbacks. Fatigue set in on the explorers. Post-expeditionary exhaustion and dysfunction, much like what Mackenzie had faced, took their toll. Jefferson pressed Lewis to bring text forward; the printer waited. The months dragged on. Jefferson grew impatient. "Everyone is impatient" for the work, he wrote to Lewis on August 16, 1809.

Lewis was appointed governor of Louisiana. His political star was now fixed high, but his obligations and worries were growing by the minute, leading to anxieties and derangement that were made worse by his mercurial disposition, worrisome nature and increasingly melancholic state. Meanwhile, there was sniping from the wings. Lewis received 1,600 acres as a gift of Congress for his achievements, and he was much honoured in several ways. Against this preferment and benefit there were unauthorized accounts published, at least one lifting material directly from Mackenzie's *Voyages from Montreal*. One cranky publisher, who thought the American discoverers were receiving too much merit for too little achievement too lately accomplished, denigrated Lewis's feats:

> With respect to the hazardous nature of the enterprise and the courage necessary for undertaking it, candour compels me to say, that public opinion has placed them on too high ground. Mr. M'Kenzie with a party consisting of about one fourth part of the number under your command, with means which will not bear a comparison with those furnished you, and without the *authority*, the *flags*, or *medals* of government, crossed the Rocky mountains several degrees north of your route, and for the *first time* penetrated to the Pacific Ocean. You had the advantage of the information contained in his journal, and could in some degree estimate and guard against the dangers and difficulties you were to meet; ... had government given an invitation, hundreds as daring, enterprising and capable of your Excellency, would have offered to engage in the expedition, and for compensations much smaller than were received by yourself and other persons composing the corps actually engaged in it.[21]

Lewis's suicide at Grinder's Stand on the Natchez Trace, in the jurisdiction of Tennessee, in October 1809 put a stop to any plans for an early completed, authorized book. There are several reasons to conclude that his death was suicide. James Neelly, US agent to the Chickasaw Nation, had found Lewis frequently deranged, in bad health and constantly worried about a war with Britain and the loss of his papers about the expedition to the Pacific. Neelly wrote to Jefferson that it was suicide by two pistol shots—one to the head, the other to the chest. In addition, Major Gilbert Russell, a US Infantry officer, said that twice previously Lewis had tried to kill himself. Jefferson added his conclusion: Lewis had been afflicted, habitually so, by hypochondria. Jefferson was inclined to believe that Lewis died at his own hand. It may have been one thing to lead a transcontinental expedition and quite another to be governor of a territory. There could have been additional medical conditions or disease. Though there is no evidence to support a case of murder, there is overridingly conclusive evidence pointing to suicide—and all those near to Lewis—Neelly, Russell, Jefferson, Clark—thought similarly.[22]

Clark took the sad news very hard, but with sympathy, writing that Lewis, suffering from the heavy use of liquor, being of a hypochondriac nature and undoubtedly being distressed by many obligations as governor of Louisiana, had been overcome by the weight of his mind.[23]

Mackenzie would have understood all of this. Lewis had not produced a line. The scientific results, the most enduring legacy, were further delayed, impossibly obfuscated by the twist of events. The president was resigned to the new state of affairs. To the German naturalist Alexander von Humboldt, Jefferson wrote that "the botanical and zoological discoveries of Lewis will probably experience greater delay, and become known to the world thro other channels before that volume will be ready."[24] Nothing else could be safely said for the moment.

The task of making the journals into a book fell to the steady, practical Clark, but he was not up to writing Lewis's narrative of events. In 1807 he became Superintendent of Indian Affairs at St. Louis, a hugely demanding task. More was in store for this capable fellow, and in 1813 he became governor of Missouri Territory. In the circumstances, the best thing he could do was engage the services of a Philadelphia lawyer and writer of great ability and care, Nicholas Biddle. Even then, Paul Allen, a journalist, completed the work, which was not published until February 20, 1814. Thus there appeared Biddle's account, a record of western exploration befitting the participants and showing the glorious exploits of adventurers. But in a distinct way the true results—that is to say the scientific, ethnographic and geographical results—got lost or had to be dealt with later. Adventure held centre stage for the moment. The west, sadly, lost scientific aura and dignity in the process, and in the eastern imaginings of what that west offered, the scientific results remained blurred. Lewis's death struck a savage blow at science, which depends on published results, and it was a cruel blow, probably inadvertent in its intent, that Jefferson had to take.

Clark remained worried that the North West Company would take possession of the Missouri River upstream from the Big Bend and toward the Rocky Mountains. As late as October 10, 1816, when writing to Jefferson from St. Louis, he spoke of the rich tracts of fine country there that watered an immense space suitable for the fur trade, mining and agrarian economies, but that was still not sufficiently used and populated. Although the section below the Great Bend was being settled fast, the section above that location, the richer portion, still had no American citizens as occupants or even traders since the demise of the Missouri Company in 1811. Clark remained apprehensive "that the British will take possession of that rich Tract by the way of Assiniboine & Saskatchewan rivers as they have done at the mouth of the Columbia." The northern shadows continued to fall over the pathway through the garden. If a large American firm could not be formed to keep out the Canadian threat, danger would ensue, and in his policies as territorial governor, Clark took liberties not in conformity with regulations. In his own words, he explained to Jefferson that he had kept peace among the tribes, but that there was considerable upheaval on the frontier: "The difficulties & responsibilities however were great, and in some instances I was compelled to vary from the principal, and Let the Missouri Tribes at war against those of the Mississippi to prevent the British influence amongst the Missouri tribes as also to prevent a Coeletion which would have destroyed our settlements at a blow."[25] In other words, it served to keep the tribes in rivalry with one another so that they would not form a grand coalition backed by the British.

We return, for a moment, to events in the federal capital around Christmas 1805. At the same time that Lewis and Clark were settling into their bivouac at Fort Clatsop, a deputation from nine different tribes inhabiting the extensive territories on the western side of the Mississippi and along the banks of the Missouri as far distant as 1,500 miles up the latter river was making its way to Washington DC. These chiefs had been invited to take this long journey by Lewis, who had encouraged them to make themselves acquainted with the people and government of the United States, who now considered the immense tract of country from whence they had come as part of Louisiana Territory. The British minister in Washington watched this event, these first rewards of the captains' frontier diplomacy, with interest.[26]

Earlier that same month, on December 3, 1805, Jefferson, in his presidential address to both houses of Congress, had spoken of how aboriginal people were abandoning the ways of the forest and realizing the benefits of agriculture. "Deputations now on their way to the seat of government, from various nations of Indians ... come charged with assurances of their satisfaction with the new relations in which they are placed with us, of their dispositions to cultivate our peace and friendship, and their desire to enter into commercial intercourse with us." The signs were promising from his point of view. Lewis and Clark's preliminary reports were en route, if not already arrived in the capital, when Jefferson wrote: "A state of our progress in exploring the principal rivers of that country, and of the information respecting them hitherto obtained, will be communicated as soon as we shall receive some further relations which we have reason shortly to expect." Before long, Jefferson was able to provide a statistical report on the people of the trans-Mississippi and Missouri.[27] Tabulation and enumeration marched west with empire. The original inhabitants were becoming government statistics. But there was more to this.

Jefferson, using Lewis and Clark as agents of empire, could now reflect on the fruits of his efforts. He had empowered the officers to gather details about the indigenous peoples and to determine their preferences in goods for trade. He intended to wean these tribes away from the Canadian and British traders. Lewis and Clark were to suggest various locations at which a government trading post could be erected, and, true to their obligation, the captains suggested that such a post ought to be put up at the spot where the Yellowstone flowed into the Missouri. Further, in all dealings with aboriginals, Lewis had instructions from the president to exhibit friendship and conciliation. To these initial instructions, dated June 1803, had been added more specific orders dated January 22, 1804. Now that the Americans had become sovereigns of the country, direct commerce could be authorized with the various tribes, "without however any diminution of the Indian rights of occupancy." Now that the Spanish were out of Louisiana and had agreed to withdraw their troops, and now that Spanish and French subjects had surrendered their lands to the United States, said Jefferson, Lewis and Clark were to advise the tribes through whose territory they passed that the United States would henceforth become "their fathers and friends, and that we shall endeavor that they shall have no cause to lament the change."

Discussion of the tragic implementation of Jefferson's Indian policy as it entered a phase beyond cultivating friendship is not within the scope of these pages. Those representatives and leaders of tribes arriving in the federal capital in 1805 came with good intentions. The diplomacy of the Corps of Discovery yielded promising results, and apart from one violent and destructive event on the return journey, often overly magnified in proportion to other proceedings, Lewis and Clark fulfilled Jefferson's estimation of what might be done. As James P. Ronda stresses, these officers were at the moment of dawn in relations with the Mandans, Shoshones, Nez Percés and Chinooks: "In tales repeated in lodge and tepee, in the faces of children paler than their brothers and sisters, in cherished flags and medals, and in individual memories now lost, Lewis and Clark seemed part of the dawn." The Shoshones had thought them Children of the Great Spirit. The Flathead chief Charlot, whom Ronda quotes, put it more darkly, years later: "We were happy when he [the white man] first came. We first thought he came from the light; but he comes like the dusk of evening now, not like the dawn of morning. He comes like a day that has passed, and night enters our future with him."[28]

Chapter 11

THE COLUMBIAN ENTERPRISE: DAVID THOMPSON, 1800–1810

In October 1800, four and a half years before Lewis and Clark left Fort Mandan on their expedition to the Pacific, David Thompson began his first of many similar journeys north of the 49th parallel. He was looking for a route to the Pacific, to the mouth of the Columbia River. Unlike Lewis and Clark's putative rationale of scientific discovery, with commerce and geopolitics as sometimes hidden byproducts, Thompson's motivation was strictly commercial at the outset, but gained a sense of urgency in the rapidly changing circumstances of trade rivalry.

Although Alexander Mackenzie's overland route to the Pacific, charted in 1792–93, had been placed on Aaron Arrowsmith's carefully authenticated maps, it offered too difficult a passage for profitable use. Neither canoes nor packhorses could overcome its topographical realities. As a result, Mackenzie's Columbian enterprise—his plan to send furs to market by both the Atlantic and Pacific—advanced by fits and starts. A workable arrangement called for much capital, labor, assistance from the aboriginal nations along the way, time-consuming exploration and,

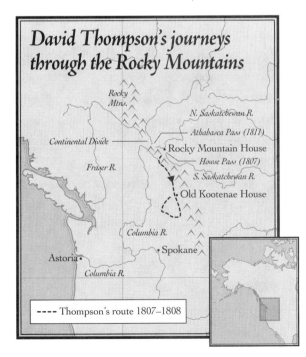

David Thompson's journeys through the Rocky Mountains

Rocky Mtns.

N. Saskatchewan R.

Athabasca Pass (1811)

Continental Divide

Rocky Mountain House

Howse Pass (1807)

Fraser R.

S. Saskatchewan R.

Old Kootenae House

Columbia R.

Astoria

Spokane

Columbia R.

---- Thompson's route 1807–1808

above all, corporate commitment and leadership. Mackenzie pressed upon Canadian governors and imperial statesmen the merits of his plan, but circumstances beyond his control delayed or slowed the project. Had the Hudson's Bay Company agreed to an alliance of convenience, it would have swept aside the impediment of the Nor'Westers' lack of access to Hudson Bay. That was not the only problem, however. Mackenzie and those of his associates who had come loyally behind him as their commercial chief in the half dozen years after his trek to and from the Pacific Ocean found themselves pitted against the more conservative element of the North West Company. Between 1799 and 1804, those two factions waged a fur-trading war (described in Chapter 9). Not until the resolution of differences and the reunion of firms in 1804 could the Columbian project be reenergized.

In these circumstances, all advances toward the Pacific were piecemeal and tentative. No field general came forward to marshal far western exploration under Canadian auspices. Mackenzie's close associate Duncan McGillivray, then in charge of the Athabasca district, shared Mackenzie's vision but lacked his zeal and was also hobbled with rheumatism. In the end, McGillivray had to cut short his own western travels, but he did encourage others to advance the plan, designating several men as advance guards or scouts—James Hughes, Finan McDonald, Joseph Howse, Jaco Finlay, Simon Fraser, Jules Quesnel and David Thompson. All played a role in unlocking the secrets of the Columbia River watershed, notably its complicated upper reaches, lakes and feeder streams. But exploration took second place to trading. For the time being, discovery remained a pay-as-you-go proposition, not a grand design backed by capital and brawn.

Thompson's task was to seek an easier route through the ramparts of the Rocky Mountains and across the Continental Divide, in more southerly latitudes than Mackenzie's trail. Such a route, if discovered, would allow a steady trade with the Pacific coast, with long sea links to Montreal, London and, especially, China. As Thompson was to find, the sole route was the tortuous Columbia River.

Thompson was no Mackenzie. He showed no imperial vision or political appreciation, no sense of urgency such as fuelled Mackenzie's restless spirit.

The Columbia River rises in Lake Columbia, a small lake in the Rocky Mountains in the Kootenay district of British Columbia. The source was located by David Thompson. Henry Warre, the artist, described this drawing in his Sketches in North America and the Oregon Territories *(1848) as "The Columbia River takes its rise."*

Had Thompson been of a different mindset and spirit or will, he might have hastened his explorations toward the mouth of the Columbia River. Perhaps timidity stalked and checked his advance, or maybe selfishness in pursuing his own more minor schemes stood in the way of urgent advance. But of greatest importance was his day-to-day preoccupation. Time and circumstance had made him a surveyor, one who methodically measures, scientifically and graphically, the land. Professionally, it is a noble calling, but it often shows the progress of the tortoise not the hare. In later years, Thompson warmed to the imperial theme and stated his bitter regrets that the British government had not been more aggressive in following discoveries with dominion. But his abundant concern in 1800, as in 1807 or 1811, was determining places of trade, setting up posts and evaluating the usefulness of corridors for transportation.[1]

What drove and defined Thompson as a figure in western exploration has long fascinated biographers and historians, and a word here about various interpretations helps explain the enduring quest to understand why Thompson took an interminable eleven years to travel from Rocky Mountain House in the foothills of the Rockies, the advance base of operations for the Columbian enterprise, to Astoria. Joseph Tyrrell, who first edited Thompson's *Narrative* for print, portrayed Thompson as blameless in his tardiness to pursue "the race to the sea" against Astor's venture. Historian Arthur S. Morton, in 1936, commenced his assault on Tyrrell's view. Morton judged Thompson as overly timid, lacking Mackenzie's and Simon Fraser's zeal. "The Canadian patriot may deplore Britain's failure through him to establish a first claim by settlement to the Pacific coast of Oregon," stated Morton.[2] Further evaluation, hard-hitting and frank, came from the pen of Richard Glover when he produced a new edition of the *Narrative* in 1962. Glover questioned Tyrrell's characterization, went after the issue of Thompson's missing journal of July 23 to October 28, 1810, and charged Thompson with deliberately destroying it so as to conceal his culpability.

The argument that Thompson dallied on his way to the coast stands up poorly under close scrutiny of the day-to-day journal entries of this explorer, trader and mapmaker.[3] It is easy for the armchair traveller to imagine that Thompson really ought to have pressed on more quickly, but Thompson moved westward toward his Pacific goal, the mouth of the Columbia River, only as circumstances allowed or dictated. Between expectation and reality there existed a yawning gap. He had little or no control over complex, even chaotic, external circumstances. His was not a military expedition, and he had no soldiers as a guard. He was obliged to trade so that he could be secure from assault by disgruntled tribes and so that he would have aboriginal allies. His partners in the North West Company looked for him to open new watersheds for trade and to satisfy shareholders in search of dividends. Thus when we meet him on his 1800 expedition, we see him moving through time and place as the requirements of the day determined.

In October of that year, from Rocky Mountain House, on the North Saskatchewan River in the Alberta foothills, Thompson began his first sortie toward a pass through the Rocky Mountains. He worked south to the Red Deer River and the Bow River. This expedition was one of reconnaissance, but the real fruits of discovery were not geographical but human, for intertribal rivalry presented itself as Thompson's preliminary obstacle. On October 6, near present-day Red Deer, Alberta, he wrote in his typical and sensitive descriptive prose: "Here we had a grand view of the Rocky Mountains, forming a concave segment of a Circle, and lying from one Point to another about SbE and NbW. All its snowy cliffs to the Southward were bright with the Beams of the Sun, while the most northern were darkened by a Tempest; those Cliffs in the Concave were alternately brightened by the Sun & obscured by the Storm, which spent it's Force only on the Summits."[4] Geology and terrain, sun and clouds, aboriginal people and their rivals, rivers and passes as vectors of trade—these preoccupied Thompson day after day.

Thompson—so much like him—pondered the nature of the riverbeds and banks of rock, and he marvelled at the quantity of particles of the mountains that had made their way to the spot on which he stood. There were also remnants of large trees that had, at one time or another, been carried down by the stream. The sight was spectacular, and the opportunity to describe the scene did not escape Thompson. He was not overpowered by the romantic; rather, he was alive to the actual, the realistic. It might be said that he was one with the environment.

He was now in the region of the Blackfoot, Bloods and especially Piegans, three kindred peoples speaking the same language and known collectively nowadays as the Blackfoot Nation or Confederacy.[5] These people valued the horse and the war bonnet above all. On one occasion, Thompson encountered two tents of Piegans who were out on an eagle hunt. They killed nine eagles (it took about thirty eagle feathers of sacred power to make one war bonnet or eagle-feather headdress). That evening the Piegans, satiated with success, feasted.

The Piegans were inveterate enemies of the Kootenay or Ktunaxa, who lived to the west. On another day, Thompson met a Kootenay chief, attended by twenty-six men and seven women, who came to offer a yellow horse and fifty beaver skins. Thompson declined the offer; he was away from his trading goods so had nothing to barter. "These poor Fellows are but poorly clothed notwithstanding the region of the Cold in these Mountains; they give me to understand that the Pekenon [Piegans] Indians have stolen most of their Horses. I said all I could to encourage them to come on to the House, and they assured me they would persevere." Thompson learned that the Piegans harassed the Kootenays' expedition, stole five horses one night and made themselves general pests. The Kootenays—"brave, undaunted, but poor"—seemed long-suffering, and Thompson concluded that they waited only for an opportunity for sweet revenge. But they reached Thompson's trading post, settled all business matters and departed. In the distance, Thompson could see ten Piegans on horseback, waiting to see what road the Kootenays would take to pass the Rocky Mountains so they could make stealthy tracks so as to lie in wait to rob them. The Kootenays took a heavily wooded route to cross the mountains.[6] The Piegans did not pursue them and waited for some distant day to prey on their foes.

On the evening of November 22, 1800, the principal chief of the Piegans, Sac o tow wow, paid a visit to Thompson and his trading party, who were camped where the Spitchee River falls into the Bow River. It was a time for diplomacy, for a frank exchange of viewpoints. Sac o tow wow listed his grievances: that the Nor'Westers had armed the Kootenays; and that by this same means the Flatheads (the Piegans' name for the Salish) "would also acquire Arms to their great Hurt." Thompson countered this. He replied that the Piegans themselves had armed the Kootenays in exchange for horses and various commodities. Then Thompson came to a new point of discussion: some Iroquois and Saulteaux hunters had asked the Nor'Westers if they could move to this area, for their own country was too poor to maintain them. Thompson had not agreed to the Iroquois–Salteaux request, not knowing, as he told Sac o tow wow, the Piegans' response to this possible intrusion. He asked for Piegan permission. "We also added that those Indians would behave quietly, would reside in the woody Hills at the foot of the Mountain & serve as a Barrier between them & their Enemies—upon these terms they gave us Permission to bring them up as soon as we pleased. Cut a Pipe of Tobacco to each Man & gave a few pints of mixed Rum to drink."[7]

Problem solving and diplomacy: these progressed hand in hand—but slowly, agonizingly so, from the company's point of view. For the moment, aboriginal America barred the traders' advance and hindered the science of measurement. Until Thompson could finesse this Piegan problem, get to the Kootenays directly, and satisfy the Iroquois and Salteaux, Nor'Wester progress would falter. And then there were the more distant aboriginal nations, the Salish among others, that he would meet and with whom he would come to an agreement.

The Nor'Westers thus advanced incrementally, snail-like almost, across ancient indigenous landscapes thrown more unexpectedly than any could know into the modern world of industry and commerce. The industrial revolution had crossed the Atlantic in the sailing ship—blanket cloth from Whitney in Oxfordshire and "stroud" from Stroud in Gloucester; rum from Jamaica and Demerara; strong tobacco from Brazil (in a rope coil and sold by the foot); muskets and ammunition from England, Scotland and New England; beads from Venice; and much else besides, including awls, iron arrow tips, fishhooks and, strangely it seems now, hawkbells. Hawkbells, those ancient requirements of falconers, had first come to America with Columbus. Now, four centuries later, Thompson still had them in his trading packs. Useful to keep bears at bay as their tinkling, advertising a walker's approach, was sufficient to chase away even a grizzly, they were equally a requirement for a ceremonial dance or entertainment. Conspicuous consumption was as much a preoccupation for the First Nations as it was for any other society. Hawkbells advertised the connection to Europe and transcended cultures. Venetian beads linked the Bow River with Venice, the queen of the Adriatic, and interlinking empires became one, transgressing cultures, modifying patterns of dress and behaviour, subverting the old. Culture had never been finite or frozen in time; now, for Thompson, for Sac o tow wow and the Piegans, and for the Kootenays, propulsion forward seemed the logical and obvious direction. Thompson acted merely as the agent or fixer, his role analogous to that of Cartier when he first came to Canadian shores and his Montagnais greeters held up beaver skins in trade, or of Cook, who had faced the same at Nootka Sound. Europe was drawn into the vortex of aboriginal America. The roots of imperialism lie in indigenous needs.[8]

That winter of 1800–1801, Duncan McGillivray, a partner of the North West Company and in charge of this department, joined Thompson at Rocky Mountain House. Then, and to the end of his days, McGillivray promoted the Columbian enterprise and became its main force even when Mackenzie was "in opposition" in the rival XY Company. "Messrs. McGilvery & Thompson are going the ensuing summer," rival HBC man James Bird wrote on February 19, 1801, "… to examine the country west of the mountain as far as the borders of the South sea & ascertain if possible whether … an advantageous trade can be carried on with those parts or not either from hence or China."[9] McGillivray had with him a copy of Captain Vancouver's mammoth, recently published (1798) book of his Pacific voyages, complete with atlas. The two pored over the text and examined its charts. They considered known facts and weighed various possibilities. Then they made plans. McGillivray withdrew from the expedition on the grounds of his health or was otherwise turned back, and there is no proof that he was the first to find a pass through the Rockies in these latitudes, though some historians have claimed he did.[10]

In June 1801, Thompson set out from Rocky Mountain House in an attempt to find a way through the Rocky Mountains and to establish a base of operations in the Columbia country. This represented a substantial outlay in capital, material and human resources for the North West Company. Thompson was an experienced canoeist in the boreal forest and shield country and was also knowledgeable about horse travel, but mountain travel was new to him, and the physical challenges in the high country of the Rockies were known to be formidable. The river bottoms and banks were exceedingly slippery and otherwise difficult, the streams were full and swift with spring runoff, and the crossing places were deep. To add to these problems, the expedition was entering a war zone: the Kootenay were being pushed west from the eastern slopes of the Rockies by the Cree, Stoney and Piegan.

The year previous, two traders, Le Blanc and Charles La Gassé, had made a similar foray with the intention of establishing friendly contacts among the Kootenay, assessing the trade potential in that country and learning some of the language. Though he gives no hint of it, Thompson likely learned of the details from the returning travellers, for they had come back to Rocky Mountain House two weeks before Thompson set out on his passage. In any event, Thompson's expedition went by horse, not canoe; and his general line of approach to the pass lay upstream on the upper reaches of the North Saskatchewan River to a lake, now known as Farley, that was well-bordered by rocky ramparts. Beyond it lay their destination.

The fourteen-person expedition consisted of Thompson and the company partner James Hughes, three Canadian traders, the Cree guide Crow (Thompson calls him "The Rook" in snide reference to what Thompson saw as his conniving tendencies) and his wife, Charlotte Small, six other men, and a Kootenay woman who would translate for them once they reached the Kootenay country. There were in all thirteen pack horses laden with trade goods, food, birch rind for canoe building, medicines and other necessities. The expedition left Rocky Mountain House on June 6, hoping to have that summer to erect a post and set up trade among the Kootenay.

The North Saskatchewan River was then in flood, and, as if that were not enough, the fallen timber from a major fire a few years earlier lay strewn about and forced the expedition to higher ground, around burned debris and windfall. They were too early in the season to avoid winter conditions, notably snow. Using creeks and cross-country tracks, they tried to break through to a river, the North Ram, that led to the small lake. They were then in the Ram Range, not far from Kootenay Plains, but it was clear to Thompson that they had reached a dead end: burned deadfall and heavy snow barred the way west. The horses, already driven hard—some nearly crippled and others feeble—and hazarded in desperate river crossings, could not be risked further; forcing these animals to swim the length of the lake and then attempt a defile among broken rocks was unthinkable. At one point rebellion rose in the ranks, and the men refused to carry packs down a ravine. Accordingly, the party returned to Rocky Mountain House, downstream almost all the way, reaching it on June 30.[11]

Thompson had much to account for, and he spread the blame for his failure. Not least to receive rebuke was his Cree guide, a reluctant fellow, who at the last minute had replaced the original and better informed guide, a Kootenay who was killed by the Stoneys. Crow was "a man so Timorous by Nature, of so wavering a disposition, & withal so addicted to flattering & lying, as to make every thing he said or did, equivocal & doubtful," said Thompson. But Thompson may have been overly critical, for trader Peter Fidler, who knew the guide, says the latter was afraid of being killed by the Kootenay—a reasonable claim, for the Crees were allied with the Stoneys against their inveterate enemies, the Kootenays. Thompson quotes Crow as saying, "This is the way with you white Men, you joke at every Thing 'till you are fairly Killed; for my Part I am certain there are strange Indians near us, who will Kill us; I dream continually of them."[12] Thompson may have been dismissive of Crow and claims to have been fearless himself (at the expense of his guide), but he did not have Mackenzie's skills of leadership nor his diplomatic ways of persuasion. Thompson was brittle and obstinate where Mackenzie would have been cajoling and encouraging: then again, Thompson never used liquor as a tool of diplomacy or bribery, but only for ceremonial purposes of trade.

In defence of Thompson, we can see that the human factor had also to contend with the environmental—the season and the weather. Had Thompson gone a month earlier or, better, later, when travel by horse would have been easier, he would more likely have breached the rocky ramparts, as backpackers retracing his trail, notably Daniel Kyba, have concluded.[13] As we shall see later in the chapter, for his second attempt, in 1807, Thompson left Rocky Mountain House a month earlier, on May 10, took a canoe upriver by line and pole, waited two weeks for snow to clear and then crossed the Continental Divide through Howse Pass on June 25.

Six years earlier, however, Thompson, practical and philosophical, concluded his first short, inconclusive sortie in search of a pass with a statement of lessons learned. To Messrs. William and Duncan McGillivray, agents of the North West Company, he wrote, on June 30, 1801, in explanatory but not apologetic terms:

> However unsuccessful this Journey has been, it has not been wholly without it's use: it has taught us to make a better choice of our Men, & take fewer of them; & never to employ an Indian of this Side the Mountains for our Guide; it has also shewn us plainly, that to employ & depend on Horses for carrying the Goods &c in such Expeditions is the most uncertain, & most expensive, of all the Modes of Conveyance. Whoever wishes to attempt to cross the Mountains for the Purposes of Commerce ought to employ a Canoe, & start early in the Spring, say the beginning of May, from the Rocky Mountain House, the Water for that Month being low & the Current not half so violent as

in the Summer; there are then also Beaches all the way, either on one Side or the other of the River even in the Mountains, by which People may track on the Shore where the Pole cannot well be used. In this Season, they would cross a great Part of the Mountains without any extraordinary Difficulty, and meet the Flushes of high Water where they would have need of it, that is, near the Head of the River—from whence there is said to be a short Road to the waters which flow on the other Side the Mountain. It is a Maxim pretty well received, that Success in Enterprizes justifies all the Measures that have been taken in such Enterprizes; on the Contrary, whatever is unsuccessful must be accounted for: it is on this Account that I have been so tedious in detailing so minutely the trifling Occurrences of the above Journey.[14]

Thompson's sortie—"the business of 1801," he later called it—got little attention from his superiors. In fact, it was "entirely forgotten or ridiculed," he said, "until the expedition of Captains Lewis and Clarke." Such was Thompson's appreciation of these events years after the fact. Old men forget, or tend to forget. Thompson may have confused what he did in 1807 or 1811, but he himself wrote in retrospect:

> In 1801 the northwest company determined to extend their Fur Trade to the west side of the Rocky Mountains, and if possible to the Pacific Ocean; this expedition was entrusted to me, and I crossed the Mountains to the head waters of McGillivray's River [Kootenay River]; but an overwhelming force of eastern Indians obliged me to retreat a most desperate retreat of six days for they dreaded the western Indians being furnished with Arms and Ammunition. The report of my attempt and defeat soon reached Washington and in 1804 the Executive of the U. States organized a plan of discovery, to be conducted by Captain Lewis and Clarke.[15]

William McGillivray, Mackenzie's close associate, had provided a powerful impetus from headquarters for westward discoveries. He gave Thompson both momentum and enhanced purpose. Moreover, Thompson had given the newly reunited North West Company a new, authorized determination to back McGillivray's scheme. But McGillivray, with hard-headed realism, knew that the transmontane passage, though theoretically feasible, was always second best in terms of import costs. Nothing could beat the access to the continental interior via Hudson Bay. In 1805, at its first rendezvous at Kaministiquia, Lake Superior, the North West Company partners agreed to offer the Hudson's Bay Company a sum not exceeding £2,000 per year for the right to transport goods through Hudson Bay and thus through the chartered territory of the old rival.[16]

The Nor'Westers continued to explore the possibility of western expansion and soon found themselves in a dangerous situation of imperial overstretch, from which they were saved by the remarkable Simon Fraser. Fraser, born in Bennington, Vermont, was another man of Alexander Mackenzie's breed but of less scientific training. He was sent by the North West Company to Athabasca in 1805 to take charge of operations beyond the mountains. By then he had served the company for nine years and had become a partner, or *bourgeois*, in the organization that he had joined when he was sixteen and living in the province of Quebec. Now, at the age of twenty-five, Fraser was assigned to discover a way across the Rockies to the Pacific at the same time as agents of his company in London were negotiating, unsuccessfully, with the Hudson's Bay Company for the right to ship goods through Hudson Bay. Fraser's physical robustness, his determination

Trader and explorer Simon Fraser built the first North West Company posts in the interior plateau of what is now central British Columbia and ventured down, or around, Hell's Gate canyon rapids. It was for this effort that David Thompson named the river after him. Fraser disproved Mackenzie's speculation that it was the Columbia River.
British Columbia Archives, PDP-02258

and energy, his indomitable courage and his knowledge of woodcraft and indigenous customs meant he was capable of extending the commercial activities of the Nor'Westers into the wilderness beyond the waterways traversed by Mackenzie more than a dozen years earlier.

Fraser, unheralded empire builder and faithful tool of his superiors, had two main tasks. First, he was to follow up Mackenzie's discoveries by developing trading posts and networks in the Pacific cordillera in those latitudes (the region now known as the central British Columbia interior based in Prince George). Second, he was to explore the various rivers and tributaries of the Peace and Columbia rivers and probe south along the powerful stream that Mackenzie left in order to walk overland, after the Dakelh advised him that to proceed downriver meant certain destruction.

Fraser arrived on the Peace River from Fort William in August 1805, and near Rocky Mountain Portage he built a post close to where Hudson's Hope stands today. This was to be the supply base for posts he intended to build farther west. During the next three years, aided by John Fraser and James McDougall, he established additional posts at McLeod Lake (Fort McLeod), Stuart Lake (Fort St. James), Fraser Lake (Fort Fraser) and the confluence of the Nechako and Fraser rivers (Fort George). The last was to serve as the starting point for Fraser's bold and hazardous descent of what Mackenzie thought was the Columbia River, to be completed before the Americans secured control of it.[17] Simon Fraser's son John recounted the circumstances, years later:

From this [Fraser] Lake my father returned and passed the winter [1806–7] with Mr. Stewart [John Stuart]. In the early part of 1807 he sent despatches, with what furs had been collected, to Athabasca, and asked for an increased force of clerks, and goods. In the Fall of 1807 he received two canoes loaded with goods, and two clerks, named Julius [Jules] Quesnel and Hugh Jones [Faries] (the former was afterwards an M.P. for Montreal). These gentlemen brought despatches from the Company, recommending my father to trace with all possible speed the "great" River to the sea,—they being apprehensive that the Americans would get ahead of the British in that quarter—particularly as in the previous year (1806) Captains Lewis and Clark had gone down the Columbia, and were extending American authority along the western coast of America; and Astor, on the part of the Americans also, was looking anxiously towards that section. The Company therefore urged my father to spare no expense in achieving the object of their desires.[18]

A delay in receiving supplies prevented Fraser from setting out on his expedition until May 22, 1808. In his journal on that date he stated, "Having made every necessary preparation for a long voyage, we embarked at 5 a.m. in four canoes at Fraser's River. Our crew consisted of nineteen men, two Indians, Mr. Stuart, Mr. Quesnel and myself, in all 24."

For the first seven days, Fraser and his companions made little progress because of the rapids in the Fort George and Cottonwood canyons. By May 29 the party was in the midst of a country with a "romantic and pleasant appearance," near the mouth of a large, clear tributary coming from the east, which Fraser named Quesnel River in honour of his second lieutenant, its explorer. The next day found them at Soda Creek, where friendly Shuswaps, repeating the advice given to Mackenzie, tried to discourage Fraser from advancing into the turbulent waters downstream. When he showed determination to continue, they advised him to send couriers ahead to let the people below know that he was coming, a suggestion he sedulously followed.[19]

On June 3, Fraser and his man met another group who had recently been across the mountains east of the Continental Divide—the key to identification was the buffalo horn. They knew Fraser was a Nor'Wester, for they recognized his canoe as the same style used by Nor'Westers in Athabasca. "They likewise say that they heard of white people having been down the first large River that flows into this on the left [the Thompson River]," wrote Fraser, "but whether it had been Capt. Lewis or some of the Fort des Prairie[s] people [David Thompson and his men] we cannot determine."

Between Soda Creek and Lillooet, Fraser's party was borne southward on turbulent waters walled in by perpendicular canyons or great overhanging rocks that appeared to make navigation impossible. On June 1, their canoes approached a fearsome, foaming stretch of water that for two miles boiled between "high banks which contracted the channel in many places to forty or fifty yards." The men had to scramble carefully along the banks, at the risk of falling at any moment into the pitiless whirlpools below.

Advancing alternately by land and water, Fraser eventually came, on June 19, to the mouth of a river that entered the main stream from the east. He named this the Thompson River in honour of the explorer who was then surveying the sourcewaters of the Columbia. At "Camchin," the village of the "Thompson Indians" (Nlaka'pamux), located where Lytton stands today, Fraser saw that the residents possessed articles of European manufacture, evidence of the inter-tribal communication between the people of the coast and those of the interior plateau.

The Nor'Westers had to abandon their canoes near the present village of North Bend, for the expedition had come into a section of the river more hazardous and terrifying than any they had seen heretofore. Fraser wrote:

> It is so wild that I cannot find words to describe our situation at times. We have to pass where no human being should venture; yet in those places there is a regular footpath impressed or rather indented upon the very rocks by frequent traveling. Besides this, steps which are formed like a ladder or the shrouds of a ship, by poles hanging to one another and crossed at certain distances with twigs, the whole suspended from the top to the foot of immense precipices and fastened at both extremities to stones and trees, furnish a safe and convenient passage to the Natives; but we, who had not the advantage of their education and experience, were often in imminent danger when obliged to follow their example.

By the end of June, Fraser arrived at a place (now Yale) from which navigable tidal waters flowed to the Strait of Georgia. With considerable difficulty, he obtained wooden canoes and, with more ease, proceeded down the broadening river that turned westward as it ran between banks lined with meadows and forests, beyond which rose foothills of the Coast Range. Finally the explorers followed the northern channel of the broad delta to its outlet at the sea, but it was the Strait of Georgia they arrived at, not the Pacific, because the latter was hidden from view by Vancouver Island. Fraser determined that he stood at 49° latitude, a disappointing revelation because he knew that his exertions had failed to bring him to the goal he had sought; the mouth of the Columbia River lay nearly three degrees farther south. This postponed the day when an easy line of transportation to the Pacific would become available to the North West Company.[20] And it ended, once and for all, any hope of a serviceable water route. The northern interior seemed closed to commerce by canoe. "This voyage has not met the wishes of the company," wrote Jules Quesnel, "and will never be of any advantage to them, this river not being navigable." Frankness shines in his letter of proceedings, but he was not about to be caught up in self-blame: "The end for which we undertook this voyage we have accomplished, so we have no reproach to make to ourselves."[21] Company aspirations faltered in the Fraser River's Devils Canyon and would have to seek new breath on what Quesnel called "the true Columbia."

Fraser's return journey to Fort George, in the district that had become known as New Caledonia, ended on August 6. The ascent of the river took thirty-four days compared to the thirty-five consumed in its descent. In reward for his discoveries, Fraser was placed in charge of a district in Athabasca. Then, after serving at Red River and on the Mackenzie, he went to Fort William and was there when the Earl of Selkirk, founder of the Red River Colony, seized the headquarters of the North West Company on Lake Superior in 1816. Five years later he retired.

While Fraser and John Stuart quickly developed the trade of the north-central cordillera, Thompson had been sent on other business to Muskrat Country, northern Manitoba, a foolish assignment of no benefit to the western push. At the 1806 rendezvous in Kaministiquia, under William McGillivray's chairmanship, Thompson received authorization and instructions to lead a new advance into the Columbia country. He travelled back to Rocky Mountain

House to make plans for southwestward surveying and trade. The Metís clerk, Jaco Finlay, had already gone forward to build a supply and resting post and to prepare canoes suitable for the western travels.

The HBC's James Bird at Edmonton House, observing Thompson's preparations for the spring of 1807, noted (in correspondence to a friend) that Thompson was getting ready for a renewed attempt to cross the Rockies, with the intention of passing through the Kootenay country and following the Columbia River to the sea. "He is to have eight men with him," Bird reported, "and the object of his enterprise is said to be to ascertain positively whether a Trade can be formed with the Country valuable enough to be worth pursuing thro the difficulties and if it should, the uniting of the commerce of the two Seas."[22]

For his 1807 venture, Thompson used lessons learned from his 1801 attempt. With a reduced number in his party, with canoes as well as horses, and with no craven and misleading guide, he commenced his second attempt from Rocky Mountain House on May 10, 1807 (just over a year before Fraser

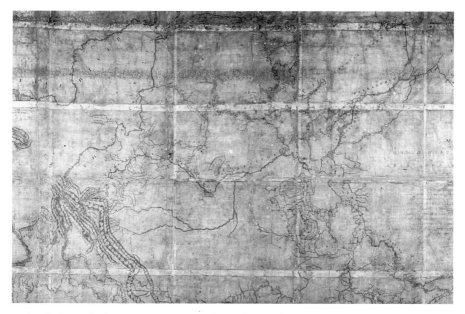

A detail of David Thompson's route across the Rockies and Continental Divide in 1807. The armchair quarterbacks of history frequently underestimate the difficulties of travel in the dangerous mountainous and riverine locales such as Thompson had to undertake with a large party. Archives of Ontario, F443, R-C(U), AO 1541

set off down the river from Fort George). Along with the requisite compact party, he took equipment and goods for the intended posts and trade. Clerks Finan MacDonald and Jules Quesnel accompanied him.

The great fear remained not only geography but also the possible hostility of the Piegans, already mentioned. They were the watchkeepers of the passes and were rich in firepower, having traded with the Nor'Westers east of the Rockies for the guns and ammunition they used to keep the Kootenays in terror west of the Rocky Mountains. The Piegans wished to keep the Kootenays unarmed, so they had barred their rivals from getting to the traders. For the same reason, they greeted any intrusion of the Nor'Westers into Kootenay lands with resistance. However, in 1807, Thompson was in luck: "The murder of two Peagan Indians by Captain Lewis of the United States, drew the Peagans to the Missouri to revenge their deaths; and thus gave me an opportunity to cross the Mountains to the defiles of the [North] Saskatchewan River, which led to the headwaters of the Columbia River."[23] Moreover, some Blackfoot had attacked a party of whites in Montana, drawing the Piegans away from the passes they controlled. This was Thompson's opportunity.

Thompson, MacDonald and Quesnel, making plans in secrecy so no word would reach the Piegans or nearby HBC traders, decided that the most feasible route would be a track used by the Kootenays a few years earlier. To make a further reconnaissance, they sent a scout, Jaco Finlay, who met the Kootenays, crossed the divide and built a small outpost. He made good his advance party's work and cached two canoes at the mouth of a stream entering what he reported to Thompson was a great river. Thompson wondered if this was the Columbia.

The main party crossed the divide with horses heavily laden. The going was rough, for the paths cleared for them by Finlay were narrow, and lack of pasture meant hungry and weak horses. Big game was not to be found; pemmican supplies dwindled. Fishing brought no results. Some Kootenays were hired as hunters and solved the problem of food. After Thompson crossed the divide, through a gap later known as Howse Pass, he found a trickle of water heading westward toward the Pacific. At that spot, Thompson noted in his diary: "May God in His mercy give me to see where its waters flow into the ocean and return in safety." That small steam was the Blaeberry, and as the party followed it downstream, crossing and recrossing it on horseback, it grew into a torrent. They eventually found themselves on the banks of the Columbia, a few miles northwest of present-day Golden, BC, and a short distance from where CPR surveyor Walter Moberly later had a headquarters.[24]

Thompson proceeded southward, that is upstream, on the upper Columbia. He came first to Windermere Lake, and there, on the bank of Toby Creek, he decided to erect a post, the first established on the Columbia River proper. It was called Old Kootenae House. Thompson's advance was less than what he had wanted for the season's work. His superiors had called for him to reach the Kootenay River—"McGillivray's River" is what Thompson called it—and put up a post there. But too many forces had stood against him, and discoveries had to be set aside for security and trade: "From the state of the Country and the Situation of my Affairs I found myself necessitated to lay aside all Thoughts of Discovery for the present and bend my whole aim to an establishment for Trade."[25]

Thompson knew he had missed an opportunity by not continuing to the Kootenay River, where food in the form of salmon and buffalo was more abundant. He and his men had brought little food with them. They had intended to live on game, but it was scarce that year. They devoured the flesh of wild horses, bear, deer, porcupine, trumpeter and whistling swans, and even, on one occasion, a dog. The party of nineteen—thirteen men and women with six children—faced starvation. "At length, thank Heaven, two Kootenay men arrived; they saw our famished looks and asking no questions, gave every one of us a sufficiency to eat which was most gratefully accepted and then traded with me provisions enough for two days."

On one occasion a forest fire threatened; on another, a violent storm blew down the tents and endangered everything. The men were fatigued and weak, unable to continue building without food. Two weirs, built to catch fish, were carried away in the swift current. They had to abandon a warehouse, measuring sixteen by sixteen feet, because no water could be collected nearby. They shifted from Lake Windermere to Toby Creek. They fished with nets but got not a single fish.

A few days later, twelve Piegans arrived on foot from the eastern side of the Rockies. Twenty-three more arrived shortly thereafter. They had learned that the Nor'Westers had entered the Kootenay country to trade. They took up a prominent spot near the gate of Old Kootenae House, and there they set up their tents. "That the Piegans are highly jealous of the Kootenaes having a trading Post in their country is certain, & equally so that they wish to find some means to drive us hence, but how they will act is yet to be learned," Thompson scratched in his journal on September 13.[26] The Piegans demanded rum, but Thompson told them he had none to give. He and his party remained within the walls of the fort, living on short rations. In late October, two of the Piegans disappeared, and Thompson feared this might mean preparations for an attack. He was wrong. A few weeks later the rest of the party quietly departed.

Then two Piegans returned. Thompson took pains to show them the loopholes cut in the walls, through which he could shoot if necessary. He pointed out the strong stockades surrounding the fort. He forthrightly told these Piegans that they were spies, and that if they attacked they would be killed. He gave them tobacco so they would not steal his horses, and he advised them to return to their people. Some Kootenays arrived at this moment, an event that hastened the departure of the troublesome Piegans.

Later Thompson learned of an intended Piegan attack. The last two Piegans were scouts of a large war party of three hundred that had been assembled under three chiefs in the mountains but had come to within twenty miles of Kootenae House. On September 13 and at other times, Thompson exercised hard-fisted diplomacy. Of his relations with the Piegans he wrote:

> I told them we were well prepared for the worst that could happen, & if any Trouble was given us, it was a very easy thing to build far out of their Power, & where they would never get a pipe of Tobacco from us, but that all their Efforts would never make us relinquish the Trade this side of the Mountains. They again repeated they had no wish for a rupture & were glad we were here to get a pipe of Tobacco in the Summer & thus we parted.

And of those with the Kootenays:

> Held a Council with the Kootenaes concerning the Blood &
> Blackfoot Indians who are said to meditate an attack on us,
> & we agreed to join the Battle the moment they appear, & for
> the Success of which we pray the mercy of the Supreme Being,
> Arbiter of Life & Death.[27]

Kootenae Appee, a prominent chief, dissuaded the Piegans from an attack, leaving the fort in safety. Then winter came, and with it deep snow arrived in the mountain passes. Kootenae House seemed sealed off from the rest of the world, including Piegan assault.

Before winter closed in, Thompson made forays to Columbia Lake and traversed the short portage to Kootenay River. Construction of the fort preoccupied him. Negotiations with Piegans, Kootenays and others commanded his urgent attention. Getting food supplies caused endless worry. Otherwise he would have taken time "to explore at least the Flat Bow Country, a[nd] by the Course of the large River, [to] determine whether it is the Columbia or not."[28]

Four months earlier, when Thompson and his men were happily putting the finishing touches to Kootenae House on August 13, 1807, a group of aboriginals brought Thompson some alarming information: about three weeks previous—that is, in late July—forty-two Americans had arrived to put up a military post at the confluence of two of the most southern and sizeable branches of the Columbia River. (In fact, what they meant were two upper tributaries of the Missouri River.) Thompson's informants also warned that the Americans were preparing to establish a small advance post lower down the river. Nowadays, historians consider such information more credible than they did in earlier times, when news from aboriginals was either dismissed or discredited. The figure (forty-two Americans) is specific, and so is the point that this was a military post, though this might have meant a trading factory under US auspices.

Thompson took the matter most seriously and wrote: "This establishment of the Americans will give a new turn to our so long delayed settling of this

Country, on which we have entered it seems too late; but, in my opinion the most valuable part of the Country still remains to us, and we have nothing to obstruct us, but the difficulty of getting Goods from Fort des Prairies, & the still more formidable poverty of the Country in Animals. Time and Perseverance will show what we can do, & if worth our Expence & Trouble."[29] The implication of all this was that Thompson must protect the trade of the Kootenay country—and keep his aboriginal trading partners from going over to the American rivals.

But who were these American agents and traders? The quest to identify them continues to this day. One fine historian, Dale Morgan, contends there was an obscure group, including a trader known as Charles Courtin, in the vicinity of the Three Forks of the Missouri River that summer. These men could have been an advance party of Manuel Lisa's Missouri Fur Company from St. Louis, with two or three members who had accompanied Lewis and Clark and were now lighting the business trail west.[30]

In December, a Kootenay chief delivered to Thompson a letter specifically addressed to him as the British merchant trafficking with the "Cabanaws" (Kootenays). It was signed by Lieutenant Jeremy Pinch and was dated September 29, 1807. The letter called for Thompson to understand that Congress had jurisdiction with the aboriginal people in these territories, "which are certainly the property of the United States both by discovery and Cession." The letter advised that military expeditions would be sent by Congress to survey the territories; merchants would also be placed there to "second the philanthropic views of Congress in the Civilization of the Natives." Soon, it said, the authority of Congress would be as strong there as in New York or Washington. Pinch called on Thompson to cease supplying "those Marauders with Arms and Ammunition," and to tell other British traders to do likewise.

Thompson was not trespassing on US territory, and it is doubtful if Pinch wrote this letter anywhere west of the Continental Divide or even in the region of the Three Forks. There is no record that Lieutenant Pinch ever even existed, but this name might have been an alias for Zachariah Perch, another name that appears in collaborative documents, itself representing none other than Lieutenant Zebulon Montgomery Pike of the 1st Regiment, US Infantry. Pike, wandering cold and lonely through the north woods in search of the course of the Mississippi River, had been sent on this reconnaissance by his superior officer in St. Louis, General James Wilkinson. He was also endeavouring to enforce US authority and customs regulations on his own hook, as it were, quite unauthorized by his instructions. His aggressive and unwarranted rudeness to Hugh McGillis and the Nor'Westers at Leech Lake post in February 1806 was doubtless generated by his desire to provide the War Department and politicians in Washington with positive proof that American interests were being furthered against subversive Canadian commerce in the Old Northwest. His heavy-handed demands that the Nor'Westers pay US customs duties, stated in a letter to McGillis, were deftly deflected by the urbane, hospitable and easygoing McGillis, whose polite but disobliging answer takes its place among the classic documents of Anglo-American diplomacy. McGillis was not to be browbeaten, and all Pike could do was make his claim. But was Pike Pinch? There is a tantalizing possibility that he was, or that someone else was acting for him in more western locales.[31]

Another possible candidate as Pinch was John McClallen, or McClellan, an artillery officer and an agent of Wilkinson who established a post in Flathead Country in western Montana. He and his men were killed by Blackfoot in hostilities with Flatheads in 1810.[32]

Historian T.C. Elliot has confirmed that Lisa's advance party had forty-two members, including George Drouillard and John Colter, both Lewis and Clark Corps of Discovery veterans. These two, who knew the country, were sent to contract Nez Percé and Kootenay buffalo hunters in the Three Forks area and invite them to trade, which confirms that the party Thompson heard of in August was in fact from Manuel Lisa's company and that one of its members had asked the Kootenay chief to carry the message to Thompson at Kootenae House.

As for General Wilkinson at St. Louis, he had been flexing his administrative muscles. On July 10, 1806, he issued a proclamation as governor and superintendent of Indian Affairs in the Territory of Louisiana, which stated that "all persons were forbidden to ascend the Mississippi and Missouri rivers and trade with the Indians" except by his permission.[33] His objectives were to control trade, to prevent foreign influence, and to draw the indigenous people into the American orbit centred on Washington and its regional capital St. Louis. A year earlier, in 1805, Wilkinson had deployed an expedition to explore the Yellowstone River. It was expected to return to St. Louis in 1807. Who composed this party and what route they took remain matters of speculation. Anthony Bettay told Jefferson by letter (January 27, 1808) that he had just returned from three years in the interior, that he had found a silver mine in the Platte River and that he had discovered an "eligible passage" across the Rocky Montains and a westward-flowing river beyond. Historian Dorothy O. Johansen suggests that Bettay may have been in the Wilkinson expedition and even that this party crossed the Continental Divide about the same time as Lewis and Clark.[34]

From St. Louis, now a burgeoning hub of Missouri commerce, Clark, the new superintendent of Indian Affairs, reported to Henry Dearborn, the Secretary of War, on May 16, 1807: "Two large companies of traders set out from this place about the first of the month intending to ascend the Missouri to the Rocky Mountains, and remain in that country two or three years—one other party set out from this place in March—one small party set (out) early in the spring for the Ceahan [Cheyenne?] Nation, and I am informed of a party of British traders having passed over by land from the North, all aiming at the same point—the head of the Missouri."[35]

Perch had stated that the US regulations of trade had been delivered to Thompson by a chief of the "Poltitopalton nation [?]" but that Thompson had not responded as he was required to do. "Your silence Sir I am to construe into a tacit disrespect," grumbled Perch.

As for Thompson, he did receive a letter from Lieutenant Perch, whoever the latter might be, for on December 26 he replied to "your polite favors" and stated that he was neither authorized nor competent to give a direct answer on the matter of US commercial and political influence, "nor am I politician enough to settle the Boundaries of our respective Countries." He added, "If prior discovery forms any right to a Country, Lieut. Broughton of the British Navy many years ago explored the Columbia for 120 miles from the sea and was the first that made known its Geography." Thompson closed his letter by stating that the high duties Perch said were required would be submitted to all the North West Company partners for their consideration and that, if complied with, would be paid as was customary at Michilimackinac.

Thompson added a private note to his copies of the surviving correspondence with Perch: "It seems this officer was on a party of Discovery when he wrote the above."[36]

Thompson forwarded the correspondence to Rocky Mountain House. There it was duly noted in the post journal of Hudson's Bay Company man James Bird at Edmonton, which confirms Thompson knew about the Perch letter. We are sure of Thompson's activities and his responses, the sole evidence giving authenticity to the shadowy activities of these Americans. And we do know that in the winter of 1809–10, Thompson found the great camp of the Nez Percés on the Flathead River, twenty miles above its confluence with Clark's Fork. He speaks of the trail from the Kootenay River to Clark's Fork as "The Great Road of the Flat Heads." John Colter, one of the former members of the Corps of Discovery, had a trading post in the vicinity of Missoula, Montana, in 1809–10, and if there were in fact American traders in the Columbia River's most inner watershed in 1807, they were Thompson's most pressing rivals.[37]

The story of Thompson and Perch is no hoax. It is only surrounded by doubts and circumspection. On the margins of the North West Company and US government influence, agents of empire were working out their equivalent of war in the shadows. The fact of the matter was that Thompson was alerted to American military, political and commercial doings. The shadows of St. Louis and of Washington were creeping across the upper Columbia River's watersheds. His superiors must have known about these encounters, but for the time being they took no countermeasures other than to give Thompson support for those active arrangements he was making at and from Kootenae House.

The Nor'Westers in the Rocky Mountains knew of Lewis and Clark's far western journey from the expedition account of Sergeant Patrick Gass, whose *Journal of the Voyages and Travels of a Corps of Discovery* had been published in Pittsburgh in 1807 and reprinted in 1808 (and afterward). Alexander Henry the Younger, at Fort Vermilion on the Saskatchewan River, perused the book in March 1810. The volume contained a report of the most interesting transactions of the expedition, a description of the continental interior and Pacific cordillera, and an account of inhabitants, soil, climate, curiosities, and vegetable and animal matters. Whether Thompson had his own copy of Gass or used or borrowed Henry's is a matter of speculation; we do know that he read it.[38]

Thompson's task was to trace the Columbia River from its source to its mouth, thereby disclosing the main features of the watershed. He worked feverishly in the next few years. The border, it must be remembered, was not then the 49th parallel of north latitude, but the extent of the watershed of the Louisiana Territory's Missouri River, which touched on British-claimed and -held territory.

Meanwhile, Duncan McGillivray used the winter of 1807–8 to advance the Mackenzie concept of the Columbian enterprise further. He wrote a widely circulated memorandum noting the company's intention of forming "a general establishment for the trade of that country on the Columbia river, ... which receives and conducts to the Ocean all the waters that rise West of the Mountains."[39] At that point he did not know if the Fraser River was a tributary of the Columbia, and thus a potential trade route, or if it entered the Pacific farther north. McGillivray also noted that the firm had now "commenced a project for extending their researches and trade as far as the South Sea."

Similarly, from his vantage point, Thompson could only imagine what river course or courses lay downstream from Toby Creek en route to the sea. That winter, Kootenay people from far and wide arrived to trade and to bolster their alliance against their enemies, and from them Thompson received encouraging news about the great river. "After drawing a Chart of their Country ... from thence to the Sea, a[nd] describing the Nations along the River, they assured me that from this House to the sea a[nd] back again was only the Voyage of a Summer Moon...."[40]

However, it would be a few years before Thompson could make that journey. In the meantime, traders from Boston and New York were hastening to the mouth of the Columbia, putting the Nor'Westers' plans in jeopardy.

Chapter 12

BOSTON AND NEW YORK
ON THE LOWER COLUMBIA RIVER:
THE WINSHIPS AND ASTOR

The eyes of Boston fixed on the Columbia River earlier than those of New York. Three brothers of the Winship family, otherwise connected to the beef-slaughtering business, launched a plan for settlement on the banks of the River of the West before John Jacob Astor did. There were essential differences between the schemes of Boston and New York, as we will see. The Winships partly pursued the Gray and Kendrick design of northwest coast fur trading (discussed in Chapter 6), but they went further by proposing a shipping base and an agricultural settlement somewhere on the lower reaches of the river. They also continued the recently successful Russian schemes, to which they themselves had been party, that used Boston ships, Russian contracts and Aleut hunters in baidarkas and other craft to search out and exploit sea otter and fur seal habitats. Theirs, then, was a scheme of international linkages, a pioneering

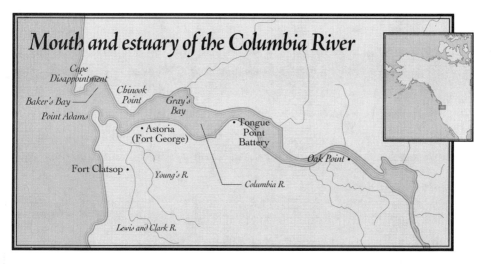

Mouth and estuary of the Columbia River

enterprise in Russian-American relations. Revolutionary it seems now, but in its time it was a marriage of convenience.

But here was the rub. Count Rezanov, the ambitious promoter of empire, had been unable to get into the Columbia River in his vessel to set up a base for the Russian-American Company in March 1806 (as recounted in Chapter 4). Perhaps the more capable Massachusetts mariners, who knew the river entrance and bar as well as any offshore sailing nation (though not better than the local Chinooks and Clatsops), had a better chance of success. Yankee enterprise could fulfill Russian destiny, and although Rezanov dearly wanted to claim the mouth of the river for the czar and use it as a shipbuilding yard and trading base, his aim surely was predicated on the benefits of trade. Nor did the Winships think solely in terms of putting down a marker for the United States there on the Columbia River so as to antedate the Russian-American Company; trade was their pre-eminent concern. They, like Mackenzie before and Astor after, valued the Columbia River as a vital link in global commerce. All these agents of empire knew that the northwest coast was, in common parlance, up for grabs, for it was the last unclaimed territory of North America, a prize still for the taking. Figuratively speaking, the mouth of the Columbia River had become the new Nootka Sound, the true river of fortune.

There is no doubt that the Winships were alive to Russian intentions to get into the Columbia and establish a base there. Rezanov had died in 1806, but his plan was taken up by others in the Russian-American Company. Thus, in early 1810, when Russian officers told Jonathan Winship Jr., who was sailing with them in a Russian vessel off the north tip of Vancouver Island, that they had their eyes covetously on the Columbia River and intended to erect a fort there, Jonathan's heart must have skipped a beat. As soon as he could, he sent word of this alarming news to his eldest brother Nathan, then at Hawaii, and told him "to proceed with all possible dispatch to the Columbia River to anticipate any movements of the Russians in that direction."[1] The Russians, for their part, were becoming increasingly alarmed by American traders—including, but not specifically, the Winships—who were running guns to the Aleuts and Tlingits, potentially subverting Russian power and causing an infinite amount of difficulty. The Russians intended, as of Rezanov's time, to put a stop to this growing aboriginal power. The Tlingit rising at old Sitka in 1802 continued to haunt them, and armed aboriginals at Yakutat Bay and elsewhere were carrying war to the Russians. The Boston gun runners posed a mounting problem to the sons of the czar.

Captain Nathan Winship, thirty-four, steered the ship *Albatross* for the wide, misty entrance of the Columbia on May 26, 1810, and crossed its shifting sands without incident. Beyond the estuary's tidal flow, he made his way upriver under sail whenever he could. The current was stiff. When the wind failed, as it often did, he resorted to the time-honoured custom of mariners in such circumstances: kedging. Lowering the long boat, he sent it ahead with the kedge anchor, which the boat crew dropped to the bottom when they had reached a certain distance from the *Albatross*. The ship hauled up against it. They did it once more, then again and yet again until, a tiring forty miles upstream, and six days after crossing the bar, they had their ship abreast of a bit of flat, dry land on the south bank (now the Oregon shore). They ran a hawser ashore and thereby secured the *Albatross* with warps to stout trees. The date was June 4, 1810. This spot came to be known as Fanny's Bottom, a rude compliment to Frances Clark, sister of Captain William Clark. Lewis and Clark had passed this way four years earlier, on March 26, 1806, and called it Fannys Island. The explorers had noted a prominent grove of oaks at the point, and oaks surely indicated dry, solid ground. Nathan Winship knew of this grove in advance, and he had it as his destination. The group of oaks at Fanny's Bottom was the first such grove that the Winship expedition came to. It was to be the seat of the Winships' western empire.

Nathan's sea captain brother, Jonathan Winship Jr., the driving force behind the scheme, planned a permanent settlement here, the first on the Columbia's lower reaches, and Nathan had brought twenty-three Hawaiians, or Kanakas, with him to do the heavy lifting. The Winships, ardent agriculturalists from Brighton, Massachusetts, a suburb of Boston, "intended that these wild Western shores [should] blossom like the rose."[2] They were God-fearing folk, these Yankee sailors, and as tough as they were courageous. The earliest historian of the Winship scheme at Oak Point, William Dane Phelps, showered abundant praise on the Winship plan as it developed in those early days when the Yankees were setting up their post: "A large building for a place of residence and trade, with the capabilities of a strong fortification, was partly erected, grounds were prepared for cultivation, and seed sown. It was the first building and planting by any white men on the banks of the [lower] Columbia; and adding, as it does, to the fact that the early development of the trade of the Northwest Coast and California was principally due to the enterprise and energy of Boston merchants and seamen, it should be truthfully recorded."[3]

Oak Point boasted good alluvial soil; a prominent place for defence; and good timber for building a palisade, a fort designed for trading, houses, barns and outbuildings. Here horticulture and animal husbandry, if successful, might sustain the shipping enterprise, and trade with Russian Sitka and Spanish California could be encouraged. The trade to China would grow. Lewis and Clark had established beyond doubt that the Columbia River offered the only feasible conduit for trade in the far west in those latitudes, and they had also discovered that trade was confined to the lower hundred miles of the river, if that. Oak Point might be a middle point between ocean and hinterland, a place to start colonization and to exploit Pacific and China trades. The scheme foreshadowed by a dozen years or so what the Hudson's Bay Company did so magnificently at Fort Vancouver, where the Willamette joins the Columbia.

The Winship brothers put up a ten-foot-high log trading post for a start and then began to build a two-storey blockhouse. Cannons were to be mounted on the upper storey, and there were to be hinged openings on the ground floor through which muskets could be fired at hostile intruders. Hog pens were thrown up. However, the local Clatsop people, fearing the American traders intended to stay permanently, aimed musket fire and arrows at the fort from a distance. Winship and his men held their ground, at least at the outset, but soon the pressure and threats became too intense. Particularly "insolent" was the group at the mouth of the Columbia, who would brook no interference in the river's trade that might affect their pre-eminent position in it. This resistance was one reason, but by no means the sole reason, that Nathan Winship was forced to abandon the enterprise.[4]

Nathan did not anticipate the further hazards that lay ahead or he would have selected higher ground. Within two weeks of the ship's arrival, the river's summer flood, perhaps unusually high this particular year, inundated the post and carried much away. The post's timbers were uprooted; the early plantings destroyed; the hog pens ruined. All of this happened that same event-filled June, and Nathan Winship realized it was too late in the season to select another site and undertake similar work elsewhere. He had no choice but to abandon the scheme and ease the *Albatross* safely down the river to Grays Bay, where the pilot told Winship what he surely had already guessed: that the Clatsops had intended to capture the ship when it was upriver. Winship continued his trade but was not altogether successful. At least he had not lost the cargo shipped from Boston, and with it he intended to continue the venture. Eventually the *Albatross* carried a mixed freight of northwest coast furs and Marquesas Islands sandalwood to China and then made a safe passage home to Boston.

Nathan Winship passes from the history of the Columbia River, little known but sympathetically remembered. He failed, though not for want of trying. Events overcame him, and when they did, Russia's chance to have a true trading ally and partner in the Columbia dissipated. But the motives of Rezanov and his successors are not entirely clear, and those of the Winships are not carved in stone either. A few years after this amazing, if stunted, attempt at a Boston base on the Columbia River, some North West Company fur traders passed by the post, noting its lovely but fatal location, oblivious to its true intent to forestall the Russians.[5] And so it was left to Astor, in a lower location on the river, to try to effect something of permanence.

John Jacob Astor, a German immigrant to the United States who developed a business in musical instruments and furs, had a longstanding connection with the fur barons of Montreal. He had visited Montreal as early as 1788, and in the course of annual trips to that shipping and banking capital of Canada, he got to know all the major traders, bankers and shippers who formed the various firms making up the North West Company and its rivals. Astor kept a residence and warehouse in that lovely quarter of old Montreal that still exists, and because he dined regularly with the business elite of Montreal, of which Simon McTavish, Sir Alexander Mackenzie and William McGillivray were solid members, he had every opportunity to learn all the tricks of the trade.

The Nor'Westers, ever cautious and defensive, were not about to let him get even a share in the company; in fact, he would not qualify technically to become a wintering partner in the interior trade, for he had no experience there. But they were certainly prepared to let him, by specific arrangements, have shares of a joint nature in what the Montrealers called the southwest trade—that is, the fur trade south and west of Michilimackinac. Traders such as Andrew Todd had done well in Michigan, Ohio and toward the juncture of the Missouri with the Mississippi, and they had helped the Spanish Missouri Company in its attempt to keep the Canadians out of the northern fringe of Louisiana (see Chapter 7). But after Louisiana passed to American sovereignty, and after the Lewis and Clark expedition had shown the flag in this quarter and upstream on the Missouri, Astor, the complete opportunist, wanted to capitalize in every way possible. The arrangement he worked out with the Nor'Westers involved trading British goods into that area via Michilimackinac and other depots. This became Astor's first thriving fur-trading business, but it was a shared arrangement with the North West Company, under the banner of the Michilimackinac Company. This company operated for a decade from 1803. At the end of this period, the Nor'Westers withdrew, for they were suffering seriously from American government prohibitions, including the Non-Intercourse Act, which forbade the ingress and egress of supplies and returns to and from the United States.

Astor's next venture bore a resemblance to Canadian endeavours, borrowing their techniques and talents, but with an American guise. Astor's business arrangements have been the subject of many outstanding historical and biographical studies.[6] These make clear the difficulties he faced and all his complications with the canny Canadian traders and bankers, mindful as they were of their pursuit of a monopoly in the interior trade of Athabasca, New Caledonia and the Columbia and Snake rivers country, the last just beginning to make its appearance as a prospect. But Astor thought he could outrange the Canadians. In early 1808 he wrote to the mayor of New York, De Witt Clinton, and described his brazen plan for a company that would expand the fur trade in the United States even farther than it had been extended by the companies in Canada. He planned a series of posts all the way from the Missouri to the mouth of the Columbia, along a corridor discovered by Lewis and Clark. Astor thought, a little rashly, that it would take only four or five years to "embrace … the whole of the fur trade & extend it to the western ocean … and to have a range of Posts or trading houses on the Rout made by Captain Lewis to the Sea."[7] The Corps of Discovery had opened the path and even suggested places to erect posts.

Astor, gripped by powerful optimism, seized on the opportunity to work out the destiny of Lewis and Clark. What they had done for science, he could do for commerce. Westward lay the course of trade and even empire. He also aimed to link St. Louis and New Orleans in the grand plan. His supreme objective was an American firm backed by the United States government, for Astor knew he faced retaliation from the North West Company as soon as his plan was launched.

Astor, then, found himself bound on a grand new departure, a dangerous one. He sought Jefferson's advice and aid for a scheme that essentially involved the granting of a monopoly to Astor's company. Astor proposed that such a scheme would really allow for a benign Indian policy, one protective of the interests of aboriginal people. But Jefferson could not grant much hope to Astor's importunities. There could be no monopoly. Besides, the Missouri Fur Company, headed by the energetic Manuel Lisa and based in St. Louis, had similar designs on the upper Missouri and Yellowstone rivers and intended to send traders across the Continental Divide as soon as possible (as we saw in Chapter 11, they may have already been busy in the vicinity of the Missouri's Three Forks). Astor was tenacious, pressuring Jefferson and the administration for various means of support—a monopoly, which he could not have; then armed assistance in the form of a warship at the mouth of the Columbia, which could only be considered in wartime.

He rose to new heights of energy when a recently appointed Russian consul-general, Andrei Dashkov, arrived in New York in June 1809 and complained about American merchant ships sailing Alaskan inshore waters. These ships subverted Russian trade and put arms into hostile hands. The Bostonians, complained Dashkov, "before our eyes shamelessly trade powder, lead, pistols, and muskets."[8] From the diplomat, Astor heard of the Russian settlements' drastic need for supplies. No matter how strongly the Russians complained of intrusions, their Alaskan and North American trade depended on American shipping and mercantile know-how. Almost immediately, Astor purchased a ship, the *Enterprise*, and sent it from New York in mid-November 1809 under the command of an old China hand, John Ebbets, who knew those seas and was also personally known to Alexander Baranov, manager of the Russian-American Company at New Archangel. As expected, Ebbets did well in Alaskan waters, giving Astor the confirmation he needed that the outlay for vessel and cargo was well worth it. But what stalled Ebbets, and gave Astor much concern, was the skipper's failure to get the *Enterprise* into the Columbia River during the winter. This meant a trading post could not be established there, which had been Astor's treasured dream. Yet again, nature ruled the sailing ship and controlled the fortunes of the lower Columbia.

Astor had tried to cut the North West Company partners into this deal, offering them a one-third share even before the ship had sailed from New York. He even proposed to tie in half of the Michilimackinac Company purchase with the arrangement. But the Nor'Westers could only decline this shrewd offer politely and with regret. The failure to fix up a co-association led to bitter rivalry at the mouth of the Columbia River. "In the end Astor's offer was rejected," writes W. Kaye Lamb, adding "the Montreal merchants decided to gamble on the future course of trading restrictions. Within a few months they had reason to regret their decision. The mid-western frontier was tightly closed to British trade; the plight of the Michilimackinac Company threatened to become desperate." The Montreal traders, having second thoughts, did seek an accommodation and travelled to New York to meet Astor, but the hard-driving Astor put a time limit on the deal; given the slow-moving nature of the North West Company's business dealings, which required agreement of both the wintering and the summer partners, meeting the deadline proved impossible. Thus Astor, making good his threatened promise, carried out his plans for the Columbia River by organizing a new corporation, the Pacific Fur Company, on June 23, 1810.[9]

Astor sought to carry out the Columbian enterprise envisioned by the North West Company, but with one exception: he would be the new premier and see the plan to fruition, unlike Alexander Mackenzie, who had failed to become the ultimate corporate chief in the rivalry with Simon McTavish. Astor would hold fifty of the one hundred shares he issued. Thirty-five of the remaining shares were assigned to eight Canadians Astor lured away from the North West Company, and the final fifteen shares were reserved for Astor's future disposal. Astor imagined that an annual council of field partners would be held at Astoria much as the Nor'Westers did at Fort William.

The new company was designed to be strong in the field and at sea, with powerful, seasoned traders and ex-Nor'Westers in key positions, backed by mighty capital at the centre. Recruiting in Montreal and St. Louis, Astor enticed many from former engagements. Wilson Price Hunt, a St. Louis merchant, came onside early as the chief agent, and he recruited Ramsay Crooks and Robert McClelland. Astor brought in three former Nor'Westers: Alexander MacKay, Donald Mackenzie and Duncan McDougall. MacKay was Astor's prize catch, for he had gone to the Pacific as lieutenant to Alexander Mackenzie in 1793 and was now to sail to the northwest coast in the *Tonquin* (making him uniquely, when this was accomplished, the first person to go to the Pacific Northwest by land and by sea from eastern North America). Donald McKenzie, a huge man characterized as perpetual motion, was later dubbed "lord of the Northwest" for his success in opening the Snake River country and other places. MacKay, McKenzie and McDougall, lured with five shares each from Astor, became powerful partners with much to gain or lose in the venture at hand. Of these, MacKay was the ranking partner in the planned seagoing expedition. Astor continued his talent hunt and recruited David Stuart and his nephew Robert Stuart, both Canadians.

Hunt, unlike MacKay, was inexperienced in frontier travel, but he was in charge of leading a large expedition from St. Louis, following Lewis and Clark's discoveries and recommendations. Hunt was also familiar with the fur-trade travels of John Colter, George Drouillard and perhaps others in the years after Lewis and Clark had completed the expedition. His party consisted of sixty-five people, including women and children. It proceeded up the Missouri at a dangerously late hour, in late October 1811. Manuel Lisa became worried about what he regarded as an incursion to the upper Missouri and Yellowstone, and for a time the Astorians and the Missouri Fur Company operated in a strange combination of antagonism and mutual need.[10] Terrible privations occurred in the Rocky Mountains that winter. An advance party from Hunt's group arrived at Astoria in January 1812, and the rest, apart from those detailed to set up interior posts on the Okanogan and Columbia rivers, arrived in June.

The sea expedition was headed by the dictatorial Jonathan Thorn, a lieutenant in the US Navy, then on a two-year furlough, who commanded the ship *Tonquin*, 269 tons, which sailed from New York on September 6, 1810. MacKay, McDougall, David Stuart and Robert Stuart embarked on the ship, as did clerks Gabriel Franchère and Alexander Ross, both chroniclers of the expedition. Thorn thought little of these traders, whom he regarded as landlubbers and braggarts. He had been selected by Astor, who apparently forgot that diplomacy, tact and care were necessary in trading with the indigenous people of the northwest coast. The ship arrived at the Columbia River entrance after a long and tedious voyage on March 22, 1811. A whole boat's crew was lost

The Tonquin, *owned by John Jacob Astor's Pacific Fur Company, sailed north from Astoria on June 5, 1811, "to trade for peltries." It is speculated that she ended her days in Clayoquot Sound, Vancouver Island. There were no survivors.* Library and Archives Canada, C-004268

at the river entrance, having been sent ahead of the *Tonquin* by the impetuous Thorn to sound and mark the perilous channel. After some days of reconnaissance, the officers selected a site for the post on the south shore of the Columbia estuary, some twelve miles from the sea.

On April 12 the whole party, thirty-three in number, left the ship and camped on shore. "However pleasing the change, to be relieved from a long and tedious voyage, and from the tyranny of a sullen despotic captain, the day was not one of pleasure, but of labor," wrote Ross, adding, "The misfortunes we had met with in crossing the fatal bar had deadened all sensibility, and cast a melancholy gloom over our most sanguine expectations. In our present position, everything harmonized with our feelings, to darken our future prospects. Silent and with heavy hearts we began the toil of the day, in clearing away brush and rotten wood for a spot to encamp on." Ross describes the place:

> From the site of the establishment, the eye could wander over a varied and interesting scene. The extensive Sound, with its rocky shores, lay in front; the breakers on the bar, rolling in wild confusion, closed the view on the west; on the east, the country as far at the Sound had a wild and varied aspect; while towards the south, the impervious and magnificent forest darkened the landscape, as far as the eye could reach. The place thus selected for the emporium of the west, might challenge the whole continent to produce a spot of equal extent presenting more difficulties to the settler: studded with gigantic trees of almost incredible size, many of them measuring fifty feet in girth, and so close together, and intermingled with huge rocks, as to make it a work of no ordinary labor to level and clear the ground. With this task before us, every man, from the highest to the lowest, was armed with an axe in one hand and a gun in the other.[11]

Thorn, impatient to a fault, was keen to get on with the next order of business: the Alaska trade as far north as Cook Inlet, with calls at trading places along the way. On June 5, 1811, with a fair wind, the *Tonquin* crossed the bar outward bound. Thorn made for Vancouver Island en route to New Archangel and a rendezvous with Baranov. He never met the lord of Alaska, for at some port on Vancouver Island—the place has never been identified conclusively, though there are many possibilities, including the most likely spot, Templar Channel in Clayoquot Sound, but also Hesquiat, Nootka and Nahwitti (at the north end of Vancouver Island)—Thorn got into a wrangle with some Natives. The source of difficulty is not fully understood, for the evidence is fragmentary, contradictory and inconclusive. Perhaps the indigenes intended to settle old scores for some previous trader's actions. Perhaps Thorn was too brittle in his

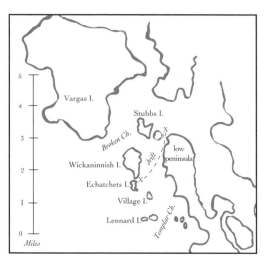

It is suspected Astor's ship Tonquin *was lost just beyond Echatchets (Echachist) Island, shown on this map (based on the July 1929 sketch by John Hosie, Provincial Archivist of British Columbia). If this information is correct, the anchor, or one of her anchors, is off Echachist Island, and whatever remains of the hull survives beyond the extremity of the low peninsula west of Tofino.*

business requirements, too cheap. Ashore, for a time, MacKay had done well in trade. He returned to the ship. However, many canoes surrounded the *Tonquin*, and their occupants swarmed the deck in increasingly worrying numbers.

Thorn ordered the crew to get the ship ready to sail, but the Natives resisted. Before long, shots were fired and vicious hand-to-hand combat ensured. Thorn and MacKay were killed, and although it is said that five sailors got away in a boat, they were never seen again. In the thick of the action, the fighting spread throughout the ship and a fire below decks ignited a keg of powder. The *Tonquin* blew up. All officers and men died in the huge blast. Chief trader MacKay never got to tell his tale of travels with Mackenzie. An interpreter named Joseachal, a Quinalt, was the sole survivor and reached Astoria more than a year later to tell the hideous tale of the last, fatal hours of Astor's vessel.[12] And so closed an eventful first chapter in the Pacific Fur Company's marine department.

At the same time as the *Tonquin* and its crew were meeting their fate on Vancouver Island in the summer of 1811, the men left behind at Astoria were putting up trading posts in the interior. Supplies, food and labourers, many of them Kanakas, or Sandwich Islanders, came from the coast. By the time Hunt's advance party arrived in January 1812, much had been accomplished as far inland as the Okanogan's confluence with the Columbia, four hundred miles upstream from the Pacific shore. In May 1812 the ship *Beaver* arrived from New York with supplies and reinforcements. Hunt sailed in this vessel to New Archangel to keep the contract with the Russians, leaving Duncan McDougall in charge of Astoria. All appeared promising. The beginnings of Astoria and the Astorian world of Pacific commerce had been launched.

Greater difficulties lay ahead for Astor and the Astorians, but a marker had been laid down on the Columbia River for the United States. Astor never got his hoped-for monopoly and, like the North West Company, had only the distant backing of government, but the *Tonquin's* expedition to the mouth of the river, and the planting of the settlement on that hillside with a commanding view of Young's Bay, marked a chapter in American empire and international rivalry that Washington could not ignore. Where the Winship scheme had faltered, Astor's bore fruit. Both were tied in with Russian contracts and designs, and both wanted to keep the British out of the Columbia River and the northwest coast lying between Russian America and Alta California.

Jefferson, though sympathetic, could not help Astor directly. But in 1813 he showered praise on Astoria. He called it "the germ of a great, free, and independent empire." Astoria would help establish liberty and self-government. The post, besides, formed the basis for the US claim to lands west of the Continental Divide, said Jefferson. John Quincy Adams, Secretary of State, even went so far as to refer to the Pacific Northwest as "the empire of Astoria."[13] It was not quite that, surely.

Even so, Astoria came to have a commanding presence in the American understanding of this early chapter of westward expansion. The settlement's place in history was assured once novelist and master storyteller Washington

Irving—using such important texts as the account of the clerk Alfred Seton, who was on the *Tonquin* voyage and remained at Astoria through its founding days—published his book *Astoria; or, Anecdotes of an Enterprise Beyond the Rocky Mountains* in 1839.

In all, Astoria's first year was an epic and tragic beginning to occupation of the lower Columbia and was characterized by misfortune, mixed leadership and violence. Before long the Canadian tide, in the person of David Thompson, the North West Company traders, and British merchant and naval ships, would arrive to dramatically alter the affairs of the Columbia.

Chapter 13

DAVID THOMPSON AND THE
VOYAGE OF A SUMMER MOON, 1811

W ord of Astor's intentions passed quickly among the Nor'Westers. From Montreal, the agents of the North West Company sent an urgent message to their counterparts in London on January 23, 1810. The letter relayed the news from the northwest interior to those who steered the company's business at the hub of empire: McTavish, Fraser and Company; Inglis, Ellice and Company; and Sir Alexander Mackenzie (the latter, though denied influence over the interior trade, was a powerful lobbyist in London. His travels, discoveries and book gave him added authenticity). These gentlemen were the ones who placed pressure on those departments of British government—particularly the Foreign Office, the Colonial and War Office, and the Board of Trade—that directed the statecraft of the empire and administered its various functions.

The Montrealers introduced the issue at hand with considerable care: "We now address you on a subject of some importance, and which in the present uncertain state of things generally, you may think ill-timed. We should be inclined to this opinion did not a particular circumstance, about to take

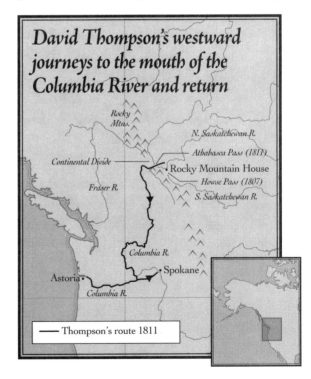

David Thompson's westward journeys to the mouth of the Columbia River and return

Rocky Mtns.

N. Saskatchewan R.

Athabasca Pass (1811)

Continental Divide

Rocky Mountain House

Howse Pass (1807)

Fraser R.

S. Saskatchewan R.

Columbia R.

Spokane

Astoria

Columbia R.

—— Thompson's route 1811

place render it necessary that some steps should, without loss of time, be taken, for ascertaining the rights and claims of Great Britain to the Columbia River and North West Coast of America, which is also connected, in this instance, with the Interests of the North West Company."

Now they came to the important business:

> Since the Expedition of Captain Lewis across the Rocky Mountains from the Head waters of the Mississourie [sic] to the Columbia, the Government and Citizens of the United States have been in the Habit of considering that River and Coasts adjacent, as belonging to their Country, either as forming part of Louisiana, or in right of the Expedition conducted by Captain Lewis. Neither of these pretensions, we presume, will be considered of any validity. Vancouver's Survey of that Coast and Sir Alexander Mackenzie's Expedition from the Peace River to the Pacific, surely, give a prior right to our discovery of these Countries: their Claims, therefore, must rest on it's forming a part of Louisiana, which, if possible, is still more preposterous. With respect to possession, that also is in our favor, for the posts of the North West Company are, and have been for several years, established on the Waters which fall into the Columbia, or on the Branches of that River.

What set the alarm bells ringing in Montreal was news that a rival American expedition, Astor's, was under immediate contemplation and in fact intended to sail from New York early the next spring, 1810, for the purpose of establishing trading posts on the Columbia River and the northwest coast. A similar expedition might sail from Boston.

> The merchants from the latter city have long traded between the North West Coast of America and China; but never attempted establishing themselves. It is now time to ascertain whether the British Government will permit these

establishments on what has hitherto been British Territory, and whether they will continue to prohibit British Subjects from carrying on a trade between China, and the North West Coast, which Aliens are allowed to enjoy unmolested. We should hope not, and that the Honorable East India Company, will not on this occasion, refuse their indulgence, on what depends on them.

This appeal followed an earlier one in which the Nor'Westers sought assistance to establish themselves on the Columbia. The object being a national one, the Nor'Westers expected some reasonable remuneration, either in a pecuniary way or through an exclusive right of trade on the Columbia River and nearby coast for a certain number of years from the time the first post was put up, either from the interior or by sea.[1] In other words, the company demanded government's backing and assurances, not for the immediate undertaking—which they intended to cover with their own resources—but for the future of its holdings, a fair enough requirement given the costs involved.[2]

Mackenzie needed no convincing by the Montrealers, for this had been his song of commerce and empire for nearly two decades, especially the last one, since the publication of his influential book. The Nor'Westers were powerful and righteous in their cause but often ineffectual lobbyists; they had to make their case over and over again and with increasing stridency. Always a deterrent to their full success was the vested interest of the Hudson's Bay Company, for that corporation boasted a royal charter, the territorial and thus commercial monopoly over at least two million square miles known as Rupert's Land, and, by implication, control of the navigation of Hudson Bay and waters leading to Hudson Strait. In commercial rivalry against the Bay traders or the Americans on the southern reaches of their influence, the Nor'westers worked on their own, largely without government support. But their trade was being followed by the flag of the United Kingdom, and they were setting in place much of what later became the southern boundary of western Canada.

In 1810, the matter of the proposed exclusive company loomed as the stumbling block, as had been the case in 1808, when Mackenzie proposed, on behalf of the Nor'Westers, that exclusive privilege of commerce be awarded in that area. This would be much better, he said, than setting up such military and naval establishments, with expensive administrative appointments to look after their well-being, as would be necessary to protect an open and general trade. In 1808, Mackenzie submitted to the government a plan for a line of posts across British territory to the mouth of the Columbia, "where a Commercial Colony might be planted, from whence a Trade could be carried on and extended, not only with the Interior but along the Coast and its adjacent Islands." In his view, the North West Company could best fulfil the plan, but the government would have to grant an exclusive right of trade in the Columbia and its tributary waters and along an extent of coast for a given period, as well as grant portions of lands necessary to carry on the general object of the undertaking. Mackenzie had also made clear that the company would have to be able to transit the territory of the Hudson's Bay Company, shipping commodities and freight in bond (which would ensure it was not sold until it reached the new settlements). The North West Company was prepared to give assurances on the matter of bonded goods. But it also called for a suspension of East India Company privileges of direct trade to China.[3] The Nor'Westers desperately needed to get a foot in the door of the China market and send ships directly to Canton.

The various departments of state considered the Nor'Westers' several appeals and petitions, now stretching over three or four years. On one occasion there was official worry that naval force would be required because of Britain's "being at war with Spain." That was later replaced by the wording "being at variance with Americans." For one reason or another, the government got cold feet. It was worried about imperial overstretch and endless complications with rivals. When in 1811 the North West Company petitioned the government for a charter of incorporation for a period of twenty-one years (precisely the terms that the Hudson's Bay Company got for its licence west of the Continental Divide in 1821), the Nor'Westers made it clear they intended to carve out a large empire in the Pacific Northwest. The petition reads:

> Your Petitioners therefore submit to Your Majesty's most
> gracious Consideration this their humble Application for

a Charter of Incorporation, for Twenty one Years, for the granting and securing to your Petitioners, and their Successors, the Sole and exclusive Trade and Commerce of that part of North America situate between the Summit of the Chain of Mountains called the Rocky Mountains on the East and the Pacific Ocean on the west, and extending from Cape Blanco in the Latitude of 42 North to 60 North, together with the Seas, Streights, Bays, Inlets, Lakes, Rivers, Creeks, and Lands which lie within these Limits and the Countries, Territories, Lands, Coasts, and Confines which border upon the different Branches, and Sources of the River Columbia or Oregan, or by whatever other name it may now or hereafter be called or designated, being the great River which falls into the Pacific Ocean in or about Latitude 46 North, and also the Countries, Lands, Territories, Coasts and Confines bordering upon all those Lakes, Rivers, Waters and Streams which are discharged into the Northern or Frozen Sea through the great Slave Lake and Mackenzie's River, in whatever Latitude or Longitude the Branches and Sources of the Said Rivers, Waters, and Streams may be situated, and of the produce of those Countries.[4]

What were they dreaming of in this proposal of commerce and empire? Something to rival the firmly entrenched Hudson's Bay Company? That certainly. They also intended to establish an empire west of the mountains equivalent to the Bay traders' domain of Rupert's Land, a great Columbian department, stretching south to where California meets Oregon today and north as far as the Gulf of Alaska. That would give them, among other things, the Snake, Columbia, Skagit, Fraser and Skeena watersheds flowing into the Pacific, and the Mackenzie River basin's waters flowing to the Arctic. The Yukon River, which flows to Bering Strait, perhaps fell outside their scheme. Around the same time as the petition, a widely circulated pamphlet of uncertain authorship, *On the Origin and Progress of the North-West Company*, warned of Astor's plans, from New York, to take possession of and settle the banks of the Columbia River.

The British government of the day, like many others, lived in a paper and legal world. Caution was the order of the day. The Mackenzie project, now in its new guise, was considered by the Board of Trade. Then it was shifted to the chambers of the Law Officers of the Crown for a determination as to the legal ramifications. The Law Officers gave the opinion that there could be no objection to the proposed articles of incorporation provided United States territory was not infringed on. They added a further proviso that no grant of sale and exclusive trade should be made, thus hobbling the project from a point of financial security and incentive.[5] No form of *imperium* along the lines of that already existing in the Hudson's Bay Company's Rupert's Land could be duplicated in the far western territory.

For the moment the Columbian enterprise was being shifted through the dispatch boxes and courier companies of London, with the Nor'Westers' London agents relaying messages to their partners in Montreal. No substantial breakthrough had occurred, though there were promising signs. Meanwhile, Astor had made his proposal to the Montreal agents to form a joint venture, much as they had done at Michilimackinac, but they had turned down the offer. The Nor'Westers, with highly principled zeal and belief in their own methods of conducting and expanding their business, intended to go it alone at all costs. They very much reflected the attitude of Mackenzie, and they did so on the basis of the continuing enormous profits of the fur trade, as new watersheds were added to old, and as transportation linkages—the mastery of which the Nor'Westers held above all others—became transcontinental: Montreal to the mouth of the Columbia River and back.

At their July 1810 rendezvous, the partners of the North West Company determined to show their hand at the mouth of the Columbia River. They instructed David Thompson to renew his attempt to travel from the source to its outlet into the Pacific, and to do so without inviting any hostility. They had heard of Astor's project and knew that he had engaged some of the clerks of the North West Company, with plans to send the *Tonquin* around Cape Horn, destined for the Columbia, later that year. There might still be time to forestall the Americans.

"Everything was changed ... I was now obliged to take 4 canoes and to proceed to the mouth of the Columbia to oppose them," Thompson wrote in response to the North West Company's directive that he oppose the Astorians in that distant quarter. He returned quickly from Lac la Pluie (Rainy Lake), where he had taken the furs he collected during the 1809 season, to Rocky Mountain House and then set off on his far western expedition of trade and examination. His objective was to reach the mouth of the Columbia River before August 1811. He would have to begin his return from the Pacific shore by that time in order to cross the Rocky Mountains in safety before wintertime.[6]

From Rocky Mountain House he worked through Athabasca Pass, where the going was tough, eventually arrived at his post near Windemere Lake and continued by way of Clark's Fork and the Pend Oreille River to Spokane House. From there he went to Kettle Falls on the Columbia, where he and his

David Thompson of the North West Company crossed Athabasca Pass in the winter of 1810, destined for the Columbia River. The Nor'Westers had learned of John Jacob Astor's scheme to develop a Pacific trading base on the river, and Thompson, in a difficult and ultimately vain attempt, was sent to forestall Astor. Library and Archives Canada, C-070258

men built a large cedar canoe, modelled on a birch-bark line. He was about to embark on what he called "Voyage to the Mouth of the Columbia by the Grace of God 1811 by D. Thompson & 7 Men on the part of the NW Company."

On July 3, with two men of the Simpoil nation, he "set off on a voyage down the Columbia River, to explore this River, in order to open out a Passage for the Interior Trade with the Pacific Ocean."[7] The next day he learned of the arrival of a vessel at the mouth of the river. It was undoubtedly Astor's *Tonquin*, and perhaps the news did not surprise the explorer.

On the morning of July 8, Thompson's canoe brigade was at the juncture of the Columbia and Snake rivers. Thompson went ashore. He had a small pole put up there, with a half sheet of paper on it, "well tied about it," he noted in his journal for that day. This was his formal claim to the whole Columbia River watershed. It read:

> Know hereby that this Country is claimed by Great Britain as part of it's Territories and that the NW Company of Merchants from Canada, finding the Factory for this people inconvenient for them, do hereby intend to erect a Factory in this Place for the Commerce of the Country around. D. Thompson. Junction of the Shawpatin [Snake] River with the Columbia, July 8th, 1811.

For the first time, Thompson's route crossed that of Lewis and Clark.[8] This was a meeting of destinies, of empires, now intersecting on the River of the West. The river had become borderland by overland discovery. The Mackenzie project was about to be realized in terms of discovery, but something was missing in terms of determined ownership and national claims by imperial Britain. Thompson was not alarmed, and he showed no anxiety, for his duty seemed confined to taking longitudes and latitudes, transiting by way of the river to the coast and insuring that the company's trade, at least upriver, was secure. He was no imperial pro-consul, only an agent of trade and science.

On his way downriver, Thompson met a man who had met the American explorers. This "Principal Chief of all the Tribes of the Shawpatin" was known to Thompson as Yellepit. Writes Thompson: "He had an American medal of 1801 Thos Jefferson & a small Flag of that Nation—he was a stately good looking Man of ab' 40 years old, well dressed .... I found him intelligent; he was also very friendly, & we discoursed a long time & settled on the Junction of the Shawatin River for a House &c."

For several weeks, perhaps longer, that half piece of paper stayed where Thompson had posted it. Then one of Astor's clerks, Alexander Ross, chanced upon it. "That he should have attempted to incite the Indians against us, in our helpless and almost forlorn state, was conduct which the world must condemn." Ross, typically hot-headed, over-reacted and misunderstood Thompson's essentially non-political purposes among the aboriginal people. Thompson was looking for trading partners and allies, but he had no intention of upsetting any arrangement entered into by Lewis and Clark or the Winships or the Astorians. He did not know that the arrangements being worked up between the North West Company and the Pacific Fur Company had not been finalized. He, like the Astorians, was uncertain of their respective companies' positions on the eve of their meeting.[9]

When Thompson arrived at the head of Rock Island Rapids, near where Wentachee is today, he was greeted by five men of the Sinkowarsin people. On occasion, the indigenous people Thompson encountered seemed shy and distant or actually hid themselves (Gass and Whitehouse from the Lewis and Clark expedition made similar observations), and the Sinkowarsins were distressed and confused by the explorer's appearance. Thompson, like Clark before him, assuaged these anxieties. He passed the pipe, the villagers gathered round, and soon nervousness was replaced by excitement and exultation. In these encounters with strangers there was natural fear and reluctance, but in the meeting of Thompson and the Sinkowarsins, the latter brought him berries and roots as presents. Imagining Thompson as somehow god-like, they clapped their hands and extended them to the sky.[10]

The Thompson expedition made its steady passage downstream, with a portage at The Dalles. Gradually the stream widened even further, and the travellers passed several aboriginal houses on either side of the river. They went ashore and traded a few half-dried salmon. Farther downriver, they camped a short distance above Point Vancouver, which was the upriver extremity of William Broughton's survey for the Royal Navy "and well described by him."[11] At one o'clock in the afternoon of July 15, 1811, the weather mild and the wind westerly at Astoria, Thompson and the brigade beached their canoe at this post near the mouth of the Columbia River.

Fully eighteen years after Mackenzie crossed to Pacific tidewater from the continental interior by way of rivers and portages, the North West Company had finally arrived at the mouth of the River of the West. There had been no alacrity in discovery since Mackenzie's time, though the Royal Navy had explored and charted much of the coast, including this river's mouth, with considerable thoroughness. The mountain passes were hazardous in winter, subject to avalanches and heavy snow. The streams were precarious in spring flood. Pathways were few and far between and often clogged with trees and brush. Aboriginal guides often proved elusive. *Engagés* could and did desert.

No one man could be expected to secure British dominion at the mouth of this river. Even so, the Nor'Westers were culpable in not backing their considerable trading interests with early claims to territory on behalf of the sovereign. The prize thus escaped them in the first instance, though they were able to play many trump cards in the game of ownership that continued over the next several years. And it must be kept in mind by all students of history that the British preferred trade to dominion. They thought mainly in terms of oceans and littoral, not continents and rivers; having sent Cook, Vancouver and Broughton on their hydrographic surveys, the British may have considered that the job was done, the claims secured on the basis of priority of discovery if not actual possession. Thompson's little act of possession was really an afterthought.

Thompson, who did not lack a sense of occasion, arrived well-dressed and in a cedar canoe, with what is generally stated to be the British flag at the prow; in fact, it was probably the North West Company duster—a red ensign, with the Union flag in the upper left-hand corner and N.W. Co. marked in white block letters on the field. There were nine boatmen in all. On shore, the Astorian Gabriel Franchère said that he and his colleagues could not imagine the canoe to be one of their own people, who were crossing the continent following the route of Lewis and Clark. This was a canoe of strangers. "A relatively well-dressed man who seemed to be in command jumped ashore," noted Franchère, "and approaching us, told us that his name was David Thompson and that he was one of the partners of the North West Company."[12] Thompson said that he had crossed the continent during the preceding season, which was virtually true, and that because some of his men had deserted, he had been forced to winter at the base of the Rockies, near the source of the Columbia. That spring, he explained, he had built a canoe and had come all the way down to Astoria. He added, oddly, that the wintering partners had thought best to abandon all their trading posts west of the mountains on condition that the Pacific Fur Company not meddle in their trade to the east. In fact, the North West Company never had any intention of abandoning the posts it had built west of the Rocky Mountains since 1805. Thompson's statement was unauthorized, incorrect, and misleading. The only possible explanation for it is that Thompson must have assumed that the two firms had entered into some sort of partnership and that the North West Company owned one third of the Astorian enterprise.[13]

Thompson told Astorian senior partner Duncan McDougall, the post manager, that he was certain a coalition of the two companies had been arranged by this time. He presented a document to this effect, written by himself, at the time of his arrival. And he handed McDougall an extract of a letter written by the wintering partners from Kaministiquia to Mr. McGillivray on the same subject. "We returned to him an answer," McDougall recorded in the head-quarters log, and this was to the effect that the two companies ought to respect their own trading activities and presumably not encroach on the interests of the rival.[14]

Alexander Ross, who was also there to observe Thompson's arrival, says: "We were all rather surprised at the unexpected arrival of a North-West proprietor at Astoria, and still more so at the free and cordial reception given to an opponent." Among Ross's associates, the general feeling may have been one of surprise, even shock. Some may have shown indifference. But completing a transcontinental journey, even in stages over many years, was no mean feat. Duncan McDougall, an ex-North West Company man, received Thompson like a brother: "Nothing was too good for Mr. Thompson," writes the crabby Ross, "he had access everywhere; saw and examined everything; and whatever he asked for he got, as if he had been one of ourselves." On that distant margin of the fur-trading realms, they were all, in fact, brothers. Ross, undeniably partisan, looked to pick a fight with the Nor'Wester. "His own visit had no other object but to discourage us—a manoeuvre of the North-West policy to extend their own trade at the expense of ours; but he failed." Ross, overly self-righteous, protests too much when he says of Thompson: "The dangers and difficulties which he took great pains to paint in their worst colors, did not deter us. He forgot that in speaking to us, he was speaking to north-westers—men as experienced and as cunning as himself." Ross had more than a little Scottish thistle in him. Washington Irving, playing to sentiment, injudiciously wrote in his novel *Astoria*: "Though Mr. Thompson could be considered as little better than a spy in the camp, he was received with great cordiality by Mr. M'Dougal."[15]

The Nor'Westers had been first west of the Continental Divide, and by 1811 they had several small posts on the waters of the Columbia, along with those in New Caledonia. "Every one knew this, and knowing it, how could we account for the more than warm and unreserved welcome Mr. Thompson met with from Astor's representative," wrote Ross. "Unless, as some thought at the time, M'Dougall was trying to pay Mr. Thompson back with his own coin, by putting on a fair face, so as to dupe him into an avowal of his real object. This is more than probable, for in point of acuteness, duplicity, and diplomatic craft, they were perhaps well matched."[16]

On July 19, accompanied by Robert Stuart of the Pacific Fur Company, Thompson and his men went in their canoe across to the Chinook village and then out to Cape Disappointment, regarded as the termination of the river, in order to have a full view of the great and fabled ocean. They remained there until the tide came in, and the grandeur of the scene was not lost on Thompson: "At ebb tide we noticed the current of the river riding in waves over the surface to the sea for about four miles; on all the shores of this Ocean, the agitation of the sea is constantly breaking against the rocky shore with high surges, and my men now allowed the great volume of water forming these high surges to be far superior to those of any Lake."[17] He gave McDougall a vial of quicksilver so that the latter might be able to make an artificial horizon for the purpose

H.J. Warre's 1848 drawing of Cape Disappointment. Located on the northern side of the entrance to the Columbia River, it was named by John Meares on July 6, 1778. The name was adopted by Captain George Vancouver. Bruno de Hezeta saw it August 17, 1775, and called it Cabo de San Roque.

of astronomical observations. McDougall, lightning-like, turned this gift of mercury into an ointment, then the common treatment for syphilis.

Thompson remained seven days at Astoria and departed for the interior with his men on July 22. With him, for the initial part of the journey, went David Stuart and eight Astorians, who were to establish a post for the Pacific Fur Company "somewhere below the Falls of the Columbia." They built Fort Okanogan at the confluence of the Okanogan and Columbia rivers, the deepest penetration eastward of the Columbia watershed to that time. Thompson went on to Spokane House and eventually returned across the Rocky Mountains and back via Fort William to the annual rendezvous. He deserved a rest, for he had completed the full course of the river from its source, which he discovered, to its mouth. It had taken a wearisome four years. The partners voted him a per annum income so that he could gather and write up his journals and complete his grand map, and they provided one hundred pounds as recompense for all the equipment and supplies he had needed to complete his astronomical findings and other scientific work.

Thompson, like Mackenzie after his western journey, never returned to the Pacific cordillera. He had a remarkably long career afterward as a boundary surveyor, laying down most of the frontier between Ontario and its bordering states. Of his western work, Thompson wrote, with stoical pride: "Thus I have fully completed the survey of this part of North America from sea to sea, and by almost innumerable astronomical Observations have determined the positions of the Mountains, Lakes and Rivers, and other remarkable places of the northern part of this Continent; the Maps of all of which have been drawn, and laid down in geographical position, being now the work of twenty seven years."[18] This is no idle boast from one who did so much in such a brief space of time.

We leave Thompson now, refreshed by the knowledge that in 1813, on well-deserved furlough, he completed his treasured great map, which now hangs proudly in the Archives of Ontario in Toronto. On it he placed Mackenzie's River, and Fraser's, too. He always gave credit where credit was due. He had completed Mackenzie's geographical and cartographic tasks, gathering details from Fraser's perilous discoveries and those of others, such as little-known John Stuart.

Thompson was faithful to the tradition of the Nor'Westers but even moreso to science, for by compiling all those innumerable longitudes and latitudes, he could establish on paper the spatial relationships of them all. "This gentleman travelled as a geographer rather than a fur-trader," observed his contemporary Gabriel Franchère, who met him at Astoria.[19] That surely was the case. Thompson had begun his work at age fourteen, when he stepped ashore at Churchill on Hudson Bay. He had conquered the west with his astronomical gear, and he takes his rightful place in the pantheon of world explorers. In later years he was to complain that the British government never backed the interests of the North West Company, but rather left them exposed to the winds of fate. That is a correct assessment.

Thompson continues to be the subject of close examination and criticism.[20] He was not the man to forestall the ships or the overland parties of John Jacob Astor, and in his defence, it surely is clear that, had he arrived at the mouth of the Columbia River before the Astorians, in and of itself it would not have been enough to secure a foothold of British Empire on that spot. No man could carve out a quarter of empire for himself, king and country. Even if he had planted the Union Jack at the river mouth in advance of the Astorians, he would not have predated the Winships. He was a factor among many forces, an actor caught up in multiple imperial rivalries. But he is not lost to history, and he grows with our better knowing him. All that he could do on the borderlands could be swept away in diplomatic arrangements or at the treaty table. Thompson knew this and distrusted the diplomats, with good cause.

Chapter 14

THE FORTUNES OF WAR

S ix years after Lewis and Clark concluded their great reconnaissance, Canadians found themselves at war with the Americans. That war now cast a long shadow over the affairs of the Columbia. It made the rivalry for control of the river estuary and fur-bearing watershed a matter of urgency.

The War of 1812, as the conflict came to be called, was fought over the impressment of American seamen by British naval commanders. Another cause was the struggle for the continental interior north of Louisiana, west of Upper Canada and south of the Hudson's Bay Company's Rupert's Land. Both these causes, especially the question of impressment, were mentioned in President James Madison's June 19, 1812, address to Congress, in which he proclaimed a state of war with Britain and the British Empire. What Madison did not say on that day was that the US government intended to employ force to back its claims to the Columbia River lands, hitherto claimed by Britain and the United States on grounds of priority of discovery or, in the case of Britain, diplomatic arrangement with a third party, Spain. Inasmuch as the intended force could not be made over land, it would have to be asserted by sea, and thus the rivalry passed from an overland phase to a seaborne one. The route via Cape Horn became the ultimate passage to the Pacific in northern latitudes.

Canadian traders, whose special pleading for protection and support in peacetime had fallen on deaf ears, reasserted their quest for primacy in the Columbia River area and redoubled their pressure on government for protection. In wartime, their fortunes were about to change for the better.

The first Astorians from overland reached the post on January 18, 1812, five months before the United States declared war. In August 1812, North West Company agents in Montreal, acting on a resolution passed at the annual meeting at Fort William, urged their London partners to press the British government for convoy support for a company ship, the *Isaac Todd*, that they planned to send to the Columbia via the Horn. As if by magic, the outbreak of war ended the British ministry's indifference to the pleas of the Nor'Westers and gave it a reason to act. In London, the Lords Commissioners of the Admiralty discussed the proposed mission with two key fur traders, both crusty fellows, Donald McTavish and John McDonald of Garth. As a result, their lordships agreed that the thirty-six–gun frigate *Phoebe* should convoy the fur-trading and supply vessel to the northwest coast, where the warship could remain to clear the coast of hostile vessels.

The *Isaac Todd*, 350 tons and carrying a letter of marque, was the pioneering ship of the company's Columbian enterprise. Fitted out in London at the expense of one of the partnerships of the North West Company, she mounted twenty guns and was well equipped in every way for a long and hazardous voyage. A slow sailer, she was also characterized by having a miserable commander and a rascally crew. The *Isaac Todd* left Portsmouth on March 25, 1813, in company with the *Phoebe*. McTavish and McDonald, as part owners, sailed as supercargoes. For the voyage they put in their own supply of barrelled beef, cheese and English porter beer, and McTavish had even engaged as his companion a flaxenhaired seamstress, Miss Jane Barnes, the first European woman to arrive at the mouth of the Columbia River (and a subject of much notoriety). Around the same time, an overland expedition of a hundred fur traders, led by John George McTavish and Alexander Henry the Younger, were to leave Fort William with the intention of meeting the ships at the Columbia sometime between May and August 1813. John George McTavish carried a message across the continent stating that the *Isaac Todd* was "accompanied by a frigate, to take and destroy everything that is American on the N.W. Coast." That would include any American shipping and the post at Astoria.

The Admiralty issued secret orders to the captain of the *Phoebe*, Commodore James Hillyar, and hoped that the destination of the vessels would not become known. The Nor'Westers, however, had loose tongues, and at Rio de Janeiro, Donald McTavish and John McDonald began to chat publicly about the mission. When Hillyar opened his "most secret orders" four days after leaving Rio, the cat was already out of the bag. "The principal object of the service on which you are employed," ran the orders, "is to protect and render every assistance in your power to the British traders from Canada, and to destroy, and if possible, totally annihilate any settlements which the Americans may have formed either on the Columbia River or on the neighboring coasts."[1] The Admiralty intended a direct voyage to the northwest coast but worried that the *Isaac Todd* might encounter the USS *Essex*, a successful raider working in the waters and islands off the Pacific coast of South America. (As it turned out, the *Phoebe* joined the British warship *Cherub* a year later, in March 1814, to find and then defeat the *Essex* outside the port of Valparaiso, forcing that vessel's surrender.)

In 1813, the *Phoebe* had rounded Cape Horn and arrived at the island of Juan Fernandez off the coast of Chile. This was the designated rendezvous for Hillyar's squadron on this assignment. There Hillyar learned from Spanish officials that the entrance of the Columbia was too shallow to admit a frigate, such as the *Phoebe* was. Accordingly, he ordered the sloop of war *Racoon*, Commander William Black, on the mission to take Astoria. Black was a seasoned officer with ten years in the navy, a good deal of fighting experience and a keen sense of responsibility to the king, the government and the naval service. He had studied history, and from the outset of his assignment he regarded the northwest coast of North America, north of Alta California, as Nova Albion—the territory claimed for Elizabeth Regina by Francis Drake in 1579. As a result, he regarded the Spanish as interlopers north of San Francisco Bay, and he attached the same label to the Russians, who had put up their Fort Ross at a spot north of Drakes Bay in 1812. Black saw the world through the narrow prism of a dedicated naval officer on state and imperial business. But if he was definite in his views, he was equally tactful and diplomatic. He was of the Nelsonic mode, determined to fulfill the mission entrusted to him by his superiors. McDonald and five Nor'Westers were transferred to the *Racoon*, and Black sailed north.

On the other side of the continent, an increasingly anxious Astor was pleading for a warship to protect his enterprise. In response to his lobbying, the Secretary of the Navy, William Jones, made urgent plans to prepare a vessel, the USS *John Adams*, a stout and well-equipped cruiser, to sail for a special service to the mouth of the Columbia River. The object was to provide specific aid to Astor, and the scheme came under the president's direction "for a special and confidential object." Jones needed an efficient corvette for this service, so he ordered the *John Adams*, a three-masted vessel, cut down by one deck. A powerful armament was to be mounted and certain stores, including anti-scorbutics and hospital supplies, were to be provided for the lengthy voyage to distant locations "where commerce and the arts do not furnish the means of replenishment." The designated captain, William Crane, thought her a strong and comfortable vessel for such a great expedition. A sailing master who knew the Columbia River entrance, Joseph Pierce, was hired on Astor's advice, and a keen crew, "truly American in their feelings and hearty in the cause," was arranged.[2]

In the end, however, getting the vessel ready consumed more time than expected, for its spars and yards were found very defective, and the demands of war on the Great Lakes that summer of 1813 resulted in the Secretary of the Navy ordering the vessel dismasted and the captain and ship's company sent to Lake Ontario. The British blockade of the eastern seaboard also prevented any sailing of an American warship. No help for the Astor scheme was forthcoming.

In the circumstances, Astor found himself thrown back on chartering two other vessels, but neither could succor Astoria. These reverses dashed his hopes of maintaining the essential link with Astoria by sea. He was disgruntled by the government's lack of support. "I fear the war will ruin if not destroy us in that quarter," he wrote a friend in July 1813, "in peace we should have done well, in war we can do nothing and are exposed to danger from the British and … the North West Company. Our government ought to have afforded us some aid, but nothing has been done and nothing is expected."[3] Astor came to feel that Jefferson had deserted him. Although Jefferson did offer aid, suggesting that the United States would represent Astoria's interest and its "independence" at any peace conference, Astor could only imagine that Jefferson no longer saw the depot as an integral part of American empire.[4] He was now cast on the whims of fate.

In January 1813, another challenge to the Astorians arose, a transcontinental one. Donald McKenzie of the Pacific Fur Company, the Astor subsidiary, brought word to Astoria from Spokane House that a state of war existed and that in two months' time a strong party of Nor'Westers, formidable in opposition, would arrive at Astoria from the interior. The object of this party was to set up a post and await a supply ship from London. The ship was said to carry everything necessary for trade with the local aboriginals, and the whole scheme had been arranged by men with experience and a thorough knowledge of the coast and interior branches of trade.[5]

Three months later, an advance party of Nor'Westers arrived overland. It consisted of no great, strong party but only three officers and sixteen men, travelling in two bark canoes. There was no sign of the rivals' supply ship, and the Astorians came to discredit the alarm that McKenzie had delivered. Nor'Wester John George McTavish bought supplies from the Astorians and took his group back to the interior forts. Winter passed into spring. Good clear days were followed by many with incessant rain. On one occasion, rain completely extinguished the fire that had been lit on the cape as a signal to approaching sailing vessels.

In August 1813, more alarming intelligence came from another quarter. Wilson Price Hunt, chief agent of the Pacific Fur Company, who had been in the Hawaiian and Marquesas islands, arrived in a chartered vessel, the *Albatross*, on August 20. He confirmed the outbreak of war and brought news, gathered from the former captain of the *Essex*, that the British were sailing for Astoria with a larger force than expected. Hunt's news confirmed the difficulties of the Astorians and underlined the precarious nature of their situation. Each passing month brought no chance of relief to the Astorians, and their prospects dimmed.

When the Nor'Westers returned to Astoria in the fall, they immediately offered the partners of the Pacific Fur Company a way out of their difficulties. The Nor'Westers would buy the post and the Pacific Fur Company's assets there and in the interior, and they would also offer the Astorians shares and employment in the new endeavour. The Astorians remained reluctant. They fought off pressures from John George McTavish, but when they realized no resistance could be safely made, Hunt gave Duncan McDougall, the ranking partner, full powers to dispose of the assets as required. The Astorians signed a bill of sale on October 16, 1813. By this arrangement, the Pacific Fur Company transferred its establishments, furs and stocks on hand in the Columbia, Okanogan and elsewhere upriver to the Nor'Westers for a price agreed to by the two parties. Astor's furs and merchandise passed into the waiting hands of the North West Company at what was later claimed to be about a third of their value. Many of the Canadians in the Pacific Fur Company entered the North West Company, and the enlarged company gained a stranglehold on the affairs of the Columbia and the interior. Astor's final yield from this fire sale was a paltry $40,000.

At last the Nor'Westers had sole possession of the Columbia, though their grasp was ever so tenuous, and at least they had control of its tributary trade and a share in the commerce of the coast. The prospects were wide. The trade with Russian America and with the Spanish in Alta California and Mexico might be promising, as was that with the Hawaiian Islands, the Marquesas and Canton.

But the partners at Astoria, as it was still called, remained in a state of acute isolation on a hostile and lonely coast, uncertain of prevailing fortunes. Neither a promised warship nor the *Isaac Todd* had yet arrived. On occasion they could hear the muffled boom of a ship's cannon through the fog offshore, and the Clatsops continued to report news of vessels offshore, but no ship was sighted. In the several accounts by traders resident at Astoria, we can sense the building drama of the next phase of events unfolding at this critical point in Canadian and American business rivalry, and we get a glimpse of the influence of sea power on the course of empire in a distant locale.

In late November 1813, on the aft end of a gale sweeping toward the coast, the sloop-of-war *Racoon* approached the mouth of the Columbia under close-reefed topsails. Onboard preparations were complete for a grand attack on the Americans at Astoria: eighty sailors and marines were ready to land from three armed boats and take the post either by surprise at daylight or under cover of fire from the ship's guns. First, though, the vessel had to cross the bar. She came to anchor six miles offshore in twenty-five fathoms. From this safe vantage point, members of the ship's company could see the headlands guarding the entrance, Cape Disappointment and Point Adams, with snow-clad Mount St. Helens in the distance. They could also see high surf breaking on the shore with only one clear patch of water indicating an unobstructed channel that would lead across the bar. Captain Black, who knew how shallow it was across the bar, sent boats ahead to sound a passage and lay down buoys readied for that purpose. Using William Broughton's small-scale plan—which was found to be perfectly correct as to the land features, though the banks were now changed—and an extract from Broughton's journal, Black steered his ship through a half-mile-wide channel.[6] The *Racoon* then dropped anchor within Cape Disappointment, the first vessel of the Royal Navy to enter the river since Broughton's command, the brig *Chatham*, attached to the Vancouver expedition, in 1792. So much had transpired in those twenty-one years.

Black had a copy of Vancouver's *Voyage of Discovery* as a ready reference about ports and passages in the North Pacific. In it, Vancouver described at length Broughton's navigation of the river entrance and lower reaches. Black also had with him a chronometer so he could determine longitudes, and, if weather permitted (it did not, as it turned out) he planned to send boat crews on various surveying duties. Some guns were fired from the south shore where the post stood as the *Racoon* crossed the bar. Astoria was ten miles from where the *Racoon* cast anchor.

Soon Duncan McDougall, formerly of Astor's firm but now one of the ranking partners of the North West Company, came out from the post in a canoe. "I soon learnt from him," wrote Black in his remark book, "that the American settlement had been given up to a party of the British North West Company who had come overland from Canada. How far Private Individuals may be authorized to treat with Enemies time must determine, but at present so ends our hopes of Prize Money at Columbia." Black noted that the Americans gave up a considerable property to the North West Company, "but I was advised by the latter there was not any American property then in the river." Black's clerk wrote similarly in his journal about the sadness felt by officers and men of the *Racoon* when they learned that they were dealing with some Canadian traders, most of them Scots, who were, in effect, consorting with the enemy.[7] Black and others may have thought that the Nor'Westers and Astorians had conspired to defraud them of prize money, but this is speculation based on hearsay evidence and is not substantiated by documentary proof. According to fur-trading sources, animosity developed between the sailors and the fur traders over the objectives and spoils of war. This confused beginning of British control at the mouth of the Columbia River tended to complicate the British diplomatic position in discussions leading to the peace treaty.

In any event, on December 12, Black, with a small party of seamen and marines, came ashore from the *Racoon*, arriving in the fur traders' coastal vessel *Dolly*, a craft that had been shipped out in frame in the *Tonquin* and had subsequently been made serviceable by the fur traders at Astoria. Black, already in a foul mood, was not impressed with what he saw ashore. "Is this the fort about which I have heard so much talking?" he is reported to have said in disgust. "D__m me, but I'd batter it down in two hours with a four pounder."[8]

The next day after lunch, with as much ceremony as could be mustered, the Union Jack, provided by Black from the *Racoon*, was hoisted by the Nor'Westers. With sailors manning the guns, and marines and company men parading with muskets, Black, true to instructions to take control of the place, mounted the stage erected for the purpose and broke a bottle of Madeira on the flagstaff. He

Fort George—formerly known as Astoria or Fort Astoria—was an extensive establishment that first belonged to the North West Company and then to the Hudson's Bay Company. In 1824, on the recommendation of Sir George Simpson, the fort was moved to a new site upriver and renamed Fort Vancouver after the famed British navigator. Library and Archives Canada, 1970-188-459(a)1

simultaneously proclaimed in a loud voice that he was taking possession of the fort and country for the king, and renamed the post Fort George in honour of His Majesty.[9] Three rounds of musketry were fired by the mixed guard, and a royal salute was fired from the fort's guns, answered by the *Racoon*. A health to His Majesty was proposed, and the ceremony ended with everyone taking a few extra glasses of wine, according to Alexander Henry the Younger, one of the participants. Black was conscious of the fact that Jonathan Thorn—"a Lieut. in the Naval Service of the United States sent out for that purpose," in Black's words—had already taken possession of the place on September 12, 1811.

Black had been diligent in his inquiries. He knew that the American traders had lately been unfortunate, for one of their ships, the *Tonquin*, had been plundered and blown up in a harbour on Vancouver Island, and Natives had murdered the crew. Another vessel had been lost on its passage out from New York. The Americans now had no settlement whatever on the Columbia River or in any part of the coast.

During the time he spent at the river estuary, Black went to visit the place where Fort Clatsop, built by Lewis and Clark, still stood, though it was now in ruins. "During the time they [Lewis and Clark and their men] remained about the Columbia the natives and them were constantly at variance: the Indians have been very inveterate against the Americans ever since," he wrote in his remark book. The captain provides some details that are totally speculative but not found elsewhere: "some of the natives had stolen a Horse from the party; the Thief was found & hung by the Americans. The Indians have never forgotten it, but take revenge whenever an opportunity offers. I understand it often happens with the N.W. Company to have a horse or horses stolen by the Natives. They never themselves punish them for it, tho' they get their Chiefs at times to do so." Alexander Henry the Younger gives further details of the expedition to find the place where Lewis and Clark had wintered: "The situation is the most pleasant spot I have seen hereabouts and by far the most eligible for them both as to security from the Natives, and for hunting &c."[10]

The next day, December 15, Black returned to the *Racoon* and prepared a report, in cipher, which he had the Nor'Westers send overland to Montreal and then to the Admiralty in London:

Country and fort I have taken possession of in name and for British Majesty; latter I have named Fort George and left in possession and charge North West Company.

Enemy's party quite broke up; they have no settlement whatever on this river or coast.

Enemy's vessels said on coast and about islands; while provisions last, shall endeavor to destroy them.[11]

The *Racoon* made sail on the morning of New Year's Eve, bound for the Hawaiian Islands. From the shore below Fort George, the officers and men of the North West Company watched the departure of the sloop of war for as long as they could. Many would have liked to have been on board. They saw the *Racoon* tack as required and then, under a full press of sail, move to the channel to exit the estuary through the wild surf rising over the bar. All seemed to go well. What they did not know was that the sloop hit the bar, twice. The vessel lost her false keel and was immediately put in desperate straits, with water coming in. The hands took turns at the pumps but only just enough to keep the vessel from disaster. In these perilous circumstances, Black knew he had no hope of making the Hawaiian Islands. He accordingly steered south for Alta California. The *Racoon* barely made the port of San Francisco, with seven feet of water in the hold and the ship's company exhausted. There Black was about to leave the wounded *Racoon*—for the Spanish authorities, though invariably polite and official, could not or would not help the interlopers—when the *Isaac Todd* made its providential appearance. Now it was time for the company to help the navy. Officers and men of the Nor'Westers' vessel gave immediate aid. At Angel Island, where the vessel was careened, repairs to the sloop were effected so satisfactorily that she was able to sail without any difficulty or hazard.

Ivan Kuskov, the Russian commander at nearby Fort Ross, recounts that Black tended to treat the Spanish as subordinates. He told Alexander Baranov that Black hinted to Kuskov that the colony at Fort Ross was an intrusion, "that the Russians disturbed the right of Great Britain as New Albion, as the name shows, is the property of the [British] empire and not of the Spaniards." Spanish documents do not show any rudeness on the part of Black, but they express impatience for the sloop of war to be readied for sailing, which would allow the Spanish to be rid of these unwelcome guests at the first instance. In any event, on April 19 the *Racoon* sailed from the Golden Gate, bound for the Hawaiian Islands to search for American shipping. Black's long cruise to the Pacific, "showing the flag," ended in success with his vessel's safe return to England.

After the departure of the *Racoon*, and with no sign of the promised supply ship from London, the Nor'Westers pondered their prospects here on the coast of chance and fortune. Their fort's defences were paltry; cannon and field pieces were in short supply. The place was vulnerable to attack and inconvenient to shipping. It lay far from the anchorage in Baker's Bay. The means of communication between ship and shore was by boat across the estuary's wide entrance, and the passage was often dangerous and sometimes fatal. (Donald McTavish, Alexander Henry the Younger and four others perished on May 22, 1814, in mid-river in a stiff gale when, owing to some mismanagement of the boat's sail, a heavy wave struck the boat, filled it and sent it to the bottom.) The Nor'Westers searched for a better location to which they could remove the post. They required an anchorage nearby; timber for construction, shipbuilding and spars; lands suitable for agriculture, animal husbandry and grazing; safe drinking water in abundant supply; security from the elements; and capabilities of defence. No such place could be found in the lower river's reaches or in the estuary or its bays. The various Native villages could not be disturbed or were otherwise unsuitable.

The immediate, critical concern being defence (from sea, if not from land), the Nor'Westers' local management decided on Tongue Point—"a very remarkable point" among marshy islands where the river proper meets the estuary, which had been seen by Lewis and Clark, though named by Broughton—as the promontory on which to mount a battery. Guns were ordered for this "Gibraltar of the West," as Alexander Ross, there at the time, called it. In February, March and April 1814, Nor'Wester crews worked at the battery, but whether guns were ever landed from supply ships and set in place is not known. This watchtower of the west haunts the margins of the river's history, suggestive, as it is, of Nor'Westers' anxieties for their future at this chokepoint of commercial empire, but equally expressive of a significant phase of North West Company enterprise in this quarter. Mounting batteries on promontories and headlands became a later preoccupation of those who came to control the Columbia River.[12]

The *Isaac Todd* reached the Columbia River entrance on April 23—thirteen weary months after leaving England. Its arrival ensured the preservation of British interests at Fort George. Foodstuffs for the traders and trading goods for the indigenous people—these and other items arrived in abundance in the hold of the ship. Both objectives of Captain Hillyar's bold mission were now achieved: the *Essex* had been captured and control of the Columbia River country was in British hands.

By the time the *Isaac Todd* reached the Columbia River, the company had sent a second vessel, the British brig *Columbia*, 185 tons, from England to the northwest coast. (This was the Nor'Westers' *Columbia*, not Robert Gray's.) Again, a ship of the Royal Navy, HMS *Laurel*, provided convoy support, but this time only as far as Rio. The *Columbia* arrived at the Columbia River and the strongly fortified Fort George on June 29, 1814, and found the *Isaac Todd* making preparations to sail to Canton. The *Isaac Todd* took all the Columbia furs from Fort George to Canton and then returned to England with tea on account for the East India Company. The supercargo, Angus Bethune, did not get a flattering price for the sea otter skins. But a profit was made, even though not such a handsome one as had been imagined. As to the *Columbia*, this vessel, having off-loaded supplies for Fort George, had an abundantly successful cruise, sailing north to the Queen Charlotte Islands and then Sitka, returning to the Columbia to gather more furs, and then sailing for the Hawaiian Islands, Macao and London. Annually, thereafter, vessels brought supplies and took away furs bound for the China market.[13] The British were thus successful in establishing the Columbian enterprise even while the War of 1812 made extensive demands on the Royal Navy in various places on the high seas. Mackenzie's dream had become a reality.

The *Columbia*, having circumnavigated the globe, returned to the coast again in 1815. Coastal trade was pursued, and this brig also sailed to Monterey to see if the Spanish authorities could be persuaded to develop a business in agricultural foodstuffs for the Nor'Westers in control of the Columbia River. The Spanish received the British officers and men handsomely, lining up fifty cavalry on the beach to pay respects. "I asked the governor if he would answer a salute; he complied, and I went on board and saluted with 11 guns, which was returned," wrote Peter Corney, first officer.[14] The captain, Anthony Robson, went ashore and obtained some fresh beef and vegetables for the crew, and Duncan McDougall, who had shipped in the *Columbia* as supercargo, informed the Spanish governor that he hoped to collect provisions for the North West Company's establishment at the Columbia River. The governor had no powers to comply, but he did say that he would consult the viceroy in Mexico. A courier was sent and came back with the predictable reply that "they could not allow any gentleman to remain in the country; we might land the goods we had brought to barter, and the governor was to see to the collecting of provisions for us against our return from Canton; but the cooper was allowed to remain (as a great favor) to superintend the curing of the beef." In effect, the British got the same response Rezanov had received nine years before—though they were formally welcomed on the spot, they were obliged to comply with rules that could not be changed. So the Nor'Westers sailed north, first to Bodega Bay and then to Fort Ross, but nothing of commercial or diplomatic consequence happened there. In 1817, *Columbia* was back once again at New Archangel and the Columbia River. The trade and trading connections were being reinforced, consolidated, extended as the Nor'Westers supplanted the Astorians—at the Columbia, in Alaskan waters, at Hawaii and at Alta California. The fruits of war, and of armed assistance to merchant trading ships during the War of 1812, were yielding outstanding dividends. The Canadian trade in the Pacific was prospering and growing.

To the *Isaac Todd* goes credit for the first legitimate trans-Pacific Canadian trade from the Columbia River to Canton. But to the *Columbia* go laurels for initiating North West Company trade (even in confined or restricted form) with the Spanish in Alta California, the Russians at Fort Ross and Bodega Bay, the Hawaiians at Kailua and the Russians again at New Archangel. The "golden round" was not now dependent only on British manufactures, northwest coast furs and Chinese tea. Such items as sandalwood, rum, livestock, tallow, provisions, naval stores, spars, timber and tobacco were conveyed by the *Columbia* within the broad confines of the Pacific rim. A third company ship, the *Colonel Allan*, visited Fort George and took furs and specie to Canton in 1816.

The East India Company continued to object to Canadian trade to Canton, however, so the North West Company reverted to the previously successful measure, first initiated by Mackenzie in 1798 (and described in Chapter 3), of having an American house facilitate its business to China. Such an arrangement, which lasted through 1821, involved a partnership with the firms of Perkins and Co. of Boston and J. and J.N. Perkins of Canton. Five or six ships sailed under this arrangement between 1815 and 1821. To make this trade more legal, in 1817 the company considered the Columbia territory to belong to the United States in order to circumvent the East India Company monopoly. American independence thus favoured the company's achievement. Canadian cargoes sailed under Yankee flags.

And so a succession of supply ships arrived at the mouth of the Columbia River to give aid and sustenance to the North West Company at Fort George. After the *Isaac Todd*, the *Columbia* and the *Colonel Allen*, the brig *Alexander* arrived from London in 1817, and the following year the ship *Levant* came as a supply ship, from Boston this time. The *Levant* came again in 1820, and the *Alexander*, last of the annual Boston ships, came in 1821.

With the union of the North West Company and the Hudson's Bay Company in 1821, the traders no longer bothered with the Canton connection but rather carried Columbia Department furs directly to England for auction and distribution as required. The shipping was all British, closing a unique chapter in the Columbia River trade when the Nor'Westers employed their own or Boston ships when they had to. The East India Company's tenacious control over the China trade did not diminish in these years, though it was in its last phase of power. Free-trading interests hoped that the company's power might be suspended, and statesmen regarded the China trade as the most likely to experience accelerated growth and profit. But the vested interests had to be pushed aside by government power, and that did not happen for many years.

Meanwhile, curiously, the Nor'Westers found themselves brought into the embrace of another monopolistic concern, the Hudson's Bay Company. However, the techniques of the Nor'Westers were the preferred pattern in the country west of the Continental Divide, and it was in the Columbia district and farther north, in New Caledonia, that the real gains were to be made in the beaver business. Fort George was replaced by Fort Vancouver in 1824, largely for political reasons. The new fort was placed on the north shore of the Columbia River one hundred miles from open ocean. Otherwise business carried on much as usual, with consolidation of trade—including coastal expansion to New Archangel and Russian America, Fort Ross and Alta California, and Hawaii and other Pacific islands—a constant preoccupation of those who directed the affairs of the Hudson's Bay Company. Altogether it was a remarkable achievement, which had its beginnings in those desperate and difficult days of the War of 1812, in the farthest west, at the mouth of the Columbia River.

Chapter 15

THE EMPIRE OF FORTUNE:
CULTIVATING THE ARTS OF PEACE

O n Christmas Eve 1814, in the ancient Flemish town of Ghent, plenipotentiaries of the United Kingdom and the United States agreed to
the terms of what became known as the Treaty of Ghent. The treaty, which
brought the War of 1812 to a close, was strangely silent on many burning questions that had been the sources of controversy leading to hostilities. Nonetheless, it established the *status quo ante bellum*, which meant that, under the first
article, all territory or places, possession of which had been taken during the

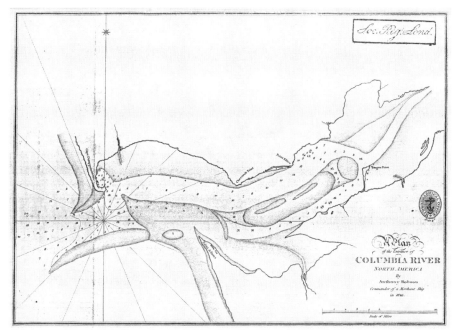

*This plan of the entrance of the Columbia River, showing safe anchorages, villages and houses,
was completed by Master Anthony Robson of the North West Company's vessel* Columbia *in
1816. In 1814, the Nor'Westers had plans to establish a battery of great guns on Tongue Point,
at the river narrows.* UK Hydrographic Record Office

war, should be restored without delay. Most promising of all, it provided for joint commissions to settle boundary disputes between the two powers. In fact, the treaty's "only definite achievement," according to one authority, "was the termination of hostilities."[1]

The Treaty of Ghent failed to make specific reference to the fort near the Columbia River mouth. In view of Anglo-American struggle to control the Columbia trade between 1810 and 1814, it is paradoxical that the British government, in contrast to its counterpart, showed little evident concern for the territory west of the Rocky Mountains when peace negotiations began at Ghent. The silence of the British plenipotentiaries on this point was later explained to the North West Company by Earl Bathurst, the Secretary for War and the Colonies, on the shocking grounds that "requiring from the Americans any recognition or guarantee of his Majesty's rights thereto, might lead to cast doubts upon a title which was sufficiently strong and incontrovertible."[2] Such spineless policy excused what was probably an oversight or, more correctly, deliberate and blatant neglect or indifference. The northwest coast and the Columbia River, both mouth and watershed, lay half a world away from London, far from the madding circumstances of a Europe recovering from hostilities of long standing. It allowed the British government to be generous and magnanimous. The North West Company could claim no charter, so its interests could be easily sacrificed, cast aside. In any event, it was trade that mattered, not dominion. These points underscored the logic behind the actions taken by the ministers of the British government. As well, Fort George was on disputed territory where British claims to sovereignty were not inviolate.

At the peace table, American plenipotentiaries acted on instructions from Secretary of State James Monroe, who insisted the fort should be returned to the United States. The diplomats argued aggressively for restoration because Astoria had been in American hands before the war. With reference to the British, Monroe noted, "It is not believed that they have any claim to territory on the Pacific Ocean."[3] Here lay the origin of a view that was stated so clearly, so repeatedly, in subsequent years by Secretary of State John Quincy Adams and that, at the end of the day, gave the United States a window on the Pacific in those latitudes without resort to war. The wily Adams had been one of the US plenipotentiaries and was ever alert to the smooth, velvet-like touch of British diplomats. Ghent negotiations taught him unforgettable lessons. The British government's objectives were simple: the security of British North America and the protection of aboriginal allies. In the end, the second of these was discarded in the face of American intransigence.

Both during and after negotiations, the Nor'Westers appealed to the British government for protection against the Americans. They hoped to safeguard their post on the Columbia, which they claimed had been acquired by purchase. They were blunt about their needs and urgently queried a permanent undersecretary if "we may rely on the protection of His Majesty's Government." Warning that their Columbia post was in danger of "forcible seizure" by Americans under the rationale that the Nor'Westers had no right to trade with aboriginal people "within the territories of the United States, which are now said to extend to the shores of the Pacific," the British traders wanted to know how secure their tenure was. They never received a satisfactory answer, and in the face of official British indifference could only conclude that maintaining a Columbia trading system was problematic.[4]

The warning signs flashed by the Nor'Westers were based on a correct assessment of the facts and circumstances of the day. After signing the treaty, the United States government took steps to recover the post on the northwest coast. On July 18, 1815, Secretary of State Monroe bluntly told Great Britain's chargé d'affaires to the United States, Anthony St. John Baker, who was resident in Washington, that inasmuch as the British force had taken possession of Astoria during the war, the United States intended to reoccupy the fort without delay.[5] Monroe gave the impression that a man-of-war flying the Stars and Stripes was about to sail for the Columbia River.

When Monroe asked that a letter be sent to the British naval commander in the North Pacific ordering the return of the fort to the Americans, the flabbergasted Baker replied that he knew very little about the fate of Astoria, although he believed that the post lay in ruins and was unoccupied. Baker's ignorance is inexcusable; his reply to Monroe lamentable. Instead of consulting his superior in London, he suggested to Monroe that Rear Admiral Sir Manley Dixon, commander-in-chief on the South American station and in charge of British warships in the distant reaches of the North Pacific, would possess authentic information and could communicate with any authorized American agent on the subject.[6]

To his credit, Baker immediately wrote to Dixon to warn him of developments in Washington. He enclosed copies of the correspondence with Monroe and emphasized that Britain did not recognize any American possession on the Pacific coast.[7] Although Baker did learn from the North West Company in Canada that the possession of Astoria was effected by purchase, he failed to press this advantageous position with the American Secretary of State.

Monroe did not, could not, act. It is generally believed that only the lack of naval units during 1815 and 1816 prevented the United States from sending a vessel on a mission of restitution to the Columbia.[8] A suggestion in the autumn of 1815 that a naval expedition explore the northwest coast won support from President James Madison, but the need for economy and for dealing with more urgent international problems caused the proposal to be set aside.[9] For instance, the USS *Congress*, which was to sail in mid-1816 for the Pacific, was sent to the Gulf of Mexico instead. Not until difficulties over Algiers and Florida were resolved did the United States government return to the matter of the northwest coast.

For two years the issue languished, but in mid-1817 the US government appointed two commissioners, Captain James Biddle and Judge John B. Prevost, to carry Monroe's earlier instructions into effect. On October 4, 1817, the American sloop-of-war *Ontario*, mounting twenty guns and under the command of Captain Biddle, slipped out of New York on a secret mission. Biddle's instructions from the Navy Department ordered him to proceed to the Columbia River "with a view to assert, on the part of the United States, the claim to the sovereignty, by some symbolical or appropriate mode adapted to the occasion." No force was to be used, even in the event that "unexpected obstructions should occur."[10] But when Simon McGillivray of the North West Company got wind of it through an intelligence leak, he immediately informed Baker's successor, Sir Charles Bagot, the British chargé d'affaires in Washington.[11] Bagot had done his homework. He confronted John Quincy Adams, US Secretary of State. Adams, who appeared "considerably embarrassed" when Bagot asked him if the rumour were true, admitted that the *Ontario* was sent to assert American sovereignty, but not to destroy the trade of the North West Company.[12]

Bagot was not satisfied with this response and was unhappy at this ill-advised gunboat diplomacy. He remonstrated against any United States attempt to occupy the country adjacent to the Columbia and informed Adams that the whole region belonged to Great Britain, "having been early taken possession of in his Majesty's name, and been ever since considered as part of his Majesty's dominions." He went further and told the Secretary of State that the establishment made there by American citizens had been voluntarily abandoned by the Astorians "under an agreement with the North West Company, which had purchased their effects, and had since retained peaceable possession of the coast."[13]

Bagot also warned London. He notified Viscount Castlereagh, the Foreign Secretary, that an American warship had been ordered "to the mouth of the Columbia River for the purpose of re-establishing the Settlement of which the United States was dispossessed during the late war."[14] The matter came up immediately for discussion in London between Castlereagh and the US diplomatic representative, Richard Rush. Castlereagh, with customary tact, said he regretted that the British government had not been notified of the intended occupation of the Columbia by the United States before the sailing of the warship *Ontario*, as Great Britain claimed dominion over that territory. In a moment of conciliation, Castlereagh suggested that the matter be put to arbitration, but this was not acceptable to Rush, who would not admit of any ground upon which Great Britain could claim dominion there. Was not the territory in American possession before the war? he asked. Did it not fall as an act of war? How then could mutual restitution, as required by the treaty, be withheld? Castlereagh had answers to these questions and would go only this far: He was prepared to admit the right of the United States as the party in possession, pending negotiations. He regretted only the manner of obtaining possession and worried that a needless war would occur in consequence of the American acts. There, for the moment, the matter rested.

In Washington, Bagot hurriedly and secretly advised the Governor General of Canada to send an overland party to warn the Nor'Westers on the Pacific coast that a US warship was on its way to Fort George to repossess it.[15] That recommendation was not acted on. Bagot also suggested to the Foreign Secretary that a British warship from England could arrive at the Columbia before the *Ontario*.[16] Further information reached the Admiralty from Commodore Sir James Lucas Yeo, commander-in-chief on the West African Coast, that indicated even larger American designs. Yeo warned that the Americans possessed a "restless and hostile spirit" toward Britain. He also reported that he learned during a recent visit to New York that the *Ontario* was sailing for the North Pacific with commissioners on board "to obtain possession of some Island or Territory in that quarter preparatory to their establishing a very extensive commerce in those Seas."[17]

The British cabinet considered this mounting difficulty and sought to avert a renewal of war. Foreign Secretary Castlereagh knew that the Nor'Westers had actually purchased Astoria. But the dilemma arose because Captain Black's report indicated that he had claimed that post and territory as a conquest of war. The first article of the Treaty of Ghent, which provided for the return to the *status quo ante bellum*, meant that Britain had to return any conquest of war, and Castlereagh, on Bagot's advice, knew that the settlement on the Columbia River had been held by the United States on the outbreak of war. Under the circumstances, the conciliatory Foreign Secretary was clearly more interested in the stability of international relations than additions to the British Empire, so he decided, decisively, to give way. In order to give the Americans what he referred to generally as "an additional motive to cultivate the arts of peace," Castlereagh concluded that the best thing was to return the post to the Americans in pursuance of the first article of the Treaty of Ghent, provided it was made abundantly clear to them that this would neither recognize United States rights nor relinquish British claims to the territory.[18] To implement this magnanimous policy, he instructed Earl Bathurst, the Secretary for War and the Colonies, to inform the fur traders of the proposed restitution of Fort George, previously Astoria, to the United States. Bathurst sent an order to any British authority, civil or military (in fact, the agents of the North West Company at the mouth of the Columbia), directing them to give no opposition to the reoccupation of the settlement by American commissioners or agents under terms of the first article of the Treaty of Ghent. At the same time, Castlereagh instructed the Admiralty to send a warship to the northwest coast to restore the post officially to American commissioners.[19] This amounted to an unusual episode in British naval-diplomatic activities, for sloop diplomacy customarily involved coercion and sometimes acquisition of territory, not restitution.

On August 19, the USS *Ontario* reached her destination well in advance of any British warship and anchored outside the bar, and on that day Captain Biddle took possession "in the name and on the behalf of the United States, of both shores of the River Columbia." In performing this service, as he reported to the Secretary of the Navy, he observed ceremonies "customary upon the like occasions of setting up a claim to national sovereignty and dominion."[20] Such was his brief report on these affairs.

Biddle's recent biographer, employing a number of correlative sources on this event, informs us that Biddle approached the shore with fifty officers and men in three boats. They landed at Cape Disappointment on the north bank of the Columbia. Biddle raised the Stars and Stripes before a crowd of Chinook people as the *Ontario*, offshore, gave a twenty-one–gun salute. "I turned up a sod of soil," recorded Biddle, "and giving three cheers, I nailed up against a tree a leaden plate in which were cut the following words:

TAKEN POSSESSION OF IN THE NAME AND ON THE
BEHALF OF THE UNITED STATES BY CAPTAIN JAMES
BIDDLE COMMANDING THE UNITED STATES SHIP
ONTARIO, COLUMBIA RIVER, AUGUST 1818."

The boats proceeded upriver, looked in on an aboriginal village and came downstream to Fort George. Biddle does not say what he found there. Lieutenant James Aulick, USN, registered his "mortification to see the British flag run up."[21] Even so, there was no altercation with the North West Company manager, James Keith, and no resistance to the American actions.

In these relaxed circumstances, Biddle quickly made plans to take his leave of the Nor'Westers and the Columbia. Easing downstream, Biddle's party stopped briefly on the south shore to allow the captain to nail a wooden board bearing the US coat of arms and an identical legend to that of the leaden plate he had put up across the river estuary at Cape Disappointment. Biddle and his officers and men boarded the *Ontario* and quickly shaped an uneventful course for Monterey, Alta California, and then for South American ports and home. At Monterey he learned of Russian activities at nearby Fort Ross, and he heard even more alarming rumours of Russian activities in the Sandwich or Hawaiian Islands. His report to Washington warned of these matters and indicates that he may have held a greater fear of Russian aggrandizement than British empire-building in the Pacific at this time.[22]

Chief Factor Keith put a different twist on Biddle's actions. He had heard a rumour that a US warship would appear and take possession, but nothing of the sort happened until midsummer 1818. "I felt perfectly easy and secure," he recalled, "till the *Ontario*'s arrival off Cape Disappointment in the morning of the 19th of August followed by Captain Biddle's appearance about 3 p.m. accompanied by a strong party including officers in three boats apparently well-armed." Only Biddle and his surgeon landed; the rest were ordered off, accompanied by one of the Nor'Westers, to cut spars at Point George. Biddle acted quietly and was extremely social and polite, not wanting to excite the local aboriginal people—or that was the impression he gave. Keith had no hint as to what was about to transpire. But after the ship departed, he found an unusually painted board nailed to a tree in a rather secluded and unfrequented place on Point George, a mile and a half from Fort George. This was Biddle's declaration of having taken possession.

Keith had been caught flat-footed. His heart was heavy. He recalled: "Such mysterious unaccountable proceedings of which the subsequent reports of the natives joined to the gloomy desponding conjectures of my own people rather aggravated the unfavourable impression [and] excited the most anxious & painful sensations at what would probably be the next step ..."[23] Keith had all guns slotted, and he redoubled the vigilance at the post. Small arms were ready for all hands. Lookouts were posted. Fort George was again on a war footing, unsure whether peace or war existed.

Thirteen months later, restitution was carried out by the British sloop-of-war *Blossom*, under the command of Captain Frederick Hickey, which had previously been engaged in protecting British commerce in ports on the Pacific side

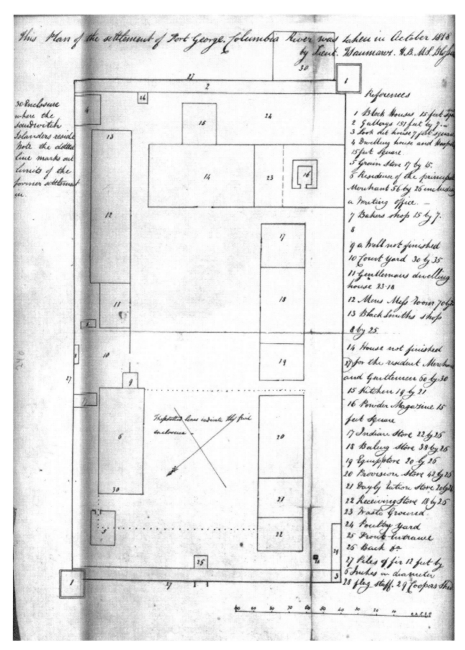

This extensive plan of Fort George, Columbia River, was taken in October of 1818 by Lieutenant Thomas Saumarez of His Britannic Majesty's Sloop **Blossom**. The Kanakas' or Sandwich Islanders' enclosure outside the fort's walls is noted as Number 30. Accession Number 228, Clatsop County Historical Society

of South America during armed confrontations between Spain and Chile. She sailed from Valparaiso for the Columbia River in July 1818, carrying government dispatches to the Nor'Westers authorizing the restitution. Onboard was the American commissioner John B. Prevost, who had been delayed on consular duties in South American ports and had not, contrary to Washington's expectations, sailed north with Biddle in the *Ontario*. The *Blossom* anchored in Baker's Bay near Fort George on October 4. Judge Prevost proved agreeable and reassuring, but Keith confided to Hickey that he was "much disappointed in my expectations relative to the pledges of security and public faith without which no commercial body can promote their own much less contribute to the national prosperity."[24]

Keith had good reason to feel as if he and the North West Company had been sold out. But Prevost, within his circumscribed powers, had little room to manoeuvre. The restitution was a *fait accompli*—and a triumph for Castlereagh's policy of giving the Americans "an additional motive to cultivate the arts of peace."

Hickey and Keith signed the "Restitution and acknowledgement of the delivery of the settlement on Columbia River" in accordance with instructions from Bathurst and the Admiralty under the first article of the Treaty of Ghent, to the Government of the United States through its agent Prevost. For his part, Prevost acknowledged receipt, on behalf of his government, of the possession of the settlement designated, in conformity with the treaty.[25] The arrangement was complete; the legalities observed. But even after the agreement of restitution was signed, Chief Factor James Keith, acting in defence of his own private interests as well as those of the North West Company, had to be satisfied that he had not given anything away needlessly. Castlereagh's, Bathurst's and the Admiralty's instructions all had to be followed. But on-the-spot clarity was still lacking. Keith needed assurance from the American that the Nor'Westers could trade unmolested.

Trader Keith was as canny a Nor'Wester as could be found, and although he was bound to follow the directions that his corporate superiors had received from Lord Bathurst, he pressed Commissioner Prevost on the meaning of the intended transaction:

Fort George, Columbia River, October 6, 1818

Sir: Now that restitution of this settlement has been made and that the North West Company are still allowed to occupy it in the prosecution of their commercial pursuits, permit me to submit to you the following important queries, to which I request a candid and explicit reply.

Whether or not you feel authorised on behalf of the United States to tender me any assurance or to afford any security that no abandonment or relinquishment of said settlement will be claimed by your government in favour of any of its subjects to the ejectment and exclusion of said North West Company prior to the final decision of the right of sovereignty to the Country between our respective governments and pending such discussion as also in the event of such sovereignty being confirmed to the United States may the North West Company implicitly rely on the justice and equity of your government? that adequate allowance will be made for any extension or amelioration of aforesaid settlement or of the trade dependent thereon, of which circumstances may from time to time suggest the propriety? I have, etc.

James Keith,
Acting for self and North West Company.[26]

Keith, we see clearly, had an eye to the future, and Prevost replied diplomatically to Keith's substantial inquiry and gave an equally thorough answer:

Sir: In answer to your note of this morning I have the honour to state that the principal object of the President in sending me thus far was to obtain such information of the place, of its access, and of its commercial importance as might enable him to submit to the consideration of Congress measures for the protection and extension of the establishment. From hence you will perceive that until the sense of the Government may be taken upon my report, any assurances I might offer to meet the wishes expressed by you would be as unauthorized as unavailing. Sir, I have, however, no hesitation in saying that should it hereafter comport with the views of the nation to foster the settlement any claim of the North West Company justified by the usages of nations will be liquidated with great liberality and that should its policy induce a system of exclusion it will never extend to your removal without sufficient notice to prevent loss and injury to the Company. I cannot conclude without expressing my approbation of the manner in which an establishment so precarious has been managed, nor without offering a hope that the same judicious course may be pursued, under the change of Flag for its success, until the pleasure of the President can be known.

J.B. Prevost.[27]

The *Blossom* sailed away, closing a chapter of sloop diplomacy at the mouth of the Columbia River. The Nor'Westers continued to use the post as their headquarters on the northwest coast for many years. It remained the chief depot of the Hudson's Bay Company, which merged with the North West Company in 1821, until Fort Vancouver was erected.

A few weeks after the *Blossom*'s visit at Fort George, the Anglo-American Convention of 1818 was signed by British and US representatives in London. During the negotiations that led to the agreement, the British proposed that an international boundary be established along the Columbia River, with joint occupancy of the land at the river mouth.[28] This was unacceptable to the United States, and the parties finally agreed to recognize each other's claims to the so-called Oregon Territory, which lay between Spanish-held Alta California to the south, Russian America to the north, the Continental Divide to the east and the Pacific coast. The Anglo-American Convention postponed negotiations between Britain and the United States on territorial claims to Oregon.

Although the contest for the Columbia country ended in Britain's favour in terms of trade, the war-weary British ministry's unwillingness to obtain recognition of British territorial control from the United States in 1815 and 1818 led to protracted negotiations during the next three decades. The non-passive stance of the State Department in Washington, on the other hand, resulted in an awakened interest in far western empire.

Through naval diplomacy, the Americans resolved one issue: the south bank of the Columbia was within the officially declared territories of the United States. The possibilities for American empire at the mouth of the Columbia now lay within the nation's grasp, but the conundrums of control continued and were to perplex a new generation of statesmen and politicians to the point of exasperation.

True to form, for the North West Company it was business as usual throughout the Columbia country. The partners had always cried out for assistance and continued to lobby the British government for protection from molestation by American citizens or the US government. They considered that Fort George did not fall within the provisions of the Treaty of Ghent because it had been acquired by purchase and not by capture.[29]

As for the placards that Captain Biddle erected on the north and south banks of the Columbia to proclaim his having taken possession of the area for the United States, it is said that the Clatsops soon took them down.[30]

Chapter 16

THE LEGACY: THE NORTH
AMERICAN FAR WEST ON THE
EVE OF THE OREGON CRISIS

E̲ven though the British had been obliged, under the Treaty of Ghent, to return the post at the mouth of the Columbia to the Americans, the Canadians and later the Hudson's Bay traders continued to hold sway over the commercial fortunes of the Columbia River basin and its adjacent coastal trades. But how long could the British and Canadians forestall new American designs in the far west? That became an increasingly urgent question in Anglo-American foreign policy dealings.

After 1815, US government policy hardened on the question of who was to control this western frontier. The United States proceeded by a number of means—including diplomatic initiatives, sloop diplomacy, purchase, compromise and war—to secure its south and southwestern frontiers.

American statesmen and traders held dear the belief that US rights, present and future, in what they called Old Oregon were clear-cut and indisputable, either by virtue of its inclusion within the boundaries of the Louisiana Purchase or by virtue of Captain Robert Gray's discovery of the Columbia River mouth and the explorations of Lewis and Clark. But before its acquisition by the United States in 1803, Louisiana, the territory west of the Mississippi, was a Spanish and French possession. Its northern and western boundaries were largely undetermined, and throughout this nearly boundless domain, traders from the North West Company and, to a lesser extent, the Hudson's Bay Company were accustomed to push their wares among the aboriginal people. When Louisiana was purchased, the area west of the Continental Divide was still without sovereignty as recognized by international law, although British traders, in the words of one scholar, "were far in the lead; they were over the Rocky Mountains before an American trader had begun to stem the current of the Missouri."[1] In 1810 the Missouri Fur Company's Andrew Henry crossed the Continental Divide; by that time the North West Company already boasted seven or eight posts in operation in the far western watersheds. US governments intended to support the rights of their mountain men; in 1816, probably at John Jacob Astor's instigation, the United States passed a law declaring that licences to trade with aboriginals within the territorial limits of the United States should not be granted to any but US citizens unless by the express direction of the president and "upon such terms and conditions as the public interest may, in his opinion, require."[2] Goods carried by unlicensed foreigners into Louisiana Territory were liable to confiscation, and the act mandated severe penalties for those found guilty of violations. At the same time, British officials had every intention of sustaining the trading rights of their nationals. Herein lay the source of future diplomatic squabbles and frontier adventures.

The Lewis and Clark expedition to the mouth of the Columbia River, and the establishment of Fort Clatsop near Point Adams on the south bank, gave added significance to the Louisiana Purchase and brought some urgency to the question of the nature and extent of the boundary between United States and British territories from the Lake of the Woods west to the Pacific. In 1807, US delegates James Monroe and James Pinckney were in London negotiating to accept the 49th parallel as the way west to the Pacific; their British counterparts agreed. No convention could be concluded, however, as difference raged on a matter of maritime rights.

Jefferson was perfectly satisfied with an extension of the 49th parallel to the Pacific Ocean in 1807, but he feared Spanish opposition.[3] He was undoubtedly overly cautious, but at the time he did not want any additional problems. It would take four more decades to sort out this issue, with no gain for the United States.

British and American diplomats had made great strides in the few years after the Treaty of Ghent. Apart from the ill-advised visit of USS *Ontario* to the Columbia River, an action that the diplomats and agents had to resolve and set to rest, London and Washington were in an amicable yet cautious mood. The Rush-Bagot Treaty of 1817 allowed for the nominal demilitarization of the Great Lakes and a controlled naval armament by the old rivals. Other clauses addressed the Great Lakes water boundaries, which were to be resolved by commission; the Newfoundland fisheries; and even the British exclusion of American merchant ships to British ports in the Caribbean, which was finally suspended. The British were in an agreeable mood. After agreeing to terms of the Rush-Bagot Treaty, Henry Goulburn, a British plenipotentiary, said to John Quincy Adams, "Well, this is the second good job we have done together." "Yes," replied Adams, "and I only hope we may do a third, going on from better to better."[4]

There was never to be another Anglo-American war, though there were numerous difficulties and even crises. Britain was entering a period of undoubted peace. The United States continued to flex its hemispheric muscles, but hardly at the expense of the British Empire. In the years after the Treaty of Ghent, the US showed increasing naval might beyond the great southern capes that marked the entrances to the Pacific and Indian oceans. The *Ontario*, which had been ordered to the Columbia River under Captain Biddle to reclaim Astoria, was then dispatched to offer protection to American commerce at South American ports. In Chile and Peru this vessel was successful in getting blockaded American vessels freed from the clutches of belligerent forces. "Showing the flag" and keeping an eye out for future problems that might involve Americans were regular duties. Scientific duties—surveying, chartmaking and preparing sailing instructions—also continued with the growth of naval power in these seas.[5]

A year after the Rush-Bagot Treaty, the Anglo-American Convention of 1818 pushed the 49th parallel west from the Lake of the Woods to the "Stony Mountains." This ceded a segment of land claimed by Britain south of the line to the United States; similarly, a banana-shaped crescent lying even farther west, fringed on the north by the natural boundary of the Louisiana Territory, passed to the British.[6] The southern limits of the Hudson's Bay Company's territory, known as Rupert's Land, were truncated, limited by the 49th parallel. A clear and certain boundary had been drawn across the prairies to the mountain rampart at the Continental Divide. An astronomical line now replaced the borderland; politics and international law were superimposed upon geographical space.

But no clear-cut division was possible from the Continental Divide to the Pacific. American negotiators had been willing to carry the 49th parallel to the sea and even to make a somewhat southerly deflection. British delegates, for a time, were unwilling to surrender their claims to lands south of this line. Both parties knew that Russian and Spanish claims still had to be reckoned with, but they trusted to compromise and openness in their relations. Under one clause, the third, they agreed "that any Country that may be claimed by either Party" west of the Rockies should be open to the vessels, citizens and subjects of both powers. Thus was established a "kind of unorganized condominium."[7]

Old Oregon, a territory the size of Western Europe, was the trading realm of "the lords of fur and forest," wrote Washington Irving in his classic *Astoria*. Here, in conjunction with aboriginal traders, the American, British and Canadian corporations and roving "freemen" pushed their wares and liquor up every creek and river valley they could locate. By 1821 this commercial war had largely been won by the Hudson's Bay Company, whose octopus-like tentacles stretched north to the Stikine River, south to Fort Ross in Alta California, and west to Hawaii, Tahiti and even Canton.

The union of the North West Company and the Hudson's Bay Company in 1821 created a British monopoly of the fur trade from Hudson Bay to the northwest coast. The HBC made rigid economies in the trade—reducing the number of establishments and employees, eliminating expenses and controlling the supply of furs to adjusted price levels. The HBC also introduced conservation measures in areas where it exercised a monopoly and pursued aggressive techniques on the borders or margins of its influence. To make its trade in the far west secure from any British rivals, in 1821 the company obtained a licence from the government giving it exclusive trade in the country outside Rupert's Land for an initial period of twenty-one years.

From Hudson Bay to the Pacific, the company reigned supreme and secure for almost half a century, an empire within an empire, with the Pacific slope as its westward commercial outpost. Governor Sir George Simpson, the HBC's "Little Emperor," wrote in 1824 that all effort ought to be made "to show ... that no exertion is wanting on our part to secure to the mother country by

Governor Sir George Simpson of the Hudson's Bay Company was a furious traveller, an acerbic judge of those who worked under him, and a businessman obsessed with economy. When the North West Company and the HBC amalgamated in 1821, he restructured the new Hudson's Bay Company and reorganized the Western or Columbia Department. It was not the fault of "the Little Emperor" that the British abandoned so much territory in 1846; the credit for that falls at the door of the British Foreign Office. British Columbia Archives, PDP-02186

discovery as much of this vast continent and the trade thereof as possible."[8] The company singled out the Columbia Department for vigorous exploration, reorganization and exploitation; within this department, two frontier areas of trade, both related to the eventual boundaries of British Columbia, came into prominence.

One of these was the Yukon territory, where in succession to Simon Fraser the company sought to forestall Russian expansion. In 1822, the governor and committee in London decided to push HBC interests as far north and west of the Fraser River as possible in order "to keep the Russians at a distance."[9] The HBC dominated the interior, and the Russian-American Company remained dependent on it for agricultural supplies. Now Chief Trader Samuel Black examined the headwaters of the Turnagain, Stikine and Finlay Rivers—all of which run parallel to and west of Mackenzie River—with a view to drawing aboriginal trade in the Stikine territory away from the Russians on the coast. This move to expand the company's northwestern margins of operation was tied to British foreign policy of checking Russian aggrandizement in northwestern North America, a policy that also supported a substantial Royal Navy project for the discovery of the Northwest Passage in 1825–28.[10] Profit and power went hand in hand in British imperial logic.

The same impulse that animated British politicians and traders to forestall the Russians on the northwest coast and in the Yukon was also active in their policies in regards to the Snake River country. The HBC and the government understood that sometime in the future, Old Oregon, claimed separately by both Britain and the United States, would have to be divided. In the Anglo-American negotiations of 1818 and 1823–24, the British government would have agreed to a partition of the territory along the 49th parallel from the Continental Divide to the Columbia River and thence along the river to the Pacific. The American negotiators would not admit to this: as in 1807, they wanted the 49th parallel to proceed as the boundary west to the Pacific. The British government reasoned that it would strengthen its case if it could consolidate the HBC's position on the north bank of the Columbia River. Accordingly, in the winter of 1824–25, Simpson, on the suggestion of the Foreign Office, arranged for Fort Vancouver to be built at the confluence of the Willamette and Columbia rivers. This ended the dominance of Fort George (Astoria), which was farther downstream and on the south bank of the river, as the port of the Columbia Department's operations. The company developed a vigorous trading policy to insulate the river's north bank from American traders and settlers. The south bank of the river would also be made secure from competition to keep the Americans at a safe distance from the Columbia River.

The rise of the Hudson's Bay Company's marine activities on the northwest coast made Russia even more paranoid about foreign encroachments. Boston traders still worked the passages and islands of southeastern Alaska, but the British were resurgent in their commercial work on the coast and in the interior.[11] The perennial problems of the Russians remained—how to feed their servants and hunters, how to get enough shipping to bring in supplies and trading goods, how to market their commodities to China. Russia would have dearly liked to gain a toehold on the Hawaiian Islands, but all attempts failed. They would have liked to establish trading relations with Japan; their overtures were turned down. On the northwest coast, the Russians found themselves at odds with the Americans as well as the British. They attempted, by an 1821 ukase or decree, to exclude all foreign shipping within a distance of 115 miles from shore. By the same bold measure they claimed sovereignty south to 51° north latitude, near the north end of Vancouver Island. But protests from the British Foreign Office and the American State Department put an end to that. Then the Russians decided to try to limit foreign influence in Alaska by establishing a border with both the British and the Americans at 54° 40' north latitude.

The British were adamant on the point of freedom of navigation and won the diplomatic fight on the grounds that the Russian maritime claim of 1821 contravened international law. On February 28, 1825, the British signed an agreement with Russia establishing the boundary at 54° 40' north latitude, with the eastern limits of Russian America set along the Portland Canal to 56° north latitude and thence by the height of land of mountains parallel to, but no nearer than ten leagues from, the coast to the 141st meridian, on which line it would run to the Arctic Ocean. The Russians acknowledged the rights of British navigation on the coast and on rivers cutting through the Russian coastal strip. The British could also trade at Sitka and on the Russian coast south of Mount Saint Elias for a ten-year period. These terms, which were essentially the same as those of a Russian-American convention of April 17, 1824, stayed Russian progress southward and eastward, while at the same time restoring British and American rights of trade and navigation. The Russian challenge, first begun by Peter the Great just over a century earlier, had been stopped at the end of the Alaskan panhandle.

In subsequent years, by contractual arrangement, the Hudson's Bay Company fed the Russian fur trade and business of Sitka, replacing the old Boston mariners of old, the Winships in particular, who could make their way north to the Alaskan ports of call. In due time, not for the telling here, the Hudson's Bay Company came to dominate that trade, exerting powers of navigation in rivers such as the Stikine, which coursed through the Alaskan panhandle. With steam navigation, certain posts that the Bay traders erected in the long inlets of Alaska became redundant. But always the commerce of the British from Fort Vancouver, and later from Fort Victoria on Vancouver Island, was essential to the Russian economy in Alaska. Canadian Pacific Railway coastal steamships continued the trade in later years, serving the inner passage and the requirements of business and communication along the Pacific coast of North America.

As for the Spanish, their experience at Nootka Sound, and the telling consequences of the British naval armament, forced them into a situation of consolidation and even retreat. They fell back on San Francisco presidio as their most northerly bastion of empire. Their shipping did not flourish in the days after their remarkable explorations north to the Gulf of Alaska by Pérez, Martínez, Malaspina, Bodega y Quadra and many others. Their scientific findings were of the highest order,[12] but their military and administrative system did not favour an extension of their territorial rule on the northwest coast. By 1819, in a treaty with the United States, Spain agreed to a delimitation of the western boundary of the Louisiana Purchase and relinquished all claims to territory on the Pacific coast north of the 42nd parallel. In other words, Spain's northern perimeter west of the Continental Divide stayed at the northern limit of Alta California, the present border of Oregon and California. It would take a war of conquest for Alta California to pass to American hands in 1846, the same year the sovereignty issue of Old Oregon was finally resolved. The full particulars of those developments do not lie within the scope of this work, but the foundations of those final dispositions were put down during those frantic and consequential years when Mackenzie, Fraser, Thompson, Lewis and Clark, the Nor'Westers, the Winships and the Astorians were seeking to control the ultimate prize, the mouth of the River of the West.

The northern extent of Spain's influence was transferred to the United States by the same 1819 treaty. This brought into play Juan Pérez's 1774 voyage to the northernmost of the Queen Charlotte Islands, Langara, at 55° 45' north latitude (discussed in Chapter 5). Spain claimed up to the 60th parallel, but John Quincy Adams as Secretary of State was content to press his Russian counterpart, Count Nesselrode, to accept Pérez's northernmost point to establish the boundary between the United States and Russian America. Nesselrode agreed, on condition that the southern tip of Prince of Wales Island remain under Russian control.[13] Thus was born the celebrated 54° 40' north, a legacy and a modification of Spanish naval discovery and colonial rights. In April 1824, the United States and Russian reached formal agreement on the southern limit of Alaska, and a year later the United Kingdom and Russia made a somewhat similar accord.

In all it had been a grand and tortuous saga, with numerous personalities crossing the pages of that time and space. In the background were the diplomats, who were propelled to their particular positions by those who exerted influence on them: the merchants. In fact, it was the merchant class—the fur traders, bankers and shippers of Canada—who were the dominant factor on the northern frontier of American influence. They shaped the direction of the farthest west out of all proportion to their numbers. They sent out exploring parties from their advance bases, brought in the indigenous people as allies, and used Canadian brawn and technique in transportation and wilderness survival. Mackenzie had shown the way. The Nor'Westers were the true lords of the wilderness, but they were also the pioneers of northern transcontinental empire, the forerunners of Canadian dominion. After 1821 the Hudson's Bay Company inherited the western rim that the Nor'Westers had so dearly bought. That the Nor'Westers never received the sort of direct help, guidance or protection from government (except in wartime) that they so desperately needed is in a way a testament to the merits of non-governmental intervention, for at the end of the day the Nor'Westers achieved their goals, winning the prize of the upper Columbia River watershed and all of the Fraser River watershed. Only the unavoidable failure of Thompson, who was caught up in the trading demands of the Columbia River interior (and with them the requirements of satisfying aboriginal trading rivalries), marred their westward progress to the river mouth. Only Castlereagh's less-than-stout diplomacy kept the British from being more forceful after winning Astoria by commerce and by war.

In later years, Thompson rightly thought that the British diplomats were too cozy with the Americans in trying to patch up differences, thus sacrificing Canadian interests. Castlereagh had wanted, as he said, to give the Americans "an additional motive to cultivate the arts of peace." In the end he was right, for the British Empire and the United States never fought another war. Jefferson's timid, careful position about westward expansion to Pacific shores was replaced by something more definite and strident. In the interim, calm directed the course of Anglo-American relations. The boundary that was put in place by convention in 1818, the demilitarization of the Great Lakes in 1817, the final extension of the 49th parallel to the Pacific (exclusive of the southern tip of Vancouver Island) in 1846 were all accomplished without war. The San Juan Islands and Alaska boundary disputes followed the same pattern. Much heat was generated, a lot of steam let off on both sides, but war was avoided. In the end, the boundary arrived at its present demarcation, abundantly more astronomical than geographical in its configuration, a representation more of politics than of rivers and terrain, the achievement of diplomats rather than corporations or armies. And it still serves to show, as its historical background relates, the highest achievement of statecraft, even brinkmanship, when two mighty empires came forth to claim the continental prize, one that neither could claim for itself alone.

It was begun by Mackenzie and countered by Lewis and Clark, and in their parallel and interlocking ways, their expeditions for commerce and science played out a telling and remarkable chapter in human enterprise, when the stakes were particularly high: the final unclaimed quarter of North America there for the taking—or the sharing.

Appendix 1

"The Theatre of All the Geographical Fictions": The Northwest and Other Passages

Romance has always been associated with the history of the search for the Northwest Passage, though it was hardly a search for adventure. Rather, it was a quest for strategic and economic advantages and was at least in part inspired by those seeking to aid or subvert Spanish hegemony in North America. However, even before the seventeenth century there are suggestions of Chinese and Japanese voyages to western North America, perhaps seeking a northeast passage.

In AD 450, Huishen and four other Buddhist monks are said to have sailed from China across the Pacific. Huishen stayed forty years in Fu-Sang and then returned to his homeland, where he was cross-examined about his travels by the emperor. James Cook's cartographer Henry Roberts showed "Foosang of the Chinese Naviagors about the years 453." The voyages of Japanese sea drifters also suggest early contact. Oddly, the most recent treatise, Gavin Menzies' *1421: The Year China Discovered the World*,[1] pays no attention to Huishen, though I agree with Gary Geddes, an expert on this Chinese navigator, that Menzies' thesis offers support for earlier, and repeated, Asian contact.[2] As to the argument in Menzies' book, Zheng He and his companions would have needed strong outboard motors fixed to the transoms of their junks to have done all that this ex-Royal Navy submariner claims.

The idea of a Northwest Passage cast a long shadow over the affairs of Europe and Asia, embroiling many states and kingdoms in the quest to find its nature and extent. The Italian geographer Toscanelli vouchsafed the idea in the fifteenth century; thereafter, innumerable expeditions were mounted by England, France, Holland and Spain to find a speedy shortcut to the seat of wealthy Indian potentates, gold-clad Chinese kings and jewel-surrounded Japanese emperors. Many centuries passed before Norway's Roald Amundsen sailed across the top of Canada and Alaska early in the twentieth century, in 1903–6. In Mackenzie's time—and that of Lewis and Clark, too—the persistent myth of a passage in more southerly latitudes continued to entice mariners and corporations into schemes beyond their financial capabilities. Ruin faced many explorers. Cartographers, on the truest and supposedly most authentic advice, swore to the accuracy of their charts and maps, in so many cases misleading monarchs, firms and adventurers into expeditions of great expense and improbable success.

Circumstances on the spot, that is, on the northwest coast, were often far different than those seen in an academy of sciences. Consider this statement, explaining the difficulties of exploration by seas: "Thus a simple inspection of the table of winds will always inform the reader of the state of the weather, and be of utility to those, who may follow us in this navigation: they, too, who may peruse with pleasure the events of our voyage, and at the same time feel interested for those who have undergone the fatigue of them, will not think with indifference on navigators, who, at the verge of the earth and having incessantly struggled against mists and storms, and scurvy, have explored an unknown coast, the theatre of all the geographical fictions, too readily embraced by modern geographers." So wrote the editor of the account of Lapérouse's voyage in the 1780s.[3] North America's west was indeed a theatre of geographical fictions. America was regarded in certain European circles as a utopia, a land of giants, an Eldorado, a place of the Seven Cities of Cibola and home of the Amazons. Romance outdistanced reality.

Not least among the proponents of the Northwest Passage were the French. After the establishment of their infant colonies in northern North America (Canada, Acadia, Louisiana), the French had much to gain by finding a wonderful waterway that could bring them directly to Japan and China. From the most august scientific headquarters in Paris, the cartographers Delisle and Buache produced doubtlessly authentic maps showing a *mer de l'ouest* (they got the dimensions of the Great Lakes wildly wrong).

Meanwhile, the Spanish pictured California as an island, seeking to confuse any interlopers, and the Russians, copycats in a way, showed Alaska as an island. There were lots of imaginary navigable passages among these lands and islands of western North America that stood between the Atlantic (and Hudson Bay) and the Pacific. It took years to unravel the truth that no Northwest Passage existed in latitudes south of 80° north latitude. Old legends die even older deaths, it seems.

When the Hudson's Bay Company was chartered by the English government and backed by the crown in 1670, its charter obliged the Company of Adventurers from England Trading into Hudson's Bay to prosecute a search for the Northwest Passage. By fits and starts the company did so, but always half-heartedly. Had they done so with zeal, the Royal Navy would not have had to expend so many lives and ships in the nineteenth century. But let us trace the steps to the origins of this problem of geography and the tangled tale of history.

Five concepts rank above all others in the European fictions of the late eighteenth century about the waters of western North America, including the western entrance to the Northwest Passage. These are, with their historical elaboration:

1. Lorenzo Ferrer Maldonado and the Strait of Anian
In 1588, a Portuguese sailor, Captain Lorenzo Ferrer Maldonado, is said to have sailed from Lisbon, across the Atlantic, and then to the Pacific by a strait, Anian. The account of this voyage was presented to the Spanish monarch in 1609. It remained unknown until 1781, when Spanish authorities began to use the document to guide the exploration of the northwest coast. Malaspina had a copy of it during his expedition.

2. The Strait of Juan de Fuca
The English consul in Venice, Michael Lok, reported that in 1596 he learned from an old man, Juan de Fuca (his true name being Apostolos Valerianos) from Cefalonia, a pilot and mariner in the employ of Spain, that in 1592 he had been in an expedition that had discovered a broad strait between 47° and 48°

north latitude, into which he entered. He then came into a much broader sea. Fuca had been compensated by the Spanish crown. The report of this voyage was published in Samuel Purchas's *Purchas, His Pilgrimes* (1625). A map of it, drawn by Delisle and Buache, appeared in 1752. No evidence of this voyage has turned up in Spanish archives, but the idea died a slow death. James Cook, in these latitudes off the mouth of the Strait of Juan de Fuca in 1778, mentions the fable.

3. Admiral Bartolomew de Fonte's Voyage

In 1708, a published account of Fonte's voyage says that in 1640 he sailed from Callao, Peru, and got as far north as 47° north latitude, where he found a great river. He encountered a ship, said to have come from Boston, Massachusetts, which was owned by a Seymour Gibbons and captained by Nicholas Shapley. Fonte concluded that no passage to the Atlantic existed. The "relation" of Fonte spread in London "mysteriously and with caution." In 1937, student of cartography Henry Raup Wagner stated his belief that this "relation" was written by Jonathan Swift or Daniel Defoe.

In 1753, Delisle, the cartographer, shows the ship's passage as into Hudson Bay and compares it to lands explored by the Russians. This chart was known to Cook, Lapérouse, Malaspina and others. Misleading cartography kept the concept alive, as it did the idea that California was an island. In the 1740s, Arthur Dobbs, a critic of the Hudson's Bay Company's inactive position on western discoveries, forced a British parliamentary inquiry, which led to parliament offering a reward of £20,000 to the discoverer of a Northwest Passage. This gave a boost to British exploration from Hudson Bay but did not result in the discovery of any strait. Mackenzie's 1789 expedition to the mouth of the Mackenzie River laid the idea of a passage in southern latitudes to rest, though the British Admiralty kept alive the idea of a northern sea route, partly to keep the Russians out and partly to provide employment for officers in the years of *Pax Britannica*. Fonte's tale was impossible, and the Delisle-Buache maps were a fantasy. However, many geographers accepted it as truth, so many maps of the latter part of the eighteenth century display Fonte's alleged discoveries and the Sea of the West.

4. The Western Sea

France's interest in the passage dates from the 1524 voyage of Giovanni da Verrazano, who was sent to find a northwest passage to counteract Spain's newly discovered passage, via Magellan Strait, to the "blessed shores of Cathay." Verrazano found the North American shore unyielding, save for a gap that he thought might lead to western waters. Jacques Cartier explored the Gulf of St. Lawrence and the River St. Lawrence. Samuel de Champlain explored west to Lake Huron. The Jesuit Marquette set out in 1673 to find a "Big Water" and, as an extension of the Verrazano misconception, imagined that he would "reach the gulf of California and thence the East Indies." Instead he went to the Mississippi. The Jesuit historian Charlevoix, who wrote a history of Canada, or New France, projected, on the basis of presumably irrefutable evidence, cartographic and historical, that a western sea existed. When Jean Nicollet reached the west end of Lake Superior and went beyond to the Illinois and the Wisconsin rivers in 1634–35, he wore a Chinese damask jacket so that he would be properly dressed at the court of the great Kublai Khan. Fur traders helped reduce speculation, but even as late as the era of Peter Pond, mistakes were made, extending the legend. French cartographers Delisle and Buache, already mentioned, showed the Western Sea prominently on their maps of the 1750s. In France, the Fonte fable shown on such maps fell out of favour. Noted authority Jacques Nicolas Bellin, whose hydrographical charts were in much demand, refused to endorse the Fuca and Fonte stories. Even so, his 1755 map of the Western Sea showed the entrance of Juan de Fuca at about 47° north and also that mentioned by another mariner, Martín Aguilar, at about 44° north. The report of Aguilar's "discoveries" spurred Spanish exploration north after 1750.

5. The River Oregon

This river was rumoured to exist in the far west. The Recollect father Louis Hennepin, beginning in 1680, spoke of the Missouri River having origins in streams in the mountains, and he speculated that beyond these mountains lay a river flowing to the Pacific. This was a fundamental postulation. Jonathan Carver, a British colonial military officer under the direction of Major Robert

Rogers (himself a believer in these prospects), went on an expedition to explore western lands and waters in 1766 and travelled for two years. He sought a rumoured pyramidial mountain, reported to be the source of all the great rivers of North America. Carver set that concept aside. From Carver's travels, and discussion of same, a growing appreciation developed for the idea of going up a branch of the Missouri and discovering the source of the Oregon, or River of the West, on the other side of the Continental Divide. By voyaging down that river, it was believed, one would come straight to the inlet or passage of Aguilar. If the traveller turned north, he would enter into the Straits of Anian and thence into the waterway discovered by Juan de Fuca. The 1778 map that accompanied the publication of Carver's narrative shows just such a configuration. On his 1796 map of the Missouri and upper Mississippi, Antoine Soulard, the surveyor general of Louisiana, showed the Missouri River's headwaters close to what he labelled "Oregan or R. of the West."

Postscript: The mind boggles now when it thinks about these assorted concepts of the Northwest Passage and various entrances and rivers and seas. But this state of disbelief is both a tribute to the complexities of the geography of western North America and a recognition of the limited knowledge of European states, geographers and cartographers. By the late eighteenth century, the Western Sea was translated into what Captain George Vancouver's advisors in London called the Hyperborean Sea, that is, the Northern Sea. The Hydrographer of the Admiralty, Alexander Dalrymple, was slow to appreciate the fact that no such passage existed in those latitudes. It served his purposes to keep the legends alive. Even when Mackenzie and Vancouver demonstrated the non-existence of such a waterway, the concept enjoyed a long after-life. Admiralty Secretary Sir John Barrow became the new torchbearer. Myths and legends die hard. Similarly, the Spanish concept of California as an island found a new lease on life when the Russians embraced the same idea.

It seems to me, though I do not have much historical foundation for the speculation, that the possible existence of these entrances, straits, rivers and seas of the west was a good talking and bargaining point when it came to getting official sponsorship for expeditions. The converse is true, for the Hudson's Bay

Company was always reluctant to pursue a northwest passage, doubting that any such existed in more southerly latitudes than the northern coast of Canada and Alaska. The HBC came under repeated attack, in and out of parliament, on this score, but the fact was that the company's reluctance to engage in expensive exploration was a correct disposition in order to keep out intruders and rivals. That Lewis and Clark were seeking a northwest passage (as many have claimed) necessarily brings up the question: what sort of passage were they seeking? Clearly when they departed on this great venture, they knew much about where they were going and what they would find: an expedition upstream via the Missouri and its tributaries, a crossing of the Rocky Mountains and then a connection with a westward-flowing stream or river leading (likely) to the Oregon or River of the West—the true Columbia River.

The existence of the Columbia had been suggested by Hezeta, pointed out by Gray, confirmed by Vancouver and Broughton, and identified at its upper reaches by Mackenzie. Lewis and Clark disclosed, or suggested, another form of northwest passage, one differing markedly from those put forward by the visionaries of previous centuries. All of these great explorers followed the idealized tracks of their predecessors. Historically conscious themselves, and guided by maps and charts, they attempted to piece together geographical truth. That many of them were misled is natural, but many of them—including Mackenzie, Lewis and Clark, and Thompson, who were in the first rank of empirical explorers and realistic discoverers—represented the new age of science and reason. Their labours in the field and in their printed works and maps chased away speculation and made finite our understanding of the true nature of North America's rivers and terrain.

[Sources: Excerpts of primary accounts relating the voyages of Lorenzo Ferrer Maldonado, Juan de Fuca and Bartolomew de Fonte are in Glyn Williams, *Voyages of Delusion: The Quest for the Northwest Passage* (New Haven, CT, and London: Yale University Press, 2002), 414–30. Various voyages of delusion are discussed in Henry Raup Wagner, "Apocryphal Voyages to the Northwest Coast of America," *Proceedings of the American Antiquarian Society* 41 (April 1931): 179–234. Among the many sources that can be consulted, the following provides an excellent introduction: David B. Quinn, "The Northwest Passage in Theory and Practice," in *North American Exploration,* vol. 1, *A New World Disclosed,* ed. John Logan Allen (Lincoln: University of Nebraska Press, 1997), 292–343. Treatment of California as an island is in Dora Beale Polk, *The Island of California: A History of the Myth* (Spokane: Arthur H. Clark, 1991). The cartographic record is harder to trace with authenticity. For a beginning, consult R. Cole Harris, ed., *Historical Atlas of Canada,* vol. 1, *From the Beginning to 1800* (Toronto: University of Toronto Press, 1987), 36 and 58. For Indian maps—of 1801, 1802 and 1810—see ibid., 59. For more details, see Henry Raup Wagner, *The Cartography of the Northwest Coast of America to the Year 1800* (1937; Amsterdam: N. Israel, 1968). Discussion of the pretended voyages of the Chinese to the northwest coast is to be found in Gavin Menzies, *1421: The Year China Discovered the World,* enlarged ed. (London: Bantam, 2003). For a recent review, consult James P. Delgado, *Across the Top of the World: The Quest for the Northwest Passage* (Vancouver: Douglas & McIntrye, 1999)].

Appendix 2

THREE FLAGS AND
THE COLUMBIA RIVER:
IDENTIFICATION AND
EXPLORATION OF THE
RIVER OF THE WEST

Mariners on the Pacific Coast were naturally drawn to seek out the River of the West, its existence so long reputed in the machinations of Louis Hennepin, Robert Rogers, Jonathan Carver and others. To complicate matters, the mariners likely also knew about the entrances rumoured by Aguilar, Fonte and Juan de Fuca, and about Pond's imagined route from Lake Athabasca to Cook Inlet. The northwest coast was a theatre of all sorts of geographical speculations, with the Northwest Passage the focal point of inquiries. I have profiled the various theories in Appendix 1 and here recount the voyages of discovery and exploration by sea.

Spanish navigator Bruno de Hezeta won the race to find the river entrance when, on August 17, 1775, in 46° 16' north, he noticed strong currents off the shore, which led him to believe they could indicate the mouth of some great river. He named the entrance Asuncion Bay. Hezeta did not examine the coast further than this mere recounting of geographical fact. Scurvy and fatigue necessitated a quick turn to the south for relief. For the moment there seemed no need to go further with inquiries, and he went on to his next assignment. But he had put this entrance on the map, a brilliant if inconclusive discovery, and the various names for it—Río San Roque (or Roc), the Bahía de las Asuncion, the Entrada de Hezeta—lured mariners who came to test the hypothesis of the River of the West.[1]

Nearly three years passed. On March 12, 1778, the British mariner James Cook, exploring "the long-looked for Coast of New Albion," coasted north from 44° 33' north. He saw a landscape that was aesthetically agreeable, for the wooded land of moderate height possessed a pleasant, fertile and diversified appearance. He and his men were aware that they were examining "so great a continent." But the weather was beastly, and Cook took out his feelings on the headlands, naming one of them Cape Foulweather. That day he came to Cape Blanco, where the Spaniard Martín Aguilar had been during Sebastián Vizcaíno's voyage in 1602–3, when Aguilar had supposedly located the southern entry to Juan de Fuca's Strait. In fact, as Captain Vancouver later discovered in 1792, Cook was too far north to observe Cape Blanco. What is important about this claimed sighting is that Cook wrote that it was in this latitude that cartographers had placed the entrance to Aguilar's Strait to the interior, which was, to Cook's way of thinking, a most improbable geographical fact. Farther north, he showed his disgust when he wrote: "It is this very latitude we were now in where geographers have placed the pretended *Strait of Juan de Fuca*, but we saw nothing like it, nor is there the least probability that ever such thing existed."

Cook was hasty in dismissing these geographical features, and he made his assessment of the Strait of Juan de Fuca when he was actually five miles south of Cape Flattery and twenty nautical miles offshore. The great mariner, at this stage of his life, was a little too contemptuous of possibilities and, in any event, despised the views of the "closet philosophers" and unskilled mapmakers whose opinions were easily cast upon the geographical features of western North America.[2]

Ten years later, John Meares sailed to resolve the puzzle of the Entrada de Hezeta. He had studied the charts of Hezeta's pilot, Francisco Antonio Mourelle, from 1775 and other sources. He sought a northwest passage entrance around 46° north, and although he hoped to trade for pelts, his real intent was geographical inquiry. This is a bit strange for a master in a trading company, but Meares sought imperial advantage and notoriety as a discoverer. Who knew what might come to him if he found a river or a strait? The off chance that there might be such a passage in this locale was something he could not pass by. His cruise south from Vancouver Island ports in the *Felice* between June 11 and July 7, 1788, was an attempt to follow on from Cook's failure ten years previously, because of haste and bad weather, to find an entrance. Once near the location indicated by Hezeta and Mourelle, Meares saw, from the masthead, breakers extending clearly across what seemed to be the river entrance. He may have lacked courage or perhaps had an abundance of prudence. Instead of entering, he chose rather to leave the names Deception Bay and Cape Disappointment. Meares concluded:

> We now discovered distant land beyond this promontory, and we pleased ourselves with the expectation of its being Cape Saint Roc of the Spaniards, near which they are said to have found a good port …. The name of Cape Disappointment was given to the promontory, and the bay obtained the title of Deception Bay [the mouth of the Columbia] …. It lies in the latitude of 46 deg 10 min North …. We can now safely assert, that there is no such river as that of Saint Roc exists, as laid down in the Spanish charts: to those of Maurelle [Mourelle] we made continual references.[3]

When T.C. Elliott, historian and yachtsman, went over the details of Meares's examination from the point of view of a mariner, he concluded that on July 5 Meares was looking into Gray's Harbor, and on July 6 he was observing Point Leadbetter, the southerly point of entrance to Willapa Bay. Currents were carrying the *Felice* southward. Elliott says that Meares "doubled" Cape Disappointment, as he claims to have done, and failed to see prominent physical features on both sides of the river. He did not, further, observe any sort of indications of a river, at a time when brown water would have been flowing into blue at the flood. "Either the weather was NOT clear on that day or Meares misrepresented the facts in his willingness to discredit the Spaniard, Heceta."[4]

At one time Meares considered coasting south as far as 42° north, where a Captain Caxon had reputedly found a good harbour. But in the end Meares determined on a more northerly course, sending a long boat into the Strait of Juan de Fuca entrance and then going north to Barkley Sound, Vancouver

Island. It seems clear that Meares lacked the daring so necessary for inshore discoveries, and it remained for Robert Gray to complete the task.

In his book of *Voyages,* Meares made observations on what he regarded as the probability of a northwest passage, but his proposals were wildly off the mark. Some details on this score suffice to make the point. He imagined a northern archipelago, somewhat akin to the Cascade Range, stretching northward from Juan de Fuca's Straits, as he called them, to southeastern Alaska in the neighbourhood of Sea Otter Sound at about 57° north. To the east of this land mass lay a sea of indeterminate size, and on this he marked "track of the American Sloop *Washington* in the Autumn of 1789." He thus imagined Vancouver Island to be connected to the main. Juan de Fuca's Straits presumably led to the great Western Sea of the French. All of this was fantastically wild and proved of no credit to Meares, but it was much debated in the pamphlet literature and in informed literary and scientific circles, especially in London and Edinburgh, and it showed the power of independent fur traders in alerting politicians and statesmen to the necessity of unlocking the secret of this western river.

Voyages by Meares, James Strange, George Dixon, and others exercised considerable influence upon Alexander Dalrymple, the cartographer, explorer, surveyor and hydrographer. Dalrymple argued for a resumption of the search for the Northwest Passage and, in the event such a passage did not exist, for the discovery of an extensive inland waterway along which Hudson's Bay Company furs could be moved to the Pacific coast. He also argued for the careful survey of the northwest coast by the Royal Navy. Dalrymple wanted to link the energies and interests of the East India Company with those of the Hudson's Bay Company. That would have combined the two monopolies in the prosecution of the fur trade, and it would have ruined the Montreal-based traders. Dalrymple's prodding produced the George Vancouver voyage, with its splendid results.[5]

The first vessel to enter the Columbia River was the *Columbia Rediviva* of Boston under Robert Gray, on May 11, 1792. Gray confirmed Hezeta's discovery but named the river after his own ship. Gray was a fur trader and his mission a commercial one. He entered into commercial arrangements with the Chinook, who lived near the river, and after a brief stay he sailed north, exiting the river on May 20. John Boit aboard *Columbia* noted that this would be a good place to set up a factory, but it was not until June 1810 that Nathan Winship arrived in the *Albatross* to do just that (though as explained in Chapter 12, he was unsuccessful).

Gray met up with George Vancouver in 1792 and handed him a copy of his newly made chart of the lower Columbia River for copying. This enabled Lieutenant William Broughton to enter the river over the turbulent bar. Had Gray had greater trade success in the lower Columbia, he might have been more secretive about the channel entrance. On the other hand, mariners share information freely for the safety of vessels and crews. Gray knew that Vancouver knew the exact location of the Columbia River entrance: it was no secret in 1792.

Later that summer, a maritime fur-trading vessel entered the river. The *Jenny*, a three-masted schooner out of Bristol, was under the command of James Baker, who had been instructed to keep his tracks and dates secret (which he did). The *Jenny* was the second vessel to enter the river.

Broughton entered the river on October 24 under Vancouver's instructions. His vessel, the *Chatham*, had a rough entry. He brought it to anchor ten miles inside the bar, just east of the present town of Megler, Washington. His crew lowered the ship's cutter and launch, and Broughton and men departed upstream, proceeding approximately 114 miles up the Columbia, a distance of about 127 miles from Cape Disappointment. Their farthest point east was some twenty miles east of the Columbia River's confluence with the Willamette River. They charted both banks of the river, and Broughton named many geographic features. He prepared an original plan chart (which is in the Hydrographic Department, Taunton, Somerset; Rv. 229), and it was published by Aaron Arrowsmith in London in 1798 under the title *Entrance of Columbia River*. It was also published, in a small insert, in Vancouver's "A Chart shewing part of the Coast of N.W. America …." in the Atlas of the 1798 edition of Vancouver's *Voyage of Discovery*. This chart, obviously, encouraged safer navigation in the river, and it was used by later mariners. For instance, Captain William Black in HMS *Racoon* had it in 1813. Broughton performed the act of taking possession on October 30, 1792.[6]

Captain Vancouver credited the discovery of the Columbia River to "the Spaniards, who call it Entrada de Ceta, after the commander of the vessel, who is said to be its first discoverer, but who never entered it …. It is the same opening that Mr. Gray stated to us in the spring … according to Mr. Gray's sketch [of the entrance to the river]."[7] If visual discovery counts for all, then honour goes to Hezeta; if exploration and actual entrance, to Gray. Pérez may have looked into Nootka Sound from offshore in 1774, but Cook entered it in 1778. Kendrick is reputed to have circumnavigated Vancouver Island, but we have proof positive that Galiano, Valdés and Vancouver actually did so. These points do not discredit the ideas and formulations and even claims of firsts, but they bring into perspective the respective achievements of discovery and exploration by land and sea.

Postscript: These discoveries were more than achievements in navigation and additions to the factual record. In due course, the United States and Spain entered into an agreement that marked the cession of Florida to the United States and the definition of the western boundary of the Louisiana Purchase. This was the Treaty of Washington, or the Floridas, 1819, sometimes called the Adams-Onis Treaty. The new line began at the Sabine River mouth and shaped itself crookedly northwesterly to the 42nd parallel (the California-Oregon border). In addition to territorial definition, Spain transferred to the United States all of its claims in the far west. The Spanish priorities of discovery were therefore inherited by the United States, and these extended north to the limits of Spanish discoveries by sea.

An Anglo-American sparring match developed over the primacy of discovery on the northwest coast. The struggle involved some of the best legal and historical minds of the age. For the basic details, compare Robert Greenhow, *Memoir, Historical and Political, on the Northwest Coast of North America, and the Adjacent Territories; Illustrated by a Map and a Geographical View of those Countries* (Washington: Blair and Rives, 1840), and Travers Twiss, *The Oregon Territory, its History and Discovery* (1846; Fairfield, WA: Ye Galleon Press, 1988).

NOTES

Preface

1. Ken Burns and Dayton Duncan, *Lewis and Clark: The Journey of the Corps of Discovery*, DVD, directed by Ken Burns (Washington, DC: WETA and Florentine Films, 1997). The film was written by Dayton Duncan, who also wrote the companion volume *Lewis and Clark: The Journey of the Corps of Discovery. An Illustrated History* (New York: Knopf, 1997).

2. Jeremy Adelman and Stephen Aron, "From Borderlands to Borders: Empires, Nation-States, and the Peoples in Between in North American History," *American Historical Review* 104, no. 3 (June 1999): 814–41.

Prologue: John Ledyard: "The Very Football of Chance"

1. Ledyard's story has recently attracted notice, though it has long been known. For the most recent accounts see Bill Gifford, *Ledyard: In Search of the First American Explorer* (Orlando, FL: Harcourt, 2007); and James Zug, *American Traveler: The Life and Adventures of John Ledyard, the Man Who Dreamed of Walking the World* (New York: Basic Books, 2005). See also James Zug, ed., *The Last Voyage of Captain Cook: Including the Siberian Journals and Selected Letters of John Ledyard* (Washington, DC: National Geographic Society, 2005).

2. Andrew Kippis, *A Narrative of the Voyages Round the World Performed by Captain James Cook; With an Account of His Life* (London: 1830), 2:126. James Burney, *Chronological History of North-Eastern Voyages of Discovery; and of the Early Eastern Navigations of the Russians* (1819; Amsterdam: N. Israel, 1969), 278, 280–81.

3. Jefferson to Charles Thomson (Secretary of the Continental Congress), September 20, 1787, quoted in John Bartlett Brebner, *The Explorers of North America, 1492–1806* (London: A. & C. Black, 1933), 459.

4. *Dictionary of American Biography* (1933), 11:93–94.

5. James Kenneth Munford, ed., *John Ledyard's Journal of Captain Cook's Last Voyage* (Corvallis: Oregon State University Press, 1963), 99.

6. J.C. Beaglehole, ed., *The Journals of Captain Cook*, vol. 1, *The Voyage of the Endeavour, 1768–1771* (Cambridge: The Hakluyt Society, 1955, repr. 1968), 449.

7. *Hordern House Catalogue* (Sydney, Australia: Hordern House, 2000), item 35, provides these details. On October 2, 1778, Ledyard led Cook's landing party ashore at Unalaska. The Russians had established a post there some years before. When the Russian leader Gerasin Izmailor returned Cook's visit, he produced maps for the celebrated navigator to use. Cook and Vancouver valued them highly. "The Russian government issued orders to cease being so helpful." Thomas Vaughan and Bill Holm, *Soft Gold: The Fur Trade and Cultural Exchange on the Northwest Coast of America*, 2nd ed. (Portland: Oregon Historical Society Press, 1990), 192.

8. Jefferson's words quoted in Gifford, *Ledyard*, 53, 104.

9. John Ledyard, *Journal of Captain Cook's Last Voyage* (Hartford, CT: Nathaniel Patten, 1783), 81.

10. Ibid., 71.

11. Ibid., 77.

12. Jared Sparks's *The Life of John Ledyard, The American Traveller* first appeared in Cambridge, MA, in 1828. It was published in London, also in 1828, as *Memoirs of the Life and Travels of John Ledyard*. The most recent edition is Jared Sparks, *The Life of John Ledyard, the American Traveller: Comprising Selections from His Journals and Correspondence* (Mystic, CT: Flat Hammock Press, 2005). I have used the first American edition.

13. Sparks, *Life of John Ledyard*, 175.

14. Brebner, *Explorers of North America*, 460. Philip Chadwick Foster Smith, *The Empress of China* (Philadelphia: Philadelphia Maritime Museum, 1984), 15–24, 43–44.

15. Ledyard Collection, New York Historical Society; noted in Stephen D. Watrous, ed., *John Ledyard's Journey through Russia and Siberia, 1787–1788: The Journal and Selected Letters* (Madison: University of Wisconsin Press, 1966), 37n6. See also the new edition by Munford, *John Ledyard's Journal*, which contains additional details, carefully researched, on the life of Ledyard.

16. Thomas Jefferson, *Notes on the State of Virginia* (first published in 1787), in *The Portable Thomas Jefferson*, ed. Merrill D. Peterson (Harmondsworth, Middlesex: Penguin, 1977), 145–50.

17. Ibid., 142–44.

18. Jefferson's correspondence with John Paul Jones and with John Jay, Secretary of State, on the motives of Lapérouse, August to October 1785, is in Julian Boyd, ed., *Papers of Thomas Jefferson* (Princeton: Princeton University Press, 1950), 8:339, 587, 593. See also Samuel E. Morison, *John Paul Jones: A Sailor's Biography* (1959; Annapolis, MD: Bluejacket Books, Naval Institute Press, 1999), 406-7.

19. Robin Inglis, "Lapérouse 1786: A French Naval Visit to Alaska," in *Enlightenment and Exploration in the North Pacific, 1741–1805*, eds. Stephen Haycox, James Barnett and Caedmon Liburd (Seattle: University of Washington Press, 1997), 53–54; and also by Inglis, *Lost Voyage of Lapérouse* (Vancouver: Vancouver Maritime Museum and Planetarium Association, 1986), 15. See also John Dunmore, ed., *The Journal of Jean-François de Galaup de la Pérouse, 1785–1788* (London: Hakluyt Society, 1994), 1:95–146.

20. Morison, *John Paul Jones*, 406–7. For sources on this venture, see ibid., p. 519, esp. Sparks, Mss.: Harvard College Library, v. 132.

21. Thomas Jefferson, "Life of Captain Lewis" (1813), in preface to Meriwether Lewis, *History of the Expedition under the Command of Captains Lewis and Clark to the Sources of The Missouri, Thence Across the Rocky Mountains and down the River Columbia, Performed during 1804, 5, 6*, ed. Paul Allen (Philadelphia: Bradford and Inskeep, 1814), 1:ix-x.

22. Sparks, *Ledyard*, 201.

23. Munford, *John Ledyard's Journal*, xxxii-xxxiii. Julian Boyd, ed., *Papers of Thomas Jefferson* (Princeton: Princeton University Press, 1950), 9:273.

24. Ledyard to Isaac Ledyard, [?] February 1786, quoted in Watrous, *John Ledyard's Journey*, 94-95.

25. Lafayette to Baron von Grimm, [?] February 1786, quoted in Watrous, *John Ledyard's Journey*, 93-94.

26. Martin Sauer, *Account of a Geographical and Astronomical Expedition* (London: 1802), 99-101.

27. These are the Reverend Andrew Kippis's words. Kippis saw Ledyard's letters to Banks, but their whereabouts is unknown. Kippis, *Narrative of the Voyages*, 2:126-27.

28. The British colony of Sierra Leone reflected these goals of Christian altruism and emancipation of slaves. It was intended as a homeland for ex-slaves returned to Africa. On this, generally, see John Gascoigne, *Science in the Service of Empire: Joseph Banks, the British State and the Uses of Science in the Age of Revolution* (Cambridge: Cambridge University Press, 1998), 179-80; also Harold B. Carter, *Sir Joseph Banks, 1743-1820* (London: British Museum of Natural History, 1988), 241-43. On Beaufoy, see *Dictionary of National Biography* (1888): 2:50-51.

29. *Proceedings of the Association for Promoting the Discovery of the Interior Parts of Africa* (London: T. Cadell, 1791), 25. British explorations in Africa, approached from the north and west, are summarized in Felipe Fernández-Armesto, ed., *The Times Atlas of World Exploration* (London: Times Books, 1991), chap. 37.

30. Thomas Paine to Jefferson, June 18, 1789, quoted in Boyd, *Jefferson Papers*, 15:198; Watrous, *John Ledyard's Journey*, 30-31.

31. Quoted in John Curtis Perry, *Facing West: Americans and the Opening of the Pacific* (Westport, CT: Praeger, 1994), 312n.38.

32. Jefferson to William Short, February 28, 1789, quoted in Boyd, *Jefferson Papers*, 14:596-98.

33. Sparks, *Ledyard*, 202.

34. Andrew Lipscomb and Albert Bergh, eds., *Writings of Thomas Jefferson* (Philadelphia: Thomas Jefferson Memorial Association, 1904-5), 1:101-2.

35. *Proceedings of the Association for Promoting the Discovery*, 67-68.

Chapter 1: Dreams, Schemes, Realities

1. Quoted in Marvin Lunenfeld, *1492: Discovery, Invasion, Encounter* (New York: D.C. Heath, 1991), xxi.

2. In 1803, the government of the Province of Upper Canada acquired legal control over the "Indian Territory," later the Canadian northwest. See Barry Gough, "Law and Empire: The Extension of Law to Vancouver Island and New Caledonia," *Western Legal History* 6, no. 2 (Summer/Fall 1993): 217-28. On Pond, see Gough "Peter Pond and Athabasca: Fur Trade, Discovery, and Empire," *Alberta* 1, no. 2 (1989): 1-18.

3. Fort Fork, which had recently been erected, was then the Nor'Westers' most western or distant settlement. Mackenzie had travelled there, from Fort Chipewyan, the previous October so as to get a head start on his 1793 voyage.

4. Quoted in Barry Gough, *First Across the Continent: Sir Alexander Mackenzie* (Norman: University of Oklahoma Press, 1997), 105.

5. The rock, now dubbed Mackenzie Rock, is in British Columbia's Alexander Mackenzie Provincial Park.

6. Stephen E. Ambrose, *Undaunted Courage: Meriwether Lewis, Thomas Jefferson, and the Opening of the American West* (New York: Simon and Schuster, 1996), 60.

7. Wistar to Jefferson, January 8, 1802, quoted in Donald Jackson, *Thomas Jefferson and the Stony Mountains: Exploring the West from Monticello*, new ed. (Norman: University of Oklahoma Press, 1993), 123–24.

8. Quoted in Jackson, *Thomas Jefferson and the Stony Mountains*, 95.

9. For further details see Gough, *First Across the Continent*, 71–72.

10. In addition, memoranda by Mackenzie of this time, and after, reflect the position taken in his *Voyages from Montreal*. They are printed in W. Kaye Lamb, ed., *The Journals and Letters of Sir Alexander Mackenzie* (Cambridge: Cambridge University Press for the Hakluyt Society, 1970).

11. Jeannette Mirsky, *The Westward Crossings: Balboa, Mackenzie, Lewis and Clark* (London: Allan Wingate, 1951), 247.

12. Quoted in Albert Furtwangler, *Acts of Discovery: Visions of America in the Lewis and Clark Journals* (Urbana: University of Illinois Press, 1993), 171–72.

13. Quoted in ibid.

Chapter 2: Visit of the Stranger from the West

1. Later the property of North West Company factor John McLoughlin, prized because of its celebrated original owner. The gun was still in use in 1827, by which time McLoughlin was working for the Hudson's Bay Company. *Journal of David Douglas during his Travels in North America, 1823–1827* (1914; New York: Antiquarian Press, 1959), 243.

2. W. Stewart Wallace, *The Pedlars from Quebec and Other Papers on the Nor'Westers* (Toronto: Ryerson Press, 1954), 3.

3 He was very close: the actual latitude is 52° 23' north, longitude 127° 28' west.

4. See Barry M. Gough, *Gunboat Frontier: British Maritime Authority and Northwest Coast Indians, 1846–1890* (Vancouver: UBC Press, 1984).

5. Mary Quayle Innis, ed., *Mrs. Simcoe's Diary* (Toronto: Macmillan of Canada, 1965), 134–35.

6. Actually 56° 8' north, 117° 27' west.

7. This was the Old Establishment on the south side of Lake Athabasca at Old Fort Point. In 1803, Fort Chipewyan was moved to the western end of the lake. Derek Hayes, *First*

Crossing: Alexander Mackenzie, His Expedition Across North America, and the Opening of the Continent (Vancouver: Douglas & McIntyre, 2001), 151.

8. Mackenzie to Simcoe, September 10, 1794, Joseph Banks Collection, Sutro Library, San Francisco; printed in *British Columbia Historical Quarterly* 16 (1952): 209–10.

9. Mackenzie to Dorchester, November 17, 1794, Colonial Office (CO) records 42/101, at the National Archive of the United Kingdom. Italics added.

10. Dorchester to Duke of Portland, November 20, 1794, ibid.

11. Alexander Mackenzie, *Voyages from Montreal, on the River St. Laurence, through the Continent of North America, to the Frozen and Pacific Oceans; in the Years 1789 and 1793. With a Preliminary Account of the Rise, Progress, and Present State of the Fur Trade of that Country* (London: Cadell and Davies, 1801), 396–97.

Chapter 3: The Mackenzie Touch

1. The first reference to their corporate name seems to be 1776.

2. Carleton to Shelburne, Quebec, March 2, 1768, quoted in Lawrence J. Burpee, *The Search for the Western Sea* (Toronto: Macmillan of Canada, 1935), 1:303.

3. Burpee, *Search for the Western Sea*, 1:289–90. Also see Major R. Rogers' Instructions to Captain Tate for the Discovery of the North West Passage, September 12, 1766, Baby Collection, MG 24, L3, vol. 40, National Archives of Canada.

4. Memorial by Peter Pond, April 18, 1785, Q/24–2, p. 418, National Archives of Canada.

5. Vincent T. Harlow, *The Founding of the Second British Empire* (London: Longman, 1964), 2:423–25.

6. Peter J. Marshall, "Britain and China in the Late Eighteenth Century," chapter 11 in *"A Free Though Conquering People": Eighteenth-Century Britain and its Empire* (Aldershot: Ashgate Variorum, 2003).

7. Marjorie Wilkins Campbell, *North West Company* (Toronto: Macmillan of Canada, 1957), 89–90.

8. Edwin E. Rich, *History of the Hudson's Bay Company* (London: Hudson Bay Record Society, 1959), 2:210–11; W. Kaye Lamb, ed., *The Journals and Letters of Sir Alexander Mackenzie* (Cambridge: Cambridge University Press for the Hakluyt Society, 1970), 28.

9. Mackenzie to McTavish, Fraser and Co., London, March 10, 1798, quoted in Lamb, *Journals and Letters of Sir Alexander Mackenzie*, 470.

10. Ibid.

11. His partners did not accept his views. When David Thompson was trading west of the Rocky Mountains, pelts he collected in the cordillera west of the Continental Divide were sent east to Rainy Lake, Grand Portage, Montreal and thence to London.

12. Lamb, *Journals and Letters of Sir Alexander Mackenzie*, 415, 417–18.

13. Enclosure in Mackenzie to Hobart, January 7, 1802, Colonial Office (CO) records 42/120, National Archives of the United Kingdom. Mackenzie knew that this project had two legal obstacles: getting rights of fishing and navigation from the East India

Company and the South Sea Company (which commerce neither company had exercised); and obtaining a licence of transit for trade goods through Hudson Bay and Rupert's Land.

14. Mackenzie to John Sullivan (for Lord Hobart), October 25, 1802, Q/293, p. 225, National Archives of Canada (also in CO 42/330, ff. 189–190 v, National Archives of the United Kingdom).

Chapter 4: Soft Gold: The Russian Thrust to Alaska, Columbia River and Alta California

1. William Coxe, *Account of the Russian Discoveries between Asia and America. To which are added, the conquest of Siberia, and the history of the transactions and Commerce between Russia and China* (London: T. Cadell, 1780). It should be noted that this work appeared before the unofficial and official accounts of Captain Cook's third and fatal voyage. By the 1787 edition of the work, Coxe had transformed his book into a comparative view of Russian discoveries with those made by Captains Cook and Clerke. The fourth edition, considerably enlarged, was published in 1804.

2. Text and explanation of this treaty are to be found in Frank A. Golder, *Russian Expansion on the Pacific, 1641–1850: An Account of the Earliest and Later Expeditions Made by the Russians along the Pacific Coast of Asia and North America; Including Some Related Expeditions to the Arctic Regions* (Cleveland: Arthur H. Clark, 1914), 33–66, 290–93.

3. Ibid., 133n296.

4. In Basil Dmytryshyn, E.A.P. Crownhart-Vaughan, Thomas Vaughan, eds., *To Siberia and Russian America: Three Centuries of Russian Eastward Expansion, A Documentary Record*, vol. 2, *Russian Penetration of the North Pacific Ocean, 1700–1789* (Portland: Oregon Historical Society Press, 1988), xxxvi.

5. Georg Wilhelm Steller, *Journal of a Voyage with Bering, 1741–1742*, ed. O.W. Frost (Stanford: Stanford University Press, 1988), 165–67.

6. Urey Lisiansky, *A Voyage Round the World in the Years 1803, 4, 5, and 6* (English trans.; London, 1814), 285; James R. Gibson, *Sea Otter Skins, Boston Ships, and China Goods: The Maritime Fur Trade of the Northwest Coast, 1785–1841* (Montreal/Kingston: McGill-Queen's University Press, 1992), 12–13.

7. Gibson, *Sea Otter Skins*, 13.

8. J.C. Beaglehole, ed., *The Journals of Captain Cook*, vol. 1, *The Voyage of the Endeavour, 1768-1771* (Cambridge: The Hakluyt Society, 1955, repr. 1968), 449.

9. Ibid., 451.

10. Nathaniel Portlock, *A Voyage Round the World, But More Particularly to the North-West Coast of America* (London: John Stockdale, 1789), 100–104.

11. [William Beresford] George Dixon, *A Voyage Round the World: But More Particularly to the North-West Coast of America* (London: George Goulding, 1789), 321.

12. Clarence L. Andrews, "Russian Plans for American Dominion," *Washington Historical Quarterly* 18 (April 1927): 83–92, quotation at 83.

13. Hector Chevigny, *Russian America: The Great Alaskan Venture, 1741–1867* (New York: Ballantine, 1965), 87; and also by Chevigny, *Lord of Alaska: The Story of Baranov and the Russian Adventure* (London: Robert Hale, 1946), 54, 56, 146.

14. Baranov's instructions of April 18, 1802, are cited in Richard A. Pierce, "The Territorial Objectives of Russia in North America" (typescript, 1982), 5.

15. Quoted from William Sturgis's account in Briton C. Busch and Barry M. Gough, eds., *Fur Traders from New England: The Boston Men in the North Pacific, 1787–1800. The Narratives of William Dane Phelps, William Sturgis and James Gilchrist Swan* (Spokane: Arthur H. Clark, 1997), 119.

16. Details of the difficult discussions are recorded in Hermann Ludwig von Löwenstern, *The First Russian Voyage Around the World: The Journal of Hermann Ludwig von Löwenstern (1803–1806)*, trans. Victoria Joan Moessner (Fairbanks: University of Alaska Press, 2003), 276–81.

17. Quoted in Hubert H. Bancroft, *History of the Northwest Coast* (New York: Bancroft, 1886), 1:321.

18. Ibid., 1:322.

19. The *Juno* was also purchased for the numerous foodstuffs and other supplies it carried. It had recently arrived from Boston. For particulars, see John D'Wolf, *A Voyage to the North Pacific* (1861; Fairfield, WA: Ye Galleon Press, 1968). D'Wolf completed Ledyard's dream voyage in reverse: he sailed from New Archangel to Petropavlovsk and then crossed Siberia, arrived in Liverpool and returned to New England.

20. Basil Dmytryshyn, E.A.P. Crownhart-Vaughan and Thomas Vaughan, eds., *To Siberia and Russian America: Three Centuries of Russian Eastward Expansion*, vol. 3, *The Russian American Colonies, 1798–1867* (Portland: Oregon Historical Society Press, 1989), 112; S.B. Okun, *The Russian-American Company* (Cambridge, MA: Harvard University Press, 1951), 121–23. Rezanov's description of attempts to enter the Columbia is in his report to Count Nikolai P. Rumiantser, June 17–29, 1806, New Archangel, quoted in Nina N. Bashkina et al., ed., *The United States and Russia: A Beginning of Relations, 1765–1815* (Washington, DC: US Government Printing Office, 1980), 443–44. Cited in Stephen Haycox, "In Search of the Great Bear: A Historiography of Russian Exploration in Alaska and California," in *Encounters with a Distant Land: Exploration and the Great Northwest*, ed. Carlos A. Schwantes (Moscow: University of Idaho Press, 1994), 56n.85.

21. Stephen W. Haycox, "Merchants and Diplomats: Russian America and the United States," in *Russian America: The Forgotten Frontier*, ed. Barbara Sweetland Smith and Redmond J. Barnett (Tacoma: Washington State Historical Society, 1990), 59.

22. Haycox, "In Search of the Great Bear," 50–51.

23. Ibid.

24. Petr A. Tikhmenev, *A History of the Russian-American Company*, trans. and ed. Richard A. Pierce and Alton S. Donnelly (Seattle: University of Washington Press, 1978), 96–99. Rezanov's visits to San Francisco, his arrangements with the governor and the commandant, and his love for Doña Concepción are of invariable interest and romance.

He had to reach a safe port, for his vessel was in need of repairs. Likely he used this as an excuse to enter San Francisco Bay. (This is confirmed in Tikhmenev.) His larger, long-range requirement was to visit the Governor of Monterey and initiate diplomacy regarding trade, especially in grains and other foodstuffs. Obtaining an anchorage was far easier than discussing any hoped-for contract.

25. E.W. Giesecke, "Discovery of Humboldt Bay, California, in 1806 from the Ship *O'Cain*, Jonathan Winship, Commander," *Terra Incognitae* 29 (1997): 51–71, and 30 (1998): 94–100.

26. Baranov was driven by the legal balance sheet and the needs of his own local power and opulence. Rezanov, by contrast, was a metropolitan-based imperialist and expansionist.

27. Kenneth N. Owens, ed., *The Wreck of the Sv. Nikolai: Two Narratives of the First Russian Expedition to the Oregon Country, 1808–1810*, trans. Alton S. Donnelly (Portland: Oregon Historical Society Press, 1985; reprint, Lincoln: University of Nebraska Press, 2000).

28. James R. Gibson, *Imperial Russia in Frontier America: The Changing Geography of Supply of Russian America, 1784–1867* (New York: Oxford University Press, 1976), 11.

29. John L. Kessell, *Spain in the Southwest: A Narrative History of Colonial New Mexico, Arizona, Texas, and California* (Norman: University of Oklahoma Press, 2002), 368. Also see Warren L. Cook, *Flood Tide of Empire: Spain and the Pacific Northwest, 1543–1819* (New Haven, CT: Yale University Press, 1973), 495–506.

30. Information from E.W. Giesecke.

31. From William Dane Phelps's account included in Busch and Gough, *Fur Traders from New England*, 49.

32. John Barrow, quoted in L.P. Kirwan, *A History of Polar Exploration* (New York: W.W. Norton, 1960), 77.

33. Quoted in Gibson, *Imperial Russia in Frontier America*, 15.

34. From William Sturgis's account published in *North American Review* 15 (1822) and reprinted in Busch and Gough, *Fur Traders from New England*, 38. The Sturgis statement was an analysis of President James Monroe's message to Congress of April 17, 1822.

Chapter 5: Rising Tides of Empire: Flags at Nootka Sound

1. Quoted in John L. Kessell, *Spain in the Southwest: A Narrative History of Colonial New Mexico, Arizona, Texas, and California* (Norman: University of Oklahoma Press, 2002), 326.

2. The Spanish learned about Russian activities and designs by vicarious, indirect means. The Russians could not contain geographical information acquired during their voyages of discovery to the east, for these benefited western science and were of advantage to the French, the British and the Spanish. See Vasilii A. Divin, *The Great Russian Circumnavigator, A.I. Chirikov*, trans. and annotated Raymond H. Fisher (Fairbanks: University of Alaska Press, 1993), 106–7, where the author echoes the Soviet-era xenophobia that science ought be kept in Russian national hands and not shared internationally. The author recounts the following details: In 1726, the cartographer Joseph Nicolas Delisle arrived in St. Petersburg, where he was assigned by the St.

Petersburg Academy of Sciences to make a great map of the Russian empire. He had his half-brother, Louis Delisle de la Croyère, an astronomer, named to the Second Kamchatka Expedition (that is the Bering-Chirikov exploring expedition). He sailed with Chirikov in 1741. Meanwhile, Delisle sent 190 copies of maps to Paris and the French Ministry of Marine. His half-brother was thought to be collecting information for him and for France. In 1747, Delisle, on the insistence of the St. Petersburg Academy of Sciences, was dismissed from the Academy, and he returned to Paris. He had brazenly assigned "the honor of the original discovery of northwestern America to his brother" (ibid., 16–17). The honour belonged to Chirikov. But Delisle's maps became global knowledge, information that Spain gained to its advantage and its alarm. The Spanish were equally suspicious and wary of letting secrets fall into the hands of rivals. (Additional information from Robin Inglis.)

3. Bucareli to Julian Arriaga, July 27, 1773, quoted in Warren L. Cook, *Flood Tide of Empire: Spain and the Pacific Northwest, 1543–1819* (New Haven, CT: Yale University Press, 1973), 55.

4. Michael E. Thurman, *The Naval Department of San Blas: New Spain's Bastion for Alta California and Nootka, 1767–1798* (Glendale, CA: Arthur H. Clark, 1967).

5. British commercial activities, coming on the heels of Cook's 1778 reconnaissance and suggestions as to trade possibilities in the sea otter business, are described in Barry M. Gough, *The Northwest Coast: British Navigation, Trade, and Discoveries to 1812* (Vancouver: UBC Press, 1992), 69–103. The Spanish did not arrive at Nootka until May 5, 1789, four years after Hanna.

6. Count Revilla-Gigedo, Report to the King, on the Affairs of the two Californias and the Dept of San Blas, April 12, 1793, trans., Foreign Office (hereafter FO) records 5/1470, pp. 353–60, National Archives of the United Kingdom (hereafter NA).

7. Bucareli's ambiguous instructions of December 24, 1773, called, in Article 7, for Pérez "to ascend to the latitude which he considers suitable, keeping in mind that the landing is to be made at sixty degrees of latitude." In the event, the mariner fell nearly four degrees short. On expectations versus results, see Herbert K. Beals, ed., *Juan Pérez on the Northwest Coast: Six Documents of His Expedition in 1774* (Portland: Oregon Historical Society Press, 1989), 33–41.

8. Martínez to Manuel Antonio Flóres, Archivo General de Indies, Seville, Mexico papers, no. 1529, quoted in Christon I. Archer, "The Spanish Reaction to Cook's Third Voyage," in *Captain Cook and His Times*, eds. Robin Fisher and Hugh Johnston (Vancouver: Douglas & McIntyre, 1979), 104.

9. Herbert K. Beals, trans., *For Honor and Country: The Diary of Bruno de Hezeta* (Portland: Oregon Historical Society Press, 1985), 86.

10. Thurman, *Naval Department of San Blas*, 257.

11. A scholarly reconstruction of the history of these outposts is contained in Katerina Solovjova and Aleksandra Vovnyanko, "The Rise and Decline of the Lebedev-Lastochkin Company: Russian Colonization of South Central Alaska, 1787–1798," *Pacific Northwest Quarterly* 90, no. 4 (Fall 1999): 191–205.

12. Jim McDowell, *José Narváez: The Forgotten Explorer, Including His Narrative of a Voyage on the Northwest Coast in 1788* (Spokane: Arthur H. Clark, 1998), 126–29.

13. John Meares, *Voyages Made in the Years 1788 and 1789, from China to the North West Coast of America* (London: Walter, 1790), 219.

14. Quoted in McDowell, *José Narváez*, 39.

15. Martínez journal, June 21 and 24, 1789, trans., FO 5/1470, pp. 501–21, NA.

16. Of these converts, it has been said: "They were prisoners of war, slaves, and outcasts whom the Indians abandoned to whatever fate the Spaniards had in store for them." Christon I. Archer, "Spain and the Defence of the Pacific Ocean Empire, 1750–1810," *Canadian Journal of Latin American and Caribbean Studies* 11, no. 21 (1986): 36.

17. Meares's thirty-one–page *Memorial*, first printed as a pamphlet, is dated April 30, 1790. It was ordered to be printed May 13, 1790, and was included in Great Britain, House of Commons *Journals* 45 (1790): 463–84. Meares's evidence before the Privy Council for Trade, May 27, 1790, is in Board of Trade (BT) files 5/6, pp. 230–33, NA. It was powerful fuel for the British diplomatic and naval fires. For a discussion of the British use of the Meares evidence, see Gough, *The Northwest Coast*, 139–41.

18. Rutledge Jr. to Jefferson, May 6, 1790, quoted in Julian Boyd, ed., *Papers of Thomas Jefferson* (Princeton: Princeton University Press, 1950), 16:413–15.

19. For more on the Beckwith mission and Dorchester's instructions, see William Ray Manning, *The Nootka Sound Controversy* (1905; New York: Arno Press, 1966), 415.

20. Ibid., 423.

21. Alexander DeConde, *This Affair of Louisiana* (New York: Charles Scribner's Sons, 1976), 53.

22. Vancouver to Evan Nepean (Undersecretary for Foreign Affairs), January 7, 1793, quoted in George Godwin, *Vancouver: A Life* (New York: D. Appleton, 1931), 219–33.

23. Pearce's account of proceedings is in John Forsyth, ed., "Documents Connected with the Final Settlement of the Nootka Dispute," *British Columbia Historical Association Second Annual Report* (1924): pp. 33–35.

24. Clarence L. Andrews, "Russian Plans for American Dominion," *Washington Historical Quarterly* 28 (April 1927): 85–86.

25. J. Richard Nokes, *Almost a Hero: The Voyages of John Meares, R.N., to China, Hawaii and the Northwest Coast* (Pullman: Washington State University Press, 1998), 81–82.

26. George Vancouver, *A Voyage of Discovery to the North Pacific Ocean and Round the World* (London: G.G. and J. Robinson, 1798), 3:285.

27. Ibid., 3:295.

Chapter 6: The Empire of Safe Harbour Retreat

1. Mary Malloy, ed., *"A Most Remarkable Enterprise": Lectures on the Northwest Coast Trade and Northwest Coast Indian Life by Captain William Sturgis* (Marstons Mills, MA: Parnassus Imprints, 2000), 6.

2. Amasa Delano, *A Narrative of Voyages and Travels* (Boston, 1817; reprint, New York: Praeger, 1970), 400. For particulars on Kendrick, see Richard A. Pierce, "John Kendrick," *Dictionary of Canadian Biography* (1979), 4:410–12.

3. Quoted in Samuel E. Morison, *The Maritime History of Massachusetts* (Boston: Houghton Mifflin, 1961), 53.

4. Quoted in Barry M. Gough, *The Northwest Coast: British Navigation, Trade, and Discoveries to 1812* (Vancouver: UBC Press, 1992), 198.

5. Instructions to J. Kendrick, September 1787, in US Senate, Report of Committee No. 335, 32nd Cong., 1st sess., 1852, 16. Printed also in Frederick W. Howay, "An Early Colonization Scheme in British Columbia," *British Columbia Historical Quarterly* 3, no. 1 (January 1939): 51–63, quote on page 51. Details of Kendrick's land schemes are drawn from this article. While I have drawn on the partial details and other particulars of Howay's valuable articles, I differ from him in interpretation, as he slights American zeal (including imperial ambitions) and fails to appreciate, strangely, the navigational capabilities of Kendrick and the aboriginal ability to negotiate treaties for their own limited benefit.

6. George Vancouver, *A Voyage of Discovery to the North Pacific Ocean and Round the World* (London: G.G. and J. Robinson, 1798), 2:254–55.

7. Translation of *La Vuelta al Mundo* [Malaspina's Voyage] (Madrid, 1885), 194; cited in Howay, "Early Colonization Scheme," 52.

8. According to F.W. Howay, "From the moment that Boston sank below the horizon in 1787, [Kendrick] paid little attention to his employers' rights or instructions." Ibid., 56.

9. Howell to Barrell and others, May 11, 1795, and December 23, 1796, quoted in Nellie B. Pipes, ed., "Later Affairs of Kendrick," *Oregon Historical Quarterly* 30, no. 1 (June 1929): 99 ff.

10. An English version of the circular is in the library of the Massachusetts Historical Society, Boston. Quoted in Howay, "Early Colonization Scheme," 60–61.

11. US Congress, House of Representatives Document 43, 26th Cong., 1st sess., 1841, and US Senate, Report of Committee No. 335, 32nd Cong., 1st sess., 1852.

12. Francis Paul Prucha, *American Indian Policy in the Formative Years: The Indian Trade and Intercourse Acts, 1790–1834* (Cambridge, MA: Harvard University Press, 1962).

13. *Moses Martin et al. v. Her Majesty the Queen et al.*, commonly referred to as the Meares Island Case (BC Supreme Court, Vancouver Registry, Action No. C845934).

14. All quotes from Howay, "Early Colonization Scheme," 58.

15. Samuel E. Morison, "The *Columbia's* Winter Quarters Located [sic]," *Oregon Historical Quarterly* 39 (1938): 3–7. Morison and his associate Edmund Hayes did not locate the actual site, which was discovered by Kenneth Gibson of Tofino. See Donald H. Mitchell, "The Investigation of Fort Defiance: Verifications of the Site," *BC Studies* 4 (1970): 3–20, and Donald H. Mitchell and J. Robert Knox, "The Investigation of Fort Defiance: A Report on Preliminary Excavation," *BC Studies* 16 (1972–73): 32–56.

16. Frederick W. Howay, ed., *Voyages of the "Columbia" on the Northwest Coast, 1787–1790 and 1790–1793* (Boston: Massachusetts Historical Society, 1941), 390–91. For Robert Haswell's version, see ibid., 312–13.

17. Hilary Stewart, ed., *The Adventures and Sufferings of John R. Jewitt Captive of Maquinna* (Vancouver: Douglas & McIntrye, 1987). The tale affords the historical basis for James Houston, *Eagle Song: An Indian Saga Based on True Events* (Toronto: McClelland and Stewart, 1983).

18. Frederick W. Howay, "The Ballad of the Bold Northwestmen: An Incident in the Life of Captain John Kendrick," *Washington Historical Quarterly* 20 (1929): 114–23.

19. William Dane Phelps, quoted in Briton C. Busch and Barry M. Gough, eds., *Fur Traders from New England: The Boston Men in the North Pacific, 1787–1800. The Narratives of William Dane Phelps, William Sturgis and James Gilchrist Swan* (Spokane: Arthur H. Clark, 1997), 9–10.

20. Mark Kaplanoff, ed., *Joseph Ingraham's Journal of the Brigantine "Hope" on a Voyage to the Northwest Coast of North America, 1790–92* (Barre, MA: Imprint Society, 1971), 2–3. All quotations from Ingraham's journal are cited by date and are drawn from this edition.

21. The urbane Ingraham supplies extensive details gathered from mariners. See Kaplanoff, *Joseph Ingraham's Journal*, 179–81.

22. Hall J. Kelley, *Discoveries, Purchases of Lands, &c on the North West Coast, Being a Part of an Investigation of the American Title to the Oregon Territory* (Boston: 1838), 1, 4.

23. Derek G. Smith, ed., *The Adventures and Sufferings of John R. Jewitt, Captive Among the Nootka, 1803–1805* (Toronto: McClelland and Stewart, 1974), 49.

24. The last aboriginal war on the coast occurred in 1855 at Clayoquot.

25. Smith, *Adventures and Sufferings of John R. Jewitt*, 128.

Chapter 7: Canadian Traders on the Missouri and the Spanish Response

1. Rufus Terral, *The Missouri Valley: Land of Drouth, Flood and Promise* (New Haven, CT: Yale University Press, 1947), 1.

2. Richard Glover, ed., *David Thompson's Narrative, 1784–1812* (Toronto: Champlain Society, 1962), 182n.

3. For instance, Alexander Henry the Younger went south from Black Cat's village and Deapolis (both in present-day North Dakota) to Cheyenne Campsite (in southern Wyoming) in July 1806. See William T. Billeck, "Alexander Henry's 1806 Route Between the Assiniboine and Missouri Rivers," *Journal of the North Dakota Archaeological Association* 4 (1990): 230–44, esp. 236–39.

4. Many editions of La Vérendrye's journals and letters exist, but the main issues about the confused nature of his actual travels are best set forth in the introduction to Lawrence J. Burpee, ed., *Journals and Letters of Pierre Gaultier de Varennes de La Vérendrye and His Sons* (Toronto: Champlain Society, 1927).

5. The original journal (1,642 pages) is in the National Archives of Canada at MG 19, A13. It has been printed in Barry M. Gough, ed., *The Journal of Alexander Henry the Younger,*

1799–1814, vol. 1, *Red River and the Journey to the Missouri*, and vol. 2, *The Saskatchewan and Columbia Rivers* (Toronto: Champlain Society, 1988, 1992).

6. See Sylvia Van Kirk, *Many Tender Ties: Women in Fur-Trade Society, 1670–1870* (Norman: University of Oklahoma Press, 1983).

7. James P. Ronda, "Foreword" in *Prologue to Lewis and Clark: The Mackay and Evans Expedition*, by W. Raymond Wood (Norman: University of Oklahoma Press, 2003), xii.

8. Quoted in William H. Goetzmann and Glyndwr Williams, *Atlas of North American Exploration* (Norman: University of Oklahoma Press, 1998), 134.

9. Warren L. Cook, *Flood Tide of Empire: Spain and the Pacific Northwest, 1543–1819* (New Haven, CT: Yale University Press, 1973), 434.

10. Goetzmann and Williams, *Atlas of North American Exploration*, 134.

11. Ibid.

12. Carondelet report, November 24, 1794, quoted in James A. Robertson, ed., *Louisiana under the Rule of Spain, France and the United States 1785–1807* (Cleveland: Arthur H. Clark, 1911), 1:335.

13. Ibid., 1:297.

14. Trudeau to Carondelet, May 31, 1794, quoted in Abraham P. Nasatir, *Before Lewis and Clark: Documents Illustrating the History of the Missouri, 1785–1804* (St. Louis: St. Louis Historical Documents Foundation, 1952), 1:228–29. "Jacques Clamorgan," in Leroy R. Hafen, ed., *The Mountain Men and the Fur Trade of the Far West* (Glendale, CA: Clark, 1965), 2:81–94.

15. Quoted in Cook, *Flood Tide of Empire*, 436.

16. Annie Heloise Abel, ed., *Tabeau's Narrative of Loisel's Expedition to the Upper Missouri* (Norman: University of Oklahoma Press, 1939), 9.

17. Quoted in Goetzmann and Williams, *Atlas of North American Exploration*, 134.

18. Lansing B. Bloom, "The Death of Jacques d'Eglise," *New Mexico Historical Review* 2 (1927): 369–79.

19. Louis Houck, *The Spanish Regime in Missouri* (Chicago: R.R. Donnelley, 1908), 2:182.

20. Annie Heloise Abel-Henderson, "Mackay's Table of Distances," *Mississippi Valley Historical Review* 10 (1923): 429–31.

21. Carondelet to Prince of Peace, June 3, 1796, quoted in Nasatir, *Before Lewis and Clark*, 1:356.

22. Milo Quaife, ed., "McKay's Journal," *Wisconsin Historical Society Proceedings* 58 (1915): 193. The Mackay-Evans correspondence and other details are found in Abraham P. Nasatir, "John Evans: Explorer and Surveyor," *Missouri Historical Review* 25 (1931): 219–39, 432–60, 585–608.

23. These societies were the Gwyneddigion (Sons of Gwynedd) and the Caradogion (Sons of Caradog/Caracticus, a Brythonic prince who fought the Romans).

24. David Williams, "John Evans' Strange Journey," *American Historical Review* 54 (January

1949): 277–95; (April 1949): 508–29.

25. Reuben G. Thwaites, ed., *The Original Journals of the Lewis and Clark Expedition* (New York: Dodd, Mead, 1904–5), 7:292.

26. Wood, *Prologue to Lewis and Clark*, 63. For discussion of the Soulard map, see ibid., 47–64.

27. Quoted in Nasatir, *Before Lewis and Clark*, 1:101.

28. Ibid., 1:106–7.

29. Ibid., 1:102.

30. Entry for November 18, 1804, in Bernard DeVoto, ed., *The Journals of Lewis and Clark* (Boston: Houghton Mifflin, 1953), 66.

31. Quoted in Lawrence J. Burpee, *The Search for the Western Sea* (Toronto: Macmillan of Canada, 1935), 2:357. Compare Gough, *Journal of Alexander Henry the Younger*, 2:225.

32. Grant to Evans, October 8, 1796, quoted in Nasatir, "John Evans," 458–59.

33. Nasatir, *Before Lewis and Clark*, 1:102–3.

34. Ibid., 1:103.

35. Ibid., 1:106.

36. The map is reproduced, in redrawn form, in Goetzmann and Williams, *Atlas of North American Exploration*, 134. See also W. Raymond Wood, "The John Evans 1796–97 Map of the Missouri River," *Great Plains Quarterly* 1, no. 1 (Winter 1981): 39–53.

37. Evans to Jones, July 15, 1797, and Morgan Rhees's notice in *Greal Neu Eurgfrawn*, 1800, both printed in Wood, *Prologue to Lewis and Clark*, 190–95.

38. Quoted in Frederick J. Taggart, "Notes Supplementary to Any Edition of Lewis and Clark," *Annual Report of the American Historical Association for 1908* (Washington, DC: Government Printing Office, 1909), 1:193.

39. Quoted in Goetzmann and Williams, *Atlas of North American Exploration*, 134.

40. Carondelet to the Prince of Peace, June 3, 1796, New Orleans, quoted in Nasatir, *Before Lewis and Clark*, 1:354–56.

41. Nasatir, *Before Lewis and Clark*, 1:108–10, provides this insight, based on a thorough reading of extant sources cited there.

Chapter 8: The View from Monticello: Jefferson's Wests

1. Paul C. Phillips, *The Fur Trade* (Norman: University of Oklahoma Press, 1961), 2:568.

2. John Logan Allen, "Imagining the West: The View from Monticello," in *Thomas Jefferson and the Changing West: From Conquest to Conservation*, ed. James P. Ronda (Albuquerque: University of New Mexico Press, 1997), 3–23; for an earlier view see George T. Surface, "Thomas Jefferson: A Pioneer Student of American Geography," *Bulletin of the American Geographical Society* 41 (December 1909): 743–50.

3. Jefferson to Robert R. Livingston, April 18, 1802, in *The Portable Thomas Jefferson*, ed. Merrill D. Peterson (Harmondsworth, Middlesex: Penguin, 1977), 485.

4. Quoted in Albert Furtwangler, *Acts of Discovery: Visions of America in the Lewis and Clark Journals* (Urbana: University of Illinois Press, 1993), 171–72. See also Stephen E. Ambrose, *Undaunted Courage: Meriwether Lewis, Thomas Jefferson, and the Opening of the American West* (New York: Simon and Schuster, 1996), 72–73.

5. This story, first told in 1824, was retold in 1856 to a son of Sir Alexander Mackenzie, George, who interviewed Bernadotte, Napoleon's surrogate on the throne of Sweden. The particulars of that interview can be found in Robert Ballantyne, *The Pioneers: A Tale of the Western Wilderness Illustrative of the Adventures and Discoveries of Sir Alexander Mackenzie* (London: James Nisbet, 1872), 124–26.

6. See Charles Ambler, *George Washington and the West* (Chapel Hill: University of North Carolina Press, 1936).

7. Quoted in John Carl Parish, *The Persistence of the Westward Movement and Other Essays* (Berkeley/Los Angeles: University of California Press, 1943), 70.

8. Thomas Jefferson, *Notes on the State of Virginia* (first published in 1787) in *The Portable Thomas Jefferson*, ed. Merrill D. Peterson (Harmondsworth, Middlesex: Penguin, 1977), 36–37.

9. Quoted in Edmund W. Gilbert, *The Exploration of Western America, 1800–1850: An Historical Geography* (Cambridge: Cambridge University Press, 1933), 7, citing *American Historical Review* 3 (July 1897): 673.

10. Gilbert, *Exploration of Western America*, 7–8.

11. Donald Jackson, *Thomas Jefferson and the Stony Mountains: Exploring the West from Monticello*, new ed. (Norman: University of Oklahoma Press, 1993), 42–43, 62, citing the correspondence in Julian Boyd, ed., *Papers of Thomas Jefferson* (Princeton: Princeton University Press, 1950), 6:371 and 15:609.

12. H.A. Washington, ed., *The Writings of Thomas Jefferson* (Washington, DC: Taylor and Maury, 1853–54) 8:483; also Meriwether Lewis, *The Lewis and Clark Expedition: The 1814 Edition*, unabridged (Philadelphia/New York: J.P. Lippincott, 1961), 1:xviii.

13. And was most recently expressed by General Charles de Gaulle in Montreal in 1967. The government of Canada requested, successfully, his departure from Canadian soil.

14. John C. Miller, *The Federalist Era, 1789–1801* (New York: Harper & Row, 1960), 134.

15. Reuben G. Thwaites, ed., *Journal of André Michaux, 1793–1796* (Cleveland: Arthur Clark, 1904); R.W. Van Alstyne, *The Rising American Empire* (Oxford: Blackwell, 1960), 80, and, by the same, "International Rivalries in the Pacific Northwest," *Oregon Historical Quarterly* 46 (1945): 185–218.

16. Jefferson's January 23, 1793, instructions to Michaux are quoted in Abraham P. Nasatir, *Before Lewis and Clark: Documents Illustrating the History of the Missouri, 1785–1804* (St. Louis: St. Louis Historical Documents Foundation, 1952), 1:164–67, which includes a synopsis of the American Philosophical Society's proceedings in the matter of Michaux's expedition.

17. Thomas Jefferson, "The Northern Boundary of Louisiana, Coterminous with the Possessions of England," in *Documents Relating to the Purchase and Exploration of Louisiana*

(Boston: Houghton Mifflin, 1904), 42. Also see Bernard DeVoto, *The Course of Empire* (Boston: Houghton Mifflin, 1952), 421.

18. DeVoto, *Course of Empire*, 420.

19. William Goetzmann, "Savage Enough to Prefer the Woods: The Cosmopolite and the West," in *Thomas Jefferson: The Man, His World, His Influence*, ed. Lally Weymouth (New York: G.P. Putnam's Sons, 1973), 114–15.

20. Quoted in Warren L. Cook, *Flood Tide of Empire: Spain and the Pacific Northwest, 1543–1819* (New Haven, CT: Yale University Press, 1973), 473.

21. Dan L. Flores, *Jefferson and Southwestern Exploration: The Freeman and Custis Accounts of the Red River Expedition of 1806*, new ed.(Norman: University of Oklahoma Press, 2002), provides the first complete account. See also David J. Weber, *The Spanish Frontier in North America* (New Haven, CT: Yale University Press, 1992), 294, and Cook, *Flood Tide of Empire*, 460–90.

22. Quoted in Elliott Coues, ed., *The History of the Expedition under the Command of Lewis and Clark, to the Sources of the Missouri River, Thence Across the Rocky Mountains and Down the Columbia River to the Pacific Ocean, Performed During the Years 1805–6, by Order of the Government of the United States* (New York: F.P. Harper, 1893), 1:xx-xxii.

23. William Clark to Meriwether Lewis, July 18, 1803, in Donald Jackson, ed., *The Letters of the Lewis and Clark Expedition with Related Documents, 1783–1854* (Urbana: University of Illinois Press, 1978), 1:110–11.

24. Elliott Coues, "Memoir of William Clark" in *The History of the Expedition*, 1:lxii-lxiii.

25. Coues, *The History of the Expedition*, 1:xx n4.

26. Gallatin to Jefferson, March 14, 1803, quoted in Jackson, *Letters of the Lewis and Clark Expedition*, 1:27–28.

27. W. Raymond Wood, "The John Evans 1796–97 Map of the Missouri River," *Great Plains Quarterly* 1, no. 1 (Winter 1981): 39–53. The original Evans map is lost; a copy is in the Beinecke Rare Book and Manuscript Library at Yale University in New Haven, CT. Also see John Logan Allen, *Passage through the Garden: Lewis and Clark and the Image of the American Northwest* (Urbana: University of Illinois Press, 1975), 137–39.

28. Quoted in Reuben G. Thwaites, ed., *The Original Journals of the Lewis and Clark Expedition* (New York: Dodd, Mead, 1904–5), 7:292.

29. Wood, "John Evans' 1796–97 Map," 46, 49.

30. Thwaites, *Original Journals*, 1:185–86; also Annie Heloise Abel, ed., *Tabeau's Narrative of Loisel's Expedition to the Upper Missouri* (Norman: University of Oklahoma Press, 1939), 124–25.

Chapter 9: Northern Shadows Across the Trail: Nor'Westers Meet Lewis and Clark

1. Victor G. Hopwood, ed., *David Thompson: Travels in Western North America 1784–1812* (Toronto: Macmillan of Canada, 1971), 150.

2. *David Thompson's Narrative, 1784–1812*, was published in a different edition by the Champlain Society in 1962, with Richard Glover as editor. Portions of the original journals held by the Archives of Ontario have been published, most notably by T.C. Elliott (in several articles), by W. Raymond Wood and Thomas D. Thiessen, and by Barbara Belyea. For a comprehensive list of these editions, see Barbara Belyea, *Columbia Journals: David Thompson* (Montreal/Kingston: McGill-Queen's University Press, 1994), 324–25.

3. Belyea, *Columbia Journals*, 152–53.

4. Fort Montagne à la Bosse lay upstream (west) of Fort Brandon, which in turn was upstream of Fort Souris. Fort Souris stood near where the Souris River flows into the Assiniboine River.

5. W. Kaye Lamb, ed., *Sixteen Years in the Indian Country: The Journal of Daniel Williams Harmon 1800–1816* (Toronto: Macmillan of Canada, 1957), 84.

6. Ibid., 87.

7. Glover, *David Thompson's Narrative*, 166.

8. Ibid., 158.

9. Carl Wheat, *Mapping the Trans-Mississippi West, 1540–1861* (San Francisco: Institute of Historical Cartography, 1957), 1:171–78. Further details on Sheheke may be found in Barry M. Gough, ed., *The Journal of Alexander Henry the Younger, 1799–1814* (Toronto: Champlain Society, 1988–92), 1:221. By this time, Jean Baptiste Lafrance was living in this village, and he was the person who introduced Alexander Henry the Younger to Sheheke. For maps of the various villages and a portrait of Sheheke (painted by Charles Balthazar Julien Fevret de Saint Memin for the American Philosophical Society), see ibid., facing 192 and 222 respectively.

10. See W. Raymond Wood, "David Thompson at the Mandan-Hidatsa Villages, 1797–1798: The Original Journals," *Ethnohistory* 24, no. 4 (Fall 1977): 329–42. This publication contains a map redrawn from Thompson's 1798 map. A copy of the latter, now in the Library of Congress, was found among the papers of William Clark. Reproduced as Map 246 in Wheat, *Mapping the Trans-Mississippi West*, 1:180.

11. Journal entry for January 5, 1798, from David Thompson's Journals, F443, Archives of Ontario, Toronto, and printed in W. Raymond Wood and Thomas D. Thiessen, eds., *Early Fur Trade on the Northern Plains: Canadian Traders Among the Mandan and Hidatsa Indians, 1738–1818. The Narratives of John Macdonnell, David Thompson, François-Antoine Larocque, and Charles McKenzie* (Norman: University of Oklahoma Press, 1985), 115–16.

12. Wood and Thiessen, *Early Fur Trade on the Northern Plains*, 128.

13. Hopwood, *David Thompson*, 189.

14. Abraham P. Nasatir, *Before Lewis and Clark: Documents Illustrating the History of the Missouri, 1785–1804* (St. Louis: St. Louis Historical Documents Foundation, 1952), 1:110.

15. That Montrealer was Alexander Henry the Elder. On this, see Barry M. Gough, *First Across the Continent: Sir Alexander Mackenzie* (Norman: University of Oklahoma Press,

1997), 173.

16. George C. Davidson, *The North West Company* (Berkeley: University of California Press, 1918), 80.

17. Daniel B. Botkin, *Our Natural History: The Lessons of Lewis and Clark* (New York: Pedigree, 1996), 106–7.

18. Larocque's name is variously spelled, but I have employed the current spelling as used by Wood and Thiessen in *Early Fur Trade on the Northern Plains.*

19. Davidson, *North West Company*, 81.

20. Bernard DeVoto, ed., *The Journals of Lewis and Clark* (Boston: Houghton Mifflin, 1953), 68; also Gary E. Moulton, ed., *The Journals of the Lewis and Clark Expedition* (Lincoln: University of Nebraska Press, 1981–2001), 3:241, which gives Clark's original spelling.

21. Moulton, *Journals*, 3:242.

22. See Davidson, *North West Company*, 81n57.

23. Moulton, *Journals*, 3:242.

24. A Canadian, Charbonneau was born about 1758, worked for the North West Company and had been an independent trader among the Hidatsas for several years by the time of the Lewis and Clark Expedition. He was husband to Sacagawea, a Lemhi Shoshone; she was a guide to Lewis and Clark, destined, after the leaders themselves, to be the most famous member of the Corps of Discovery. See Moulton, *Journals*, 3:228–29n1 and n2.

25. DeVoto, *Journals*, 69.

26. Wood and Thiessen, *Early Fur Trade on the Northern Plains*, 137–38.

27. Later, in 1806, they approached Hugh Heney to help them with First Nations diplomacy in the foothills.

28. Moulton, *Journals*, 3:281n1.

29. Wood and Thiessen, *Early Fur Trade on the Northern Plains*, 230 –39.

30. Excerpted from ibid., 232.

31 Ibid.

32. Ibid., 233.

33. Ibid.

34. Ibid., 238.

35. Ibid.

36. Larocque's comments here and in following paragraphs are from Ida Amanda Johnson, *The Michigan Fur Trade* (1919; Grand Rapids, MI: Black Letter Press, 1971), 102–16.

37. Of all the attempts to explain and analyze this system, the best introduction remains Johnson, *Michigan Fur Trade*, 102–16. The various (twelve) acts to regulate the trade with aboriginals by the factory system are listed on pages 104 to 105. The system began in 1796 and was abolished in 1822.

38. Lamb, *Sixteen Years in the Indian Country*, 88.

39. *Journal of Larocque from the Assiniboine to the Yellowstone, 1805,* Publications of the Canadian Archives, No. 3 (Ottawa: Government Printing Bureau, 1910; French edition, 1911). Reprinted as *The Journal of François Laroque* (Fairfield, WA: Ye Galleon Press, 1981). Quote at p. 33.

40. For more on how this was arranged, see Larocque narrative, June 25, 1805, in Wood and Thiessen, *Early Fur Trade on the Northern Plains,* 170. A map of Larocque's route from the Assiniboine River to the Bighorn Mountains and return is found in ibid., facing page 160.

41. DeVoto, *Journals,* 84. See also Moulton, *Journals,* 3:308n1.

42. Paul C. Phillips, *The Fur Trade* (Norman: University of Oklahoma Press, 1961), 2:310.

43. David Freeman Hawke, *Those Tremendous Mountains: The Story of the Lewis and Clark Expedition* (1980; New York: W.W. Norton, 1998), 92.

Chapter 10: Lewis and Clark to the Pacific and Return

1. See "Fort Mandan Miscellany," in Gary E. Moulton, ed., *The Journals of the Lewis and Clark Expedition* (Lincoln: University of Nebraska Press, 1981–2001), 3:333–503, from which details in this chapter are drawn.

2. Clark's 1805 map is in Moulton, *Journals of Lewis and Clark,* 1: maps 32 a, b and c.

3. David L. Nicandri, "Lewis and Clark: Exploring under the Influence of Alexander Mackenzie," *Pacific Northwest Quarterly* 95, no. 4 (Fall 2004): 171–81.

4. R. Cole Harris, ed., *Historical Atlas of Canada,* vol. I, *From the Beginning to 1800* (Toronto: University of Toronto Press, 1987), plate 62.

5. Lewis's report, in Moulton, *Journals of Lewis and Clark,* 3:363.

6. Ibid., 405.

7. Ibid., 487.

8. Bernard DeVoto, *The Course of Empire* (Boston: Houghton Mifflin, 1952), 480.

9. To begin analysis of the American, British and aboriginal knowledge, including maps, that Lewis and Clark had for possible evaluation, consult, in the first instance, Barbara Belyea, "Mapping the Marias: The Interface of Native and Scientific Cartographies," *Great Plains Quarterly* 17 (Summer 1997): 163–82.

10. Moulton, *Journals of Lewis and Clark,* 4:359–62.

11. Ibid., 359.

12. Donald Jackson, *Thomas Jefferson and the Stony Mountains: Exploring the West from Monticello,* new ed. (Norman: University of Oklahoma Press, 1993), 197.

13. Gary E. Moulton, ed., *The Journals of Lewis and Clark,* vol. 10, *Patrick Gass* (Lincoln: University of Nebraska Press, 1996), 132.

14. Comparing journals of the Corps of Discovery against those of Meares and Vancouver presents a sobering reminder that Lewis and Clark knew precisely what to expect (hardly a moment of triumph). David L. Nicandri, "The Illusion of Cape Disappointment," *We Proceeded On* (journal of the Lewis and Clark Trail Heritage

Foundation) 30, no. 4 (November 2004): 15–21.

15. No conclusive evidence exists that confirms the Boston vessel *Vancouver*, under Captain Brown, was deployed on a specific mission to link up with the Corps of Discovery.

16. This story is told by John Jewitt, who was aboard the *Lydia*.

17. Clark to Lewis, July 24, 1803, quoted in Donald Jackson, ed., *The Letters of the Lewis and Clark Expedition with Related Documents, 1783–1854* (Urbana: University of Illinois Press, 1978), 1:112.

18. John Logan Allen, *Passage through the Garden: Lewis and Clark and the Image of the American Northwest* (Urbana: University of Illinois Press, 1975), 369–70.

19. Jefferson to Lacépède, July 14, 1808, quoted in Jackson, *Letters of the Lewis and Clark Expedition*, 2:443.

20. James P. Ronda, "'The Writingest Explorers': The Lewis and Clark Expedition in Historical Literature," *Pennsylvania Magazine of History and Biography* 112, no. 4 (October 1988): 611.

21. [David McKeehan] to Lewis, Pittsburg *Gazette*, April 7, 1807, 7. Quoted in Jackson, *Letters of the Lewis and Clark Expedition*, 2:401–2.

22. The points leading to this conclusion can best be followed in Jackson, *Letters of the Lewis and Clark Expedition*, 2:467–68, where Neelly's letter to Jefferson of October 18, 1809, and Jefferson's correspondence with Russell are found (2:466–67, 573–75).

23. Clark to Jonathan Clark, October 28, 1809, in ibid., 2:726–27.

24. Jefferson to Lewis, August 16, 1809, and Jefferson to Von Humboldt, December 6, 1813, in ibid., 2:458 and 596 respectively.

25. Clark to Jefferson, October 10, 1816, in ibid., 2:623–25.

26. A.W. Merry to Lord Mulgrave, January 3, 1806, no. 2, Foreign Office (FO) records 5/48, pp. 14–15, National Archives of the United Kingdom.

27. Thomas Jefferson, "A Statistical View of the Indian Nations," *American State Papers, 2, Indian Affairs* 1:705–43.

28. James P. Ronda, *Lewis and Clark among the Indians* (Lincoln: University of Nebraska Press, 1984), 255.

Chapter 11: The Columbian Enterprise: David Thompson, 1800–1810

1. Barbara Belyea, ed., *Columbia Journals: David Thompson* (Montreal/Kingston: McGill-Queen's University Press, 1994), 200.

2. A.S. Morton, "The North West Company's Columbian Enterprise and David Thompson," *Canadian Historical Review* 17 (1936): 266–88, quotation at 284; and by the same, *A History of the Canadian West to 1870*, 2nd ed. (Toronto: University of Toronto Press, 1973), 491. Belyea, *Columbia Journals*, xiv-xv, provides excellent analysis of this biographical theme.

3. Barbara Belyea, "The 'Columbian Enterprise' and A.S. Morton: A Historical Exemplum," *BC Studies* 86 (Summer 1990): 3–27; and for a review of the historiography, Barry Cotton, "In Search of David Thompson," *British Columbia Historical News* 37, no. 4 (Winter 2004): 23–27.

4. Journal entry for October 6, 1810, David Thompson's Journals, F443, Archives of Ontario, Toronto.

5. The Piegans, or Picaneaux, according to Alexander Henry the Younger, dwelt along the foot of the Rocky Mountains. His extensive description of them, dated 1809, is in Barry M. Gough, ed., *The Journal of Alexander Henry the Younger, 1799–1814* (Toronto: Champlain Society, 1992), 2:376–81. Henry grouped the Blackfoot Confederacy as Slave Indians, a term he adopted from the Crees.

6. Journal entries from October 17 to 23, 1800, Thompson's Journals.

7. Ibid., November 22, 1800.

8. This is a demonstration of the argument put forward by Ronald Robinson in "Non-European Foundations of European Imperialism: Sketch for a Theory of Collaboration" in *Imperialism: The Robinson and Gallagher Controversy*, ed. William Roger Louis (New York: Franklin Watts, 1976), 128–51.

9. Sylvia Van Kirk and Jennifer Brown, "Duncan McGillivray," in *Dictionary of Canadian Biography* (Toronto/Sainte-Foy QC: University of Toronto Press and Les Presses de l'Université Laval, 1983), 5:530–32. For full bibliographic details of the McGillivray-Thompson arrangements, see Arthur S. Morton, ed., *The Journal of Duncan M'Gillivray of the North West Company at Fort George on the Saskatchewan, 1794–95* (Toronto: Macmillan of Canada, 1929), Appendix, 8–13.

10. For a review of this controversy, see Harold A. Innis, *The Fur Trade in Canada: An Introduction to Canadian Economic History*, rev. ed. (New Haven, CT: Yale University Press, 1962), 259–60.

11. This account is based on Daniel A. Kyba, "David Thompson's 1801 Attempt to Cross the Rocky Mountains," *Alberta History* 46, no. 1 (Winter 1998): 1–25, and additional advice from the author. See also Jane Ross and Daniel Kyba, *The David Thompson Highway: A Hiking Guide* (Calgary: Rocky Mountain Books, 1995).

12. Frederick W. Howay, ed., "David Thompson's Account of his First Attempt to Cross the Rockies," *Queen's Quarterly* 40 (1933): 333–56, quotation at 348.

13. Kyba, "David Thompson's 1801 Attempt," 25.

14. Belyea, *Columbia Journals*, 34.

15. Thompson to Sir James Alexander, May 9, 1845, Foreign Office (FO) records 5/441, National Archives of the United Kingdom; also Belyea, *Columbia Journals*, 207.

16. W. Stewart Wallace, ed., *Documents Relating to the North West Company* (Toronto: Champlain Society, 1934), 203; Edwin E. Rich, *The Fur Trade and the Northwest to 1857* (Toronto: McClelland & Stewart, 1967), 197.

17. Each of these three posts — McLeod, St. James and Fraser — was of vital importance in this cordilleran trade, but Fort St. James was the principal depot for the whole country north of the forks of the Fraser up to the Russian (later US) boundary, including the Babine highlands, with waters draining to the Arctic via the Peace River and to the Pacific via the Skeena River.

18. Quoted in W. Kaye Lamb, ed., *The Letters and Journals of Simon Fraser, 1806–1808* (Toronto: Macmillan of Canada, 1960), 273–74. All unattributed quotations from Simon Fraser are from this book.

19. This was "to prove perhaps the most desperate expedition in the history of western exploration," according to Bruce Hutchinson, *The Fraser* (Toronto: Clarke Irwin, 1950), 39.

20. This was finally achieved in 1820 when packhorses and trails linked the upper Fraser with the lower Columbia, travelling overland from Fort McLeod, alongside Okanagan Lake, to the conjunction of the Columbia and Snake rivers.

21. Jules Quesnel to J.M. Lamothe, May 1809, in *Report of the Public Archives for the Year 1919* (Ottawa: King's Printer, 1940), 58.

22. Quoted in Morton, *A History of the Canadian West*, 480.

23. Quoted in ibid., 481.

24. Clara Graham, *Fur and Gold in the Kootenays* (Vancouver: Wrigley, 1945), 22–23.

25. Thompson's words through here are from Belyea, *Columbia Journals*.

26. Ibid., 66.

27. Ibid., 226.

28. Ibid., 218.

29. Ibid., 60, 223.

30. Cited in Dorothy O. Johansen, *Empire of the Columbia*, 2nd ed. (New York: Harper & Row, 1965), 86–90, which provides the outline for the analysis that follows here. Courtin left no trace of his travels and died in 1810, another source lost to history.

31. T.C. Elliott, "The Strange Case of David Thompson and Jeremy Pinch," *Oregon Historical Quarterly* 40, no. 2 (June 1939): 190. See Pike's hot letter to McGillis, February 6, 1806, and the cool reply from McGillis, February 15, 1806, in Donald Jackson, ed., *The Journals of Zebulon Montgomery Pike with Letters and Related Documents* (Norman: University of Oklahoma Press, 1966), 1:87–88, 90, 256–68.

32. Pierre Cruzatte, Joseph Field, and John B. Thompson of Lewis and Clark's party may have returned up the Missouri after reaching St. Louis. Perhaps, too, they joined McClallen, and were among those killed with him. Gough, *Journal of Alexander Henry the Younger*, 1:183n.

33. Elliott, "Strange Case," 195–98.

34. Johansen, *Empire of the Columbia*, 87.

35. Quoted in Elliott, "Strange Case," 199.

36. Thompson to J. Perch, December 26, 1807, and note of copyist, ibid., 191.

37. Joseph B. Tyrrell, "Letter of Roseman and Perch, July 10th 1807," *Oregon Historical Quarterly* 38, no. 4 (December 1937): 391–97.

38. Gough, *Journal of Alexander Henry the Younger*, 2:434n.

39. Duncan McGillivray, "Some Account of the Trade Carried on by the North West Company," Royal Commonwealth Society Collection, Cambridge University Library.

40. Belyea, *Columbia Journals*, 227. This Kootenay map is not known to have survived, which is a pity. Peter Fidler, HBC trader and surveyor, held the view that aboriginal maps conveyed much information where European documents failed; besides, they showed rivers and other remarkable places, even though indigenous draftsmen were "utterly unacquainted with any proportion in drawing them." Fidler's praise was echoed by William Clark, who transcribed indigenous maps, and by François-Antoine Larocque's evidence that Crow and Shoshone dressed-skin maps were very good and allowed them to show the places where at different seasons they could be found. See Moulton, "Introduction," in vol. 1, *The Journals of the Lewis and Clark Expedition*; and W. Raymond Wood and Thomas D. Thiessen, eds., *Early Fur Trade on the Northern Plains: Canadian Traders Among the Mandan and Hidatsa Indians, 1738–1818. The Narratives of John Macdonnell, David Thompson, François-Antoine Larocque, and Charles McKenzie* (Norman: University of Oklahoma Press, 1985), 182.

Chapter 12: Boston and New York on the Lower Columbia River: The Winships and Astor

1. Samuel Furgerson, "Journal of a Voyage from Boston to the North-West Coast of America, in the Brig *Otter*, Samuel Hill Commander, May 26, 1810," ms 207, Beinecke Library, Yale University, New Haven, CT; Robert H. Ruby and John A. Brown, *The Chinook Indians: Traders of the Lower Columbia River* (Norman: University of Oklahoma Press, 1988), 120.

2. E.W. Giesecke, "1810 Winship Settlement Near Clatskanie First on Columbia River," *The Clatskanie Chief*, June 15, 1995.

3. Phelps's account, "Solid Men of Boston," is in Briton C. Busch and Barry M. Gough, eds., *Fur Traders from New England: The Boston Men in the North Pacific, 1787–1800. The Narratives of William Dane Phelps, William Sturgis and James Gilchrist Swan* (Spokane: Arthur H. Clark, 1997), 52–53.

4. Information on the arrival at Oak Point and the events of June 1810 comes from William Gale's (Nathan Winship's assistant) journal entries, quoted in Hubert H. Bancroft, *History of the Northwest Coast* (New York: Bancroft, 1886), 2:133–34; Samuel E. Morison, *The Maritime History of Massachusetts* (Boston: Houghton Mifflin, 1961), 58–59. Ruby and Brown, *Chinook Indians*, 120–24, provides fuller details.

5. Barry M. Gough, ed., *The Journal of Alexander Henry the Younger, 1799–1814* (Toronto:

Champlain Society, 1992), 2:641 and 673. Henry was at Oak Point on at least two occasions, January 11 and February 3, 1814. Henry, who seldom worried about aboriginal resistance, says that the reason the Oak Point project came to an end was that this most delightful situation for a fort unfortunately overflowed in the summer season.

6. Most recently, John Denis Haeger, *John Jacob Astor: Business and Finance in the Early Republic* (Detroit: Wayne State University Press, 1991). In connection with the Astoria project, see James P. Ronda, *Astoria and Empire* (Lincoln: University of Nebraska Press, 1990).

7. Astor to Clinton, January 25, 1808, Clinton Papers, quoted in Paul C. Phillips, *The Fur Trade* (Norman: University of Oklahoma Press, 1961), 2:270.

8. Quoted in Ronda, *Astoria and Empire*, 68. The Russian negotiations with the United States are described and analyzed in this work, pp. 65–86.

9. Correspondence between the concerns is in the Astor Papers, Coe Collection of Western Americana, Yale University, and is printed in Dorothy Wildes Bridgwater, ed., "John Jacob Aster [sic] Relative to His Settlement on the Columbia River," *Yale University Library Gazette* 24, no. 2 (October 1949): 53–54. The quote from W. Kaye Lamb is in *Journal of a Voyage to the North West Coast of North America during the Years 1811, 1812, 1813 and 1814* [by Gabriel Franchère] (Toronto: Champlain Society, 1969), 6–11. For a structural analysis, see David Lavender, "Some American Characteristics of the American Fur Company, 1808–1834," *Minnesota History* 40, no. 4 (Winter 1966): 178–87.

10. Described in Ronda, *Astoria and Empire*, 133–64.

11. Reuben G. Thwaites, ed., *Adventures of the First Settlers on the Oregon or Columbia River, 1810–1813* [by Alexander Ross] (Cleveland: Arthur H. Clark, 1904), 88–89.

12. E.W. Giesecke, "Search for the *Tonquin*," *Cumtux* 10, no. 3 (Summer 1990): 3–8; 10, no. 4 (Fall 1990): 3–14; and 11, no. 1 (Winter 1990): 23–40. The Tonquin Foundation (www.tonquinfoundation.org), based in Tofino, BC, was established after an anchor, believed to have come from the *Tonquin*, was found in Templar Channel. The foundation has applied to do further research in the area to establish the anchor's provenance. On the identification of the interpreter, see Robert F. Jones, ed., *Annals of Astoria: The Headquarters Log of the Pacific Fur Company on the Columbia River, 1811–1813* (New York: Fordham University Press, 1999), xviii.

13. Quoted in Ronda, *Astoria and Empire*, xii.

Chapter 13: David Thompson and the Voyage of a Summer Moon, 1811

1. McTavish, McGillivrays and Company; John Ogilvy; Thomas Thain, Agents North West Company, to McTavish, Fraser and Co; Inglis, Ellice and Co; and Sir Alexander Mackenzie, January 23, 1810, MG 11, Q/113, 228–30, National Archives of Canada.

2. Victor G. Hopwood, ed., in *David Thompson: Travels in Western North America 1784–1812* (Toronto: Macmillan of Canada, 1971), 274–75, details the pressure William McGillivray, in London, placed on the Foreign Office on December 15, 1810.

3   Mackenzie's letter of March 10, 1808, and related correspondence is in Board of Trade (BT) files 1/59/14 and 39, National Archives of the United Kingdom (hereafter NA); also BT 5/18, p. 208. For subsequent appeals, see George C. Davidson, *The North West Company* (Berkeley: University of California Press, 1918), 124–32.

4.   Petition of North West Company, for a Charter, June 22, 1811, BT 1/61/12, NA. There is a further petition of similar nature, dated November 9, 1812, in BT 1/70/16.

5.   Law Officers of the Crown report, March 12, 1812, and Board of Trade report by Butler to McTavish, Fraser and Co., May 13, 1812, BT 1/70/16.

6.   David Thompson journal entry for April 15, 1810, also commentary by Thompson regarding advice given him circa July 22, 1810, by partners at Fort William, in David Thompson journals, vol. 35, F443, Archives of Ontario. Quoted in James K. Smith, *David Thompson: Fur Trader, Explorer, Geographer* (Toronto: Oxford University Press, 1971), 84–85, which also contains a useful discussion of North West Company motives.

7.   Quoted in Barbara Belyea, ed., *Columbia Journals: David Thompson* (Montreal/Kingston: McGill-Queen's University Press, 1994), 142.

8.   Joyce and Peter McCart, *On the Road with David Thompson* (Calgary: Fifth House Publishers, 2000), 232.

9.   Belyea, *Columbia Journals*, 274; also James P. Ronda, *Astoria and Empire* (Lincoln: University of Nebraska Press, 1990), 232–35.

10. David L. Nicandri, "Twisted Hair, Tetoharsky, and the Origin of the Sacagawea Myth," *Columbia* 19, no. 2 (Summer 2005): 6.

11. Richard Glover, ed., *David Thompson's Narrative, 1784–1812* (Toronto: Champlain Society, 1962), 358. In 1843, Joseph Howse referred to a manuscript, or publication, "David Thompson's Lieut. Broughton," but despite an extensive search I have not yet been able to trace it. See Joseph Howse's "Journey West of the Rocky Mountains," copy, Selkirk College Library, Castlegar, BC.

12. W.Kaye Lamb, ed., *Journal of a Voyage to the North West Coast of North America during the Years 1811, 1812, 1813 and 1814* [by Gabriel Franchère] (Toronto: Champlain Society, 1969), 86.

13. Ibid., 87–88.

14. Thompson to D. McDougall, David Stuart and Robert Stuart, July 15, 1811, and the reply, July 16, 1811, ibid., 11–12. Robert F. Jones, ed., *Annals of Astoria: The Headquarters Log of the Pacific Fur Company on the Columbia River, 1811–1813* (New York: Fordham University Press, 1999), 33–35, 158n25.

15. Washington Irving, *Astoria; or, Anecdotes of an Enterprise Beyond the Rocky Mountains* (1839; London: KPI Press, 1985), 75. Alexander Ross's comments are from Reuben G. Thwaites, ed., *Adventures of the First Settlers on the Oregon or Columbia River, 1810–1813* [by Alexander Ross] (Cleveland: Arthur H. Clark, 1904), 101–2.

16. Thwaites, *Adventures of the First Settlers*, 101–2.

17. Glover, *David Thompson's Narrative*, 358.

18. Ibid., 359.

19. Lamb, *Journal of a Voyage*, 88.

20. The interested reader can do no better than to begin with Barbara Belyea, "The 'Columbian Enterprise' and A.S. Morton: A Historical Exemplum," *BC Studies* 86 (Summer 1990): 3–27, and to search out the various interpretations of Morton, Joseph Tyrrell and Richard Glover. Too much was placed on Thompson's head by the North West Company, which failed to give him adequate resources. Furthermore, the British government, lukewarm to the North West Company's aspirations (until war drove them to action in 1812), always preferred trade to dominion. At least twice the Hawaiian Kingdom offered the British sovereignty; each time it was declined with regretful and polite thanks. An authoritative edition of Thompson's journals are being prepared for publication by the Champlain Society of Toronto. The most recent general biography is D'Arcy Jenish, *Epic Wanderer: David Thompson and the Mapping of the Canadian West* (Toronto: Doubleday Canada, 2003).

Chapter 14: The Fortunes of War

1. Admiralty orders are in Admiralty records (hereafter Adm.) 2/1380, National Archives of the United Kingdom (hereafter NA), quoted in George C. Davidson, *The North West Company* (Berkeley: University of California Press, 1918), 137.

2. William Jones to William Crane, April 16, 1813, RG 45, Entry 7, Confidential Letters Sent, and Crane to Jones, May 12 and June 22, 1813, RG 45, Master Commandant's Letters Received, 1813–1814, both in the Naval Records Collection of the Office of Naval Records and Library, US National Archives, Washington.

3. Quoted in John Denis Haeger, *John Jacob Astor: Business and Finance in the Early Republic* (Detroit: Wayne State University Press, 1991), 160.

4. Ibid., 161–62.

5. Robert F. Jones, ed., *Annals of Astoria: The Headquarters Log of the Pacific Fur Company on the Columbia River, 1811–1813* (New York: Fordham University Press, 1999), 171–72.

6. Broughton's journal seems not to have survived, but Vancouver used it in writing his *Voyage of Discovery*.

7. John A. Hussey, ed., *The Voyage of the "Racoon": A Secret Journal of a Visit to Oregon, California and Hawaii, 1813–1814* (San Francisco: Book Club of California, 1958), 5. All further quotations from Black are from this book.

8. Ross Cox, *Adventures on the Columbia River* (London: H. Colburn and R. Bentley, 1831), 1:266.

9. Described by Alexander Henry the Younger in his journal entry for December 13, 1813, from Barry M. Gough, ed., *The Journal of Alexander Henry the Younger, 1799–1814* (Toronto: Champlain Society, 1992), 2:622. Also see W. Kaye Lamb, ed., *Journal of a Voyage to the North West Coast of North America during the Years 1811, 1812, 1813 and 1814* [by Gabriel Franchère] (Toronto: Champlain Society, 1969), 133–34.

10. Henry journal, December 14, 1813, from Gough, *Journal of Alexander Henry the Younger*, 2:624.

11. Black's report, December 15, 1813, Adm.1/22, NA.

12. Alexander Ross was the first to make public the Nor'Westers' attempts at Tongue Point (in *Fur Traders of the Far West: A Narrative of Adventures in the Oregon and Rocky Mountains*, 2 vols. [London: Smith, Elder, 1855]), but laurels go to Ronald Corbyn, an archaeologist of the US National Park Service, who examined the site and whose research indicated possible adverse impacts from existing or future federal projects, management actions or neglect (information from the Naval Historical Center, Washington, to author, November 8, 1988). See also Ronald C. Corbyn, "The North West Company Fort at Tongue Point, Oregon," *Northwest Anthropological Research Notes* 23, no. 2 (Autumn 1989): 195–216.

13. Peter Corney, *Early Voyages in the North Pacific 1813–1818* (1896; Fairfield, WA: Ye Galleon Press, 1965), 93–188. See also Barry M. Gough, "The North West Company's 'Adventure to China'," *Oregon Historical Quarterly* 76, no. 4 (December 1975): 309–31, where further references to sources are given. Fuller particulars on the California connection are given in Marion O'Neil, "The Maritime Activities of the North West Company, 1813–1821," *Washington Historical Quarterly* 21, no. 4 (October 1930): 243–67.

14. Corney, *Early Voyages*, 118.

Chapter 15: The Empire of Fortune: Cultivating the Arts of Peace

1. Alfred L. Burt, *The United States, Great Britain and British North America from the Revolution to the Establishment of Peace after the War of 1812* (New Haven, CT: Yale University Press, 1940), 371. However, the Treaty of Ghent was significant in regard to the future of First Nations. It ended the British-backed scheme for a pan-Indian homeland. The tribes south of the international boundary were now abandoned by the British.

2. "Statement relative to the Columbia River [1815]," enclosed in a letter from Simon McGillivray to Sir Charles Bagot, November 15, 1817, fur traders' demands, May 7, 1814, and related correspondence, Foreign Office (hereafter FO) records 5/123, National Archives of the United Kingdom (hereafter NA). For an analysis of the fluctuating positions of British plenipotentiaries, consult Neville Thompson, *Earl Bathurst and the British Empire, 1762–1834* (Barnsley: Leo Cooper, 1999), 82–83.

3. J. Monroe to Plenipotentiaries, March 22, 1814, *American State Papers*, 1, *Foreign Relations*, 3:731.

4. North West Company to Henry Goulburn, Undersecretary of State for War and the Colonies, July 28, 1815, and August 2, 1815, Colonial Office (CO) records 42/164, NA. Also Katherine B. Judson, "The British Side of the Restoration of Fort Astoria," *Oregon Historical Quarterly* 20 (1919): 243–60, 305–6.

5. Monroe to Baker, July 18, 1815, encl. in Baker to Viscount Castlereagh, July 19, 1815, FO 5/107, NA.

6. Baker to Monroe, July 23, 1815, encl. in Baker to Castlereagh, August 13, 1815, FO 5/107, NA.

7. Baker to Dixon, July 24, 1815, encl. in ibid. The full diplomatic interplay may be traced in Burt, *United States, Great Britain and British North America*, 411–22.

8. See Frederick Merk, "The Genesis of the Oregon Question," *Mississippi Valley Historical Review* 36 (March 1950): 593–94.

9. The two powers were then reaching an agreement on the demilitarization of the Great Lakes. Both countries knew that there was an urgent need for economies, and the Americans knew that the arrangement rested on fragile grounds. This was not a time for adventures in planting the flag.

10. Benjamin Homans to Biddle, September 30, 1817, Private Letters of the Secretary of the Navy, RG 45, 241–2, Naval Records Collection of the Office of Naval Records and Library, US National Archives (hereafter USNA); quoted in K. Jack Bauer, ed., *The New American State Papers, Naval Affairs*, vol. 2, *Diplomatic Affairs* (Wilmington, DE: Scholarly Resources, 1981), 93.

11. McGillivray to Bagot, November 15, 1817, encl. in Bagot to Castlereagh, December 2, 1817, FO 5/123, NA.

12. Bagot to Castlereagh, November 24, 1817, cypher, FO 5/123, NA.

13. Ibid.

14. Quoted in Robert Greenhow, *Memoir, Historical and Political, on the Northwest Coast of North America, and the Adjacent Territories; Illustrated by a Map and a Geographical View of those Countries* (Washington: Blair and Rives, 1840), 164.

15. Bagot to Sir John Sherbrooke (Governor-in-Chief of Canada), December 1, 1817, FO 5/123, NA.

16. Bagot to Castlereagh, December 2, 1817, FO 5/123, NA.

17. Yeo to J.W. Croker, August 30, 1817, encl. in J. Barrow to Hamilton (Foreign Office), September 3, 1817, FO 5/128, NA.

18. Castlereagh to Croker, January 26, 1818, copy, FO 5/1470, NA, pp. 116–17. See also Charles K. Webster, *The Foreign Policy of Castlereagh, 1812–1815* (London: G. Bell & Sons, 1931), 196; Gerald S. Graham, *Empire of the North Atlantic: The Maritime Struggle for North America*, 2nd ed. (Toronto: University of Toronto Press, 1958), 262–64.

19. Admiralty draft orders, January 26, 1818, copy, FO 5/1470, NA, pp. 116v–17.

20. James Biddle, Journal, RG 45, roll M 902, Naval Records Collection, USNA; see also David F. Long, *Sailor-Diplomat: A Biography of Commodore James Biddle, 1783–1848* (Boston: Northeastern University Press, 1983), 77.

21. Quoted in Long, *Sailor-Diplomat*, 77, 78.

22. Biddle to the Secretary of the Navy, August 19, 1818, RG 45, AF 9/287, Naval Records Collection, USNA; quoted in Bauer, ed., *New American State Papers*, 2:95.

23. J. Keith to Capt. F. Hickey, October 7, 1818, encl. in Barrow to Hamilton, August 10, 1819, FO 5/147, NA. Another copy is in FO 5/1470, pp. 121–26.

24. Keith to Hickey, October 4, 1818, encl. in Barrow to Hamilton, August 10, 1819, FO 5/147, NA. Another copy is in FO 5/1470, pp. 121–26. Also see F.V. Longstaff and

W. Kaye Lamb, "The Royal Navy on the Northwest Coast, 1813–1850, Part I," *British Columbia Historical Quarterly* 9 (January 1945): 6; Bowles to Croker, April 29, 1818, Adm. 1/23, NA.

25. Restitution, signed by Hickey and Keith, October 6, 1818, and receipt by Prevost, October 6, 1818, FO 5/1470, NA, pp. 128–29.

26. Keith to Prevost, October 8, 1818, copy, FO 5/1470, NA, pp. 126–27.

27. Prevost to Keith, October 8, 1818, copy, FO 5/1470, NA, pp. 127–28.

28. Burt, *United States, Great Britain and British North America*, 422.

29. "Statement relative to the Columbia River [1815]," FO 5/123, NA.

30. Hubert H. Bancroft, *History of the Northwest Coast* (New York: Bancroft, 1886), 2:293.

Chapter 16: The Legacy: The North American Far West on the Eve of the Oregon Crisis

1. Frederick W. Howay quoted in F.W. Howay, W.N. Sage and H.F. Angus, *British Columbia and the United States: The North Pacific Slope from Fur Trade to Aviation* (New Haven, CT: Yale University Press, 1942), 42.

2. Kenneth W. Porter, *John Jacob Astor, Business Man* (Cambridge, MA: Harvard University Press, 1931), 2:694. *Statutes at Large of the United States of America, 1789–1873*, vol. 3, chap. 165, April 29, 1816; cited in Howay, Sage and Angus, *British Columbia and the United States*, 42.

3. This was *after* Louisiana passed from Spanish and French hands. See Thomas Falconer, *The Oregon Question*, 2nd ed. (London: Samuel Clarke, 1945), 33n. Also Samuel Flagg Bemis, *John Quincy Adams and the Foundations of American Foreign Policy* (New York: Alfred A. Knopf, 1956), 281.

4. The first was the Treaty of Ghent. Quoted in H.C. Allen, *Great Britain and the United States: A History of Anglo-American Relations (1783–1952)* (New York: St. Martin's Press, 1955) 356.

5. Robert Erwin Johnson, *Thence Round Cape Horn: The Story of United States Naval Forces on Pacific Station, 1818–1923* (Annapolis, MD: Naval Institute Press, 1963).

6. See map in Allen, *Great Britain and the United States*, 259.

7. The text of the Anglo-American Convention of 1818 is to be found in Hunter Miller, ed., *Treaties and Other International Acts of the United States* (Washington, DC: Government Printing Office, 1931–48), 2:658 ff.

8. Simpson to Samuel Black, July 25, 1824, quoted in Edwin E. Rich and A.M. Johnson, eds., *A Journal of a Voyage From Rocky Mountain Portage in Peace River to the Source of Finlays Branch and North West Ward in Summer 1824* [by Samuel Black] (London: Hudson's Bay Record Society, 1955), xlviii.

9. Governor and Committee to Simpson, February 27, 1822, quoted in R. Harvey Fleming, ed., *Minutes of Council of Northern Department of Rupert Land 1821–31* (London: Hudson's Bay Record Society, 1940), 303.

10. For the interplay of territorial and maritime factors in the making of British imperial policy for northwestern North America at this time, see Barry M. Gough, ed., *To the Pacific and Arctic with Beechey: The Journal of Lieutenant George Peard of H.M.S. "Blossom,"* *1825–1828*, Hakluyt Society, 2nd Series, no. 143 (Cambridge: Cambridge University Press, 1973), 6–18.

11. The strategy of the HBC was largely directed by two giants, Sir George Simpson and Dr. John McLoughlin, who had competing and sometimes overlapping agendas. The rise of the corporation in the Pacific Coast trade is a classic case of informal empire leading to formal empire, laying the groundwork for the present province of British Columbia. See Richard Somerset Mackie, *Trading Beyond the Mountains: The British Fur Trade on the Pacific, 1793–1843* (Vancouver: UBC Press, 1997); and John S. Galbraith, *The Hudson's Bay Company as an Imperial Factor, 1821–1869* (Berkeley/Los Angeles: University of California Press, 1957).

12. Beginning with José Mariano Moziño, *Noticias de Nutka: An Account of Nootka Sound in 1792*, trans. and ed. Iris H. Wilson Engstrand, with an introduction by Richard Inglis (Seattle: University of Washington Press, 1991).

13. Bemis, *John Quincy Adams*, 317–40.

Appendix 1: "The Theatre of All the Geographical Fictions": The Northwest and Other Passages

1. An enlarged edition was published by Bantam in 2003.

2. Gary Geddes, review of *The Island and Seven Cities: Where the Chinese Settled When They Discovered North America*, by Paul Chaisson, *Globe and Mail*, May 27, 2006.

3. L.A. Milet-Mureau, ed., *A Voyage Round the World Performed in the Years 1785–1788, by J.F.G. LaPerouse*, English ed. (London: Hamilton, 1799), 1:357.

Appendix 2: Three Flags and the Columbia River: Identification and Exploration of the River of the West

1. Herbert K. Beals, ed., *For Honor and Country: The Diary of Bruno de Hezeta* (Portland: Oregon Historical Society Press, 1985), 86.

2. For further particulars and discussion, as well as references, consult Barry M. Gough, *The Northwest Coast: British Navigation, Trade and Discoveries to 1812* (Vancouver: UBC Press, 1992), 30–55, esp. 40–43, on Cook's navigation on the coasts of Oregon and Washington states and Vancouver Island.

3. John Meares, *Voyages Made in the Years 1788 and 1789, from China to the North West Coast of America* (London: Walter, 1790), 167–68.

4. T.C. Elliott, ed., "John Meares' Approach to Oregon," *Oregon Historical Quarterly* 29 (September 1928): 279. Elliott excerpts Meares's *Voyages* for July 3 to August 10, 1788. For further analysis see, J. Richard Nokes, *Almost a Hero: The Voyages of John Meares, R.N., to China, Hawaii and the Northwest Coast* (Pullman: Washington State University Press, 1998), 61–63 and 77.

5. Howard T. Fry, "The Fur-Trade and the Search for the North-West Passage," chapter 7 in *Alexander Dalrymple and the Expansion of British Trade* (Toronto: University of Toronto Press, 1970).

6. Information from E.W. Giesecke. For an introduction to the literature on Broughton and the river, see Gough, *Northwest Coast*, 226n33, where the key references are given. Broughton's proceedings form part of Vancouver's narrative; see W. Kaye Lamb, ed., *The Voyage of George Vancouver, 1791–1795,* (London: Hakluyt Society, 1984), 2:747–70.

7. Lamb, ed., *Voyage of George Vancouver,* 2:768.

BIBLIOGRAPHY

Documentary Sources: Manuscript

Canada

Baby Collection. MG24-L3, vol. 40: Tate. National Archives of Canada, Ottawa.

Howse, Joseph. "Journey West of the Rocky Mountains." Selkirk College Library, Castlegar, BC.

Masson Collection. MG19-C1, vol. 3: Laroque. National Archives of Canada, Ottawa.

Q series, 24-2: Peter Pond; 113: North West Company deputation; 293: Mackenzie. National Archives of Canada, Ottawa.

Thompson, David, Journals (F443). Archives of Ontario, Toronto.

Great Britain

Admiralty (Adm) Records. Adm 1/22: Black; Adm 2/1380: orders. National Archives of the United Kingdom, Kew.

Board of Trade (BT) Records. BT 1/16/12 North West Company petition; BT 1/17/16: Law Officers; BT 1/59/14 and 39: Mackenzie; BT 5/6: Meares; BT 5/18: Mackenzie. National Archives of the United Kingdom, Kew.

Colonial Office (CO) Records. CO 42 series, especially 101, 120, 164: all Mackenzie and North West Company. National Archives of the United Kingdom, Kew.

Foreign Office (FO) Records. FO 5 series (America), FO 5/48: Lewis and Clark; FO 5/107: Baker-Monroe; FO 5/123: Columbia River; FO 5/415, 418 and 441: Thompson; FO 5/1470: Martínez journal (Nootka). National Archives of the United Kingdom, Kew.

McGillivray, Duncan. "Some Account of the Trade Carried on by the North West Company." Royal Commonwealth Society Collection. Cambridge University Library, Cambridge.

United States

Draper Manuscripts, George Rogers Clark Papers, 52 J 93–95; also AJ–140. Wisconsin Historical Society, Madison (www.americanjourneys.org).

Furgerson, Samuel. "Journal of a Voyage from Boston to the North-West Coast of America, in the Brig *Otter*, Samuel Hill Commander, May 26, 1810." Ms 207. Beinecke Library, Yale University, New Haven, CT.

Joseph Banks Collection. Sutro Library, San Francisco.

Naval Records Collection of the Office of Naval Records and Library. RG 45, Entry 7: Confidential Letters: Crane; RG 45: Master Commandant's Letters Received. RG 45, roll M 902: Biddle. US National Archives (USNA), College Park, MD.

Tongue Point report, 1988. Naval Historical Center. Washington Navy Yard, DC.

Documentary Sources: Printed

Abel, Annie Heloise, ed. *Tabeau's Narrative of Loisel's Expedition to the Upper Missouri*. Norman: University of Oklahoma Press, 1939.

Abel-Henderson, Annie Heloise. "Mackay's Table of Distances." *Mississippi Valley Historical Review* 10 (1923): 429–31.

American State Papers, Foreign Relations. 6 vols. Washington, DC: Government Printing Office, 1832–59.

Bauer, K. Jack, ed. New *American State Papers, Naval Affairs*. Vol. 2, *Diplomatic Affairs*. Wilmington, DE: Scholarly Resources, 1981.

Beaglehole, John C., ed. *The Journals of Captain Cook*. Vol. 1, *The Voyage of the Endeavour, 1768–1771*. 1955. Reprint, Cambridge, UK: The Hakluyt Society, 1968.

———. *The Journals of Captain Cook*. Vol. 3, *The Voyage of the Resolution and Discovery, 1776–1780*. Cambridge, UK: The Hakluyt Society, 1967.

Beals, Herbert K., trans. *For Honor and Country: The Diary of Bruno de Hezeta*. Portland: Oregon Historical Society Press, 1985.

———, ed. *Juan Pérez on the Northwest Coast: Six Documents of His Expedition in 1774*. Portland: Oregon Historical Society Press, 1989.

Belyea, Barbara, ed. *Columbia Journals: David Thompson*. Montreal/Kingston: McGill-Queen's University Press, 1994.

[Beresford, William] George Dixon. *A Voyage Round the World: But More Particularly to the North-West Coast of America*. London: George Goulding, 1789.

Billeck, William T. "Alexander Henry's 1806 Route Between the Assiniboine and Missouri Rivers." *Journal of the North Dakota Archaeological Association* 4 (1990): 230–44.

Boyd, Julian, ed. *Papers of Thomas Jefferson*. 18 vols. Princeton: Princeton University Press, 1950–.

Bridgwater, Dorothy Wildes, ed. "John Jacob Aster [sic] Relative to His Settlement on the Columbia River." *Yale University Library Gazette* 24, no. 2 (October 1949): 47–69.

Burney, James. *Chronological History of North-Eastern Voyages of Discovery; and of the Early Eastern Navigations of the Russians*. 1819. Amsterdam: N. Israel, 1969.

Burpee, Lawrence J., ed. *Journals and Letters of Pierre Gaultier de Varennes de La Verendrye and His Sons*. Toronto: Champlain Society, 1927.

Busch, Briton C., and Barry M. Gough, eds. *Fur Traders from New England: The Boston Men in the North Pacific, 1787–1800. The Narratives of William Dane Phelps, William Sturgis and James Gilchrist Swan*. Spokane: Arthur H. Clark, 1997.

Corney, Peter. *Early Voyages in the North Pacific, 1813–1818*. 1896. Fairfield, WA: Ye Galleon Press, 1965.

Coues, Elliott, ed. *The History of the Expedition under the Command of Lewis and Clark, to the Sources of the Missouri River, Thence Across the Rocky Mountains and Down the Columbia River to the Pacific Ocean, Performed During the Years 1805–6, by Order of the Government of the*

United States. 4 vols. New York: F.P. Harper, 1893.

Cox, Ross. *Adventures on the Columbia River.* 2 vols. London: H. Colburn and R. Bentley, 1831.

David, Andrew, Felipe Fernandez-Armesto, Carlos Novi, Glyndwr Williams, eds. *The Malaspina Expedition, 1789–1794: The Journal of the Voyage by Alejandro Malaspina.* 3 vols. London: Hakluyt Society, 2001, 2003, 2005.

Delano, Amasa. *A Narrative of Voyages and Travels.* Boston, 1817. Reprint, New York: Praeger, 1970.

DeVoto, Bernard, ed. *The Journals of Lewis and Clark.* Boston: Houghton Mifflin, 1953.

Dmytryshyn, Basil, E.A.P. Crownhart-Vaughan, and Thomas Vaughan, eds. *To Siberia and Russian America: Three Centuries of Russian Eastward Expansion, A Documentary Record.* Vol. 2, *Russian Penetration of the North Pacific Ocean, 1700–1789.* Portland: Oregon Historical Society Press, 1988.

———. *To Siberia and Russian America: Three Centuries of Russian Eastward Expansion.* Vol. 3, *The Russian American Colonies, 1798–1867.* Portland: Oregon Historical Society Press, 1989.

Douglas, David. *Journal of David Douglas during his Travels in North America, 1823–1827.* 1914. New York: Antiquarian Press, 1959.

D'Wolf, John. *A Voyage to the North Pacific.* 1861. Fairfield, WA: Ye Galleon Press, 1968.

Elliott, T.C., ed. "John Meares' Approach to Oregon." *Oregon Historical Quarterly* 29 (September 1928): 278–87.

Fleming, R. Harvey, ed. *Minutes of Council of Northern Department of Rupert Land 1821–31.* London: Hudson's Bay Record Society, 1940.

Flores, Dan L. *Jefferson and Southwestern Exploration: The Freeman and Custis Accounts of the Red River Expedition of 1806.* New edition. Norman: University of Oklahoma Press, 2002.

Glover, Richard, ed. *David Thompson's Narrative, 1784–1812.* Toronto: Champlain Society, 1962.

Gough, Barry M., ed. *The Journal of Alexander Henry the Younger, 1799–1814.* Vol. 1, *Red River and the Journey to the Missouri.* Toronto: Champlain Society, 1988.

———, ed. *The Journal of Alexander Henry the Younger, 1799–1814.* Vol. 2, *The Saskatchewan and Columbia Rivers.* Toronto: Champlain Society, 1992.

———, ed. *To the Pacific and Arctic with Beechey: The Journal of Lieutenant George Peard of H.M.S. "Blossom," 1825–1828.* Hakluyt Society, 2nd Series, no. 143. Cambridge: Cambridge University Press, 1973.

Greenhow, Robert. *Memoir, Historical and Political, on the Northwest Coast of North America, and the Adjacent Territories; Illustrated by a Map and a Geographical View of those Countries.* Washington: Blair and Rives, 1840.

Hopwood, Victor G., ed. *David Thompson: Travels in Western North America 1784–1812.* Toronto: Macmillan of Canada, 1971.

Howay, Frederick W., ed. *Voyages of the "Columbia" on the Northwest Coast, 1787–1790 and*

1790–1793. Boston: Massachusetts Historical Society, 1941.

Hussey, John A., ed. *The Voyage of the "Racoon": A Secret Journal of a Visit to Oregon, California and Hawaii, 1813–1814*. San Francisco: Book Club of California, 1958.

Innis, Mary Quayle, ed. *Mrs. Simcoe's Diary*. Toronto: Macmillan of Canada, 1965.

Irving, Washington. *Astoria; or, Anecdotes of an Enterprise Beyond the Rocky Mountains*. 1839; London: KPI Press, 1985.

Jackson, Donald, ed. *The Journals of Zebulon Montgomery Pike with Letters and Related Documents*. 2 vols. Norman: University of Oklahoma Press, 1966.

———, ed. *The Letters of the Lewis and Clark Expedition with Related Documents, 1783–1854*. 2 vols. Urbana: University of Illinois Press, 1978.

Jefferson, Thomas. "Life of Captain Lewis" (1813). Preface to Meriwether Lewis, *History of the Expedition under the Command of Captains Lewis and Clark to the Sources of The Missouri, Thence Across the Rocky Mountains and down the River Columbia, Performed during 1804, 5, 6*. Vol. 1. Edited by Paul Allen. Philadelphia: Bradford and Inskeep, 1814.

———. "The Northern Boundary of Louisiana, Coterminous with the Possessions of England." In *Documents Relating to the Purchase and Exploration of Louisiana*. Boston: Houghton Mifflin, 1904.

———. "A Statistical View of the Indian Nations." *American State Papers*. Class 2, *Indian Affairs*. Washington, DC, 1806, 1:705–43.

Jones, Robert F., ed. *Annals of Astoria: The Headquarters Log of the Pacific Fur Company on the Columbia River, 1811–1813*. New York: Fordham University Press, 1999.

———, ed. *Astorian Adventure: The Journal of Alfred Seaton, 1811–1815*. New York: Fordham University Press, 1993.

Kaplanoff, Mark, ed. *Joseph Ingraham's Journal of the Brigantine "Hope" on a Voyage to the Northwest Coast of North America, 1790–92*. Barre, MA: Imprint Society, 1971.

Kelley, Hall J. *Discoveries, Purchases of Lands, &c. On the North West Coast, Being a Part of an Investigation of the American Title to the Oregon Territory*. Boston: n.p., 1838.

Lamb, W. Kaye, ed. *Journal of a Voyage to the North West Coast of North America during the Years 1811, 1812, 1813 and 1814* [by Gabriel Franchère]. Toronto: Champlain Society, 1969.

———, ed. *The Journals and Letters of Sir Alexander Mackenzie*. Cambridge: Cambridge University Press for the Hakluyt Society, 1970.

———, ed. *The Letters and Journals of Simon Fraser, 1806–1808*. Toronto: Macmillan of Canada, 1960.

———, ed. *Sixteen Years in the Indian Country: The Journal of Daniel Williams Harmon 1800–1816*. Toronto: Macmillan of Canada, 1957.

———, ed. *The Voyage of George Vancouver, 1791–1795*. 4 vols. London: Hakluyt Society, 1984.

Larocque, François-Antoine. *The Journal of François Laroque*. Fairfield, WA: Ye Galleon Press, 1981.

Ledyard, John. *Journal of Captain Cook's Last Voyage*. Hartford, CT: Nathaniel Patten, 1783.

Lewis, Meriwether. *The Lewis and Clark Expedition: The 1814 Edition, Unabridged*. 3 vols. Philadelphia/New York: J.P. Lippincott, 1961.

Lipscomb, Andrew, and Albert Bergh, eds. *Writings of Thomas Jefferson*. 20 vols. Philadelphia: Thomas Jefferson Memorial Association, 1904–5.

Lisiansky, Urey. *A Voyage Round the World in the Years 1803, 4, 5 and 6*. English translation. London: 1814.

Lunenfeld, Marvin. *1492: Discovery, Invasion, Encounter*. New York: D.C. Heath, 1991.

Mackenzie, Alexander. *Voyages from Montreal, on the River St. Laurence, through the Continent of North America, to the Frozen and Pacific Oceans; in the Years 1789 and 1793. With a Preliminary Account of the Rise, Progress, and Present State of the Fur Trade of that Country*. London: Cadell and Davies, 1801.

Malloy, Mary, ed. *"A Most Remarkable Enterprise": Lectures on the Northwest Coast Trade and Northwest Coast Indian Life by Captain William Sturgis*. Marstons Mills, MA: Parnassus Imprints, 2000.

Manning, William Ray. *The Nootka Sound Controversy*. 1905. New York: Argonaut Press, 1996.

Meares, John. *Voyages Made in the Years 1788 and 1789, from China to the North West Coast of America*. London: Walter, 1790.

Milet-Mureau, L.A., ed. *A Voyage Round the World Performed in the Years 1785–1788, by J.F.G. LaPerouse*. English edition. London: Hamilton, 1799.

Miller, Hunter, ed. *Treaties and Other International Acts of the United States*. 8 vols. Washington, DC: Government Printing Office, 1931–48.

Morton, Arthur S., ed. *The Journal of Duncan M'Gillivray of the North West Company at Fort George on the Saskatchewan, 1794–95*. Toronto: Macmillan of Canada, 1929.

Moulton, Gary E., ed. *The Journals of the Lewis and Clark Expedition*. 13 vols. Lincoln: University of Nebraska Press, 1981–2001.

Moziño, José Mariano. *Noticias de Nutka: An Account of Nootka Sound in 1792*. Translated and edited by Iris H. Wilson Engstrand, with an introduction by Richard Inglis. Seattle: University of Washington Press, 1991.

Munford, James Kenneth, ed. *John Ledyard's Journal of Captain Cook's Last Voyage*. Corvallis: Oregon State University Press, 1963.

Nasatir, Abraham P. *Before Lewis and Clark: Documents Illustrating the History of the Missouri, 1785–1804*. 2 vols. St. Louis: St. Louis Historical Documents Foundation, 1952.

Owens, Kenneth N., ed. *The Wreck of the Sv. Nikolai: Two Narratives of the First Russian Expedition to the Oregon Country, 1808–1810*. Translated by Alton S. Donnelly. Portland: Oregon Historical Society Press, 1985. Reprint, Lincoln: University of Nebraska Press, 2000.

Peterson, Merrill D., ed. *The Portable Thomas Jefferson*. Harmondsworth, Middlesex: Penguin, 1977.

Portlock, Nathaniel. *A Voyage Round the World, But More Particularly to the North-West Coast of*

America. London: John Stockdale, 1789.

Rich, Edwin E., and A.M. Johnson, eds. *A Journal of a Voyage From Rocky Mountain Portage in Peace River to the Source of Finlays Branch and North West Ward in Summer 1824* [by Samuel Black]. London: Hudson's Bay Record Society, 1955.

Robertson, James A., ed. *Louisiana under the Rule of Spain, France and the United States 1785–1807*. 2 vols. Cleveland: Arthur H. Clark, 1911.

Ross, Alexander. *Fur Traders of the Far West: A Narrative of Adventures in the Oregon and Rocky Mountains*. 2 vols. London: Smith, Elder, 1855.

Sauer, Martin. *Account of a Geographical and Astronomical Expedition*. London: 1802.

Smith, Derek G., ed. *The Adventures and Sufferings of John R. Jewitt, Captive Among the Nootka, 1803–1805*. Toronto: McClelland and Stewart, 1974.

Steller, Georg Wilhelm. *Journal of a Voyage with Bering, 1741–1742*. Edited by O.W. Frost. Stanford: Stanford University Press, 1988.

Stewart, Edgar I., and Jane R. Stewart, eds. *The Columbia River* [by Ross Cox]. Norman: University of Oklahoma Press, 1957.

Stewart, Hilary, ed. *The Adventures and Sufferings of John R. Jewitt Captive of Maquinna*. Vancouver: Douglas & McIntyre, 1987.

Thwaites, Reuben G., ed. *Adventures of the First Settlers on the Oregon or Columbia River, 1810–1813* [by Alexander Ross]. Cleveland: Arthur H. Clark, 1904.

———, ed. *Journal of André Michaux, 1793–1796*. Cleveland: Arthur H. Clark, 1904.

———, ed. *The Original Journals of the Lewis and Clark Expedition*. 8 vols. New York: Dodd, Mead, 1904–5.

Tyrrell, Joseph B., ed. *David Thompson's Narrative of his Explorations in Western America, 1784–1812*. Toronto: Champlain Society, 1916.

———. "Letter of Roseman and Perch, July 10th 1807." *Oregon Historical Quarterly* 38, no. 4 (December 1937): 391–97.

U.S. Congress. House. House of Representatives Document 43. 26th Cong., 1st sess. 1841 [memorial of Charles Bulfinch et al.].

———. Senate. Report of Committee, No. 335. 32nd Cong., 1st sess. 1852 [Kendrick and Gray claims].

Vancouver, George. *A Voyage of Discovery to the North Pacific Ocean and Round the World*. 3 vols. London: G.G. and J. Robinson, 1798.

von Löwenstern, Hermann Ludwig. *The First Russian Voyage Around the World: The Journal of Hermann Ludwig von Löwenstern (1803–1806)*. Translated by Victoria Joan Moessner. Fairbanks: University of Alaska Press, 2003.

Wallace, W. Stewart, ed. *Documents Relating to the Northwest Company*. Toronto: Champlain Society, 1934.

Washington, H.A., ed. *The Writings of Thomas Jefferson.* 9 vols. Washington, DC: Taylor and Maury, 1853–54.

Watrous, Stephen D., ed. *John Ledyard's Journey through Russia and Siberia, 1787–1788: The Journal and Selected Letters.* Madison: University of Wisconsin Press, 1966.

White, Catherine M., ed. *David Thompson's Journals Relating to Montana and Adjacent Regions, 1808–1812.* Missoula: Montana State University Press, 1950.

Wood, W. Raymond, and Thomas D. Thiessen, eds. *Early Fur Trade on the Northern Plains: Canadian Traders Among the Mandan and Hidatsa Indians, 1738–1818. The Narratives of John Macdonell, David Thompson, François-Antoine Larocque, and Charles McKenzie.* Norman: University of Oklahoma Press, 1985.

Monographs, Studies and Reference Works

Adelman, Jeremy, and Stephen Aron. "From Borderlands to Borders: Empires, Nation-States, and the Peoples in Between in North American History." *American Historical Review* 104, no. 3 (June 1999): 814–41.

Allen, H.C. *Great Britain and the United States: A History of Anglo-American Relations (1783–1952).* New York: St. Martin's Press, 1955.

Allen, John Logan. "Imagining the West: The View from Monticello." In *Thomas Jefferson and the Changing West: From Conquest to Conservation,* edited by James P. Ronda, 3–23. Albuquerque: University of New Mexico Press, 1997.

———. *Passage through the Garden: Lewis and Clark and the Image of the American Northwest.* Urbana: University of Illinois Press, 1975.

Ambler, Charles. *George Washington and the West.* Chapel Hill: University of North Carolina Press, 1936.

Ambrose, Stephen. *Undaunted Courage: Meriwether Lewis, Thomas Jefferson, and the Opening of the American West.* New York: Simon and Schuster, 1996.

Andrews, Clarence L. "Russian Plans for American Dominion." *Washington Historical Quarterly* 18 (April 1927): 83–92.

Archer, Christon I. "Spain and the Defence of the Pacific Ocean Empire, 1750–1810." *Canadian Journal of Latin American and Caribbean Studies* 11, no. 21 (1986): 15–41.

———. "The Spanish Reaction to Cook's Third Voyage." In *Captain Cook and His Times,* edited by Robin Fisher and Hugh Johnston, 99–120. Vancouver: Douglas and McIntyre, 1979.

Ballantyne, Robert. *The Pioneers: A Tale of the Western Wilderness Illustrative of the Adventures and Discoveries of Sir Alexander Mackenzie.* London: James Nisbet, 1872.

Bancroft, Hubert H. *History of the Northwest Coast.* 2 vols. New York: Bancroft, 1886.

Bannon, John Francis, ed. *Bolton and the Spanish Borderlands.* Norman: University of Oklahoma Press, 1964.

Bashkina, Nina N., et al., ed. *The United States and Russia: A Beginning of Relations, 1765–1815.* Washington, DC: U.S. Government Printing Office, 1980.

Beckey, Fred. *Range of Glaciers: The Exploration and Survey of the Northern Cascade Range.* Portland: Oregon Historical Society, 2003.

Belyea, Barbara. "The 'Columbian Enterprise' and A.S. Morton: A Historical Exemplum." *BC Studies* 86 (Summer 1990): 3–27.

———. "Mapping the Marias: The Interface of Native and Scientific Cartographies." *Great Plains Quarterly* 17 (Summer 1997): 163–82.

Bemis, Samuel Flagg. *John Quincy Adams and the Foundations of American Foreign Policy.* New York: Alfred A. Knopf, 1956.

Binnema, Theodore. *Common and Contested Ground: A Human and Environmental History of the Northwestern Plains.* Norman: University of Oklahoma Press, 2001.

Black, Lydia T. *Russians in Alaska 1732–1867.* Fairbanks: University of Alaska Press, 2004.

Bloom, Lansing B. "The Death of Jacques d'Eglise." *New Mexico Historical Review* 2 (1927): 369–79.

Botkin, Daniel B. *Our Natural History: The Lessons of Lewis and Clark.* New York: Pedigree, 1996.

Brebner, John Bartlett. *The Explorers of North America, 1492–1806.* London: A. & C. Black, 1933.

Burns, Ken, and Dayton Duncan. *Lewis and Clark: The Journey of the Corps of Discovery,* DVD. Directed by Ken Burns. Washington, DC: WETA and Florentine Films, 1997.

Burpee, Lawrence J. *The Search for the Western Sea.* 2 vols. Toronto: Macmillan of Canada, 1935.

Burt, Alfred L. *The United States, Great Britain and British North America from the Revolution to the Establishment of Peace after the War of 1812.* New Haven, CT: Yale University Press, 1940.

Campbell, Marjorie Wilkins. *North West Company.* Toronto: Macmillan of Canada, 1957.

Carter, Harold B. *Sir Joseph Banks, 1743–1820.* London: British Museum of Natural History, 1988.

Chevigny, Hector. *Lord of Alaska: The Story of Baranov and the Russian Adventure.* London: Robert Hale, 1946.

———. *Russian America: The Great Alaskan Adventure, 1741–1867.* New York: Ballantine, 1965.

Cook, Warren L. *Flood Tide of Empire: Spain and the Pacific Northwest, 1543–1819.* New Haven, CT: Yale University Press, 1973.

Corbyn, Ronald C. "The North West Company Fort at Tongue Point, Oregon." *Northwest Anthropological Research Notes* 23, no. 2 (Autumn 1989): 195–216.

Cotton, Barry. "In Search of David Thompson." *British Columbia Historical News* 37, no. 4 (Winter 2004): 23–27.

Coxe, William. *Account of the Russian Discoveries between Asia and America. To which are added, the conquest of Siberia, and the History of the transactions and Commerce between Russia and China.* London: T. Cadell, 1780.

Cutter, Donald C. *Malaspina and Galiano: Spanish Voyages to the Northwest Coast, 1791 and 1792.* Vancouver: Douglas & McIntyre, 1991.

Davidson, George C. *The North West Company.* Berkeley: University of California Press, 1918.

DeConde, Alexander. *This Affair of Louisiana.* New York: Charles Scribner's Sons, 1976.

Delgado, James P. *Across the Top of the World: The Quest for the Northwest Passage.* Vancouver: Douglas & McIntrye, 1999.

DeVoto, Bernard. *The Course of Empire.* Boston: Houghton Mifflin, 1952.

Divin, Vasilii A. *The Great Russian Circumnavigator, A.I. Chirikov.* Translated and annotated by Raymond H. Fisher. Fairbanks: University of Alaska Press, 1993.

Duncan, Dayton, and Ken Burns. *Lewis and Clark: The Journey of the Corps of Discovery. An Illustrated History.* New York: Alfred A. Knopf, 1997.

Dunmore, John. *French Explorers in the Pacific.* Vol. 1, *The Eighteenth Century.* Oxford: Clarendon Press, 1965.

———. *French Explorers in the Pacific.* Vol. 2, *The Nineteenth Century.* Oxford: Clarendon Press, 1969.

———, ed. *The Journal of Jean-François de Galaup de la Pérouse, 1785–1788.* 2 vols. London: Hakluyt Society, 1994, 1995.

Elliott, T.C. "The Strange Case of David Thompson and Jeremy Pinch." *Oregon Historical Quarterly* 40, no. 2 (June 1939): 188–99.

Falconer, Thomas. *The Oregon Question.* 2nd edition. London: Samuel Clarke, 1945.

Fernández-Armesto, Felipe, ed. *The Times Atlas of World Exploration.* London: Times Books, 1991.

Forsyth, John, ed. "Documents Connected with the Final Settlement of the Nootka Dispute." *British Columbia Historical Association Second Annual Report* (1924): 33–35.

Fry, Howard T. "The Fur-Trade and the Search for the North-West Passage." Chapter 7 in *Alexander Dalrymple and the Expansion of British Trade.* Toronto: University of Toronto Press, 1970.

Furtwangler, Albert. *Acts of Discovery: Visions of America in the Lewis and Clark Journals.* Urbana: University of Illinois Press, 1993.

Galbraith, John S. *The Hudson's Bay Company as an Imperial Factor, 1821–1869.* Berkeley/Los Angeles: University of California Press, 1957.

Gascoigne, John. *Science in the Service of Empire: Joseph Banks, the British State and Uses of Science in the Age of Revolution.* Cambridge: Cambridge University Press, 1998.

Gibson, James R. *Feeding the Russian Fur Trade: Provisionment of the Okhotsk Peninsula, 1639–1856.* Madison: University of Wisconsin Press, 1969.

———. *Imperial Russia in Frontier America: The Changing Geography of Supply of Russian America, 1784–1867.* New York: Oxford University Press, 1976.

———. *Sea Otter Skins, Boston Ships, and China Goods: The Maritime Fur Trade of the Northwest Coast, 1785–1841.* Montreal/Kingston: McGill-Queen's University Press, 1992.

Giesecke, E.W. "Discovery of Humboldt Bay, California, in 1806 from the Ship *O'Cain*, Jonathan Winship, Commander." *Terrae Incognitae* 29 (1997): 51–71, and 30 (1998): 94–100.

———. "Search for the *Tonquin*." *Cumtux* 10, no. 3 (Summer 1990): 3–8; 10, no. 4 (Fall 1990): 3–14; and 11, no. 1 (Winter 1990): 23–40.

Gifford, Bill. *Ledyard: In Search of the First American Explorer.* Orlando, FL: Harcourt, 2007.

Gilbert, Edmund W. *The Exploration of Western America, 1800–1850: An Historical Geography.* Cambridge: Cambridge University Press, 1933.

Godwin, George. *Vancouver: A Life.* New York: D. Appleton, 1931.

Goetzmann, William. "Savage Enough to Prefer the Woods: The Cosmopolite and the West." In *Thomas Jefferson: The Man, His World, His Influence,* edited by Lally Weymouth, 107–27. New York: G.P. Putnam's Sons, 1973.

——— and Glyndwr Williams. *Atlas of North American Exploration.* Norman: University of Oklahoma Press, 1998.

Golder, Frank A. *Russian Expansion on the Pacific, 1641–1850: An Account of the Earliest and Later Expeditions Made by the Russians along the Pacific Coast of Asia and North America; Including Some Related Expeditions to the Arctic Regions.* Cleveland: Arthur H. Clark, 1914.

Gough, Barry M. "British-Russian Rivalry and the Search for the Northwest Passage in the early 19th Century." *Polar Record* 23, no. 144 (1986): 301–17.

———. *First Across the Continent: Sir Alexander Mackenzie.* Norman: University of Oklahoma Press, 1997.

———. *Gunboat Frontier: British Maritime Authority and Northwest Coast Indians, 1846–1890.* Vancouver: UBC Press, 1984.

———. "Law and Empire: The Extension of Law to Vancouver Island and New Caledonia." *Western Legal History* 6, no. 2 (Summer/Fall, 1993): 217–28.

———. "The North West Company's 'Adventure to China,'" *Oregon Historical Quarterly* 76, no. 4 (December, 1975): 309–31.

———. *The Northwest Coast: British Navigation, Trade, and Discoveries to 1812.* Vancouver: UBC Press, 1992.

———. "Peter Pond and Athabasca: Fur Trade, Discovery and Empire." *Alberta* 1, no. 2 (1989): 1–18.

Graham, Clara. *Fur and Gold in the Kootenays.* Vancouver: Wrigley, 1945.

Graham, Gerald S. *Empire of the North Atlantic: The Maritime Struggle for North America.* 2nd edition. Toronto: University of Toronto Press, 1958.

Grinev, Andrei V. *The Tinglit Indians in Russian America, 1741–1867.* Lincoln: University of Nebraska Press, 2005.

Haeger, John Denis. *John Jacob Astor: Business and Finance in the Early Republic.* Detroit: Wayne State University Press, 1991.

Harlow, Vincent T. *The Founding of the Second British Empire.* 2 vols. London: Longman, 1952, 1964.

Harris, R. Cole, ed. *Historical Atlas of Canada*. Vol. 1, *From the Beginning to 1800*. Toronto: University of Toronto Press, 1987.

Hawke, David Freeman. *Those Tremendous Mountains: The Story of the Lewis and Clark Expedition*. 1980. New York: W.W. Norton, 1998.

Haycox, Stephen W. "Merchants and Diplomats: Russian America and the United States." In *Russian America: The Forgotten Frontier*, edited by Barbara Sweetland Smith and Redmond J. Barnett, 55–71. Tacoma: Washington State Historical Society, 1990.

———. "In Search of the Great Bear: A Historiography of Russian Exploration in Alaska and California." In *Encounters with a Distant Land: Exploration and the Great Northwest*, edited by Carlos A. Schwantes (Moscow: University of Idaho Press, 1994).

Hayes, Derek. *First Crossing: Alexander Mackenzie, His Expedition Across North America, and the Opening of the Continent*. Vancouver: Douglas & McIntyre, 2001.

Houck, Louis. *The Spanish Regime in Missouri*. 2 vols. Chicago: R.R. Donnelley, 1908.

Howay, Frederick W. "The Ballad of the Bold Northwestmen: An Incident in the Life of Captain John Kendrick." *Washington Historical Quarterly* 20 (1929): 114–23.

———, ed. "David Thompson's Account of his First Attempt to Cross the Rockies." *Queen's Quarterly* 40 (1933): 333–56.

———. "An Early Colonization Scheme in British Columbia." *British Columbia Historical Quarterly* 3, no. 1 (January 1939): 51–63.

———, W.N. Sage and H.F. Angus. *British Columbia and the United States: The North Pacific Slope from Fur Trade to Aviation*. New Haven, CT: Yale University Press, 1942.

Hutchinson, Bruce. *The Fraser*. Toronto: Clarke Irwin, 1950.

Inglis, Robin. "Lapérouse 1786: A French Naval Visit to Alaska." In *Enlightenment and Exploration in the North Pacific, 1741–1805*, edited by Stephen Haycox, James Barnett and Caedmon Liburd, 49–64. Seattle: University of Washington Press, 1997.

———. *Lost Voyage of Lapérouse*. Vancouver: Vancouver Museum and Planetarium Association, 1986.

Innis, Harold A. *The Fur Trade in Canada: An Introduction to Canadian Economic History*. Revised edition. New Haven, CT: Yale University Press, 1902.

Jackson, Donald. *Thomas Jefferson and the Stony Mountains: Exploring the West from Monticello*. New edition. Norman: University of Oklahoma Press, 1993.

Jenish, D'Arcy. *Epic Wanderer: David Thompson and the Mapping of the Canadian West*. Toronto: Doubleday Canada, 2003.

Johansen, Dorothy O. *Empire of the Columbia*. 2nd edition. New York: Harper & Row, 1965.

Johnson, Ida Amanda. *The Michigan Fur Trade*. 1919. Grand Rapids, MI: Black Letter Press, 1971.

Johnson, Robert Erwin. *Thence Round Cape Horn: The Story of United States Naval Forces on Pacific Station, 1818–1923*. Annapolis, MD: Naval Institute Press, 1963.

Judson, Katherine B. "The British Side of the Restoration of Fort Astoria." *Oregon Historical Quarterly* 20 (1919): 243–60 and 305–6.

Kendrick, John. *Alejandro Malaspina: Portrait of a Visionary*. Montreal/Kingston: McGill-Queen's University Press, 1999

Kessell, John L. *Spain in the Southwest: A Narrative History of Colonial New Mexico, Arizona, Texas, and California*. Norman: University of Oklahoma Press, 2002.

Kippis, Andrew. *A Narrative of the Voyages Round the World Performed by Captain James Cook; With an Account of His Life*. 2 vols. London: 1830.

Kirwan, L.P. *A History of Polar Exploration*. New York: W.W. Norton, 1960.

Kyba, Daniel A. "David Thompson's 1801 Attempt to Cross the Rocky Mountains." *Alberta History* 46, no. 1 (Winter 1998): 1–25.

Lavender, David. "Some American Characteristics of the American Fur Company, 1808–1834." *Minnesota History* 40, no. 4 (Winter 1966): 178–87.

Long, David F. *Sailor-Diplomat: A Biography of Commodore James Biddle, 1783–1848*. Boston: Northeastern University Press, 1983.

Longstaff, F.V., and W. Kaye Lamb. "The Royal Navy on the Northwest Coast, 1813–1850, Part I." *British Columbia Historical Quarterly* 9 (January 1945).

Mackie, Richard Somerset. *Trading Beyond the Mountains: The British Fur Trade on the Pacific, 1793–1843*. Vancouver: UBC Press, 1997.

Marshall, Peter J. *"A Free Though Conquering People": Eighteenth-Century Britain and its Empire*. Aldershot: Ashgate Variorum, 2003.

McCart, Joyce, and Peter. *On the Road with David Thompson*. Calgary: Fifth House Publishers, 2000.

McDowell, Jim. *José Narváez: The Forgotten Explorer, Including His Narrative of a Voyage on the Northwest Coast in 1788*. Spokane: Arthur H. Clark, 1998.

Menzies, Gavin. *1421: The Year China Discovered the World*. Enlarged edition. London: Bantam, 2003.

Merk, Frederick. "The Genesis of the Oregon Question." *Mississippi Valley Historical Review* 36 (March 1950): 583–612.

Miller, John C. *The Federalist Era, 1789–1801*. New York: Harper & Row, 1960.

Mirsky, Jeannette. *The Westward Crossings: Balboa, Mackenzie, Lewis and Clark*. London: Allan Wingate, 1951.

Mitchell, Donald H. "The Investigation of Fort Defiance: Verifications of the Site." *BC Studies* 4 (1970): 3–20.

——— and J. Robert Knox. "The Investigation of Fort Defiance: A Report on Preliminary Excavation." *BC Studies* 16 (1972–73): 32–56.

Morison, Samuel E. "The Columbia's Winter Quarters Located [sic]." *Oregon Historical Quarterly* 39 (1938): 3–7.

———. *John Paul Jones: A Sailor's Biography.* 1959. Annapolis, MD: Bluejacket Books, Naval Institute Press, 1999.

———. *The Maritime History of Massachusetts.* Boston: Houghton Mifflin, 1961.

Morton, A.S. *A History of the Canadian West to 1870.* 2nd edition. Toronto: University of Toronto Press, 1973.

———. "The North West Company's Columbian Enterprise and David Thompson." *Canadian Historical Review* 17 (1936): 266–88.

Nasatir, Abraham P. "Jacques Clamorgan." In *The Mountain Men and the Fur Trade of the Far West,* vol. 2, edited by Leroy R. Hafen, 81–94. Glendale, CA: Arthur H. Clark, 1965.

———. "John Evans: Explorer and Surveyor." Parts 1–3. *Missouri Historical Review* 25 (January 1931): 219–39; (April 1931): 432–60; (July 1931): 585–608.

Nicandri, David L. "The Illusion of Cape Disappointment." *We Proceeded On* (journal of the Lewis and Clark Trail Heritage Foundation) 30, no. 4 (November 2004): 15–21.

———. "Lewis and Clark: Exploring under the Influence of Alexander Mackenzie." *Pacific Northwest Quarterly* 95, no. 4 (Fall 2004): 171–81.

———. "Twisted Hair, Tetoharsky, and the Origin of the Sacagawea Myth." *Columbia* 19, no. 2 (Summer 2005): 3–8.

Nisbet, Jack. *The Mapmaker's Eye: David Thompson on the Columbia Plateau.* Pullman: Washington State University Press. 2005.

———. *Sources of the River: Tracking David Thompson Across Western North America.* Seattle: Sasquatch Books, 1994.

Nobles, Gregory H. *American Frontiers: Cultural Encounters and Continental Conquest.* New York: Hill and Wang, 1997.

Nokes, J. Richard. *Almost a Hero: The Voyages of John Meares, R.N., to China, Hawaii and the Northwest Coast.* Pullman: Washington State University Press, 1998.

Okun, S.B. *The Russian-American Company.* Cambridge, MA: Harvard University Press, 1951.

O'Neil, Marion. "The Maritime Activities of the North West Company, 1813–1821." *Washington Historical Quarterly* 21, no. 4 (October 1930): 243–67.

Parish, John Carl. *The Persistence of the Westward Movement and Other Essays.* Berkeley/Los Angeles: University of California Press, 1943.

Perry, John Curtis. *Facing West: Americans and the Opening of the Pacific.* Westport, CT: Praeger, 1994.

Phillips, Paul C. *The Fur Trade.* 2 vols. Norman: University of Oklahoma Press, 1961.

Pipes, Nellie B., ed. "Later Affairs of Kendrick." *Oregon Historical Quarterly* 30, no. 1 (June 1929).

Polk, Dora Beale. *The Island of California: A History of the Myth.* Spokane: Arthur H. Clark, 1991.

Porter, Kenneth W. *John Jacob Astor, Business Man*. 2 vols. Cambridge, MA: Harvard University Press, 1931.

Prucha, Francis Paul. *American Indian Policy in the Formative Years: The Indian Trade and Intercourse Acts, 1790–1834*. Cambridge, MA: Harvard University Press, 1962.

Quaife, Milo, ed. "McKay's Journal." *Wisconsin Historical Society Proceedings* 58 (1915): 193.

Quinn, David B. "The Northwest Passage in Theory and Practice." In *North American Exploration*. Vol. 1, *A New World Disclosed*, edited by John Logan Allen, 292–343. Lincoln: University of Nebraska Press, 1997.

Rich, Edwin E. *The Fur Trade and the Northwest to 1857*. Toronto: McClelland & Stewart, 1967.

———. *History of the Hudson's Bay Company*. 2 vols. London: Hudson Bay Record Society, 1959.

Richards, Rhys. *Captain Simon Metcalfe: Pioneer Fur Trader in the Pacific Northwest, Hawaii and China 1787–1794*. Kingston: Limestone Press, 1991.

Robinson, Ronald. "Non-European Foundations of European Imperialism: Sketch for a Theory of Collaboration." In *Imperialism: The Robinson and Gallagher Controversy*, edited by William Roger Louis, 128–51. New York: Franklin Watts, 1976.

Ronda, James P. *Astoria and Empire*. Lincoln: University of Nebraska Press, 1900.

———. *Lewis and Clark among the Indians*. Lincoln: University of Nebraska Press, 1984.

———. "'The Writingest Explorers': The Lewis and Clark Expedition in Historical Literature." *Pennsylvania Magazine of History and Biography* 112, no. 4 (October 1988): 607–30.

Ross, Jane, and Daniel Kyba. *The David Thompson Highway: A Hiking Guide*. Calgary: Rocky Mountain Books, 1995.

Ruby, Robert H., and John A. Brown. *The Chinook Indians: Traders of the Lower Columbia River*. Norman: University of Oklahoma Press, 1988.

Smith, James K. *David Thompson: Fur Trader, Explorer, Geographer*. Toronto: Oxford University Press, 1971.

Smith, Philip Chadwick Foster. *The Empress of China*. Philadelphia: Philadelphia Maritime Museum, 1984.

Solovjova, Katerina, and Aleksandra Vovnyanko. "The Rise and Decline of the Lebedev-Lastochkin Company: Russian Colonization of South Central Alaska, 1787–1798." *Pacific Northwest Quarterly* 90, no. 4 (Fall 1999): 191–205.

Sparks, Jared. *The Life of John Ledyard, The American Traveller*. Cambridge, MA: Hilliard and Brown, 1828.

Surface, George T. "Thomas Jefferson: A Pioneer Student of American Geography." *Bulletin of the American Geographical Society* 41 (December 1909): 743–50.

Taggart, Frederick J. "Notes Supplementary to Any Edition of Lewis and Clark." In the *Annual Report of the American Historical Association for 1908*. 2 vols. Washington, DC: Government Printing Office, 1909.

Terral, Rufus. *The Missouri Valley: Land of Drouth, Flood, and Promise.* New Haven, CT: Yale University Press, 1947.

Thompson, Neville. *Earl Bathurst and the British Empire, 1762–1834.* Barnsley: Leo Cooper, 1999.

Thurman, Michael E. *The Naval Department of San Blas: New Spain's Bastion for Alta California and Nootka, 1767–1798.* Glendale, CA: Arthur H. Clark, 1967.

Tikhmenev, Petr A. *A History of the Russian-American Company.* Translated and edited by Richard A. Pierce and Alton S. Donnelly. Seattle: University of Washington Press, 1978.

Twiss, Travers. *The Oregon Territory, Its History and Discovery.* 1846. Fairfield, WA: Ye Galleon Press, 1988.

[University of Virginia Library]. *Lewis and Clark: The Maps of Exploration, 1507–1814.* Charlottesville, VA.: Howell Press, 2002.

Van Alstyne, R.W. "International Rivalries in the Pacific Northwest." *Oregon Historical Quarterly* 46 (1945): 185–218.

———. *The Rising American Empire.* Oxford: Blackwell, 1960.

Van Kirk, Sylvia. *Many Tender Ties: Women in Fur-Trade Society, 1670–1870.* Norman: University of Oklahoma Press, 1983.

——— and Jennifer Brown. "Duncan McGillivray." In *Dictionary of Canadian Biography,* 5:530–32. Toronto/Sainte-Foy QC: University of Toronto Press and Les Presses de l'Université Laval, 1983.

Vaughan, Thomas, and Bill Holm. *Soft Gold: The Fur Trade and Cultural Exchange on the Northwest Coast of America.* 2nd edition. Portland: Oregon Historical Society Press, 1990.

Wagner, Henry Raup. "Apocryphal Voyages to the Northwest Coast of America." *Proceedings of the American Antiquarian Society* 41 (April 1931): 179–234.

———. *The Cartography of the Northwest Coast of America to the Year 1800.* 1937. Amsterdam: N. Israel, 1968.

Wallace, W. Stewart. *The Pedlars from Quebec and Other Papers on the Nor'Westers.* Toronto: Ryerson Press, 1954.

Weber, David J. *The Spanish Frontier in North America.* New Haven, CT: Yale University Press, 1992.

Webster, Charles K. *The Foreign Policy of Castlereagh, 1812–1815.* London: G. Bell & Sons, 1931.

Wheat, Carl. *Mapping the Trans-Mississippi West, 1540–1861.* San Francisco: Institute of Historical Cartography, 1957.

Williams, David. "John Evans' Strange Journey." *American Historical Review* 54 (January 1949): 277–95; (April 1949): 508–29.

Williams, Glyn. *Voyages of Delusion: The Quest for the Northwest Passage.* New Haven, CT/ London: Yale University Press, 2002.

Wood, W. Raymond. "David Thompson at the Mandan-Hidatsa Villages, 1797–1798: The Original Journals." *Ethnohistory* 24, no. 4 (Fall 1997): 329–42.

———. "The John Evans 1796–97 Map of the Missouri River." *Great Plains Quarterly* 1, no. 1 (Winter 1981): 39–53.

———. *Prologue to Lewis and Clark: The Mackay and Evans Expedition.* With a foreword by James P. Ronda. Norman: University of Oklahoma Press, 2003.

Zug, James. *American Traveler: The Life and Adventures of John Ledyard, the Man Who Dreamed of Walking the World.* New York: Basic Books, 2005.

———, ed. *The Last Voyage of Captain Cook: Including the Siberian Journals and Selected Letters of John Ledyard.* Washington, DC: National Geographic Society, 2005.

INDEX

Note: references to illustrations in bold numerals

More Great History Titles From Harbour Publishing:

Stanley Park's Secret: The Forgotten Families of Whoi Whoi, Kanaka Ranch and Brockton Point
Jean Barman
Officially opened in 1888, Stanley Park was not pristine wilderness—it was home to a number of settlements. Barman skillfully weaves forgotten stories with official records to reveal a troubling, important facet of BC's history.
978-1-55017-420-5 • 6 x 9, paper, 288 pages
80 b&w photos

Desolation Sound: A History
Heather Harbord
Desolation Sound, a popular cruising destination along the BC coast is an area full of ghosts, an area with a storied past. Harbord brings these ghosts to life and in doing so, fills a crucial hole in the history of the province.
978-1-55017-407-6 • 6 x 9, paper, 260 pages
80 b&w photos

Raincoast Chronicles Fourth Five
Edited by Howard White
Fourth Five, a collection of the complete Raincoast Chronicles 16-20, expounds on such diverse matters as supernatural deer, the cannery village of Ceepeecee, fishing-fleet superstitions and the coveted recipe for donkey boiler coffee.
978-1-55017-372-7 • 8.5 x 11, cloth, 420 pages
100+ b&w photos

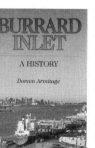

Burrard Inlet: A History
Doreen Armitage
Winner of the 2004 Heritage Advocacy Award, this engaging history traces the development of the Burrard Inlet from First Nations settlement to the modern-day metropolis that surrounds the inlet.
978-1-55017-272-0 • 6 x 9, cloth, 324 pages
80 b&w photos

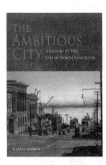

The Ambitious City: A History of the City of North Vancouver

Warren Sommer

Published in honour of the City of North Vancouver's 2007 centennial, this popular history includes first-person accounts as well as a host of archival photos and illustrations. Sommer skilfully covers ethnic relations, labour history and politics.

978-1-55017-411-3 • 8.5 x 11, cloth, 342 pages
100+ b&w photos

One River, Two Cultures: A History of the Bella Coola Valley

Paula Wild

Starting with the prehistory of the Nuxalk First Nations, Wild documents the arrival and impact of the rough and ready mix of "outsiders" who embraced the challenges of living in a remote wilderness area.

978-1-55017-354-3 • 6 x 9, paper, 288 pages
60 b&w photos

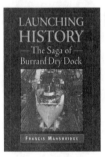

Launching History: The Saga of the Burrard Dry Dock

Francis Mansbridge

A fascinating history of one of the West Coast's major ship builders. Includes stories of some of the famed Union Steamship Company ships, the BC Ferry fleet, warships and workboats.

978-1-55017-280-5 • 8.5 x 11, cloth, 266 pages
150 b&w photos

These and other titles are available at bookstores or from:

Harbour Publishing
Box 219 Madeira Park, BC V0N 2H0

Toll free order line: 1-800-667-2988
www.harbourpublishing.com • orders@harbourpublishing.com